CONVERGENCE AND DIVERGENCE OF FAMILY LAW IN EUROPE

AF184215

EUROPEAN FAMILY LAW SERIES

Published by the Organising Committee of the
Commission on European Family Law

Prof. Katharina Boele-Woelki (Utrecht)
Prof. Frédérique Ferrand (Lyon)
Prof. Cristina González Beilfuss (Barcelona)
Prof. Maarit Jänterä-Jareborg (Uppsala)
Prof. Nigel Lowe (Cardiff)
Prof. Dieter Martiny (Frankfurt/Oder)
Prof. Walter Pintens (Leuven)

CONVERGENCE AND DIVERGENCE OF FAMILY LAW IN EUROPE

MASHA ANTOKOLSKAIA
Editor

intersentia
Antwerpen – Oxford

Distribution for the UK:
Hart Publishing Ltd.
16C Worcester Place
Oxford OX1 2JW
UK
Tel: + 44 1865 51 75 30
Fax: + 44 1865 51 07 10

Distribution for North America:
Gaunt Inc.
Gaunt Building
3011 Gulf Drive
Holmes Beach
Florida 34217-2199
USA
Tel: + 1 941 778 5211
Fax: + 1 941 778 5252

Distribution for Switzerland and Germany:
Stämpfli Verlag AG
Wölflistrasse 1
CH-3001 Bern
Switzerland
Tel: + 41 (0)31 300 63 18
Fax: + 41 (0)31 300 66 88

Distribution for other countries:
Intersentia Publishers
Groenstraat 31
BE-2640 Mortsel
Belgium
Tel: + 32 3 680 15 50
Fax: + 32 3 658 71 21

Convergence and Divergence of Family Law in Europe
Masha Antokolskaia (ed.)

© 2007 Intersentia and Masha Antokolskaia
Antwerpen – Oxford / Amsterdam
http://www.intersentia.com

ISBN 978-90-5095-690-1
D/2007/7849/28
NUR 822

No part of this book may be reproduced in any form, by print, photoprint, microfilm or any other means, without written permission from the publisher.

LIST OF AUTHORS

Prof. Masha Antokolskaia
Professor of Civil and Family Law at the VU University Amsterdam

Prof. Katharina Boele-Woelki
Professor of Private International, Comparative and Family Law at the University of Utrecht; Chair of the Commission on European Family Law

Dr. Bente Braat
Lecturer-researcher at the University of Utrecht

Prof. Miquel Martin-Casals
Professor of Civil Law and director of the Observatory of European and Comparative Private Law University of Girona

Prof. Caroline Forder
Professor of Family Property Law at the University of Antwerp

Dr. Olga Khazova
Associate Professor at the Institute of State and Law within the Russian Academy of Sciences

Prof. Ingrid Lund-Andersen
Associate Professor of Family Law at the University of Aarhus

Prof. Marie-Thérèse Meulders-Klein
Professor Emeritus of Family law at the University of Louvain-la-Neuve; Past President of the International Society of Family Law; Titular Member of the International Academy of Comparative Law; D.H. of the University of Uppsala (Sweden)

Prof. Esin Örücü
Professorial Research Fellow and Professor Emeritus of Comparative Law at the University of Glasgow; Professor Emeritus of Comparative law at the Erasmus University Rotterdam

Mr. Kees Saarloos
Junior Researcher at the University of Maastricht

Prof. Ingeborg Schwenzer
Professor of Private Law at the University of Basel

Prof. Frederik Swennen
Professor of Family Law at the University of Antwerp

Dr. Velina Todorova
Associate Professor of Family Law at University of Plovdiv

Prof. Bea Verschraegen
Professor of Law at the Law Faculty of the University of Vienna; Head of the Department of Comparative Law, Harmonised Law and Private International Law

TABLE OF CONTENTS

PART III. CONVERGENCE AND DIVERGENCE IN SPECIFIC FIELDS OF FAMILY LAW

INTRODUCTION

This volume contains the written versions of the presentations held at the international conference 'Convergence and Divergence of Family Law in Europe', organised in Amsterdam in September 2006. The main objective of this conference was instigating an in-depth discussion of various facets of the convergence/divergence discord. Theoretical issues of convergence, recent examples of regional convergence/divergence developments in Europe, and convergence/divergence tendencies in several central fields of family law: marriage, divorce, cohabitation and matrimonial property law were thereby examined. Another objective was to give the floor to scholars that take different sides in the ongoing debate surrounding convergence, divergence and deliberate harmonisation activities in the field of family law.

The question whether family law in Europe has been converging in the past and is converging at present remains controversial. One may find it puzzling that while the idea of convergence has been supported in the last decennia by a number of eminent scholars, the existence of convergence has at the same time been persistently denied by equally renowned opponents. Convergence-optimism gained support during the radical reforms of family law in the 1960s-1980s. Consequently, Jacques Fayer wrote in 1978 that: 'a classical aphorism of comparative law: that while the law of property and obligations tends towards homogeneity, family law remains the seat of national idiosyncrasies, [...] which has been beyond dispute for some ten year ago', is losing its validity since 'the laws of the majority of the countries of Western Europe tended to converge towards a uniform model, and this evolution has been very rapid'.[1] In 1989 Mary-Ann Glendon submitted that '[...] despite contrasts in the legal and political context of law reforms, the national differences among Western family law systems have diminished steadily over the past two decades'.[2] Yet, later developments were somewhat disappointing for the convergence-optimists. The events in the field of divorce law provide an illustrative example thereof. In the 1980s, the advance of no-fault divorce throughout Western Europe evoked the idea that Europe was moving towards a spontaneous harmonisation of family law. The momentum of the no-fault movement was initially so great that many reputable scholars saw it as a token of a

---

1 FOYER, J., 'The Reform of Family Law in France', in: CHLOROS, A., (ed.), *The Reform of Family Law in Europe*, Kluwer, Deventer, 1978, p. 75.

2 GLENDON, M.A., *The Transformation of Family Law*, The University of Chicago Press, Chicago and London, 1989, p. 1.

spontaneous convergence of divorce law in Europe. It was even optimistically spoken of as 'entering into the period which is marked by a kind of *ius commune*'.[3] At a certain point in time it indeed looked this way. For example, in 1960 fault-based divorce existed in thirteen Western European countries, divorce upon the irretrievable breakdown of the marriage in seven, and mutual consent divorce in six,[4] while four countries allowed no divorce at all. In 1980 fault grounds remained in just eight jurisdictions, while no-fault divorce had extended to twelve, as had mutual consent divorce.[5] However, as the turn of millennium approached, the no-fault movement gradually lost much of its momentum. Attempts to get rid of the fault grounds failed in England and Wales in 1996, in France in 2005, and also in Belgium in 2007.[6] Two Eastern-European countries, Latvia and Lithuania, have recently re-introduced fault grounds into their divorce law. Moreover, the no-fault laws of different European countries appear to be functionally highly divergent when it comes to the easiness, costs and duration of marriage dissolution.[7] These recent developments have encouraged the convergence-pessimists. The most radical stance against the idea of convergence of laws is taken by Pierre Legrand, who plainly stated that 'if one forgoes surface examination at the level of rules and concepts to conduct a deep examination in terms of legal *mentalités*, one must come to the conclusion that legal systems, despite their adjacency within the European Community, have not been converging, are not converging and will not be converging'.[8]

To some extent, this difference in opinions with regard to the existence of convergence and divergence seems easy to explain. The different appreciation of convergence or divergence of family law has often to do with the fact that the history of family law in Europe includes both periods showing a clear tendency to divergence as well as periods when the convergence trend was dominant. Thus the mere choice of the period of investigation can be decisive for one's conclusions. What is more difficult

---

3 NEUMAYER, K., 'General Introduction', in: CHLOROS, A., (ed.), *The Reform of Family Law in Europe*, Kluwer, Deventer, 1978, p. 1. In a similar sense see also: PINTENS, W., VANWINCKELEN, C., *Casebook. European Family Law*, Leuven Univ. Press, Leuven, 2001, p. 16 and PHILLIPS, R., *Putting asunder: A history of divorcé in Western Society*, Cambridge University Press, Cambridge, 1988, p. 570.

4 PHILLIPS, R., *Putting Asunder* (1988), p. 570.

5 Ibid.

6 The Belgian divorce law is changed by Law of 12 April 2007 (in force from 1 September 2007). This law proclaimed the irretrievable breakdown of marriage and the mutual consent to be the only two grounds for divorce. However, the breakdown can be established upon the proof of specific 'circumstances'. Culpable behaviour is maintained among such circumstances (Art. 229 para. 1 CC). Therefore, the Belgian solution somehow resembles the current English one.

7 See my analysis in: *Harmonisation of Family Law in Europe: A Historical Perspective. A Tale of Two Millennia*, Intersentia, Antwerp, 2006, p. 352–365.

8 LEGRAND, P., 'European Legal Systems Are Not Converging', *45 International and Comparative law Quarterly*, 1996, p. 61–62.

to explain is the fact that sometimes the same historical examples are employed by both proponents and opponents of the convergence thesis in support of their opposite conclusions. The reforms introducing no-fault divorce in the 1970s are a recurrent example. On the one hand, the advance of no-fault divorce has been pointed to as evidence of convergence, as it has led to the eradication, or at least the attenuation, of the fault grounds.[9] On the other hand, it has been suggested that no evidence of a convergence tendency can be derived from the no-fault movement, as, due to the fact that in spite of the similar general trend, the results of divorce reforms have not been the same in every country.[10] Perhaps even more illustrative in this respect is the difference in the appreciation of the results of harmonisation of family law in the framework of the Nordic co-operation. While two prominent Scandinavian scholars estimate the Nordic family laws at the heyday of this co-operation as 'almost identical'[11], David Bradley lays the emphasis on the remaining differences.[12] This allows the suggestion that the result of one's findings also depend on what one is looking for. It seems that the convergence/divergence debate sometimes comes to resemble an argument as to whether a glass is half full or half empty.

The main argument evoked by the opponents of the idea of convergence is the so-called 'cultural constraints argument', submitting that the differing family laws are embedded in unique and cherished national cultural heritages; that this cultural and historical diversity is unbridgeable and therefore family laws are not converging spontaneously and cannot be harmonised deliberately.[13] The most radical interpretation of this argument is again given by Pierre Legrand, who claims that the current diversity of law in Europe is an emanation of the irredeemable dissimilarity of national

---

9 See for instance: NEUMAYER, K., 'General Introduction' (1978), p. 1; PINTENS, W., VANWINCKELEN, C., *Casebook. European Family Law* (2001), p. 16; PHILLIPS, R., *Putting asunder* (1988), p. 570.

10 See for example: BRADLEY, D., 'A Family Law For Europe? Sovereignty, Political Economy and Legitimation', in: BOELE-WOELKI, K., (ed.), *Perspectives for the Unification and Harmonisation of Family Law in Europe*, European Family Law Series No. 4, Intersentia, Antwerp, 2003, p. 96.

11 AGELL, A., 'Is There one System of Family Laws in the Nordic Counties', *3 European Journal of Law Reform*, (2001), p. 314; SCHMIDT, T., 'The Scandinavian Law of procedure in Matrimonial Causes', in: EEKELAAR, J.M., KATZ, N., (eds.), *The Resolution of Family Conflicts*, Butterwoths, Harvard, 1984, p. 80.

12 BRADLEY, D., *Family Law and Political Culture. Scandinavian Laws in Comparative Perspective*, Sweet & Maxwell, London, 1996, p. 12; BRADLEY, D., 'A Family Law For Europe? Sovereignty, Political Economy and Legitimation' (2003), p. 68 and 82–88.

13 On the use of this argument see, for instance: OLIVEIRA, G., DE, 'A European Family Law? Play it again, and again ... Europe!', *12 Tijdschrift voor familie- en jeugdrecht* (2000), p. 272, and A *Civil Code for Europe*, Coimbra editora, Coimbra, 2002, p. 127; HOHNERLEIN, M., 'Konturen eines einheitlichen europäischen Familien- und Kindschaftsrecht – die Rolle der Europäischen Menschenrechtskonvention', *4 European Legal Forum* (2000–01), p. 252.

cultures.[14] Accordingly, he postulates the principle impossibility of convergence and deliberate harmonisation.

Although the use of the cultural constraints argument is not been restricted to family law, family law has long been seen as its paradigmatic playground. Thus, Wolfram Müller-Freienfels wrote in 1968: 'Family law concepts are especially open to influence by moral, religious, political and psychological factors; family law tends to become introverted because historical, racial, social and religious considerations differ according to country and produce different family law systems'.[15] Therefore the cultural constrains argument was long perceived with regard to family law as almost self-evident and not requiring much scrutiny.

This unquestioning acceptance of the cultural constrains argument led to the assumption that family law is unsuitable for taking part participation in the pending deliberate harmonisation of private law.[16] The reasoning behind this assumption is quite straightforward: in the same way that the cultural embedment of family law makes family law unsusceptible to spontaneous harmonisation (convergence), it will necessarily impede its deliberate harmonisation.

Without serious reassessment of the cultural constrains argument, and slightly out of step with the developments in the convergence/divergence debate within family law circles, the general attitude towards the harmonisation of family law gradually became more positive in the late 1990s.[17] The most tangible result of this development was the establishment of the *Commission on European Family Law* (CEFL)[18] – an academic initiative, uniting scholars from 23 European jurisdictions, whose purpose is the elaboration of non-binding *Principles of Family Law*. The CEFL puts a considerable effort into promoting the idea of harmonisation of family law. Apart

14 LEGRAND, P., *Fragments on Law-as-Culture*, Tjeenk Willink, Deventer, 1999.

15 MÜLLER-FREIENFELS, W., 'The Unification of Family Law', *16 The American Journal of Comparative Law* (1968–69), p 175.

16 For instance: KOOPMANS, T., 'Towards a New "*Ius Commune*"', in: WITTE, B., DE, FORDER, C., (eds.), *The common law of Europe and the future of legal education*, Kluwer, Deventer, 1992, p. 50; DROBNIG, U., 'Scope and General Rules of a European Civil Code', *5 European Review of Private Law* (1997), p. 493; KERAMEUS, K., 'Problems of Drafting a European Civil Code', *5 European Review of Private Law* (1997), p. 479; ALPA, G., 'European Community Resolutions and the Codification of "Private Law"', *2 European Review of Private Law* (2000), p. 326; BASEDOW, J., 'Codification of Private Law in the European Union: the making of a Hybrid', *1 European Review of Private Law* (2001), p. 35–37.

17 BOELE-WOELKI, K., 'Comparative Research-based Drafting of Principles of European Family Law', in: M. Faure, et al. (eds.), *Towards a European Ius Commune in Legal Education and Research*, Intersentia, Antwerp, 2002, p. 175–177, PINTENS, W., 'Europeanisation of Family Law', in: BOELE-WOELKI, K., (ed.), *Perspectives for the Unification and Harmonisation of Family Law in Europe*, European Family Law Series No. 4, Intersentia, Antwerp, 2003, p. 4 ff.

18 For more information see the CEFL website: http://www2.law.uu.nl/priv/cefl/.

from drafting Principles, it has held three conferences[19] in order to broaden the theoretical basis for the harmonisation of family law. However, in spite of the wealth of literature[20] and the budding drafting activities of the CEFL, harmonisation of family law remains a highly controversial issue, and the discussion whether it is possible at all is far from closed. The main reason for this is that the cultural constraints argument has not been so much overcome, but rather, more or less passed over.

The persistent disagreement on the fundamental issue of whether the harmonisation of family law is possible at all led to the situation that, while the popularity of the idea of harmonisation has been notably increasing throughout the last decade, the resistance to it has not diminished. On the contrary, the advancement of harmonisation activities has only sharpened the debate. The opponents of harmonisation continue to rely on the notion of the cultural and historical embedment of family law as their key argument. The perseverance of their opposition is, *per se,* no indication of weakness of the idea of deliberate harmonisation. It also does it not mean that the CEFL has started its work prematurely without awaiting sufficient consensus. Consensus on such a controversial issue would probably never have been reached. This means that if harmonisation activities were ever to be started, they could have been started only in spite of serious opposition. Nevertheless, the mere fact that such opposition is inevitable does not mean that the proponents of harmonisation can simply disregard the opposition's arguments altogether in the spirit of the old Persian proverb 'the dog barks but the caravan moves on'. Their objections are too serious to be ignored.

Consequently, more clarity with regard to the convergence/divergence discord and the controversy surrounding the cultural constraints argument is crucial for the future of deliberate harmonisation of family law. If the opponents of harmonisation are right in their contention that the family laws in Europe are not converging at present and have never actually converged in the past, and the current diversity is an emanation of the irredeemable dissimilarity of the national cultures, any attempt to harmonise family law is doomed to create only a virtual reality alien to, and thus alienated by, the social reality. If the convergence tendency does exist, the deliberate harmonisation activities are in line with the natural course of events and obviously have more chance

---

19 In 2002, 2004 and 2007. The conference papers of the first two conferences are published in two volumes respectively: BOELE-WOELKI, K., (ed.), *Perspectives for the Unification and Harmonisation of Family Law in Europe*, European Family Law Series No. 4, Intersentia, Antwerp, 2003, and BOELE-WOELKI, K. (ed.), *Common Core and Better Law in European Family Law,* European Family Law Series No. 10, Intersentia, Antwerp, 2005. The proceedings of the third conference are in process.

20 For a recent overview see: MARTINY, D., 'Is Unification of Family Law Feasible or Even Desirable?' in: *Towards a European Civil Code,* HARTKAMP, A., et al (eds.), Ars Aequi Libri, Nijmegen, 2004, p. 328–333 and the CEFL website: http://www2.law.uu.nl/priv/cefl/ under the rubric 'publications'.

for success. One could even say that, if the convergence tendency is as strong as some allege, family law in Europe will be spontaneously harmonised in due time without any deliberate harmonisation activities. More insight with regard to convergence/divergence can provide an important theoretical basis for both the deliberate harmonisation of family law, as well as for the rejection thereof.

With the purpose of acquiring this insight, the Royal Dutch Academy of Arts and Sciences awarded a grant to the present author for conducting a comparative historical study of convergence and divergence tendencies in several central fields of family law in Europe during the last two millennia. The results of this study are published in the monograph *Harmonisation of Family Law in Europe: A Historical Perspective. A Tale of two Millennia.*[21] As I have tried to show in this study, a thorough examination of the cultural constraints argument involves two dimensions, one empirical and the other theoretical. With regard to the contention that family law has never really converged in the past and is not converging in the present, the enquiry is in principle a historical-empirical one. With regard to the contention that convergence and the deliberate harmonisation of family law are not possible at all, the enquiry also seems empirical at first sight – but an analysis of the debate on this issue reveals that the essence of the discord is on the theoretical, rather than the empirical level. It is this theoretical dimension that provides clarification as to how different scholars can derive opposing conclusions from the analysis of the same historical events. The contrasting appreciation of the same historical events is rooted in the different positions that the observers take in the theoretical controversy surrounding the correlation between law and society, and comparative law methodology. With regard to the correlation of law and society, the cultural constraints argument relies on the so-called strong 'mirror' theory of law, which postulates that this correlation is very strong. With regard to comparative law methodology, the argument is related to the so-called 'relativist' epistemology, which induces the observer to search for differences rather than for similarities.[22]

In the historical part of my study I provide an inventory and analysis of the convergence and divergence tendencies as well as a scrutiny of the attempts at deliberate harmonisation of family law during the last two millennia. In order to enrich this analysis and to broaden its scope it was decided to discuss the contemporary convergence/divergence tendencies in the setting of an international conference devoted to this subject. This was the conference 'Convergence and Divergence of Family Law in Europe', held in Amsterdam in September 2006, and the present volume is the result of this conference.

---

21 Intersentia, Antwerp, 2006.

22 See: Chapter 2 of the aforementioned monograph, p. 15–51.

The structure of this volume generally follows the patterns of the discussion held during the conference. The first part contains the written versions of two presentations given during the first theoretical session of the conference. The aim of this session was to discuss the historical and theoretical issues of the convergence/divergence debate and the controversy surrounding the cultural constraints argument. This part commences with the article by the present author, in which I delve into the historical aspects of the convergence/divergence dichotomy on the basis of the results of the empirical-historical part of the above mentioned study. The second article by Esin Örücü tackles the theoretical issues of the convergence/divergence discord from a broader comparative-theoretical perspective.

The second part of this volume gives a picture of the contemporary role of convergence/divergence tendencies on a regional level in various part of Europe. It starts with an article by Ingrid Lund-Andersen in which she gives an overview of the recent trends in the renowned Nordic co-operation in the approximation of family laws, which is generally perceived as the most successful example of regional harmonisation of family laws in Europe. The next article by Miquel Martin-Casals deals with convergence/divergence tendencies in the development of the family law of the Spanish autonomous communities. The two following contributions offer a summary of the convergence and divergence trends in Eastern-Europe against the background of such sweeping events as the fall of the Soviet Union, the disintegration of the Eastern-Block and the accession of a majority of the Central European countries to the EU. The first of these articles, written by Velina Todorova, uses Bulgaria as an example to provide a synopsis of the state of affairs in the whole of the Eastern-European region. The second article, by Olga Khazova, gives an account of the integrative and contrastive tendencies at work in the countries formally belonging to the Soviet Union.

The third part of this volume deals with the convergence and divergence tendencies in some particular fields of family law. This part includes an article by Frederik Swennen on the implication of convergence and divergence on the laws on marriage; an article by Ingeborg Schwenzer, analysing convergence and divergence in the field of same-sex relationships; an article by Caroline Forder and Kees Saarloos, challenging the thesis that the laws on the establishment of parenthood provide a story of successful convergence; and an article by Bente Braat, on convergence and divergence trends in matrimonial property law.

Near the end of this volume the reader finds a contribution written by CEFL chairwomen Katharina Boele-Woelki, giving an insider's view in the experience of the *Commission on European Family Law* (CEFL) with convergence and divergence tendencies. The volume concludes with the observations of Marie-Thérèse Meulders-

Klein, which confront the reader with a critical perspective on the subjects discussed during the conference.

The convergence/divergence debate continues to burn and as yet shows no tendency to come to a conclusion. One can only hope that the efforts of the authors who contributed to this volume will provide to attaining more insight into the different aspects of the convergence divergence-debate and to more understanding between those who hold different standpoints.

Masha Antokolskaia

PART I
THE CONVERGENCE AND DIVERGENCE DEBATE: A NEVERENDING STORY

HARMONISATION OF FAMILY LAW IN EUROPE: A HISTORICAL PERSPECTIVE

MASHA ANTOKOLSKAIA

1. INTRODUCTION

In this article I aim to summarize some results of my five year study into convergence and divergence of family law in Europe.[1] The idea of this study first crossed my mind in 1999 when I was asked to contribute to a report on the perspectives of the harmonisation of family law in Europe for the Netherlands Comparative Law Association.[2] I was challenged by the idea of exploring the main objection to family law harmonisation, the so-called 'cultural constraints argument'. This argument suggests that it is principally impossible to harmonise family law because the family laws of the different European countries are deeply embedded in their unique national cultures and history. The aforementioned study revealed that the cultural constraints argument produces two main questions. The first question, whether family law has converged in the past and is still converging in the present, is in principle a historical-empirical one. The second question; whether convergence and the deliberate harmonisation of family law are possible at all, is more theoretical in nature. In this article I will restrict myself to presenting my findings with regard to the first question.

2. TENDENCY TOWARDS CONVERGENCE AND TENDENCY TOWARDS MODERNISATION

The question whether or not family law within Europe has been converging in the past and is still converging remains highly controversial. The idea of convergence is

---

1 This study, financed by the Dutch Royal Academy of Sciences and Arts, resulted in a monograph *Harmonisation of Family Law in Europe: A Historical Perspective. A Tale of Two Millennia*, Intersentia, Antwerp, 2006.

2 ANTOKOLSKAIA, M., HONDT, W., de, STEENHOFF, G, *Naar een Europees Familierecht, Report for the Netherlands Comparative law Association,* Kluwer, Deventer, 1999.

supported by some eminent contemporary scholars. At the same time the existence of convergence is persistently denied by others. Both sides are able to invoke empirical evidence since the history of family law in Europe includes periods showing divergence as well as periods of convergence. Thus the mere choice of the period of investigation can be decisive for the outcome of the research. In order to be able to avoid selectiveness and provide comprehensive empirical material I have conducted a comparative historical study of convergence and divergence in the field of marriage, divorce, extramarital cohabitation, the status of extramarital children and matrimonial property law in Europe during the last two millennia. The idea behind this choice was that after discussing two thousand years of developments in several core fields of family law it should be possible to suggest an answer to the question of whether family laws in Europe have converged in the past and are converging at present. Looking through the history of family law during the whole of the last two millennia rather than at selected short-term periods, allows this issue to be seen from a broader perspective. This broad analysis reveals that the history of family law in Europe more closely resembles a spiralled rather than a linear process. During the first spin of this spiral, the permissive Classical Roman family law was replaced by the restrictive canon family law of the Middle Ages. During the second spin, the medieval canon family gave way to the permissive law of our times. The informal, secular, private character of Classical Roman family law almost disappeared at the end of the High Middle Ages only to return again in our times, albeit as part of a much more sophisticated legal system. The last centuries of the development of family law in Europe can be depicted as a progressive evolution, the pace of which varied from time to time and from one country to another, but the direction has clearly been the same everywhere: from patriarchal, restrictive, transpersonalistic law, to modern, permissive, personalistic law.[3] The studies of several renowned scholars support this vision. The image of this progressive evolution clearly follows from the seminal work of Mary-Ann Glendon.[4] Extensive historical study of divorce law in Europe brought Roderick Phillips to the same conclusion.[5] According to Harry Willekens: 'Changes in different legal systems

---

3 I have already argued elsewhere that 'looking at the history of family law in Europe, it is possible to see that ever since the Middle Ages, when canon family law was uniform, all European countries were developing in the same direction. The substance, the tendencies and the driving forces of the reform of family law were essentially the same everywhere. The only true differences are in the timing.' See: ANTOKOLSKAIA, M., 'Development of Family Law in Western and Eastern Europe: Common Origins, Common Driving Forces, Common Tendencies', *28 Journal of Family History* (2003), p. 65. Earlier, Harry Willekens had come to a similar conclusion. See: WILLEKENS, H., 'Explaining Two Hundred Years of Family Law in Western Europe', in: WILLEKENS, H., (ed.), *Het gezinsrecht in de sociale wetenschappen*, Vuga, The Hague, 1997, p. 60.

4 GLENDON, M.A., *The Transformation of Family Law*, The University of Chicago Press, Chicago and London, 1989.

5 Phillips notices that 'for the most part, the history of divorce since the sixteenth century has been one of movement away from the Roman Catholic doctrines of marriage. This movement has varied in place and significance over time and place and has not always followed a lineal progression.'

do not take place simultaneously nor at the same pace, but when change occurs the direction is always the same'.[6] David Bradley also acknowledges that 'general trends – liberty, equality and secularity – are clearly apparent in the family laws of developed countries'.[7]

As was indicated above, the spiral development of family law in Europe during the last two millennia can be divided into two major periods: from the Roman times to Protestant Reformation, and from the Reformation to the present. The main event of the first period is the transformation from the diversity of Roman law and various 'barbarian' customary laws, to the uniformity of the medieval canon family law. This period could be considered as an era of overwhelming 'convergence'; that is, in the meaning of 'approximation of laws', rather than a spontaneous process. The mediaeval family law unification by no means occurred spontaneously, but was the result of considerable and deliberate efforts on the part of the Catholic Church. In the sixteenth century the Reformation divided Europe into Protestant and Catholic countries. Thereby the period of uniformity of canon family law and the legislative monopoly of the Catholic Church in family matters came to an end. The Enlightenment, the French Revolution and the subsequent Restoration brought about further division. Since the Enlightenment, Europe has been split by the ideological discord between the 'progressive' camp (seeking modernisation of family law under the influence of the ideas of the Enlightenment), and the 'conservative' camp (opposing this modernisation in the name of 'traditional' family values).[8] In general, it is possible to conclude that the Reformation theology and later the Enlightenment progressive thought instigated the second period of development of family law in Europe: from medieval uniformity to the present-day diversity. When compared to the first period, the main characteristic of this second period is undoubtedly increasing divergence rather than convergence.

The existence and importance of the convergence tendency during the second period is the main issue of the present-day convergence/divergence debate. The proponents

---

PHILLIPS, R., *Putting asunder: A history of divorce in Western Society*, Cambridge University Press, Cambridge, 1988, p. 1.

6 WILLEKENS, H., 'Explaining Two Hundred Years of Family Law in Western Europe', in: WILLEKENS, H., (ed.), *Het gezinsrecht in de sociale wetenschappen*, Vuga, The Hague, 1997, p. 60. See in the same sense also: ANTOKOLSKAIA, M., 'Development of Family Law in Western and Eastern Europe: Common Origins, Common Driving Forces, Common Tendencies', *28 Journal of Family History* (2003), p. 52–69.

7 BRADLEY, D., *Family Law and Political Culture, Scandinavian Laws in Comparative Perspective*, Sweet & Maxwell, London, 1996, p. 238.

8 It is worth noting here that in domestic debates the cultural constraints argument is by far more popular in the 'conservative' camp. Rodolfo Sacco has mentioned that 'The ideology of cultural self-sufficiency is merely the name given to the ideology of cultural delay'. SACCO, R., 'Diversity and Uniformity in the Law', *49 The American Journal of Comparative Law* (2001), p. 177.

of the cultural constraints argument allege the persistence and even increase of the differences, while the opposite side suggests that the tendency towards convergence came to dominate family law at least in the latter part of the twentieth century. The persistence of this debate finds its explanation in the fact that after the Reformation, the development of family law in all European countries generally followed the same pattern, but the profundity and pace of these developments differed significantly.[9] The proponents of the idea of convergence lay the emphasis on the overall similarity of these developments, while its opponents stress the difference in profundity and pace.

From the sixteenth century onwards, the driving forces of this progressive evolution – the Reformation, the Enlightenment, industrialisation, urbanization, liberalism, socialist and feminist ideas, etc. – were pan-European events. In addition, the general economic, social and political developments in the whole of Europe were rather similar. Consequently, the evolution of family law also displayed similarities at a general level in the sense that under the impact of pan-European cultural, economic and ideological trends the family laws of different countries were moving in the same direction – from a traditional restrictive family law, built upon communitarian transpersonal premises, to a more permissive family law, based upon modern personalistic ideology.

The existence of a century long pan-European modernisation trend, however, does not necessarily mean that there is also a tendency towards convergence.[10] David Bradley rightly warns against such a short-cut in reasoning.[11] Convergence is brought on by this similar evolutionary development only when, within the framework of this development, the differences between national family laws are steadily diminishing. It is therefore important to distinguish between two questions: whether there is a general tendency towards modernisation of family law in *Europe*, on the one hand;

---

9 Mary Ann Glendon suggested that 'the degree and timing of changes in patterns of family relationships differed according to regions and population groups'. GLENDON, M.A., *The New Family and the New Property*, Butterworth, Toronto, 1981, p. 12.

10 In a number of my earlier works I erroneously derived evidence of convergence from the fact that family laws in Europe were evolving in the same direction. See: ANTOKOLSKAIA, M., 'Geschiedenis van het familierecht: gelijke ontwikkeling', 'Gezamenlijke tendensen en beginselen' en 'Drie voorbeelden van harmonisatie en unificatie van het Familierecht in de 20ste eeuw. Vergelijking van het onvergelijkbare?', in: ANTOKOLSKAIA, M., HONDT, de, W., STEENHOFF, G, *Naar een Europees Familierecht, Report for the Netherlands Comparative Law Association*, Kluwer, Deventer, 1999, p. 33–81; ANTOKOLSKAIA, M., The Process of Modernisation of Family Law in Eastern and Western Europe: Difference in Timing, Resemblance in Substance', *4.2 Electronic Journal of Comparative Law* (2000), http://law.kub.nl/ejcl/42/art42-1.html; ANTOKOLSKAIA, M., 'Development of Family Law in Western and Eastern Europe: Common Origins, Common Driving Forces, Common Tendencies', *28 Journal of Family History* (2003), p. 52–69.

11 BRADLEY, D., 'A Note on Comparative Family Law: Problems, Perspectives, Issues and Politics,' *Oxford University Comparative Law Forum* (2005), ouclf.iuscomp.opg, p. 10.

and whether there is a general tendency towards convergence of the *family laws of the European countries*, on the other.

The answer to the first question, whether family law has converged in the past, is obviously in the affirmative. The overall similarity of the development of family law towards modernisation calls for a fundamental qualification of the thesis of the embedment of family law in unique national cultures, and therefore of the cultural constraints argument. Yet it is clear that there has always been a significant divergence in pace and profundity of modernisation of family laws from one European country to another. The examinations in my aforementioned study suggest that from all societal factors that one could consider, it is, above all, the differences in the balance of political power between 'progressive' and 'conservative' forces, that make the various countries respond to the pan-European challenges in dissimilar ways.[12] For those who oppose the idea of convergence, the ensuing differences constitute the evidence that family laws did not converge in the past and are not converging in the present.

The answer to the second question, whether family is converging at present, seems less clear. On the basis of the image of the spiral development of family law, I have just submitted that the main characteristic of the period from the Reformation onwards is increasing divergence rather than convergence. Nonetheless, this period witnessed several episodes that were clearly characterised by increased similarity at the pan-European or regional level. The most notable example of pan-European developments is the spread of the Napoleonic *Code Civil* over a large part of Europe in the early nineteenth century. The best example of successful regional approximation of family laws is the twentieth-century Nordic co-operation. It is worth mentioning, that in both cases the approximation of laws was a result of deliberate harmonisation activities, rather than a spontaneous convergence process.

3. HAVE FAMILY LAWS BEEN CONVERGING IN THE PAST?

3.1. SELECTION OF PERIOD IS CRUCIAL

It seems impossible to suggest a sensible answer to this question without further delineation of the period one is talking about. Except for the examples mentioned

---

12 BRADLEY, D., 'A Family Law For Europe? Sovereignty, Political Economy and Legitimation', in: BOELE-WOELKI, K., (ed.), *Perspectives for the Unification and Harmonisation of Family Law in Europe*, European Family Law Series No. 4, Intersentia, Antwerp, 2003, p. 81.

above, the historical overview of the preceding chapters reveals no evidence of durable diminishment of diversity before the second half of the twentieth century. In the 1960s-1970s the acceleration of modernisation of family law throughout Western Europe led the many scholars of that time to believe that Europe had started to move towards spontaneous harmonisation.

It seems that any unqualified contention of the existence of convergence can only be based on the analysis of a period with a relatively short time-span. Several choices of such a period would predetermine an outcome confirming the existence of convergence. For instance, if one takes as a starting point the transitional period of the beginning of the twentieth century, when dissimilarities between the countries had become sharper due to the radical breakthroughs in Scandinavia, Russia and Portugal, and compares this with the present time, one will no doubt be led to conclude that similarity has increased. A similar picture arises if one chooses to compare the initial period of the radical reforms commencing in the 1960s-1970s, when some European countries were already affected by these reforms while others kept their old laws, with the present situation, when the rearguard have significantly caught up with the vanguard.

However, since the perception that family laws are converging is clearly associated with the ongoing process of modernisation, it seems logical to compare the present-day situation not with some moment when this process accelerated (for instance the first radical reforms in the early twentieth century, or the mass reforms commenced in the 1960s), but rather with the situation that existed on the eve of the period of modernisation. This would be the state of affairs before the implementation of the Enlightenment ideas into family law – roughly at the middle of the eighteenth century. The period thus defined about the last 250 years seems to be the one to produce the outcome most relevant to the convergence/divergence debate of our time. An investigation of this period allows one to examine the fruits of family law modernisation up to the present as a whole, not just a limited episode of it.

The analysis of this period gives no indication that the level of similarity of family laws as a whole has become higher now than it was 250 years ago. This remains the case if one compares family laws on the level of functional equivalence, and disregards the outer forms and technical details. The following summary of the relevant chapters of my aforementioned book shows that the level of diversity/similarity not only varies in time but also differs significantly from one field of family law to the other.

3.2. HAS THERE BEEN CONVERGENCE OF THE LAWS ON MARRIAGE?

Before the 1960s the laws of European countries uniformly recognised only one form of intimate relationship: legal marriage.[13] In contrast, in the Europe of today a whole range of varieties of such relationships are legally recognised:[14] heterosexual and homosexual marriage, registered partnerships, intermediary forms between a status and a contract *a la PACS*, and non-institutionalised cohabitation. Two hundred and fifty years ago, the unanimity with which Europe regarded the concept of marriage as a heterosexual union was total and self-evident. Today, opening up marriage for homosexuals and transsexuals has turned this uniformity into a heated controversy. Consequently, in the area of marriage law, one single uniform legal concept of marriage and one single legal form of intimate relationships has been replaced by a variety of diverging legal concepts and forms.

In the field of spousal equality the picture is rather different. The high level of similarity of 250 years ago (women everywhere were legally subordinate to their husbands as the head of the family) has evolved through a period of considerable diversity (due to differences in pace of the equalising of the rights of the spouses) towards an almost total similarity in our time (the spouses are all but completely legally equal everywhere in Europe). There and back again, so to say. Moreover, the whole issue of the equality of men and women in family relationships has become a matter of mandatory European Human Rights Law. This is an interesting example of a particular issue where modernisation could be considered 'completed'. It appears that in respect of the particular issue of spousal equality, this expectation has become true. However, it should be noted that on the balance of things, even this particular issue of 'completed' modernisation as a whole did not witness any increase in convergence, if one compares the equality of the spouses attained at the end of the period in question, with the universality of spousal inequality that existed at the beginning of this period 250 year ago.

---

13 Mary Ann Glendon concluded that 'by the turn of the twentieth century, Western family law systems had come to share, generally speaking, a common set of assumptions. Domestic relations were organized around a unitary conception of the family as marriage centred and patriarchal. Marriage was treated as an important support institution and a decisive determinant of the social status of spouses and children.' GLENDON, M.A., *The Transformation of Family Law*, The University of Chicago Press, Chicago and London, 1989, p. 291.

14 MEULDERS-KLEIN, M.-T., 'Les concubinages: diversités et symboliques', in: RUBBELIN-DEVICHI, J., *Des concubinages: droit interne, droit international, droit compare*, Litec, Paris, 2002, p. 606.

3.3. HAS THERE BEEN CONVERGENCE OF THE LAWS ON DIVORCE?

In the Catholic part of Europe divorce as such did not exist at all in the mid-eighteenth century. The only possibility to terminate marriage there was annulment. The Protestant and Orthodox countries provided for divorce upon a limited number of fault grounds. The difference between those countries that did not permit divorce and those that allowed for divorce was, of course, a very significant one. However, a more homogeneous picture arises if one analyses these laws from a functional perspective: the availability of divorce or annulment in terms of accessibility and costs in time, money and infringement in the private life of the spouses. Two hundred and fifty years ago divorce was almost as rare, costly, time-consuming and difficult to obtain, as annulment.

An analysis of present-day divorce laws reveals that it should be concluded that diversity has more likely increased than the opposite – even if one leaves aside Malta, the only remaining European country not allowing divorce, as if it were merely the exception that proves the rule. No European country maintains fault as the sole ground for divorce. Nevertheless, fault is still preserved alongside other grounds in a significant number of European jurisdictions. On the other side of the spectrum, an easy divorce on demand has been introduced in Sweden, Finland, Spain and indirectly in Russia. A functional analysis of the current divorce legislation leads to the conclusion that the fault/no-fault dichotomy is no longer indicative of the availability and accessibility of divorce. Looking at the accessibility of divorce in terms of cost in time, money and infringement to private life, reveals considerable differences between countries with an easy, rapid and cheap divorce without inquiry, separation or a waiting period (for example the immediate divorce in Sweden) and countries with time and money consuming divorces with extensive judicial inquiry and a long period of separation (for example the four year separation in Ireland).

3.4. HAS THERE BEEN CONVERGENCE OF THE LAWS ON EXTRAMARITAL COHABITATION?

Europe was unanimous, 250 years ago, in giving non-marital cohabitation no legal recognition. Currently there is a hesitant unanimity in recognising that the rights of cohabitees should be protected one way or another. However, there is a whole range of legal constructions employed for providing such protection. The level of institutionalisation of both same- and opposite-sex cohabitation varies, from granting cohabitees only some limited rights in the field of public and private law, to a complete functional equivalent to marriage (registered partnership 'Nordic style'). There is also a persistent diversity in Europe regarding how far the State should go in imposing regulation on opposite-sex couples who have chosen not to institutionalise their relationship.

3.5. HAS THERE BEEN CONVERGENCE OF THE LAWS GOVERNING POSITION OF EXTRAMARITAL CHILDREN?

Two hundred and fifty years ago, illegitimate children were strongly disadvantaged everywhere in Europe. At present, the legal status of children born to unmarried parents exhibits only some rudimentary differences as compared to the status of children whose parents are married. As the equality of marital and extramarital children is now prescribed by European Human Rights Law, the remaining differences can be expected to disappear in the near future. Along with the equality of the spouses, the law governing the status of extramarital children provides a second example of a case where modernisation could be considered more or less 'completed'. Important as that may be, it should be noted here that this law was again no less similar at the beginning of modernisation than it is at its 'end'.

3.6. HAS THERE BEEN CONVERGENCE OF THE LAWS GOVERNING MATRIMONIAL PROPERTY?

Contrary to the laws on marriage, divorce, cohabitation and illegitimacy, the matrimonial property laws of the European countries do not share a common legal past. However, this seems to make little difference with regard to the issue of convergence and divergence. The matrimonial property law of mid-eighteenth century Europe was typified by a great diversity of regimes, each applying different legal techniques in order to achieve similar objectives: enabling the husband to use his wife's property to the benefit of the family, on the one hand, and simultaneously safeguarding the heritable property of the wife for her children and kin, on the other. This similarity of objectives predetermined a considerable level of similarity on a functional level. Irrespective of the matrimonial property regime, the law was generally characterised by reserving for the husband the right to administer his wife's property, and by the legal incapacity of married women.

From the end of the nineteenth century until the 1980s matrimonial property law experienced a period of transition from the old, male dominated model to the modern model, based on the equality of the spouses. This transitional period was characterised by large differences between the vanguard and the rearguard countries. During this period the spousal equality in patrimonial matters and the legal capacity of married women were highly politically controversial issues.

At present this transitional period has all but ended. Diversity of legal regimes of matrimonial property law from country to country is as typical for contemporary matrimonial property law as it was 250 years ago. Yet these technically different legal regimes display a far-reaching commonality on the functional level because the objectives of the modern matrimonial property laws are the same everywhere in Europe. The common functional objectives of present-day matrimonial property law are: ensuring the equality of the spouses and achieving a proper balance between the principles of solidarity and autonomy. With respect to the formal equality of the spouses the similarity of the laws of various European countries is almost total. Irrespective of the matrimonial property regime, everywhere in Europe a woman can enjoy full legal capacity, and all European legal systems provide both spouses with equal rights of administration of their own property and (where such funds exists) of common funds. The issues of equality of the spouses in patrimonial matters and the legal capacity of married women have completely lost their controversial character. On a functional level, however, a considerable similarity can be delineated in regard to the *de-facto* equality of the spouses; as well the balance between the principles of autonomy and solidarity, but the level of similarity here is noticeably lower.

A two-fold conclusion can be derived from this analysis. On the one hand, matrimonial property law in Europe has reached a rather high level of similarity both on the level of the objectives of the regulation and on the level of the actual accomplishment of these objectives. On the other hand, these functionally similar results are achieved in the various systems of matrimonial property law by means of dissimilar legal techniques. The main differences between these techniques go along the lines of the two main systems of matrimonial property in present-day Europe: the system of limited community of property and that of deferred community of property. With regard to these systems and techniques there is very little similarity, and this will most likely continue to be the case.

Interestingly, it would appear that the level of similarity of matrimonial property law in Europe seems to have come full circle in the last 250 years. The technical diversity of legal regimes combined with a similarity of objectives and a considerable functional equivalence is typical both for the end and the beginning of this period.

3.7. CONCLUSION

The answer to the question whether family laws in Europe have converged in the past is thus dependent on the period one has in mind. Convergence has definitely existed in certain periods, areas and places. However, the main characteristic of the whole period from the Reformation onwards is an increasing divergence rather than convergence. In the light of the fact that the modernisation of family law is considered to be the main driving force behind convergence, it is interesting to note that during the period of modernisation as a whole, convergence cannot be considered to have been the prevailing tendency either. On the contrary, apart from the limited differentiation that already came into being during the Reformation, it was the differences in the profundity and pace of modernisation that led to the diversity of family law in the first place. It is above all the acceleration of the modernisation of family law in the second half of the twentieth century, and especially from the 1960s onwards, that has in turn led to a reduction in this diversity and created a perception that convergence, rather than divergence, is the main effect of modernisation. Among the fields of family law analysed in this study, there are two examples where this development has come full circle, and the present situation shows the same high level of similarity as did the situation of 250 years ago: the equality of the spouses, and the equality of children born in and outside wedlock. On these particular issues, a final point has been reached (namely: full legal equality) from which it seems reasonable to expect that it will not be subjected to major changes in the foreseeable future. Here, modernisation could be considered 'completed'. The remaining question seems to be whether similar developments are taking place in other areas of family law. Can what is presently going on in family law in Europe be considered as the 'final part' of modernisation, in the sense that what first has diverged because of differences in profundity and pace, is now converging again?

4. ARE FAMILY LAWS CONVERGING AT PRESENT?

4.1. WOULD THE REARGUARD EVER REACH THE VANGUARD?

The analysis of the more recent history of family law in the preceding chapters reveals many examples of the phenomenon that, at the same time that the countries which lag behind in the modernisation of family law make a step forward (for example by giving limited protection to same-sex couples or introducing no-fault divorce), the countries in the vanguard of modernisation make another step forward (like allowing same-sex marriage or introducing divorce on demand), so that the gap between them remains. This phenomenon seems to be so persistent that it leads one to expect that the rearguard will never catch up with the vanguard and lasting convergence will never take place. Paraphrasing the paradox of Zeno, it is possible to ask whether or not Achilles could overtake a tortoise, but it is quite clear that a tortoise could never overtake Achilles, unless it suddenly sprouts wings. It is interesting to see that in family law, there are some historical examples of tortoises sprouting wings and overtaking Achilles. Such were the breakthroughs in the modernisation of family law following the Portuguese Revolutions of 1910 and the Russian Revolution of 1917, or the introduction of divorce on demand and same-sex marriage in 2005 in 'Catholic' Spain. But these are exceptions rather than rules. Normally the tortoises (generally the South European countries plus Ireland) remain slow and the Achilleses (for example the Nordic countries) keep moving fast. While countries lagging behind in, for instance, the liberalisation of divorce approach one stage, the vanguard has already moved to the next, and in this way the distance remains constant, and the common core on the level of positive law remains limited.

4.2. THE END OF HISTORY OF FAMILY LAW?

The question to be answered here is whether this process will come to an end when some 'final' stage of evolution is reached, as seems to be the case with spousal equality and the equality of children born in and out of wedlock. It seems possible to say that if family law is evolving everywhere from less permissive to more permissive, there must be a point in the future where the highest level of permissiveness will be reached by all so that no further development will be possible. One could oppose the picture of ongoing competition between Achilleses and tortoises with the suggestion that all Achilleses and tortoises will unavoidably meet each other at the finish line. It could for instance be suggested that divorce on demand is the final point of the development of divorce law. Perhaps the same could be suggested of same-sex marriage. Comprehensive convergence could be expected if the countries that presently have divorce on demand and same-sex marriage have thereby reached the summit of the modernisation of divorce, marriage and same-sex cohabitation law, where they will later be joined by the other countries that are developing in the same direction but at a lesser speed. This would be the 'final point' of family law evolution – a kind of 'end of history'. At this point the family laws of all European countries would have reached uniformity by way of a spontaneous modernisation/convergence process.

While obviously no one can exclude such future possibility altogether, there is no empirical indication that the modernisation of family law will ever actually be 'finished'.[15] The 'end of history' may have been suggested by several religious and political theories but there has been no such undertaking in the field of family law. For good reason, I propose since such an interpretation of the modernisation process of family law seems far too speculative.[16] Although for some particular issues, like the equalisation of the position of spouses and illegitimate children, 'final points' of modernisation appear to be very well conceivable, this does not say much about the overall development of family law. No one could claim to know how family law will develop further. How could one know whether divorce on demand will be the final point of development of divorce law? It is certainly no less plausible that divorce law will develop further. Divorce on demand granted by a state official could evolve into a private informal declaration, a kind of *repudium,* given by one spouse to the other without any involvement of the State, as it was in classical Roman law. Indeed, maybe at some stage of history, marriage and divorce will no longer be regulated by law at all? Maybe some day the legal regulation of civil marriage will become superfluous, as legal protection will be given on the basis of *de facto* relationships? Maybe same-sex couples, once genuine equality has been acquired, will no longer be interested in the status civil marriage can grant them? Without a crystal ball, we can only guess the future. If we stop guessing and return to the solid ground of facts, there is no sound indication that the ongoing evolution of family law will come to an end in the near future.

The arrival of an 'end point' of developments in family law is also rather unlikely due to technical developments such as medically-assisted procreation, surrogate motherhood and – who knows –possibly even cloning, keep generating new challenges for family law. New possibilities like these continue to provide food for new controversies, which will keep the diversity of family laws existing. There are also family law problems that cannot be described in simple terms of modernisation or protection of human rights. These are dilemmas involving merely conflicts of interest between two individuals. Who should be considered the legal mother of a child born from a surrogate mother: the genetic mother, or the woman who has carried the child? Whose interests should be protected when a child wishes to have the

---

15 In the second chapter of my book, mentioned in note 1 above, I have laid a link between the idea of end point modernisation of family and the unfinished 'modernity project'- a concept introduced by Jean-François Lyotard into the modernist/postmodernist discord. (LYOTARD, J-F., *Het postmoderne uitgelegd aan onze kinderen,* vertaald door Janssen, C., Kok Agora, Kampen, 1987, p. 31–32). The 'Modernity' project is based on a belief in the possibility of emancipating man and improving human conditions according to the law of reason and universally valid values. Developing towards the ideal family law is exactly in line with this modus of thinking.

16 Also Willekens pointed out that a general trend towards similar developments does not allow implying 'that all legal systems [...] are fated to develop towards the same horizon.' WILLEKENS, H., 'Explaining Two Hundred Years of Family Law in Western Europe', in: WILLEKENS, H., (ed.), *Het gezinsrecht in de sociale wetenschappen,* Vuga, The Hague, 1997, p. 60.

name of its begetter revealed, appealing to the right to know one's origins, and the mother opposes this, referring to the protection of her private life? Such dilemmas know no obvious solution and will probably remain a source of unending disagreement among the European legislatures.

CONVERGENCE AND DIVERGENCE: THEORETICAL ISSUES

Esin Örücü

1. INTRODUCTION

At present the convergence and non-convergence debate dominates 'theoretical comparativism'. It is said by many that today comparative law is used predominantly to suppress the difference and promote the similar – at least within Europe[1] – and that comparative lawyers are working for convergence and are not neutral observers.[2] It might even be asked whether comparative law has indeed become an instrument of integration in Europe.

There are of course many who prefer to stress non-convergence and difference, thereby 'insulation'. For them, cultural identity, mentality, difference, and 'living apart together' are important tenets of States within which cultural pluralism, and beyond that, legal pluralism, are discussed. These are the critics of convergence and 'transplants', who see an intimate connection between law and culture, tradition and heritage, that is, local context.[3]

At the outset, I would like to point out that I believe there are lessons to be learnt from the following observation. A researcher involved in the Scottish nationalist movement,

---

1 Among the factors creating unity and integration in Europe are cited: Christendom, Roman law, an inherited body of classical culture, a trans-European educational network, capitalism, and eventually, the industrial mode of production, culminating today in the EU, though divided between 'euromaximalists' and 'eurominimalist'. See: Giner, S., Guibernau, M., 'Conclusion: One Europe? The democratic governance of a continent', in: Guibernau. M., (ed.), *Governing European Diversity*, Sage, London, 2001, p. 259, 261.

2 See: Ward, I., 'Limits of Comparativism: Lessons from UK-EC Integration', 2 *Maastricht Journal of European and Comparative Law* (1995), p. 23.

3 Among the factors leading to diversity in Europe are cited: wars, religion, ideological conflicts, massive economic imbalance, as well as cultural and political imbalance, a network of sovereign states with divergent economic and political interests and thriving on mutual hostility. See: Giner, S., Guibernau, M., 'Conclusion: One Europe? The democratic governance of a continent' (2001), p. 263.

for example, might prefer to stress the differences between the English and the Scottish legal systems – and there are many – in order to show that they are insurmountable for even partial harmonisation of the two legal systems. A Scottish researcher believing in the unity of the UK however, and perhaps also wanting to pave the way for European unity, might pick on the similarities between the English and the Scottish legal systems – and again there are many – in the hope of generating a unification movement at home as a first step to a harmonisation movement within Europe. Thus it is possible to claim, according to this type of political choice, that the Dutch and the English legal systems for instance, are quite different and 'never the twain shall meet'. But it is also possible to emphasise the similarities between these two if there is the will to facilitate European co-operation within the European Union. Both approaches stem from ideological assumptions and are legitimate research strategies as long as the strategy is clearly laid down at the start of the project. Which approach is preferred depends more on the political and theoretical orientation of the researcher rather than inherent theoretical truth.

Over the years there has been voluminous rhetoric on convergence and, by the opposing camp, on divergence. In my valedictory lecture in Rotterdam I myself looked at the reality of convergence under a number of sub-headings: First, I approached legal systems in order to illustrate the thesis of 'original convergence' and make a case for the overlaps of legal systems within and across the classically accepted legal families. I then looked at the convergence occurring now, that is, 'ongoing convergence' within the context of the ever-enlarging Europe, and assessed this convergence at a number of levels. I eventually made predictions for 'future convergence'.[4]

Of course, legal systems that may not appear to be converging in one area of law may be converging in another. Legal systems that may be grouped together for the purposes of one subject, may be re-grouped differently with others for the purposes of another subject. Legal systems that belonged together at a certain time period may shift their positions in another time period. Borders are constantly changing and legal systems remain in one position for only a limited period of time, though this time span may be quite long. This shows how legal systems can never be placed in fixed positions for all time and in all areas of law. Furthermore, this, coupled with the overlaps to be exposed through the deconstruction of legal systems into their original components, can only strengthen the 'original convergence' thesis.

---

4 Örücü, E., 'Looking at Convergence through the Eyes of a Comparative Lawyer', *9–2 EJCL* (2005), p. 1–15 http://www.ejcl.org/92/issue92/art92–1.html. I have already dealt with some of these issues elsewhere: See: Örücü, E., *Enigma of Comparative Law: Variations on a Theme for the Twenty-First Century,* Martinus Nijhoff Publishers, Leiden, 2004.

In fact, when we look beyond rules, substance and structure towards legal tradition and legal culture, the interrelationships become even more obvious. This may sound like the reverse of the usual claim that rules and solutions may look alike but legal cultures and traditions differ. The 'original convergence' thesis puts forth that in essence rules and structures may have developed differently and diverged over time but their legal traditions and cultures overlap.

This view has been strengthened more recently by Patrick Glenn's 'On Common Laws',[5] where he demonstrates that universality and particularity, unity and diversity, unity in diversity, and expansion and local sensibility appear as the defining moments in the history of legal systems. Glenn observes that the concept of common law, not as it lives in the name of the Common Law tradition but in its primary historical sense, is common in relation to law that is not common, in that, it lives as 'relational common law' surviving and functioning in relation to the particular law that has priority over it. It is present only in a manner compatible with the local law, with no obligatory content, and no binding or unifying authority. Thus common laws have 'a relational character', in that, they define themselves in relation to others, and 'they are in a constant dynamic state'.[6] He demonstrates that the Common Law, the *ius commune, le droit commun, el derecho comun, il diritto commune* and *das gemeine Recht*, with their different experiences, all share these characteristics. In addition, multiple, interactive common laws, reflecting the essential diversity of European law, 'each radiating out from major centers of population or influence', variously accommodated '*iure propria* internal to each of them'.[7] This leads Glenn to make the point that today the hypothesis of multiple common laws is 'as plausible as that of a single overarching common law'[8] for our understanding of the *ius commune*: a point that is crucial for a number of projects in different fields working towards the creation of common cores for 'European laws'.

Glenn traces the *ius commune*, the common law as originating in England, in France, in Germany and in Spain, and other common laws of Europe, and deals with the early expansion of *ius unum* and the common law. He also reminds us that there were a number of common laws 'free of a territorial base', such as canon law and commercial law.

More important, Glenn considers the relations of common laws with each other. His claim is that common laws, tolerant to particular laws, were also tolerant of each other.

---

5 Glenn, H.P., *On Common Laws*, Oxford University Press, Oxford, 2005.

6 Ibid, p. 43.

7 Ibid, p. 21.

8 Ibid, p. 25.

Not being aggressive, they shared information. Thus interrelationship and interaction were crucial, and we know that interrelationship breeds convergence.

He also referred to 'mixed jurisdictions'. He sees these as places of confluence of common laws, as 'ongoing interdependence'; places where we see an unsuccessful 'process of exclusive appropriation of one of the common laws'.[9] However, Glenn also points out that 'with the increase in importance in the world of overlapping laws',[10] their significance may decline, possibly because more and more legal systems become mixed.

Since state law is in the process of 'losing its complete and exclusive nature', Glenn argues, the idea *of ius commune* should be re-examined, and to this end it is worthwhile to look at 'the multiple forms of common law which have existed in western law'.[11] So, teaching 'common laws' becomes essential as we must reflect on the relations of different laws and different peoples while developing an awareness of normative history, in order to help in resolving today's problems. 'The notion of the common law was the most important instrument for conceptualising legal relations in Europe for hundreds of years'.[12] Thus, common laws were, and will be, contemporary means of 'reconciliation and equilibrium'.[13]

At this point I would like to move on to theories of convergence and divergence.

2. THEORIES OF CONVERGENCE AND DIVERGENCE FROM THE VANTAGE POINT OF A COMPARATIST

2.1. INTRODUCTION

Now, the fact is that the issue of convergence and divergence is usually approached within the context of European integration. Integration theories were born within the political sub-field of international relations, which is essentially divided between the neo-functionalists, who see integration as a gradual self-sustaining process, and the inter-governmentalists, who stress the role of national governments. In relation to European integration, there are debates going on among realists, liberals, rational-

9 Ibid, p. 119.
10 Ibid.
11 Ibid, viii.
12 Ibid, p. 43.
13 Ibid, p. 143.

choice institutionalists and constructivists theorists.[14] However, in these debates, theorising concerns integration rather than convergence or divergence, which are seen only as bye-products of integration, the view being that there is empirical evidence that European integration has a 'transformative' impact on the European state legal systems.[15] In fact, it is this transformation that has to be assessed. Within European integration other notions such as globalisation, institutionalisation, norm-diffusion and identity-change are also discussed.

Again in the context of European integration, 'convergence' has been defined as, 'the adaptation or adjustment of policy making patterns in the member states under the influence of European integration towards a uniform, Union wide policy.'[16] Following on from this definition then, divergence would be born out of the reaction or resistance to these policies. However, there could also be divergent pattern of adaptation and reaction at the national levels, labelled as 'differentiated integration' and 'flexibility' arrangements.[17] What is essential then is to identify the conditions and factors that may account for such patterns. However, Antoaneta Dimitrova and Bernard Steunenberg conclude that their review does not show any 'clear and unambiguous trend towards convergence due to the influence of European integration.'[18] Most researchers have found that convergence and policy differences co-exist. No researcher has ever found a self-contained or impervious legal system.

For example, in the area of 'divergence', 'game theoretical models' have been used to explain disparities between EU member states. Another approach indicates 'partial implementation' as the factor that leads to divergence. Yet another model is presented as the 'stage' or 'growth' model of institutional change and adaptation.[19] Obviously policy differences are due to differences in institutional political structures, to geographic and geopolitical conditions, and to costs, rather than to political choices and cultural differences alone. Only by empirical testing in a number of specific fields can we demonstrate whether convergence or divergence is taking place and reveal the factors leading to convergence and divergence.

---

14 For example, Mark Pollack has analysed various of these approaches to European integration. See: POLLACK, M.A., 'International Relations Theory and European Integration' 39 *Journal of Common Market Studies* (2001), p. 221–244.

15 Ibid, p. 234.

16 DIMITROVA, A., STEUNENBERG, B., 'The Search for Convergence of National Policies in the European Union – An impossible Quest?' *1:2 European Union Politics* (2000), p. 201–202.

17 Ibid, p. 203.

18 Ibid, p. 207. For the workings of the EU to maintain integration but allow divergence through ideas of 'differentiated integration', 'win set', 'preference set', 'opt-out', 'opt-up' and 'general safeguard clauses' see: ibid, p. 207–214.

19 Ibid, p. 204–205.

There seems to be no direct positive impact of European integration on convergence. Contextual factors, 'institutional embeddedness', and 'implementation effectiveness' are among the factors to be considered for this loose connection. Dimitrova and Steunenberg's research suggests that convergence leading to uniformity within the context of the EU needs two conditions to be fulfilled: the EU Council must agree on a uniform policy at the legislative stage which does not include exemptions; all national governments must fully implement a directive without national incentives leading them to deviate from the policy.[20] Only in this case can we talk of convergence; otherwise we can only talk of either partial convergence or non-convergence.

As already noted, these debates and approaches are related to 'integration'. Theorising on 'convergence' and 'divergence' may need other frameworks.

Let us note that convergence implies initial separation and subsequent approach. Divergence implies initial common origin and subsequent separation. Convergence comes about through interrelationship, interaction and contact, so that two adjacent systems increasingly have more in common, though their starting points may have been quite different. Divergence arises in isolation and insularity and is often a random process. It is the separation with no contact that leads to marked differences even when originally the starting point may have been the same. Usually divergence is gradual.

A number of models could be envisaged: (a) common origins + original divergence + subsequent divergence, (b) common origins + original divergence + ensuing convergence + ongoing convergence, (c) common origins + original divergence + ensuing convergence + ongoing divergence (d) separate origins + original convergence + ongoing convergence, (e) separate origins + original convergence + later divergence + ongoing convergence. The picture can be enriched by two additional models: (f) 'concerted parallel development' which entails neither further convergence nor divergence, and (g) 'harmony in diversity'.

Convergence can be further refined: For instance, Lord Bingham, delivering his opinion in *Fairchild*,[21] made a most pertinent observation indicating a 'convergence of policy', a 'convergence of solutions' or even a 'convergence of reasoning'. Guy Canivet, while looking at the issues of convergence, differentiated between

---

[20] DIMITROVA, A., STEUNENBERG, B., 'The Search for Convergence of National Policies in the European Union – An impossible Quest?' (2000), p. 219.

[21] Joined Cases of *Fairchild* v *Glenhaven Funeral Services Ltd and others*; *Fox* v *Spousal (Midlands) Ltd* and *Mathews* v *Associated Portland Cement Manufacturers (1978) Ltd and others* [2002] KHL 22, [2002] 3 All ER 305.

'imposed convergence' (which can also be called regulatory convergence) – which he sees as brought about by imposed European Union regulations, directives, legal reasoning and solutions – and 'spontaneous convergence' brought about by convergence of reasoning and convergence of solutions.[22] We can talk of 'even convergence' and 'uneven convergence'. So we see how co-existing normative and legal orders or indeed legal traditions interact in many complex ways.

Below we will consider some theoretical bases for both convergence and divergence such as 'contamination', 'diffusion', 'derivation', 'transposition', 'appropriation of common laws', and the 'tree model' and the 'wave theory'. 'Globalisation' is an overused term to explain cross-frontier mobility of peoples and businesses, and convergence and integration, and is not considered as an appropriate theoretical framework in this work.

2.2. CONTAMINATION

Pier Guiseppe Monateri for example, has suggested 'contamination' as the basis for understanding the world of legal systems: 'the actual legal world is more to be seen as a world of "contaminations" than a world split up into different families'.[23] He claims that this idea is neither new nor linked to globalisation, since 'practically every system, even in antiquity has grown through "contaminations"',[24] the practice of borrowing having always been a normal path of development. Legal systems 'mutating' over time borrow from each other by the process of contamination. In his view the 'widespread cross-diffusion of French and German patterns within Civil law, and the overcoming of American models at the present, shape a similar legal landscape all across the world, with a wilderness of local variants'.[25] A comparative lawyer can detect cross-pollination, cross-fertilisation and 'horizontal transfers' between systems in all places and at all times.

Further, Monateri focuses on history rather than deliberate efforts of import/export patterns and claims that a 'weak' legal tradition, in the sense of one being widely open to foreign 'cultural intruders', is formed by borrowings and presenting the process as evolutive. Strong proximate systems rather than distant ones, prestigious patterns rather than discredited ones contaminate the weaker system. He then analyses

[22] Canivet, G., 'La convergence des systémes juridique du point de vue du droit privé français' *1 R.I.D.C* (2003), p. 7–22.

[23] Monateri, P.G., 'The "Weak" Law: Contaminations and Legal Cultures' in: *Italian National Reports to the XVth International Congress of Comparative Law, Bristol 1998*, Giuffrè editore, Milano, 1998, p. 83, 107.

[24] Ibid.

[25] Ibid.

developments in Italian law, which he presents as a 'weak' tradition. Monateri also suggests that 'legal borrowing calls for special explanation only in so far as it differs from other kinds of cultural diffusion'[26] Thus, such a study should concentrate on 'cultural sharing' and 'selection' evolving through the efforts of 'competing elites in search of legitimation'.[27] 'Contamination' is one theoretical approach to convergence.

2.3. DIFFUSION

So, it is said, the 'diffusion' theory can also explain the forces of convergence.[28] William Twining believes that this theory rather than transplant theories should be taken up by comparatists to explain the phenomenon of convergence. Challenging the simplified notions of 'identifiable exporters and importers', 'export/import between countries', 'direct one way transfers', the classical beliefs related to 'objects' and 'agents' of receptions, 'parent systems and dependents', Twining advocates the use of social science sources.[29] A particular innovation, networks for and agents and channels of diffusion, and the adoption of the innovation, are processes that have to be studied. Diffusionism seems to have gone out of fashion in anthropology but not in sociology. In this approach, the spread of ideas is pitched against the concept of innovation. As diffusion also implies interaction or 'inter-legality' born out of a spreading in space, Twining talks of cross-level diffusion.[30] There is obviously a 'diffusion of innovations', but once the 'knock-on-effect' starts, very little remains of the original innovation, but there is probably further independent innovation. Diffusion is regarded as an 'informal spread', as a general and abstract term, 'embracing contagion, mimicry, social learning, organized dissemination' and in other ways.[31]

In fact, the diffusion theory is a glorified transplant theory put into social science terminology indicating the spread of ideas – a special type of communication (autopoiesis). Seemingly, the theory as such suffers from an 'export bias' as it looks at the innovator-exporter (diffuser), and therefore may lead to virtual convergence.

---

26 Ibid, p. 91.

27 Ibid.

28 See: Twining, W., 'Diffusion of Law: A Global Perspective' *49 Journal of Legal Pluralism* (2004), p. 1–45 and *1:2 The Journal of Comparative Law* (2006), p. 237–260. Also Twining, W., 'Social Science and Diffusion of Law', 32 *Journal of Law and Society* (2005), p. 203–40. Twining refers to the 'diffusion of law' research carried out by Everett Rogers. See: Rogers, E. M., *Diffusion of Innovations,* Free press, New York, 1995.

29 Twining, W., *The Journal of Comparative Law* (2006), p. 238–239.

30 Ibid, p. 249.

31 Strang, D., Soule, S., 'Diffusion in Organisation and Social Movement' *24 Annual Review of Sociology* (1998), p. 265–266.

It does not deal with 'infusion' that is, the 'importers' point of view' and therefore cannot measure genuine or actual convergence, which involves internalisation of the received.

2.4. DERIVATION

'Derivation', is of great significance in the historical development of many legal systems. Mostly relevant for colonial relationships, it is yet another explanation of convergence. As almost all legal systems are related historically and are derivatives of each other, the relationship between a legal system and its socio-cultural context does not stand in the way of its relationship with other legal systems or even with other socio-cultural contexts. Derivation however, implies a special relationship of parent and child. It usually refers to colonial experiences and rests on the belief that there are minor legal systems whose laws derived from major ones. An inherent belief in 'dependency' forms the basis of this explanation of convergence. It is mostly eurocentric and does not imply cross-fertilisation or overlap.

2.5. TRANSPOSITION

Contamination, diffusion and derivation are all variations on the theme of 'transfrontier mobility of law',[32] which shows that legal systems live in contact and interaction, and are interrelated. Systems may have common roots or may have heavily borrowed from each other or, through some historical accident, be derivatives from a parent system. Convergence should be the overall outcome. However, when laws are moved and then 'transposed', that is, 'tuned' to create the 'fit', variations occur.[33] That is why I have defined transposition thus:

> *'The term "transposition" is more apt in instances of massive change based on competing models, in that here the pitch is changed. In musical transposition, each note takes the same relative place in the scale of the new key as in the old, the "transposition" being made to suit*

---

[32] In some languages, such as the German, and for instance in Turkish by derivation, the general word used for these activities is reception (*rezeption*). However, for me reception is a specific instance of 'transfrontier mobility of law', which involves the willingness on the part of the recipient, other forms being, imposition, imposed reception, imitation and the like. See generally for terminology: WATSON, A., *Legal Transplants: An Approach to Comparative Law,* Scottish Academic Press, Edinburgh, 1974; ÖRÜCÜ, E., 'A Theoretical Framework for Transfrontier Mobility of Law', in: JAGTENBERG, R., ÖRÜCÜ, E., ROO, A., DE, (eds.), *Transfrontier Mobility of Law,* Kluwer, The Hague, 1995, p. 5.

[33] See: ÖRÜCÜ, E., 'Law as Transposition', *51 International and Comparative Law Quarterly* (2002), p. 205.

the particular instrument or the voice-range of the singer. So in law. Each legal institution or rule introduced is used in the systems of the recipient, as it was in the systems of the model, the transposition occurring to suit the particular socio-culture and needs of the recipient.'[34]

Borrowing, whether by way of imposition or reception, leads to virtual convergence, as it does not tell us anything of the outcome but only of the process. 'Transposition' on the other hand, leads to both true convergence and to divergence occurring in the process of 'tuning'. Thus, some distortion occurs which leads to healthy growth, nothing retaining its previous identity but following the 'separate origins + original convergence + ensuing divergence + ongoing convergence', 'common origins + original divergence + ensuing convergence + ongoing convergence' or 'common origins + original divergence + ensuing convergence + ongoing divergence' patterns noted above (2.1). This shows how transposition can be used as a theoretical framework to explain both convergence and divergence.

2.6. APPROPRIATION OF COMMON LAWS

'Appropriation of common laws' can also form the basis of an explanation of convergence.[35] As mentioned earlier, according to Patrick Glenn, although the English common law and the *ius commune* have been widely discussed within the context of Europe, the fact that there were many more common laws and that these common laws themselves were in dynamic relationship, has been neglected. Through this interaction and because individual legal systems appropriated notions, rules, institution and principles from these common laws, another explanation of convergence in Europe emerges. Until the nineteenth century the numerous common laws of Europe – French, German, Spanish, Dutch and English – lived in constant interaction with the local particular and with each other. As these common laws expanded both within and outside Europe, particular laws they met appropriated them. There was constant contact and intermingling. Common laws were the main instrument of 'conciliation' of laws. Claims of universality were reconciled with claims of particularity at a time when law was not seen as an exclusive product of the State. Even later, at a time of legal nationalism this continued to be the case. The resultant convergence, which takes us beyond the State, also supports State and other local forms of normativity. It only challenges 'exclusivity'. We should be able to extend this analysis to our day, as conciliation also means accommodating diversity and creating at least minimum commonality.

---

34 Ibid, p. 207.

35 GLENN, H.P., *On Common Laws* (2005).

2.7. 'FAMILY TREE' MODEL AND 'WAVE THEORY'

'For our purposes, the most significant theories however, come from linguistics. They can shed light on both convergence and divergence.'[36]

2.7.1.

In linguistics, the theory of the 'family tree model' of language development reflects an evolutionary approach and is the one generally used to explain ramification and divergence. The 'family tree' model (*stammbaum*) in linguistics was proposed by Augustus Schleicher in 1862.[37] This model assumed that resemblances arose from common origin (understood in terms of parenthood), and languages closely similar and linked were thought to have separated or diverged from each other, with original divergence and further subsequent divergence. The underlying human reality was originally thought to be migration of peoples.[38] Thus, when speakers are no longer in contact, they drift apart linguistically and they become isolated (evolutionary theory). The family tree model is coherent but only takes into account one of the ways in which change, difference and diversity occur. Exclusive reliance on the 'tree-model' of development can only explain ramification and divergence. The model overlooks 'the possibility that two languages may have passed through a period of common development, usually when their speakers occupied adjacent territories.'[39] In response, the 'wave theory' was developed.

2.7.2.

The 'wave theory' or 'wave hypotheses', showing how changes spread like waves and disperse over a wide area, can also handle the equally important forces of convergence.[40] This hypothesis was introduced again in the 19th century by another German linguist, Johannes Schmidt in 1872.[41] According to this hypothesis, different linguistic changes may spread like waves over a speech area thus leading to convergence. A subsequent wave may also move to areas not covered by the earlier wave. Schmidt drew lines (isoglosses) on a map to separate places where there were language differences, one isogloss enclosing one area with a particular linguistic form

---

36 See for an exposition and analysis of these theories: RENFREW, C., *Archaeology and Language: The Puzzle of Indo-European Origins*, Jonathan Cape, London, 1987, p. 244–248 (105).

37 SCHLEICHER, A., *Die Darwinsche Theorie und die Sprachwissenschaft*, Böhlau, Weimar, 1963. For the French edition: *La Théorie de Darwin et la Science du Langage* in *Receuil de Travaux Originaux ou Traduit relatifs à L'Histoire Littérraire* 1, Franck, Paris, 1968.

38 RENFREW, C., *Archaeology and Language* (1987), p. 101–102.

39 Ibid, p. 104.

40 Ibid, p. 105.

41 SCHMIDT, J., *Die Verwandtschaftsverhaltnisse der indogermanischen Sprachen*, Böhlau, Weimar, 1872.

(divergence). Successive waves create a network of isoglosses. If however, 'one dialect gains a political or commercial predominance of some sort over adjacent dialects, those nearest to this central dialect may give up their own peculiarities and come in time to speak only that central dialect.'[42] Colin Renfrew says that it is possible to imagine that the entire area covered by Indo-European languages or language groups was 'occupied initially by people who spoke a single Proto-Indo-European language.'[43] Following various local divergences (the tree model), the subsequent groupings would then have come about by the operation of the wave model. In this hypothesis, two or more closely related languages may each have features in common with their own neighbours that they do not share with each other. The relationships are far more complicated than any which could be conveyed simply by means of a family tree, as the wave model caters both for convergence and divergence.

However, similarities do not always arise from genetic relationships, neither does resemblance necessarily indicate common origin. There can be 'horizontal transfers' between adjacent systems. 'Horizontal transfer' can also explain why a borrowed concept or institution does not always exactly retain its original meaning. Areas nearest or adjacent to the initial change will change first and may even give up their own peculiarities. Subsequent re-groupings may come about on the 'wave model' mentioned above. Thus convergence can occur between concepts or systems originally very different.

It follows from the foregoing that a wave need not start from a fixed centre either. Developments can take place in steps with no one locale as the prime innovating centre. It is not necessary to depict one as the donor and the other the recipient. In this perspective, there is no one localised homeland but 'cumulative mutuality'. Interaction is the essence. The 'tree model' and the 'wave model' can be used together to explain developments. So can the 'knock-on-effect', which can also be regarded as the 'ripples' of the wave. As Renfrew says, 'it is, in fact, the resemblances between languages most distant from each other spatially which can least easily arise from the wave-like diffusion of an innovation, and are thus most likely to be the result, rather, of a relationship explicable in family tree terms.'[44]

2.7.3.

In short, as Renfrew shows, one language was spoken in historical terms, being simply the result of convergence, contact and interaction. 'That is to say that languages in

---

42 Renfrew, C., *Archaeology and Language* (1987), p. 105.
43 Ibid, p. 106.
44 Ibid, p. 111.

different areas which were not themselves necessarily related, became Indo-Europeanised through the process of contact.'[45] Contact leads to convergence and convergence to uniformity. It was later suggested instead, that there was some 'common origin', that is, 'the family tree model has to apply, at least in part, to explain some of the observed uniformity.'[46] However, 'that does not exclude the operation of the wave model.'[47] Thus, both on the 'tree model' and the 'wave model', a common ancestral origin is assumed. Yet, similarities can develop through time, by the process of convergence through contact. Therefore, common parentage is not in issue, since the ancestors could have been quite dissimilar, but through continuing contact, mutual influence and borrowing, the languages become significantly closer to each other, though never becoming identical. Thus waves cause diffusion and dispersals occurring spontaneously through contact.[48]

Replace the term 'language' by 'law', and one can see that this combined approach could also indicate a way forward for an understanding of how legal systems function, change and develop; converge or diverge. These combined theories cater for our understanding of both.

3. ORIGINAL AND ONGOING CONVERGENCE

3.1.

While developing the 'original convergence' thesis, I regarded relationships to be of the utmost importance.[49] This is not necessarily a claim at 'derivation', though that is also of great significance in the historical development of legal systems. In fact, historically most legal systems are related. The relationship between a legal system and its socio-cultural context does not exclude its relationship with other legal systems or even with other socio-cultural contexts. There is never 'exclusivity'.

When we take a fresh look at the classification of legal systems and re-assess their positions in relation to each other according to their parentage, their constituent elements and the resulting blend, and then re-group them on the principle of

---

45 Ibid, p. 45.

46 Ibid.

47 Ibid.

48 A variant, 'wave of advance model', was also proposed to explain the random, unsystematic, slow, gradual and continuous convergence, as opposed to colonisation, which also creates convergence, but through intentional and deliberate settlement. See: AMMERMAN, A.J., CAVALLI-SFORZA, L.L., 'The wave of advance model for the spread of agriculture in Europe', in: RENFREW, C., COOKE, K.L., (eds.) *Transformations, Mathematical Approaches to Cultural Change*, Academic press, New York, 1979, p. 275–294.

49 See: ÖRÜCÜ, E., 'Looking at Convergence through the Eyes of a Comparative Lawyer' (2005).

predominance, we immediately observe that legal systems that appear to be individually distinctive and even irreconcilable, are in fact parts of intertwined and overlapping family trees.[50] This supports my 'original convergence' thesis.

In Europe[51] we find evidence of 'common origins', of 'original convergence' and of 'ongoing convergence' if the legal systems are reassessed according to the old and the new overlaps and blends and as to how the existing constituent elements have mingled and are mingling with new elements entering them. For instance, English common law was an overlap of Roman law, civilian ideas, canon law, equity and domestic common law. Some continental systems in Europe are combinations of canon law, Roman law, French law and German law such as the Italian, some of Roman law, French law, German law and indigenous law such as the Dutch, some of customary law, neo-canon law, French law, German law, Swiss law, Greek law and Roman law, and even Ottoman law, as in Greece, and some such as Cyprus, of ancient Greek, Roman, Byzantine, Franco-Venetian, Ottoman and British laws. Roman law itself has elements of the laws of Hammurabi and ancient Greek laws. Overlaps of different ingredients account for French law and German law. So we see that all legal systems are crosses,[52] the basis of the 'original convergence' thesis.

European Law reflects combinations of Common Law, such as Irish, English and American Laws, and Civil Law in its many varieties, such as German, French, Dutch and Danish Laws, as well as mixed jurisdictions such as Scottish Law. All these have their own diverse historic ingredients. An enlarged Europe has even more to accommodate since it has to engage with the remnants of socialist law and legal culture and other varieties of the Civilian tradition.[53] In addition, an important subject of study today is the status of Islamic Law and its impact in Europe. Just as people are on the move in Europe today, so are legal systems.

---

50 See: ÖRÜCÜ, E., 'Family Trees for Legal Systems: Towards a Contemporary Approach', in: HOECKE, M., VAN, (ed.) *Epistemology and Methodology of Comparative Law*, Hart Publishing, Oxford, 2004. The idea of 'family trees' here should not be read to coincide totally with the 'tree model' discussed earlier (above 2.7.1.) as I envisage a number of family trees.

51 Here we are only concerned with Europe, but if we broaden our gaze, we see other regions where convergence is discussed. See: e.g., NIEKERK, G., VAN, 'The convergence of legal systems in Southern Africa' *3 The Comparative and international law journal of Southern Africa 35* (2002), p. 308–318.

52 For some more extreme crosses, one could look at Cyprus, Malta and Turkey, see: ÖRÜCÜ, E., 'Family Trees for Legal Systems: Towards a Contemporary Approach' (2004).

53 The opposite view has been expressed: '... we see more examples of flexibility at all levels and more differentiation in policies as diversity in the Union increases further with enlargement.' See: DIMITROVA, A., STEUNENBERG, B., 'The Search for Convergence of National Policies in the European Union – An impossible Quest?' (2000), p. 221.

Looking at Malta,[54] a new member of the EU for instance, we see more complicated crosses. In Malta, legal history began with the Phoenician settlement and continued with the Roman conquest bringing the *Corpus Iuris*. Then the Normans invaded and brought feudal law as applied in Spain, Naples and Sicily. The invasion of the Moors had direct influence on the Maltese language. The sovereignty of the Knights of St. John recognised local usage and issued declarations of private law drawing on laws of other countries, mostly Italian. Then came the French with their Napoleonic laws. Finally the British brought the Common Law. So here we see a good example of an eclectic Criminal Code drafted under strong Italian influence but with pervasive English and Scottish impact, and a Commercial Code largely based on the French, with maritime law following English Law. The 1873 Civil Code is predominantly based on the French and Italian Codes and also on the Municipal Code de Rohan, the Civil Code of Louisiana and the Austrian Civil Code. Canon law applies in family law where there is also the influence of English Law, German Law, Italian Law and French Law. Constitutional law is mainly British. The official languages are Maltese and English. The ingredients work cumulatively and interactively.

As pointed out by Luigi Moccia, whose working hypothesis is that 'Continental (Civil) law and English (Common) law stood together in past centuries as component parts of a same cultural context not yet affected by legal nationalism and positivism',[55] these are two traditions on a path of convergence as part of 'European culture'.[56] In many parts of the world, as well as at home, English law met the civilian tradition and happily lived with it. 'The two have never been strangers'.[57] English law borrowed from the civilian tradition, internalised various Roman law concepts into equity and common law, and thus enriched its common law. In addition, in the fields of contract law, commercial law and criminal law there were attempts at home to codify the law in the nineteenth and twentieth centuries. So it is clear that, common law and codification can co-exist. Examples can be found in other common law jurisdictions such the United States, where there is a variety of Codes such as the Uniform Commercial Code and the Californian Civil Code, and in Australia, where one talks of Code States with codified Criminal Law.

---

54 See: GANADO, J.M., 'Malta: A Microcosm of International Influences' in: ÖRÜCÜ, E., ATTWOOLL, E., COYLE, S., *Studies in Legal Systems Mixed and Mixing,* Kluwer law International, London, 1996, p. 225–247.

55 MOCCIA, L., 'Historical Overview on the Origins and Attitudes of Comparative Law', in: WITTE, B., DE, FORDER, C., (eds.), *The common law of Europe and the future of legal education*, Metro, Kluwer, Deventer, 1992, p. 609.

56 ZIMMERMANN, R., 'Savigny's legacy: Legal history, comparative law, and the emergence of a European legal science', *112 Law Quarterly Review* (1996), p. 557, 602.

57 Ibid.

In the early part of the last century, feelings of fairness and justice were seen to demand uniform laws for all, when the utopian idea of 'one law for the civilised nations' if not 'one law for the world' was expressed. It was soon realised that this was a dream, but many aspired to it. Harmonising the laws in certain regions such as in the Nordic Union and the Benelux countries, brought variations of this dream to life. Model laws, convention law and the like are all attempts to create uniform standards, often for the sake of convenience and to ease the way for economic integration as part of a political agenda. Furthermore, it is commonplace to wish to get closer together in times of peace and the reverse is true in times of conflict.

When considering 'ongoing convergence', we note that convergence is seen in many fields of law. It extends beyond the fields of private law, commercial law and procedural law. In fact, the mere existence of the European Union itself implies an active role for comparative lawyers in the development of general principles. The number of 'common core' projects and Commissions set up to prepare European Codes, General European Principles, European Case Books and Restatements, and to develop theories of 'competing legal systems', in addition to regulations, directives and conventions of the European Union and the Council of Europe, and the European Convention of Human Rights, bear witness to a plethora of activity in building the groundwork for further convergence and integration. Moreover, to provide answers to shared problems from this new pool of 'rule of reason', a *communis opinion doctorum novum* is developing.

3.2.

The existence of a common 'legal heritage' is indicated for instance in an Opinion of Advocate-General Warner of the European Court of Justice, who points out that the Court 'in developing the general principles of Community law, draws on what has been termed "the legal heritage" of all the Member States.' Having established a general principle by looking at the Danish, English, German, Italian, Scots and French laws, he says: 'What matters here, of course, is the existence of the principle, not the scope or mode of its application in the law of any particular Member State.'[58] The fact that this principle also exists in public international law under its English name 'estoppel', and that it has its origin in Roman law, strengthens his position.

In another case, Advocate-General Geelhoed specifically mentions resort to *ius commune*. He states that, 'regard must be had to the changes which have occurred in the legal systems of Western Europe over the last 50 years.' Legislators have catered

---

[58] *Boizard* v *Commission* 63 and 64/79 [1980] ECR 3002, (Advocate-General Warner).

for these developments, but 'individuals and interests not included in the scope of the legislation may not rely on the special protection provided by it. Therefore, they must rely on general rules of private law, such as *ius commune*.'[59]

In the context of Europe today, there is an effort to create an 'ever closer union', and although some see this only as a means of facilitating economic ties, others regard legal and cultural integration as the ultimate goal. Whether the starting point is 'common core' or 'better law', a number of areas are prepared for harmonisation and unification and in the search for closer integration in Europe, many hitherto neglected areas are being looked at. For example, though as yet there is no uniform family law for Europe, efforts are being made to create standardisation in aspects of family law through European law and Conventions related to respect for family life, the equal treatment of men and women, the equal treatment of legitimate and illegitimate children and the recognition of divorce, maintenance and custody judgements. The belief that family law, being culture bound, does not lend itself to comparison, let alone harmonisation, has been refuted,[60] and there is lively comparative law research activity in this field.

In addition, an increasing number of areas of law are designated as 'European' today, such as European competition law, European contract law, European tort law and European family law with European Commissions of academics working to produce general principles in these fields using either the 'common core' or the 'better law' approach. Treaty law also brings together rules in various branches of substantive law and private international law. To date several areas such as commercial law, trade and labour law, transport by rail, sea and air, copyright and industrial law and procedural law have been brought closer together and in some cases unified.

Moreover, a 'common law of human rights' is developing fast and there is already unity within Europe between both the Member States of the European Union and the jurisdictions subject to the Council of Europe Conventions. For example, within the European Union, both the European Court of Justice (ECJ) and the Court of First Instance (CFI) have jurisdiction – limited though it be – to ensure respect for fundamental rights arising 'from the constitutional traditions common to the Member States, as general principles of Community law.' Human rights or fundamental

---

59 The Advocate-General's opinion is both for *Gonzalez Sanchez* v *Medicina Asturiana SA* Case C-185/00, para. 66 and 67, and *Commission of the European Communities* v *French Republic* Case C-52/00.

60 See: BOELE-WOELKI, K., (ed.), *Perspectives for the Unification and Harmonisation of Family Law in Europe*, European Family Law Series No. 4, Intersentia, Antwerp-Oxford, 2003 and contributions to that volume. Also see: CRUZ, P., DE, 'Legal Transplants: Principles and Pragmatism in Comparative Family Law', in: HARDING, A., ÖRÜCÜ, E., (eds.) *Comparative Law in the 21st Century*, Kluwer Law International, London, 2002, p. 101–120.

freedoms and rights are seen as constitutive elements of European integration, part of a pre-existing 'common heritage'. These general principles now extend to the relevant rights arising under the European Convention on Human Rights. These principles, claims Advocate-General de Lamothe, 'contribute to forming that philosophical, political and legal substratum common to the Member States from which through the case law an unwritten Community law emerges.' Furthermore, 'fundamental principles of the national legal systems contribute to enabling Community law to find in itself the resources necessary for ensuring, where needed, respect for the fundamental rights which form the common heritage of the Member States.'[61]

There are also moves to create a 'common criminal law' for Europe, particularly for crimes that extend beyond the borders of a single nation state. Entities such as the European Union and the Council of Europe are regarded as facilitators for the realisation of these aspirations.

Administrative law systems in Europe are also converging and common rules, common principles and a common mentality are emerging. However we cannot yet talk of a common law of public law. Nevertheless, many concepts developed on the basis of the European Convention of Human Rights have seeped into domestic legal systems in Europe either directly or by way of European Community law. Mentalities, cultures and legal constructions are mixing to bring about such a common law. This is extremely significant.

The above show that ongoing convergence is inevitable. The repercussions will widen our so-called 'globalising' world.

Simplifying considerably, and ignoring 'original convergence', we can say that it was necessity that led to these efforts towards the creation of Europe-wide areas of law. The very fact that such European law is being developed indicates its feasibility. This only leaves open the question of desirability, which can be tied to political agenda. So, once one aligns oneself with the convergence approach, then discussion is needed as to how best to achieve the end of further convergence and on what is the right course of action. If one does not so align oneself, then, the 'contrarian challenge' must be followed to its bitter end, which might even render comparative law research a futile exercise!

---

61 Case 11/70 *Internationale Handelsgesellschaft* [1970] ECR 1125 at 1146–7.

4. PATHS OF CONVERGENCE

At this point, we need to return to a number of paths of convergence, presented on a spectrum, to assess developments in Europe today.

4.1.

The simplest path to take is the path of 'waiting' for gradual and incremental evolution of convergence. This is at one end of the spectrum of possibilities. Yet, to wait for gradual development may not be regarded as practical, in which case one way forward towards convergence or even uniformity would be through codifying basic principles in the fields under consideration – the most extreme option at the other end of the spectrum. Alan Watson, for instance, believes that one cannot look for 'satisfactory' law in 'the most common solutions, themselves the result of borrowing' or in established rules or 'in immediate positions of various mixed systems'. According to him, what is needed is 'authority': 'a common law for Europe requires the acceptance of a uniform system of adjudicating differences within a standard framework of the necessary sources of law. Authority is paramount, because it alone can constitute the common element.'[62] He then suggests that a standard system of authority can only be created by legislation, 'and this can only be achieved by a common civil code. The idea may be unpalatable in some jurisdictions, but it alone is workable.'[63]

In fact the European Parliament adopted Resolutions calling for the codification of European Private Law in 1989 and again in 1994. However, whether at present a European Civil Code is practicable, or even desirable, is under debate, though the project has found support in some quarters.

There are other options here. For instance, a European Code of Contracts could be a slightly watered down version of a European Civil Code.

4.2.

Another possibility is to unify the General Principles of Contract law and this has indeed been achieved. The Commission set up in 1980 for this purpose has completed its work, which could be the first step towards the production of a future Civil Code. Such projects on unifying General Principles which can then be used as Restatements,

---

62 WATSON, A., 'A Common Private Law for Europe?' *9 Maastricht Journal of European and Comparative Law 4* (2002), p. 330.

63 Ibid, p. 332.

are being undertaken in other fields also: thus another way forward is in American style Restatements. In this connection the work of the Commission on European Family Law (CEFL) related to aspects of family law must be mentioned.[64]

4.3.

The case-books approach has already produced its first fruits and 'law and economics' scholars suggest that when legal systems are in competition in a 'market of solutions', the 'best solution' will always win the day.

4.4.

An 'evolutionary theory' has also been suggested, as a variation of the 'law and economics' approach, whereby gradual and organic convergence could take place based on spontaneous 'cultural evolution' without any compulsory principles.[65] This more or less takes us back to the first position on the spectrum.

4.5.

Finally and at worst, transnational rules could function alongside national rules and eventually become congruent with them.[66]

4.6.

To support developments in Europe, legal education embracing both European and national principles could become compulsory in Law Schools and text books be produced to this end. Today, European Law Schools have been set up and new relationships between universities forged.

---

64 See for instance: CEFL's first product *Principles of European Family Law Regarding Divorce and Maintenance between Former Spouses.* BOELE-WOELKI, K., et al (eds.), Intersentia, Antwerp-Oxford, 2004.

65 SMITS, J.M., 'The Harmonisation of Private Law in Europe: Some Insights from Evolutionary Theory', *31 Georgia Journal of International & Comparative Law* (2002), p. 79–99.

66 HARTLIEF, T., 'Towards a European Private Law? A Review Essay', *1 Maastricht Journal of European and Comparative Law* (1994), p. 175

5. AN EXAMPLE STRADDLING TWO WORLDS

One way of looking at convergence would be to look at the example of the United Kingdom which straddles two worlds, with one foot in the *ius commune novum* with legal systems of the continental Europe, and the other in the 'unity of common law' with the legal systems in the Commonwealth and the USA. The United Kingdom, of which Scotland, a mixed jurisdiction, is a part, can be regarded as a point of confluence. This position can best be illustrated by recent cases. For instance in the *Fairchild* case,[67] inspiration was drawn from other common law jurisdictions such as Australia, New Zealand, Canada and the USA, from Scotland, a mixed jurisdiction, and also from civilian jurisdictions such as France, Germany, the Netherlands, Greece, Spain and Norway, as well as from Roman law. The aim was to create a 'convergence of reasoning' and a 'convergence of solutions', leading to 'interlocking' of legal systems.

> '*This survey shows, as would be expected, that though the problem underlying the cases such as the present is universal the response to it is not. [...] But [...] most jurisdictions would, it seems, afford a remedy to the plaintiff. Development of the law in this country cannot of course depend on a head-count of decisions and codes adopted in other countries around the world often against a background of different rules and traditions. The law must be developed coherently, in accordance with principle, so as to serve, even-handedly the end of justice. If however, a decision is given in this country which offends one's basic sense of justice, and if consideration of international sources suggests that a different and more acceptable decision would be given in most other jurisdictions, whatever their legal tradition, this must prompt anxious review of the decision in question. In a shrinking world [...] there must be some virtue in uniformity of outcomes whatever the diversity of approach in reaching that outcome [emphasis added].*'[68]

English law lives mainly in the 'unity of common law', a unity born of a process of colonial expansion within which English common law played and still plays a crucial role as the basis of harmony in the common law world and maintains this harmony by laying down paths of cross-fertilisation. For instance, in *Cheali* v *Equiticorp Finance Group Ltd and another*, Lord Browne-Wilkinson stated that, 'It is manifestly desirable that the law on this subject should be the same in all common law jurisdictions.'[69] Again, in *Bennet* v *Horseferry Road Magistrates' Court and another*: 'Whatever differences there may be between the legal systems of South Africa,

---

67 See above note 21.

68 Ibid, p. 334.

69 [1991] 4 All ER 989 PC.

the United States, New Zealand and this country, many of the basic principles to which they seek to give effect stem from common roots.'[70]

Judges use cases from other jurisdictions within this unity, attributing to them persuasive effect and sometimes even preferring one such decision over the domestic one. The different socio-cultures within, face the same legal culture: the common law. Specific to this unity, there is still the consciousness that common law is a whole and provides a strong tie between the several jurisdictions within the 'unity of common law'. Here convergence is striking and lessons can be drawn from this example.

6. CONCLUDING REMARKS

Rejecting both the 'dominance' and 'dependency' models and models of 'complete independence' in favour of 'interaction' models, we can conclude that though there are processes at work separating out individual systems, other processes are keeping them together but distinguishing them in their individuality.[71] Convergence, the result of contact and interaction, does not in any way reject diversity. If we regard legal systems in Europe as having started on equal footing, and now developing together a 'cumulative mutual Europeanness', then it is not necessary to see one region as the donor, the other the recipient. In the development process a combination of the '*stammbaum*' and 'wave' theories could effectively provide explanations. At an early stage some legal systems have separated like the branches of a tree, while others were formed by waves spreading out from secondary centres, especially when an 'innovation' set off a process of development. The picture is of overlapping waves as well as of spread. Rather than a wave emanating from a single central location, one can envisage an area where network linkages are intense and effective, such as that occurring today within the European Union. Here the wave model is harmonised with contact and interaction.

As a generalist comparatist I must stress that the place of comparative law and the comparative lawyer in all this is crucial. First, comparative law is a fundamental source of any Europe-wide project, in fact, of European law itself. It is the main tool for working towards the convergence of legal systems in Europe. It aids in overcoming exclusive nationalism and shows that convergence must be based on intercultural

---

[70] *Bennet* v *Horseferry Road Magistrates' Court and another* [1993] 3 All ER 138 HL.

[71] The suggestion and explanation in this paragraph is a calque inspired by Colin Renfrew, see: RENFREW, C., *Archaeology and Language* (1987), p. 246–248, who also uses the work of the Spanish linguist Antonio Tover (1977).

communication while leaving room for diversity. The mere existence of the European Union implies that comparative law has a serious role in the developing of principles, in the search for common roots, common principles and common solutions to bring about rapprochement.

Second, the kind of comparative law that facilitates intercultural communication needs comparative lawyers trained in interdisciplinary research problems, with knowledge of, and familiarity with, different legal cultures, a good command of languages, knowledge of history, economics and politics, and also methodology.

The comparative approach in the activities of EU judges should be regarded as 'a "quasi-compelling" method of interpretation of Community law intrinsically linked to the continuous integration process which characterises the European construction.'[72] As put by Koen Lenaerts, the European Union, 'has its own variant of *E pluribus unum*, that is a set of interlocking legal orders, showing mutual respect for each other based on equivalent levels of judicial protection of the rule of law. That constitutes the common platform for the legal underpinnings of European integration, a *ius commune* built with the bricks of the comparative law method'.[73]

Within Europe today, 'common core' projects regard legal systems as being multi-level and consider comparative law as an 'integrative' enterprise.[74] Regarding cultural diversity in law as an asset while not taking a preservationist approach for its own sake, the aim must be to work towards building European culture on a map of multi-level legal systems. This building of a common culture puts strong emphasis on legal education – education that recognises the crucial place of comparative law teaching.

To reiterate, at one end of the spectrum any 'unification' or 'harmonisation' project is integrationist and based on the search for 'common cores' – leading eventually to convergence – while at the other, difference and distinction are used to create and defend national legal identity by an 'insulation' project – leading eventually to divergence. The drive towards a common 'European identity' is achievable by cross-border import and export of ideas and collaboration to create further convergence. Restricting Europeanisation to new legislation and scholarly publications alone cannot achieve this however. When and if the rules of national legal systems are regarded as local variations of uniform European subject matter,

---

72 Lenaerts, K., 'Interlocking Legal Orders in the European Union and Comparative Law' 52 *International and Comparative Law Quarterly* (2003), p. 873–906, 878–879.

73 Ibid, p. 906.

74 Bussani, M., 'Current Trends in European Comparative Law: The Common Core Approach' 21 *Hastings International and Comparative Law Review* (1998), p. 785.

then it is clear that there is room for both convergence and divergence. The ultimate aim is for congruous development with natural convergence in a loosely connected unity. As noted above, convergence does not preclude diversity since differentiation and flexibility are not in the way of 'convergence', though they may be in the way of complete 'integration' or total 'Europeanisation'. Juxtaposed against the reality of 'ongoing convergence', theories of convergence must trump theories of divergence.

PART II
FROM DIVERSITY TO SIMILARITY: REGIONAL TENDENCIES

APPROXIMATION OF NORDIC FAMILY LAW WITHIN THE FRAMEWORK OF NORDIC COOPERATION

INGRID LUND-ANDERSEN

1. INTRODUCTION

Dating back to the time of the Vikings there has been a special relationship between the three Scandinavian countries, Denmark, Norway and Sweden. They are neighbours, and in the more distant past they went to war against each other in order to take possession of each other's territories. This has meant that, through the ages, in various ways there have been different forms of union between these countries or parts of them.

Today this has resulted in the languages of the three countries being very similar. It is easy to read the languages of the other countries, though there are clear differences of pronunciation and each spoken language has a different melody.

The legal cooperation between the Scandinavian countries is based on these two factors: common cultures and similar social conditions which go back over hundreds of years, and languages which are substantially similar.

The intensity of harmonisation of laws has varied at times but it now seems to be entering a new era. Finland and Iceland which, together with the Scandinavian countries, constitute the Nordic countries are increasingly involved in this cooperation.

2. DEMOGRAPHICS

The relationships between the peoples of Denmark, Norway and Sweden can be compared with the kind of love-hate relationship that exists between many siblings.

Sweden is the big sister; it has a population of around 9 million, which is nearly twice that of either of the other two. At 5.4 million, *Denmark's* population is a little larger than that of Norway's 5.0 million. *Norway* is the little sister who has been held down, having been subject to the rule both of Denmark and of Sweden. From 1387 to 1814 Norway was in a union with Denmark, and from 1814 to 1905 it was in a union with Sweden. In 1905, Norway became an independent sovereign state with its own king, who had originally been a prince of Denmark.

Today these three countries are held to be among the best countries in the world to live in. In Scandinavia the policy of equality is well established and there are extensive social security systems. The same applies to Finland and Iceland.

Finland can be regarded as a kind of step-sister, linked to Sweden – the big sister. In terms of its population, Finland is about the same size as Denmark. From1154, Finland was joined to Sweden for about 700 years until 1809, when it became a part of the Russian Empire. Finland claimed its independence shortly after the Russian Revolution in 1917. Finnish children learn Swedish in school and about 6% of Finns have Swedish as their mother tongue. The Finnish language is part of a totally different language group and it is not at all understandable for Scandinavians.

Iceland is like a little foster child which is now standing on its own feet. The population, which numbers about 300,000, speaks and writes Icelandic, which is an old Nordic language which cannot be read or understood in the other Nordic countries. Iceland was previously a Danish colony, together with Greenland and the Faeroes.[1] Iceland became independent in 1918. Danish is taught in schools in Iceland.

Today the problem of language is the greatest hindrance to closer cooperation between the Scandinavian countries and Finland and Iceland, as their laws and law books are mostly written in Finnish or Icelandic.

3. NORDIC LEGAL COOPERATION – A SHORT HISTORY

Since 1872, every three years lawyers from the Nordic countries have been able to take part in *Nordic Lawyers Meetings,* where a number of the most current legal issues are discussed. At the first meetings the topics discussed included issues such as the

1 Greenland and the Faeroes are self-governing regions, which are part of the Danish state. Most of the laws adopted by the Danish Parliament do not apply to Greenland and the Faeroes. Åland has a corresponding status in relation to Sweden.

property of married people and the property rights of spouses. There are generally several hundred participants – judges, advocates, law professors etc.

After World War II there was a great desire to strengthen cooperation between the 5 Nordic countries. Two official bodies were established, both having the development of legal cooperation as one of their aims. In 1952 the *Nordic Council* was set up; this is a body for promoting cooperation between the parliaments of the Nordic countries. And in 1971, as an addition to this, the *Nordic Council of Ministers* was set up, to promote cooperation between governments.

In the area of family law, since 1980 a *Nordic Family Law Seminar* has been held each alternate year. This is an association for cooperation on family law in the Nordic countries. The seminars are arranged in turn in one of the Nordic universities and last for 2–3 days. The number of participants is limited to a maximum of 40 specially invited family law experts. In addition to legal academics, the participants include advocates and representatives from government ministries with responsibilities for family law.

It can thus be said that a good framework has been established for the discussion and development of ideas.

Legal cooperation between the countries during the last 100 years can be divided into 4 phases:

Phase 1: 1909–1927. This was a period *of major law reforms in the Scandinavian countries with the aim of full harmonisation.* Cooperation was both intense and successful. The discussions at the first meetings of Nordic lawyers concerning property rights between spouses led to invitations being issued to a conference in Stockholm in 1909 for the preparation of the most appropriate common Scandinavian legislation in the area of family law. The topics selected were: rules on separation and divorce, property rights as between spouses, and the resolution of international conflicts of law in these areas. Among other things, there was emphasis on areas where individual countries had a pressing need for reform of their legislation, and where it was important for the relations between the countries to reach agreement.[2] A three-member committee was then appointed in each country. What characterised the work at that time was that the committees had very few members, the meetings between

2 See the Danish Report 'Udkast til lov om ægteskabs indgaaelse opg opløsning', København, 1913, p. 1, and the Danish Report 'Udkast til lov om ægteskabets retsvirkninger', København, 1918, p. 3–4.

the delegates of the three countries were lengthy (up to several weeks),[3] in each of the three countries the draft laws were the same on questions of principle, and the laws were forward looking.

This cooperation led to the implementation of new core rules for married couples (the Act on Contraction and Dissolution of Marriage and the Act on the Legal Effects of Marriage in Denmark, and corresponding legislation in Norway and Sweden) in the period 1913–1927, based on the recommendations of the committees. The rights to separation on the grounds of incompatibility and to divorce on the grounds of a certain period of separation were introduced, thereby acknowledging that marriages were not to be preserved at any price. The basis for the legislation on property rights between spouses was the legal equality between man and wife. Consideration for the housework of wives argued against arrangements for separate property, and each of the three countries introduced deferred community of property instead. An important precondition for this successful Nordic cooperation lay at the political level. At this time a small group of experts could prepare a relatively short draft law, which was largely accepted both by governments and parliaments.[4]

Phase 2: 1955–1969. After a long period without changes being made, there was a period of *minor reforms with only partial harmonisation.* In 1955 the Nordic Council recommended that the governments should examine the conditions for a revision of the legislation in the Nordic countries on marriage and the property rights of spouses. Again expert committees were appointed which had only very few members. Thus, in Denmark there were 5 expert committee members. There was good cooperation between the committees, but this was less intensive than it had been at the beginning of the century. The joint meetings lasted only a few days, and as the extent of revision varied between countries, not all the issues were discussed. Finland and Iceland were also included in this work.[5] Among other things, the rules on separation and divorce were changed to make it easier to dissolve a marriage.

Phase 3: 1970–1998. The youthful uprisings of 1968 had an influence on family law rules, as family law suddenly became politically interesting. In Sweden, the Social Democrats had a firm hold on the government and here there was a desire for radical reform. Politically, there was no time to be lost in discussions within the Nordic framework, nor was there felt to be a need for Nordic legal unanimity. In all the

---

3 See the Danish Report 'Udkast til lov om ægteskabs indgaaelse og opløsning', København, 1913, p. 2.

4 Cf. Danielsen, S., Lødrup, P., 'Det nordiske samarbejde på familierettens område', *Tidsskrift for Rettsvitenskab* (1988), p. 567. Some of the information given in this review is taken from this article.

5 For more detail on the Nordic cooperation see the Danish Report No. 369/1964, 'Ægteskabs indgåelse og opløsning samt forældremyndighed og samkvemsret', p. 5–6.

Nordic countries committees were appointed to revise the marriage laws. By this time the committees had grown in size, and for the first time a number of politicians were appointed as members. In Sweden six politicians were appointed as members of the committee – three from the Social Democrats and three from the right of centre parties – with a lawyer as the chairman.[6] The Danish committee finally consisted of 18 members, of whom, 11 were politicians, one from each political party represented in Parliament.[7]

The general attitude was that the debate within one's own country mattered most. This *acceptance of the weakening of Nordic cooperation* meant that *harmonisation* was only *sporadic*. In any event, family laws developed very differently in each country. An important exception is the law on registered partnerships for same-sex partners, which I will return to shortly.

Phase 4: 1998 to the present. In 1998 the Nordic Council of Ministers, in the form of the Nordic Ministers for Justice, asked 3 professors from Denmark, Norway and Sweden to undertake a comparative study of Nordic family law. The aim was to assess the possibilities for and benefits of harmonising the laws. This was an official acknowledgement of a desire to strengthen cooperation. The new initiative is characterised by the fact that a fundamental review of the rules is to be made and the most important differences are to be identified. Further, a description is to be made of where there is a practical need for cooperation, as well as the issues, which are suitable for harmonisation in the short, medium and long term. Family law in Finland and Iceland are also described and concrete proposals for uniform rules are to be made for each sector. The discussions are conducted on the basis of a 'better lawmaking' assessment.

The practical basis for the new cooperation is that a large number of citizens move around within the Nordic area, marry and have children. It has also been pointed out that if the Nordic countries harmonise their laws they will be able to speak with one voice in international forums and thereby obtain greater influence.[8]

---

6 See the Swedish Report No. 1981:85, 'Äktenskapsbalk', p. 4.

7 See the Danish Report No. 915/1980, 'Samliv uden ægteskab I', p. 7.

8 For many years Danish interest in participating in international cooperation in the area of family law has been limited and this has been criticised by DANIELSEN, S., in 'Internationalt samvær', in: IVERSEN, T., KRISTENEN, L.H., WERLAUFF, E., *Hyldestskrift til Jørgen Nørgaard*, København, 2003, p. 318.
Neither Norway nor Iceland is a member of the European Union, and Denmark has reserved its position with regard to legal cooperation. Iceland is the only Nordic country which is not represented in the Commission on European Family Law.

The Nordic Council of Ministers has given financial support, and several university departments have agreed to carry out research in support of this work. Since 1998 the group of experts has added a couple of members, including members from Finland. So far, 4 major books have been issued; one on the law of marriage, one on inheritance, and two on the law of children – on parental authority, paternity, and child support.[9] The next step is planned to be a book on the cohabitation of unmarried partners, but surprisingly, in November 2006, the Nordic Council of Ministers rejected the application for funding – in any case for the time being.

This initiative is a return to the model used in Phase 1, with few legal experts making concrete proposals on the basis of close cooperation. *The aim is more harmonisation.* Several of the tasks, which were carried out in Phase 1 as part of the work of the committee itself, are now performed by legal academics. This means that professors and lecturers who participate in Nordic writing projects use their research resources to create a basis which makes it easier for civil servants and politicians to decide whether the time is right to initiate work on reform. Likewise, the committees appointed benefit from the descriptions made of the law in the other Nordic countries. Today this division of labour is more justified than previously, as in recent years committees have often had to work within tight deadlines and under close political scrutiny.

In contrast to the situation in Phase 3, politicians are no longer members of family law committees. Instead representatives of special interest groups and professional experts are appointed.

4. EXAMPLES

Nordic cooperation on these books has already had a clear influence on Danish thinking in the new report on *parental authority and contact*, which was published in May 2006.[10] In the terms of reference for the committee preparing the report it was stated that the committee should take account of developments in the other Nordic countries, as recently set out in the Nordic book on Children Law II.[11] The influence of this book is seen in the fact that the committee's recommendation refers to the existing rules in Finland – which is not often the case in such recommendations – as

9 AGELL, A., *Nordisk äktenskapsrätt*, Nord 2003:2, København, 2003, LØDRUP, P., *Nordisk arveret*, Nord 2003:3, København, 2003, LØDRUP, P., AGELL A., SINGER, A., *Nordisk børneret I*, Nord 2003:4, København, 2003 and DANIELSEN, S., *Nordisk Børneret II*, Nord 2003:14, København, 2003.

10 Danish Report No. 1475/2006, 'Barnets perspektiv'.

11 DANIELSEN, S., *Nordisk Børneret II*, Nord 2003:14, København, 2003.

well as including a description of the rules in Iceland – which is extremely rare. Moreover, the descriptions of the existing laws in the other Nordic countries are more detailed than is usual in committee recommendations. The fact that the author of the book was also a member of the committee may have been a factor in this.

Finally, it is interesting that, encouraged by the good experiences in Finland, Norway and Sweden, the majority of the committee proposed that, in special cases, the courts can decide to grant joint parental authority against the objections of one of the parties, and decide where the child shall live. The Danish Parliament went a step further and introduced a rule according to which the court only may revoke joint parental authority due to weighty reasons. Hitherto such rules have been rejected in Denmark, as they have been considered to be contrary to the basic idea of joint parental authority constituting a framework for cooperating parents. The committee also proposed that, in certain circumstances, a child should have a legal entitlement to have contact with people other than its parents. This proposal too was based on the experience of the rules on this in Iceland, Norway and Sweden. Thus, steps towards harmonisation have been taken in the area of the legal relationships between parents and children, even if the rules are not identically expressed.

I will now give two examples to illustrate both circumstances, which can form the basis for wide-ranging harmonisation in the Nordic countries, and circumstances which are not favourable to harmonisation.

In 1989, as the first country in the world, Denmark introduced a law allowing *registration of civil partnerships between people of the same sex.*[12] Registered partners were given almost the same legal rights as married people, apart from rights in relation to children and the right to marry in church.

During the work of the commission, which preceded this legislation, there had been considerable disagreement between its members about the way forward, and there was virtually no cooperation with the other Nordic countries. A minority of 5 members recommended the introduction of a law on registered civil partnerships, but a majority of 6 members, including the legal experts, opposed this.[13] There was much debate on the question in the media, so that even before the commission published its report proposals had been made in Parliament for the introduction of

12 Act No. 372 of 7 June 1989 on registered partnerships, with effect from 1 October 1989. The Act is described by LUND-ANDERSEN, I., 'The Danish Registered Partnership Act', in: BOELE-WOELKI, K., FUCHS, A., (eds.), *Legal Recognition of Same-Sex Couples in Europe*, Intersentia, Antwerp, 2003, p. 13- 23.

13 See the Danish Report No. 1127/1988, 'Homoseksuelles vilkår'.

a law on civil partnerships. The Members of Parliament had a free vote and the law was adopted with 71 votes in favour and 47 against.

This model recognises certain fundamental values of Danish society:

1. *Equality* is granted to partners, regardless of their sexual orientation. Gay and lesbian groups are strongly organised in Denmark, and on this point the law had important symbolic value.
2. The law is based on *freedom of choice*: it is up to same-sex couples to decide whether or not they want to register their relationships.
3. The law does *not affect church matters*. For most Danish people the church is only of ceremonial importance, and the church's influence on society is small. Accordingly, registered partnerships are entered into at register offices.

Since 1989 the same basic model has been adopted in Norway (1993),[14] Sweden (1994),[15] Iceland (1996)[16] and most recently in Finland in 2001.[17] In part this can be explained by the fact that the values referred to above are also considered important in the other Nordic countries. And in part this has been an issue of significant political interest, so it has been natural to introduce a model, which is in accordance with the wishes of homosexuals when the same model has worked well in other Nordic countries.

When one compares the laws, there appears to be *almost complete harmonisation.*[18] From the perspective of harmonisation it must therefore be considered that the introduction of registered partnerships has been a success story in the Nordic countries. This agreement has presumably influenced the introduction of arrangements for registered partnerships in many other countries, which are similar to the Nordic model to a greater or lesser extent.[19]

In contrast to this is the legal situation on the *division of the property of unmarried cohabitants upon dissolution of cohabitation.*

14 Act No. 40/1993.

15 Act No. 1117/1994.

16 Act No. 87/1996.

17 Act No. 950/ 2001.

18 However, on one important question Sweden stands alone – or has gone ahead of the other countries – as on 5 June 2002 the Swedish Parliament adopted a law allowing registered partners to adopt children, including international adoptions, see Prop. 2001/02:123.

19 See BOELE-WOELKI, K., FUCHS, A., (eds.), *Legal Recognition of Same-Sex Couples in Europe*, Intersentia, Antwerp, 2003, and CURRY-SUMMER, I., *All's well that ends registered?*, Intersentia, Antwerp, 2005.

In the 1970s in Denmark, Norway and Sweden it was up to the courts to find a solution when, on the termination of a cohabiting relationship, one cohabitant claimed part of the other cohabitant's property, and in particular part of the value of the shared home.

The lower courts in each country chose a solution similar to joint ownership, presumably inspired by the concept of constructive trusts, as known in common law jurisdictions.

In the course of the 1970s the Norwegian Supreme Court developed a joint-ownership solution in which housework was considered as equivalent to making a financial contribution, both in respect of married partners and cohabitants.[20] The Supreme Court justified this on the basis that 'any other conclusion would be contrary to the view of modern society and the sense of justice'.[21] What may have been decisive for this finding was that, in the key case in the Supreme Court, some of the judges were women.

The same issue was decided in the opposite direction in Denmark where in 1980 the Danish Supreme Court rejected the concept of joint ownership and instead introduced the possibility of the financially weaker party obtaining a compensatory amount on the basis of an enrichment principle.[22] In a later case in 1984 it was stated that only in extraordinary cases could emphasis be put on housework and care.[23] No woman judge took part in either of the decisions.[24]

In Sweden, legislation was introduced in 1987, which regulated the division of the property of unmarried cohabitants on the termination of cohabitation – the Cohabitants (Joint Homes) Act. This provided that the value of the joint home and the household goods must be divided between the cohabitants, provided they are acquired during the cohabitation.[25] This is a solution which often gives the same result as joint ownership but which is in fact a rule for the division of property which,

20 For more details, see SVERDRUP, T., 'Maintenance as a separate issue – The Relationship Between Maintenance and Matrimonial Property', in: BOELE-WOELKI, K., (ed.), *Common Core and Better Law in European Family Law*, Intersentia, 2005, Antwerp, 2005, p. 122–124.

21 See the so-called 'Housewife case', *Norsk Retstidende,* 1975, p. 220.

22 See *Ugeskrift for Retsvæsen* 1980, p. 480.

23 See *Ugeskrift for Retsvæsen* 1984, p. 166.

24 For more details, see LUND-ANDERSEN, I., 'The Legal Status of Cohabitants in Denmark', in: SCHERPE, J., YASSARI, N., *Die Rechtsstellung nichtehelicher Lebensgemeinstschaften – The Legal Status of Cohabitants*, Max-Planck-Institut Hamburg, Mohr Siebeck, Tübingen, 2005, p. 460–463.

25 For more details, see RYHRSTEDT, E., 'The Legal Status of Cohabitants in Sweden', in: SCHERPE, J., YASSARI, N., *Die Rechtsstellung nichtehelicher Lebensgemeinstschaften – The Legal Status of Cohabitants*, Max-Planck-Institut Hamburg, Mohr Siebeck, Tübingen, 2005, p. 418–426.

with regard to domestic assets treats, cohabitants in the same way as married partners with community property. The legislation is an expression of a political decision to establish neutrality as between different forms of family structures.

In all three countries the aim has been the same – to ensure that the financially weaker party does not end up empty-handed upon the termination of cohabitation. However, it must be noted that the law in Norway and Sweden gives the weaker party greater protection than is given under the Danish model. This is because under Norwegian law – in contrast to Danish law – housework is considered equivalent to making a financial contribution, and the law in Sweden gives cohabitants who are covered by the Cohabitants (Joint Homes) Act the same rights as married couples with community of property as regards the marital home and contents. Furthermore, the methods used have been quite different. In Denmark and in Norway the law has been established by the courts, so the choice of judges who heard the case in question in the Supreme Court was important. In contrast, in Sweden the property rights of unmarried cohabitants are regulated by legislation, which reflects the political climate of the time. *Harmonisation in this area would appear to be almost impossible.*

Looking at the situation in a wider international context, no other country has introduced rules corresponding to the Swedish Cohabitants (Joint Homes) Act, and no other country appears to have gone as far as Norway in recognising housework as being equivalent to other contributions to the common property of cohabitants. On the other hand, the Danish model of giving compensation for unjustified enrichment appears to be quite common.[26]

5. CONCLUSION

The Nordic model for civil partnerships has inspired the introduction of similar arrangements in many other countries, and this shows that joint action by the Nordic countries can have an influence on international developments.

The year 1998 was a turning point for Nordic cooperation and harmonisation in the area of family law. Thus, the basis for *information* about the law in the other countries has been greatly improved by the considerable efforts made in preparing books on existing Nordic law. Furthermore, discussions between legal experts and joint

26 See Law & Policy, Volume 26, No. 1, *Special Issue on Family Law and Policy: Cohabitation and Marriage Promotion*, January 2004, and SCHERPE, J., YASSARI, N., *Die Rechtsstellung nichtehelicher Lebensgemeinstschaften – The Legal Status of Cohabitants*, Max-Planck-Institut Hamburg, Mohr Siebeck, Tübingen, 2005.

proposals for harmonisation can give significant *inspiration for law reforms.* A group of civil servants regularly evaluates the practical possibilities and need for harmonisation of Nordic laws.

It will be seen that there are clearly points of similarity between the extensive comparative studies of Nordic family law and the work of the *Commission on European Family Law.* However, *Nordic cooperation* has some particular advantages. First, the social conditions and legal traditions are more similar in the Nordic region than in the rest of Europe. Second, the analyses of the legal situations are made in greater depth, as only the 5 Nordic countries are involved. Third, in the concluding chapters in the Nordic books it is possible to refer to nuanced recommendations, as there are no proposals for guiding principles and the more restricted formulations, which arise from them.[27] It is these differences that mean that the Nordic cooperation and the work of the Commission on European Family Law can fruitfully supplement each other.

---

[27] See the principles of the Commission on European Family Law in BOELE-WOELKI, K., et al, *Principles of European Family Law Regarding Divorce and Maintenance Between Former Spouses,* Intersentia, Antwerp, 2004.

FAMILY LAW OF SPANISH AUTONOMIES: FOLLOWING A SIMILAR PATTERN?

MIQUEL MARTÍN-CASALS

1. FAMILY LAW WITHIN THE CONTEXT OF NON-UNIFIED CIVIL LAW IN SPAIN

As is well known, the Spanish codification process failed to unify civil law in the Spanish Civil Code 1889. Several Spanish territories continued to apply their historical private law, the Spanish Civil code in these parts of Spain being subsidiary applicable law only. Under Franco's dictatorship, in a process starting at the end of the 1950s and lasting until 1973, the law of these territories was laid down, with some restrictions, in a series of "Compilations" (*Compilaciones*). With the recovery of democracy, the Spanish Constitution 1978 set a new framework for the survival of private law in these parts of Spain, establishing a distribution of legislative powers between the Central State and the Autonomous Communities which has given rise to a great deal of debate over the last three decades.[1] For the purposes of this paper, it is useful to emphasise from the outset that:

[1] Artículo 149. 1. El Estado tiene competencia exclusiva sobre las siguientes materias:... 8. Legislación civil, sin perjuicio de la conservación, modificación y desarrollo por las Comunidades Autónomas de los derechos civiles, forales o especiales, allí donde existan. En todo caso, las reglas relativas a la aplicación y eficacia de las normas jurídicas, relaciones jurídico-civiles relativas a las formas de matrimonio, ordenación de los registros e instrumentos públicos, bases de las obligaciones contractuales, normas para resolver los conflictos de leyes y determinación de las fuentes del derecho, con respeto, en este último caso, a las normas de derecho foral o especial [Translation of the author: Art. 149. 1. The State shall have exclusive competence over the following matters:... 8. Civil legislation, without prejudice to the preservation, modification and development by the Autonomous Communities of their civil law, foral or special, whenever this exists. In any event, rules for the application and effectiveness of legal provisions, civil relations referring to the forms of marriage, keeping of records and drawing up of public instruments, bases of contractual liability, rules for resolving conflicts of law and determination of the sources of law in conformity, in this last case, with the rules of foral or special law.

(1) Not all Spanish Autonomous Communities are empowered to legislate on civil law, but only those Autonomous Communities that had historically had their own private law and had kept it in force over the centuries. This means that out of the 17 Spanish Autonomous Communities only 6 (Aragon, the Balearic Islands, Catalonia, Galicia, Navarra and the Basque Country) have, according to the Constitution, the power for the "preservation, modification and development" of their own Civil law.

(2) As regards family law, the Constitution sets out the boundaries of the legislative powers of these Autonomous Communities by stating that, in any event, the State will keep the power to legislate on what it calls "civil relations arising from the forms of marriage". There is a general consensus that this means that these 6 Communities cannot pass family law rules on marriage dealing with aspects such as capacity to marry, formalities of marriage, its celebration or, in general, personal aspects of marriage. However, it is also clear that they have the power to legislate on the economic relationships of marriage. It is also generally accepted that the personal aspects of divorce (but not the economic ones) are to be legislated on by the Central State only and, so far, no Autonomous Community has made any attempt to pass legislation on this subject matter.

In the wake of the Spanish Constitution 1978, in 1981 the Spanish legislature passed two Acts introducing into the Spanish Civil Code far-reaching family law reforms: (1) An extensive amendment of filiation, parental responsibility and matrimonial property[2] and (2) An amendment to the regulation of marriage, including separation and annulment, and reintroducing divorce into Spanish law.[3]

In the 1980s political parties and social groups at local level tried to cope with the new problems posed by the need to reduce bitterness appearing in cases of separation and divorce, especially if children were involved, and to deal with an increasing number of cohabiting partners. It is precisely in these two areas of family mediation and of opposite- and same-sex partnerships where the legislatures of many Spanish Autonomous Communities have been very active over the last decade.

---

2 Ley 11/1981, de 13 de mayo, *de modificación del Código civil en materia de filiación, patria potestad y régimen económico matrimonial* (BOE num. 119. from 19.5.1981).

3 Ley 30/1981, de 7 de julio, *por la que se modifica la regulación del matrimonio en el Código civil y se determina el procedimiento a seguir en las causas de nulidad separación y divorcio* (BOE num. 172, from 20.7.1981)

2. THE INTRODUCTION OF FAMILY MEDIATION AND OF A SCHEME FOR OPPOSITE- AND SAME-SEX COUPLES BY THE AUTONOMOUS COMMUNITIES

2.1. INITIAL IDLENESS OF THE SPANISH LEGISLATURE AND CATALAN ACTIVISM

Family mediation was introduced in Spain at the beginning of the 1980s by establishing multidisciplinary teams assisting family law courts. At the end of the decade a service of family mediation had been created in the Basque country and pilot programmes on family mediation were brought into operation in some courts in Barcelona,[4] Madrid and some other cities in Spain.[5] Although the 1981 reforms in the law of marriage did not even mention family mediation, the regulation of separation and divorce allowed for the parties to establish an agreement on most of the effects of the marriage breakdown (*convenio regulador*), which was mandatory when both parties agreed to separate or divorce. The rules also provided that in these cases of uncontested proceedings, both parties could be represented by a single lawyer. Although the agreement of the effects of separation or divorce had to be approved by the judge, it could be reached without his intervention and this opened up the possibility that third neutral and impartial parties could help parties to resolve their disputes in an informal way.

In the case of cohabitation, at the end of the 1980s many Spanish city councils established municipal registers where opposite-sex cohabitants, initially, and also same-sex cohabitants, afterwards, could declare that they were living together not only for the purposes of obtaining the small benefits that city councils could afford to award them, but, mainly, to furnish proof of cohabitation as regards a possible future breakdown, in order to claim the meagre benefits that case-law was ready to give them in those days.

---

4 ORTUÑO, P., 'La aprobación judicial de los acuerdos en mediación familiar', 2,3 *Apuntes de Psicología* (2000), p 287–302; Consol BALDELLOU, M., *Hacia un nuevo derecho de familia. Una visión desde el ejercicio de la abogacía*, *ibid*, p. 303–316.

5 See, instead of many, RIPOLL-MILLET, A., *Familias. Trabajo social... y mediación Barcelona*, Paidós, 2001, p. 74; HINOJAL, A., *La mediació familiar en l'àmbit de les administracions públiques. La mediació familiar en el divorci o procés legal de separació*, en GENERALITAT DE CATALUNYA. DEPARTAMENT DE JUSTÍCIA *La mediació familiar*, Barcelona, Generalitat de Catalunya. Departament de Justicia. Centre d'Estudis Juridics i Formació Especialitzada, 2001, p. 103–138; Osma, M. A.., LOZA, S., 'Mediación familiar: Experiencias y reflexiones desde el ámbito público', 5 *Anuario de Sexologia A.E.P.S* (1999), p. 85–99.

During the 1990s, however, the Spanish legislature did not seem to perceive the need to pass legislation on these matters. No legislative action at all was taken as regards family mediation and for many years the Spanish Parliament struggled unsuccessfully with a Bill presented by the conservative *Partido Popular* on what was called in Spain "contrato de unión civil", and which followed the model of "contrat d'union civile" then discussed in France.[6]

On the recovery of self-government in 1980, the coalition of conservative nationalist parties in the Catalan government developed an ambitious legislative programme in Catalan civil law, which could not ignore that it was necessary to deal with problems not previously regulated. In 1998 the Catalan Parliament passed the Catalan Family Code,[7] which mentioned family mediation and the need to prepare an Act on this matter. In the same parliamentary session it passed another Act – which the government did not want to include in the Family Code – on what was called "Stable Unions of Couples" (hereafter LUEP).[8]

As regards family mediation, a Final Provision of the Family Code established that the Government had to prepare a draft Bill on family mediation and introduce it into the Catalan Parliament within a maximum of six months after the Family Code had entered into force. This provision also set out the main guidelines of the future regulation by establishing that mediation should be based upon confidentiality, voluntary participation of the parties, judicial approval of the agreements and a short duration of the mediation proceedings, i.e. mediation could last three months only and, when necessary, could be extended for a maximum period of another three months (Third Final Provision). The Catalan government met the deadline and presented a Bill on family mediation,[9] but the Bill was dropped due to oncoming elections. After the elections, the new Government, supported by the same conservative coalition, presented a slightly amended Bill to Parliament,[10] which, after a few months, became the 2001 Catalan Family Mediation Act.[11]

---

6 Instead of many, see, TRÍAS SAGNIER, J., 'El contrato de unión civil y las modificaciones legislativas que introduce', *Actualidad Jurídica Aranzadi, Num. 215*, 30.10.1997, p. 1–5 and GARCÍA GÓMEZ, R., 'El contrato de unión civil. Reflexiones sobre la conveniencia de una regulación de las uniones de hecho', in: MARTÍNEZ GALLEGO, E., (Coord.), *Matrimonio y uniones de hecho*, Ediciones Universidad de Salamanca, Salamanca, 2001, p. 117–154.

7 Llei 9/1998, de 15 de juliol, *del Codi de família* (DOGC num. 2687, 23.7.1998; correction of mistakes DOGC num. 2732, 28.9.1998). An English translation can be found at http://www.gencat.net/justicia/normes/angl/l9preame.htm.

8 Llei 10/1998, de 15 de juliol, *d'unions estables de parella* (DOGC num. 2687, 23.7.1998). An English version of this Act can be found at http://www.gencat.net /justicia/doc/doc_10614500_1.pdf.

9 See: *Projecte de Llei de mediació familiar de Catalunya*, BOPC num. 384, 29.3.1999, p. 31721–31726.

10 See: *Projecte de Llei de mediació familiar de Catalunya*, BOPC num. 83, 12.6.2000, p. 34–40.

11 See: Llei 1/2001, de 15 de març, *de mediació familiar de Catalunya*, DOGC num. 3355, 26.3.2001 (hereafter LMFC).

As regards opposite and same-sex partnerships, the 1998 Act on the Stable Unions of Couples, also promoted by the same conservative coalition, provided that persons meeting certain conditions, such as being of age, not having a certain degree of kinship and not being previously married, were eligible to establish opposite or same-sex partnerships according to the scheme of the Act. The regulation of opposite and same-sex couples was very similar, but same-sex unions could be established by public deed only and were granted more rights than opposite-sex unions, since the idea underpinning the Act was that whereas opposite-sex couples had an alternative scheme (i.e. marriage), same-sex couples did not.

2.2. FAMILY MEDIATION ACTS

2.2.1. Main Characteristics of the Acts of the Autonomous Communities

In 2001, a few months after the Catalan Family Mediation Act was passed, two other Autonomous Communities: Galicia[12] and Valencia[13] – passed their own Acts. In 2003 the Canary Islands[14] passed the fourth, Castile-La Mancha[15] followed suit in 2005 with the fifth and finally, Castile and Leon[16] and the Balearic Islands[17] passed their respective family mediation Acts in 2006.

It is worth mentioning that some of the Autonomous Communities that have passed family mediation Acts do not have legislative powers on civil law and, in spite of that, have made a regulation that touches upon some private law family matters on the grounds of legislative powers for "Social Services".

To a greater or lesser extent, all these Acts follow the model of the Catalan Act, but also show differences in aspects referring, for instance, to:

---

12 Ley 4/2001, de 31 de mayo, *reguladora de la mediación familiar* (DOG num. 117, 18.6.2001) (hereafter, LMFG).

13 Ley 7/2001, de 26 de noviembre, *reguladora de la Mediación Familiar en el ámbito de la Comunidad Valenciana* (DOGV num 4.138, 29.11.2001, p. 25105–25116) (hereafter LMFV).

14 Ley 15/2003, de 8 de abril, *de la Mediación familiar* (BOC num. 85, 6.5.2003, p. 7136 et seq., slightly amended in 2005 (cf. Ley 3/2005, de 23 de junio, *para la modificación de la Ley 15/2003, de 8 de abril, de la mediación familiar* [BOC num. 130, 5.7.2005, p. 12259 et seq.]) (herafter LMFIC).

15 Ley 4/2005, de 24 de mayo, *del Servicio Social Especializado de Mediación Familiar* (DOCM num. 111, 2.6.2005, p. 1149 et seq.) (hereafter LMFCLM).

16 Ley 1/2006, de 6 de abril, *de mediación familiar de Castilla y León* (BO Castilla y León, num. 75, 12.4.2006) (hereafter LMFCL).

17 Ley 18/2006, de 22 de noviembre, *de mediación familiar* (BO Illes Balears, num. 170, 30.11.2006) (hereafter LMCIB). When proofreading this text two new Autonomous Communities have passed their Acts on family mediation: Madrid (Ley 1/2007, de 21 de febrero, *de mediación familiar* [BO Comunidad de Madrid, num. 54, 5.3.2007]) and Asturias (Ley 3/2007, de 23 de marzo, *de mediación familiar* [BO del Principado de Asturias 9 abril 2007, num 81]).

a) Practice of family mediation: All Spanish Acts devote a large part of their provisions to dealing with the principles of family mediation, the professional conditions that must be met to become mediator, the mediation procedure, the duties of the mediator and, if infringed, to which sanctions this gives rise. However, most of the Acts of the Spanish Autonomous Communities do not pretend to govern all types of mediation and their provisions apply to public mediation only. Public mediation is organised by the Autonomous Government, sometimes as a service attached to the Ministry of Justice and, occasionally, through a Centre of Family Mediation (as is the case in Catalonia), while in other cases it is treated as any other Social Service and attached to the corresponding ministry (as, for instance, in the case of Castile-La Mancha). A novelty in this respect is the Balearic Act, which provides not only that mediation must be performed by certified and registered mediators (cf. Art. 29 LMFIB), but also that they must pertain to officially approved mediation centres. These mediation centres may be established by professional associations and both private and public legal entities which, in all cases, i.e. even if they are private entities, are governed by the Act and "are considered as to be included within the scope of social services specialised in the area of family" (cf. Art. 30 LMFIB).

b) Persons entitled to enter mediation: The different Acts show a clear trend towards widening the circle of persons who are entitled to submit their disputes to family mediation. Thus, whereas in the case of purely *de facto* couples, i.e. couples not governed by the Catalan Act on Stable Unions, the Catalan Act restricts mediation to matters affecting children and more precisely, to conflicts arising from parental responsibility (cf. Art. 5.3 LMF), other Acts, such as the Galician one (cf. Art. 4.2 LMFG), do not establish any restriction with regard to cohabitants. More expansionist is the Valencia Act, which although also limiting family mediation to couples established according the legislation of the Community (cf. DA 2ª), provides that mediation can take place between family members up to the fourth degree of consanguinity or affinity (cf. 3.a LMFV). This means in practice that the Act considers that the same model of family mediation is suitable for solving conflicts, for instance, not only between grandparents and children but also between cousins or between the wives of two brothers. Additionally, the Valencian Act provides for mediation between adult persons given up for adoption when they were children and their biological parents (cf. Art. 3 y Art. 13 LMFV). Also very wide is the understanding of "family" for the purpose of family mediation in the Canary Islands' Act (cf. Art. 3 LMFIC) and even wider in the Act of Castile-La Mancha, where family mediation can solve conflicts not only between family members but also personal conflicts between children and their family members or "close persons" (*allegados*) (cf. Art. 3 LMFCLM).

c) Sorts of conflicts which can be submitted to family mediation: As we can see, to lay down who is eligible for family mediation already gives us an idea about the types of conflicts that can be submitted to mediation. However, it does not offer a complete picture. Thus, the Catalan Act, for instance, provides that conflicts on maintenance arising between all family members can also be submitted to mediation (cf. Art. 5.2 LMFC) and, the Valencia Act establishes that the provisions of the Family Mediation Act can also be applied to conflicts arising in a family business (cf. Art. 13.1.a).6 LMFV). By contrast, the Balearic Act does not enumerate all the specific conflicts which may be submitted to family mediation and provides that "There is no mediation if there is no family conflict...In any case, questions which may be submitted to family mediation must always refer necessarily to matters of civil family law which, according to this law, are at the disposal of the parties and which are eligible to be raised in a court" (cf. Art. 8 LMFIB).

2.2.2. The State's Proposal on Mediation

The 2005 Act modifying the Civil Code and the Civil Procedure Act on separation and divorce,[18] established in one of its Final Provisions that "[T]he government will submit to Parliament a Bill on mediation based upon the principles established by the provisions of the European Union and, in any case, on voluntary participation, impartiality, neutrality and confidentiality and respecting the services of mediation established by the Autonomous Communities" (Third Final Provision). To promote mediation, this Act also amends the Civil Procedure Act (hereafter LEC) by adding a new rule providing that the parties may temporarily suspend civil proceedings in order to enter mediation (cf. Art. 770, 7ª LEC) and that, among the documents included when filing a separation or divorce by common agreement, they may also include the document recording the agreement that the parties have reached through mediation (Art. 777.2 LEC).

It is worth stressing that the provision referring to a future Bill on mediation, does not speak about a Bill on "family mediation", but just of a Bill on "mediation". And it does not say that what must be respected are the "mediation Acts" of the Autonomous Communities, but the "services of mediation" they have established.

At the end of 2005 the Commercial Section of the Spanish Codification Commission prepared a draft Bill on "Voluntary Jurisdiction",[19] i.e. a proceeding in which the intervention of the judge is requested or is necessary without there being actual

[18] Ley 15/2005, de 8 de julio, *de modificación del Código civil y de la Ley de Enjuiciamiento Civil en materia de separación y divorcio* (BOE num. 163, 9.7.2005, p. 24458 et seq.).

[19] Boletín de Información del Ministerio de Justicia, *Anteproyecto de Ley de Jurisdicción Voluntaria*, Octubre 2005, núm. 1999 (Suplemento).

litigation. This draft Bill provided for a general regulation on court-connected mediation without any further qualifications, i.e. without confining mediation to family law conflicts. In a short regulation of 7 articles only, the draft Bill provided that at any stage of the proceedings the parts could ask for the adjournment of the proceedings "in order to reach an agreement counting on the mediation activity of a third party" (cf. Art. 34.1) and that the court, on its own motion, could also adjourn proceedings and send the parties to a free information session (Art. 34.2) stressing, nevertheless, that "participation of the parties in this mediation activity will be voluntary" (cf. Art. 38.2). Other provisions referred to the adjournment of the proceedings (Art. 35) the appointment of the mediator (Art. 36), and included some references to traditional principles of family mediation such as neutrality and impartiality of the mediator (Art. 37) or wilfulness and confidentiality of the mediation (Art. 38). Finally, the last two provisions referred to the mediation agreement and its effects and to the termination of the mediation without having reached any agreement (cf. Arts. 39 and 40, respectively). This draft Bill would have brought the Spanish treatment of mediation close to the most recent European trends which, in countries such as Austria[20] and Belgium,[21] point at general private law mediation Acts, i.e. not confined to family law matters.[22] However, the Bill finally presented to Parliament by the Spanish government[23] has dropped the regulation of mediation altogether without giving any sort of explanation.

2.2.3. Practical Results

Unfortunately, there is no data available on the success of family mediation in the different Autonomous Communities during these years. In some cases, the period elapsed since the corresponding Act was passed is too short. In any case, the Autonomous Communities do not publish this data and it is an extremely complicated process to obtain it. However, as regards family mediation in Catalonia, although the number of mediations is increasing, it is far from satisfactory. By the end of 2006 the Catalan Family Mediation Centre considered that around 700 family

---

[20] *29. Bundesgesetz über Mediation in Zivilrechtssachen (Zivilrechts-Mediation-Gesetz-ZivMediatG) sowie über Änderungen des Ehegesetzes, der Zivilprozessordnung, der Strafprozessordnung, des Gerichtsgebührengesetzes und des Kindschaftsrechtsänderung-gesetzes 2001* (BGBl Teil I, 6. Juni 2003, Nr. 29) (available at http://www.mediatorenliste.justiz.gv.at/mediatoren/mediatoren.nsf/vwFiles/Gesetz/ $FILE/ 2003a029.pdf.

[21] 21 février 2005, *Loi modifiant le Code judiciaire en ce qui concerne la médiation, Moniteur Belge/ Belgisch Staatsblad*, 22.03.2005, Ed. 2, pp. 12772-12778, available through http://www.ejustice.just.fgov.be/doc/rech_f.htm.

[22] See, in more detail: MARTÍN-CASALS, M, 'Divorce Mediation in Europe: An Introductory Outline', *l 9.2 Electronic Journal of Comparative Law* (2005), http://www.ejcl.org/92/art92–2.html.

[23] *Proyecto de Ley de Jurisdicción voluntaria para facilitar y agilizar la tutela y la garantía de los derechos de la persona y en materia civil y mercantil*, Boletín Oficial de las Cortes generales – Congreso de los Diputados, Serie A, num. 109–1, of 27.10.2006.

mediation proceedings had taken place according to the scheme provided by the Act since it came into force in 2001. If we consider that we are talking about a population of 7 million people experiencing around 20,000 legal separations and divorces per year and that in Catalonia there are about 1,400 trained and registered mediators, these figures should oblige the Catalan legislature to re-examine whether the established scheme should be improved or not.

2.3. OPPOSITE-SEX AND SAME-SEX PARTNERSHIPS ACTS

2.3.1. Main Characteristics of the Acts of the Autonomous Communities

The model established by the Catalan Unions of Stable Couples Act provides that an opposite-sex couple can be established either by cohabitation for two years or by public deed. A period of cohabitation is not necessary when the cohabitants have a common child. By contrast, same-sex couples can be established solely by common agreement of the parties formalised in a public deed. Registration in a public register is not necessary either for opposite-sex or same-sex couples.

With reference to the rights of these two types of couples, the most striking difference is that, in the case of death, the surviving same-sex partner has more rights than the surviving opposite-sex partner. Thus whereas opposite-sex partners are entitled to limited rights only, such as the right to continue on living in the common home for one year, surviving same-sex partners have, additionally, rights in the intestate succession of their pre-deceased partner. By contrast, originally only opposite-sex couples could adopt jointly, but this difference was abolished in 2005.

Regarding the bundle of rights and duties established in the Act, most of them are part of a default scheme and partners can establish the rules governing the relationship by an agreement that does not require any specific form.[24] However, some rights cannot be excluded, either because they are implicitly considered public policy (for instance, joint liability for common expenses [Art. 5 LUEP] or the reciprocal duty of maintenance [Art. 8 LUEP]) or because the Act expressly lays down a "minimum of rights" that the partners cannot exclude.

24 Art. 3.1 LUEP provides that "[T]he members of the stable couple may regulate validly, either verbally or in writing by means of a private or public instrument or deed, the personal and patrimonial relations deriving from the cohabitation and the respective rights and duties. They may also regulate and govern the economic payments that are appropriate in the event of termination of the cohabitation, with the minimum of the rights that are governed in this chapter, which cannot be renounced until they become enforceable."

This "minimum of rights" refers to cases where the relationship ends while the two cohabitants are alive and: (a) firstly, to the need to grant economic compensation to the partner who suffers a detriment because he or she has worked for the benefit of the common household, receiving no compensation or insufficient compensation in exchange and because life in common has given rise to a situation of inequality between the wealth of both partners that amounts to an unjust enrichment (cf. Art. 13 and 16.3 LUEP) and (b) secondly, to the need to grant maintenance for a maximum period of three years to the partner to whom life in common has decreased his or her earning capacity or, in the case where the partner has to continue on taking care of a common child, until the child is emancipated or comes of age (cf. Arts. 14 and 16.4 LUEP).

Although it is possible for the parties to agree on how to fulfil these "minimum rights" (for instance, by the payment of a lump sum or with assets instead), the Act does not allow them to exclude these rights entirely, probably aiming at preserving a minimum of protection for the weaker party. However, it cannot be denied that this limitation runs counter the self-determination of the parties and that the protection of adult persons in full possession of their senses could have been better served by establishing procedural and substantial safeguards for their agreements.

From 1999 to 2006, another 12 Autonomous Communities[25] have passed Acts on opposite-sex and same-sex partners. This means that currently 13 out of the 17 Spanish Autonomous Communities have their own Acts.

---

[25] This is the case of Aragon (1999) Navarre (2000), Balearic Islands (2001) and the Basque Country (2003), i.e., Autonomous Communities with legislative powers on family law, and also of Valencia (2001), Madrid (2001), Asturias (2002), Castile and Leon (2002), Andalusia (2002), Canary Islands (2003), Extremadura (2003) and Cantabria (2005), which are Communities that do not enjoy these powers.
See: Aragon: Ley 6/1999, de 26 de marzo, *relativa a parejas estables no casadas* (BOE num. 95, 21.04.1999). Navarre: Ley Foral 6/2000, de 3 de julio, *para la igualdad jurídica de las parejas estables* (BOE num. 214, 6.9.2000); Balearic Islands: Ley 18/2001, de 19 de diciembre, *de Parejas Estables* (BOE num. 14, 16.1.2002; Basque Country: Ley 2/2003, de 7 de mayo, *reguladora de las parejas de hecho* (BOPV num. 100, 23.5.2003) and Valencia: Ley 1/2001, de 6 de abril, *por la que se regulan las uniones de hecho* (BOE num. 112, 10.5.2001); Comunidad Autónoma de Madrid: Ley 11/2001, de 19 de diciembre, *de Uniones de Hecho de la Comunidad de Madrid* (BOE num. 55, 5.3.2002); Asturias: Ley 4/2002, de 23 de mayo, *de Parejas Estables* (BOE num. 157, 2.7.2002); Andalusia: Ley 5/2002, de 16 de diciembre, *de Parejas de Hecho* (BOE num. 11, 13.1.2003); Canary Islands: Ley 5/2003, de 6 de marzo, *para la regulación de las parejas de hecho en la Comunidad Autónoma de Canarias* (BOC num. 54, 19.3.2003); Extremadura: Ley 5/2003, de *Parejas de Hecho de la Comunidad Autónoma de Extremadura* (DOE num. 42, 8.4.2003); Cantabria: Ley 1/2005, de 16 de mayo, *de parejas de hecho* (BO Cantabria num. 98, 16.5.2005). See also in Castile and Leon a regulation also dealing with partnerships but whose main aim is to establish a register: Decreto 117/2202, de 24 de octubre, *Registro de Uniones de Hecho* (BO Castilla y León num. 212, 31.10.2002).

One could ask to what extent these Acts follow the Catalan model. The answer is not easy, but in general it can be said, that they follow the structure of the Catalan Act and its provisions, although they introduce some changes which are crucial. So, for instance:

a) The emphasis on private rights or on public or social rights: An important difference can be drawn between the Acts of those Autonomous Communities that have powers to legislate on private law and those that do not have them. When they do, their Acts tend to recognise family and succession rights for couples similar to those recognised by the law of the Autonomous Community to married couples. When they do not have these powers, the Act concentrates on bringing opposite- and same-sex couples into line with married couples in social rights resulting from public law issued by the Autonomous Community and referring to areas such as public housing, medical treatment, civil-servant law and tax law.[26] The impact is limited, though, since many of these areas are mainly governed by the law of the State, not of the Autonomous Community.

b) Divergences in family law and succession law: Even in those Communities having legislative powers on private law, the final result regarding the rights of opposite- and same-sex couples on family property matters and in the law of succession is very different, since family law and law of succession are vary greatly from Community to Community and the Acts tend to mirror their regulation with the matrimonial property and succession law of the corresponding Community. For instance, in Aragon, where married couples can issue a joint or reciprocal will, the right is extended to couples under the new scheme (cf. Art. 15). This is not the case in Catalonia, where joint or reciprocal wills are forbidden.

A common characteristic is, however, that they do not recognise a matrimonial property regime for opposite- and same-sex couples such as married couples have, but some basic rules only.

c) Positive discrimination: The Catalan Act introduces positive discrimination in favour of same-sex partners, on the grounds that "same-sex partners cannot marry even if they want to",[27] by awarding them rights in the intestate succession of the pre-deceased partner. By contrast, all the other Acts treat opposite-sex and same-sex partners equally in the case of succession rights, without introducing positive discrimination. It must be emphasised that the opening of marriage to same-sex

[26] See for instance: the Act of Andalucia, Arts. 14 to 22.

[27] See: Preamble of the Catalan Act.

partners in 2005 by the amendment of the Spanish Civil Code has left the positive discrimination of the Catalan Act without a rationale.

d) The constitution of the relationship: The Catalan Act provides that a condition for a couple entering the scheme is, among others, that none of the partners is still married or a member of another recognised stable union which has not been dissolved. All the other Acts also include this requirement. However, as regards the way of entering the relationship, the Acts are very different.

Catalonia establishes a "double track" (cohabitation / public deed) for entering into a partnership in the case of opposite-sex partnerships, whereas same-sex partnerships can be established by a public deed only. The rules in force in 3 other Autonomous Communities, however, accept these two forms of constitution both for opposite and same-sex partnerships.[28]

By contrast, in all the other Autonomous Communities, the two-track model encompassing cohabitation and public deed has been replaced by registration in a specific register. The declaration of will embodied in this registration is, in these Autonomous Communities, a formal condition for the validity of all sorts of partnerships.[29] Thus, for instance, the Act of the Basque Country provides that registration "... will have constitutive character, so that this Act shall not apply to those [couples] who are not registered" (cf. Art. 3.1).

2.3.2. Practical Results

A question that may arise with regard to all these regulations is how effective they are, which sorts of problems they have solved, of which sorts of couples, etc. The same that has already been said regarding mediation can be repeated here: on the one hand, in many cases where Acts have been in force for such a short time that it is difficult to analyse their impact. Moreover, in all cases it is extremely difficult to obtain reliable data in order to carry out an impact analysis of these Acts.

But let us use the data available about Catalonia as a simple example. According to the data of the census of 2001, there were in Catalonia almost 1.5 million married couples[30] and more than 130,000 unmarried couples.[31] Out of these 130,000

---

28 In this sense see: the Acts of Aragon (Art. 3.1), Navarre (Art. 2.2) and Asturias (Art. 3.2).

29 See, for instance: the Acts of the Balearic Islands Act (Art. 1.2), the Basque Country (Art. 3.1), Cantabria (Art. 1), the Community of Valencia (Art. 1.1 and 1.2), Extremadura (Art. 4) and Madrid (Art. 1.1).

30 Exactly, 1,412,522.

31 Precisely, 131,856.

unmarried couples roughly 70% only qualified for entering the scheme provided by the law. This means that there were around 90,000 who could enter the scheme, but by the end of 2005 only around 2,400 couples had entered a "stable union" according to the scheme provided by the Catalan Act "formally", i.e. by public deed. In short: the percentage of couples using the formal constitution is very small (around 2.5% of all couples).[32] This means that, under the Catalan Act and others that are similar, most couples will become stable unions by cohabitation during a certain period. In the case of those Communities where couples must register, the estimate is also that the number of registered couples is quite low.

More worrying is the condition of not being married for being able to enter the scheme even in a factual way, i.e. by mere cohabitation. This condition, in Catalonia at least, is leaving almost one third of cohabiting couples out of the scheme, which in the case of widows, normally elderly women, living together with undivorced men increases to around 42%.[33]

2.3.3. The State's Silence and New Catalan Activism: What's Coming Next?

It cannot be denied that the proliferation of Acts in the Spanish Autonomous Communities was driven more by the need to give a legal framework to same-sex couples than to establish an alternative to marriage for opposite-sex couples. Now that Spain has joined the small club of countries that allow same-sex marriage, a reconsideration of these schemes seems to be necessary.

Once again the Spanish legislature has failed to give guidance on this point. In 2004 the Spanish Ministry of Justice announced the preparation of an Act "addressed to governing other forms of living together, such as unmarried couples, which also have a place in a free, open and plural society where different options of life in common exist".[34] However, over the last two years no preliminary text or draft Bill has been produced, something which probably can be interpreted in the sense that after opening marriage to same-sex couples and establishing divorce at will in the 2005 reforms, the Spanish legislature does not consider that this matter is urgent any longer. This is at least the interpretation given by the Supreme Court, which after the reform

---

32 For a detailed overview of these and other data see: MARTÍN CASALS, M., *'La regulació de la parella de fet: Lleis i models'*, in: ÁREA DE DRET CIVIL DE LA UNIVERSITAT DE GIRONA (ED.), 'Nous reptes del Dret de família', *Materials de les Tretzenes Jornades de Dret Català a Tossa*, Documenta Universitaria, Girona, 2005, p. 335 ff.

33 See : MARTÍN CASALS, M., 'La regulació de la parella de fet: Lleis i models', *ibid.*

34 *Libertad digital*, 4.10.2004 http://www.libertaddigital.com. See also: the intervention of the speaker of the Socialist parliamentary group during the debate on the different bill proposals dealing with cohabiting couples (Sr. Pedret Marzà) (DS, Congreso, VIII Legislatura, Pleno, n. 21, 29.6.2004, 925).

has changed its paternalistic approach in the protection of weaker cohabitants not governed by any specific Act[35] and has declared that "cohabitation is an institution that has nothing to do with marriage, although both of them are within family law" and that "after same-sex marriage and unilateral divorce are in existence it can be stated that unmarried unions are made up of people who absolutely do not want marriage and its consequences".[36]

Will the Catalan legislature now take the lead once again? Although it is too early to say, the new Catalan Statute of Autonomy (hereafter EC) tackles the issue. The new Statute of Autonomy is a political constitution of the Autonomous Community, which in a difficult debate that has lasted two years has fuelled up the traditional mixture of dislike and admiration that many Spaniards feel for their Catalan countrymen. In a part of the Statute of Autonomy devoted to rights and duties and within a section dealing with "the protection of persons and families", it provides that"[P]ublic authorities will promote equality between different stable unions of couple, taking into account their characteristics, irrespective of the sexual orientation of their members. An Act shall regulate these unions and other forms of life in common and their effects" (cf. Art. 40.7 EC). The Catalan Statute of Autonomy has opened up a second political transition in Spain and is being imitated by other Autonomous Communities currently amending their Statutes. It is very likely that they will include similar provisions and if they include this particular provision on stable unions this may perpetuate the current situation of plurality of regulations.

Hopefully, the other Communities will not imitate the amendment on the regulation of opposite-sex and same-sex couples prepared in 2006 by the Catalan legislature which, fortunately enough, for now will not become law since the call for new elections for November 2006 led to the dissolution of the Catalan Parliament. In the Bill of the 2nd Book of the Catalan Civil Code referring to persons and family, the Catalan government made a regulation which, in my opinion, gives rise to many doubts, not only about the constitutionality of the proposed regulation, but also about its rationality.

The Bill keeps the double track for entering the relationship, i.e. by cohabitation and by public deed, but provides for a status that is more comprehensive than before, so that couples governed by the scheme are almost indistinguishable from married couples. However, according to the proposed regulation, a basic condition for establishing a stable union of couples has disappeared: people still married to third

---

35 See, among many others: the decisions SSTS 17.1.2003 (RJ 2003\4); 31.12.2003 (RJ 2003\9005); 17.6.2003 (RJ 2003\4605); 14.5.2004 (RJ 2004\403) and 23.11.2004 (RJ 2004\7385).

36 In this sense STS 12.9.2005 (RJ 2005\7148 = La Ley 2005, 1826).

persons are eligible for establishing a stable union, not only through cohabitation but also through a formal declaration vested in a public deed (cf. Art. 234–2 PCCC). By contrast, once the union has been established, a subsequent marriage or a subsequent union dissolves the previous one (Cf. Art. 234–6 PCCC).[37] In practice this means that establishing a stable union creates a status, which is practically identical to marriage, even when a previous marriage has not been dissolved and even if cohabitants have made no declaration about the effects they want to give to their cohabitation. The proposal opens up the opportunity to leave marriage without any content, since although entering cohabitation does not give rise to divorce because it does not break marriage, it has all its practical effects: it replaces the status of a non-dissolved marriage still in force by a cohabitation status having the same effects. In my opinion, the Act has wrongly followed the principle "one fits all" and has deepened the confusion between a cohabitation (or factual) model and a registered partnership (or formal) model existing in the regulation in force and the current mismatch of rules. Let us hope that the new Catalan government revises past decisions or, at least, that in the other Autonomous Communities common sense prevails.

[37] See: *Projectes de llei del Codi Civil de Catalunya*, Barcelona, Generalitat de Catalunya, 2006.

THE ACCESSION OF BULGARIA TO THE EUROPEAN UNION: A PATH TO THE HARMONISATION OF FAMILY LAW?

Velina Todorova

To the memory of Vladi

1. INTRODUCTION

This chapter aims to explore the correlation between the current changes of Bulgarian Family law and the process of Europeanisation in Bulgaria. The analysis will refer to the rich body of literature both on Europeanisation and on the harmonisation of family law in Europe.

Accession to the EU was the dominating political and legal discourse in Bulgaria after the fall of Iron Curtain in 1989.[1] Bulgaria applied for EU membership in 1995, opened accession negotiations in 2000, concluded them in December 2004 and achieved full membership in January 2007. Accession negotiations, without any reservations, were the most powerful factor for reforms during that period. The literature has portrayed the process of Europeanisation[2] from the viewpoints of

[1] The strategic objective of integration with the EU has been maintained by consensus by all governments since 1990. Bulgaria's application for Union membership, backed by a virtually unanimous endorsement from the National Assembly, was lodged on 14 December 1995. The Government Memorandum accompanying the application states: "Bulgaria's membership of the European Union constitutes a strategic goal and is a matter of national interest. It will consolidate the results of the democratic reforms which have been carried out since the beginning of the 1990s and will represent a political acknowledgement of their success. Commission Opinion on Bulgaria's Application for Membership of the European Union, p.8. DOC/97/11 Brussels, 15.07.1997. At: http://ec.europa.eu/enlargement/archives/pdf/dwn/opinions/bulgaria/bu-op_en.pdf.

[2] The term "Europeanisation" is borrowed from the relevant literature. I accept all the concerns of those authors who regard it as ambiguous, in particular when it is used to describe the process of accession of post communist countries to the EU. In this case the term embraces not only meeting accession requirements but also the coinciding processes of post-communist transition and modernisation. See: Grabbe, H., *The EU's transformative power: Europeanisation through conditionality in Central and Eastern Europe*, Palgrave Macmillan, New York, 2006, p. 4–5.

its actors, discussing its "transformative effect"[3] on the country's laws, institutions, policies and the differences between the 'Europeanisation West' and 'Europeanisation East'.[4] In my chapter I will use this conceptualization to outline the changes in the area of family legislation, but I will refrain from discussing its implementation.

The policy of the EU towards Central and Eastern European countries (CEE) in the process of enlargement has most often been described as a 'policy of conditionality'.[5] The continuing adjustment of Bulgarian legislation is a good illustration of this policy. Its major driving force is the external pressure explained as 'top-down' influences from the Union on the Government, which produces the transformative effects. This description is valid for the conditionality not only to comply with the *acquis communàètaire* but also to meet the so-called 'democratic conditionality' for accession. This chapter aims to set out the way that family legislation in Bulgaria has been influenced by both the requirements of the *acquis* and 'democratic conditionality', even not particularly projected.

The impact of the process of Europeanisation on the harmonisation of family law in Europe has been discussed in the literature, though mainly with regard to the existing member states and less so with regard to prospective member states. The debate is focused on the power and ethics of the EU legislating on family matters.[6] No doubt the Union has no unified body of substantive family law to be used as *acquis*

---

3 GRABBE, H., 'The process of EU Accession: What will it bring to Southeast Europe?', 2003, p. 7, *Global Development Network for Southeast Europe*, available at: http://www.wiiw.ac.at/balkan/files/GDN_EU_Grabbe_EUaccessionprocess.pdf.

4 The academic debate makes distinction between the Europeanisation in member states and in the accession countries, particularly in Central and Eastern Europe. Several specific points of the impact of the accession process on the candidate countries have been defined in the literature, including: 1/ the coincidence of Europeanisation in the East with the post-communist transition process, 2/ the asymmetrical relationship between the EU and the candidate countries that gives the EU more coercive power and influence in the negotiations, making accession more a 'top down' rather than an interactive 'top down' and 'bottom up' process, 3/ the uncertainty and diffuseness of the process of EU enlargement into the East, 4/ the need to go beyond the *acquis communautaire* (the standards accession countries are required to meet) and to promote democracy via 'democratic conditionality'. In: GRABBE, H., 'The process of EU Accession: What will it bring to Southeast Europe?' (2003); HERITIER, A., 'Europeanization Research East and West: A Comparative Assessment', in: SCHIMMELFENNING, F., SEDELMEIER U., (eds.), *The Europeanization of Central and Eastern Europe*, Cornell University Press, New York, 2005; PEEVA, S., *Childcare Reform in Bulgaria – a Case of Europeanization?*, Dissertation completed as a Candidate No. 16322 for the MSc European Politics and Governance, the LSEPS, 2006 (unpublished).

5 GRABBE, H., 'The process of EU Accession: What will it bring to Southeast Europe?' (2003); PEEVA, S., *Childcare Reform in Bulgaria – a Case of Europeanization?* (2006).

6 See: MEULDERS-KLEIN, M.-T., 'Towards a European Civil Code of Family Law? Ends and Means', in: BOELE-WOELKI, K., (ed.), *Perspectives for the Unification and Harmonisation of Family Law in Europe*, European Family Law Series No. 4, Intersentia, Antwerp-Oxford, 2003; MARTINY, D., 'Is Unification of Family Law Feasible or even Desirable?', in: HARTKAMP, A., et al (eds.), *Towards a European Civil Code,* (third edition), Ars Aequi Libri, Nijmegen, 2004. MCGLYNN, C., 'The Europeanisation of Family Law' in: *1 Child and Family Law Quarterly 13* (2001).

conditionality for applicant countries. However, as the experience of Bulgaria suggests, accession to the EU has the potential to harmonise the family legislation of the aspirant countries or at least some parts of it. Not only the rich body of international conventions that serve as the basic principles of the judicial cooperation in civil matters within the framework of the 'Justice and Home Affairs" *acquis*[7] but also some specific conditions that the Commission sets out for each applicant country produce this effect. For example, the 'democratic conditionality' that steadily evolved for Bulgaria shaped overall reform in the human rights and child protection legislation that eventually pushed the Government to include the drafting of a new Family Code in its strategy for judicial reform.

An important aspect of Bulgaria's Europeanisation is its coincidence with the transformation of the country's economy and social values.[8] The accession provided a positive environment for domestic actors to have their interests structured and empowered and for them to become influential in shaping domestic policies. As Grabbe points out: "... Europeanisation has the effect of empowering modernizers to change specific policies".[9] The new child protection legislation, administration and policies, as well as some regulations in the Draft Family Code, are a good example of this so-called 'bottom up' process. Thus I claim that Europeanisation was a significant factor in accelerating the convergence in certain areas of Bulgarian family law with the family laws in the member states. This aspect of harmonisation will also be explored in more detail.

2. THE POLICY OF 'CONDITIONALITY' AS A MEANS TO THE 'TOP-DOWN' HARMONISATION OF BULGARIAN FAMILY LAW

The conditions for CEE enlargement were set out at the 1993 Copenhagen European Council.[10] Apart from the so called 'economic' conditionality[11] they include the ability

7 It derives from the framework for cooperation set out in Title VI (Art. K) of the Treaty on European Union – the "third pillar". See: Commission Opinion on Bulgaria's Application for Membership of the European Union, p. 96. DOC/97/11 Brussels, 15.07.1997.

8 GRABBE, H., 'The process of EU Accession: What will it bring to Southeast Europe?' (2003), HERITIER, A., 'Europeanization Research East and West: A Comparative Assessment' (2005), p. 203.

9 GRABBE, H., 'The EU's transformative power: Europeanisation through conditionality in Central and Eastern Europe' (2006), p. 51.

10 The Copenhagen Council marked the EU commitment to enlargement voiced in the pre-accession strategy. See GRABBE, H., Ibid, p. 7.

11 'A functioning market economy and the capacity to cope with competitive pressures and market forces within the Union'. European Council in Copenhagen 21–22 June 1993 conclusions of the presidency. At: http://ue.eu.int/ueDocs/cms_Data/docs/pressdata/en/ec/72921.pdf.

to take on the obligations of membership – not only to accept the *acquis*[12] but to be able to apply it, and a number of political criteria called 'democratic conditionality' – the stability of the institutions guaranteeing democracy, the rule of law, human rights, and respect for and protection of minorities.[13] The pre-accession and accession strategies for Bulgaria involve conditions in both the *acquis* and the political criteria for membership that have led to pressure for the harmonisation of family law,[14] even though it was not explicitly targeted.

2.1. THE 'ACQUIS' CONDITIONALITY

The approximation of domestic legislation with the Justice and Home Affairs (JHA) *acquis,* for instance, was the first area in which family legislation experienced harmonising effects. In its Opinion of 1997 the Commission noted that in order to meet the requirements of JHA *acquis,* Bulgaria would have to make a sustained long term effort. The need to tackle the Hague Conventions[15] was particularly stated as part of that effort.[16] In this context, the most evident line along which unification of Bulgarian Family Law had to proceed was the requirement to ratify promptly all international conventions constituting European private international law.[17] For a period of four years (2002 to 2006), the main private international law conventions of the Hague Conference and the Council of Europe concerning the relations between

12 Community law as an autonomous legal order apart from international law and national law. In: OTT, A., 'Enlarging the European Union: An Introduction.' At: http://www.asser.nl/eurlaw/index.asp?c_nr=2&l2=&sub_categorie=11.

13 The European Council in Copenhagen in June 1993 concluded that: "The associated countries in Central and Eastern Europe that so desire shall become members of the Union. Accession will take place as soon as a country is able to assume the obligations of membership by satisfying the economic and political conditions. Membership requires: – that the candidate country has achieved stability of institutions guaranteeing democracy, the rule of law, human rights and respect for and protection of minorities; – the existence of a functioning market economy, as well as the capacity to cope with competitive pressure and market forces within the Union; – the ability to take on the obligations of membership, including adherence to the aims of political, economic and monetary union. The Union's capacity to absorb new members, while maintaining the momentum of European integration, is also an important consideration in the general interest of both the Union and the candidate countries". European Council in Copenhagen 21–22 June 1993 conclusions of the presidency. At: http://ue.eu.int/ueDocs/cms_Data/docs/pressdata/en/ec/72921.pdf.

14 The term 'harmonisation' is used to express the changes in the law resulting from 'top-down' (forced) or 'bottom-up' (evolutionary) processes that lead to a certain degree of uniformity. Another term that is used in the relevant literature is 'convergence'. It is defined as 'spontaneous' or 'evolutionary harmonisation' of the legal systems. See: ANTOKOLSKAIA, M., *Harmonisation of Family Law in Europe: A Historical Perspective*, Intersentia, Antwerp-Oxford, 2006, p. 16–18.

15 Commission Opinion on Bulgaria's Application for Membership of the European Union, p. 101. DOC/97/11 Brussels, 15.07.1997.

16 Bulgaria became a member to the Hague Conference of Private International Law only in 1999.

17 MARTINY, D., 'Is Unification of Family Law Feasible or even Desirable? (2004), p. 317–318.

parents and children were ratified: the Hague Convention on Protection of Children and Co-operation in Respect with Intercountry Adoption (1993);[18] the Hague Convention on the Civil Aspects of International Child Abduction (1980),[19] the European Convention on Recognition and Enforcement of Decisions Concerning Custody of Children and on Restoration of Custody of Children (1980)[20] and the Hague Convention on Jurisdiction, Applicable Law, Recognition, Enforcement and Cooperation in respect of Parental Responsibility and Measures for the Protection of Children (1996).[21] All these Conventions, although rapidly incorporated into domestic law, have been brought into an environment already prepared to some extent to accept and apply them. It was the Child Protection Act passed in 2000 that created that environment by setting out a new administration mandated for the protection of children and the 'best interests of the child'. The ratifications were followed by changes in domestic law. The Civil Procedure Code (CPC) was amended to determine the competent court on hearing such cases (Art. 307à – b of the Civil PC), the execution of court orders and judicial cooperation in this area.[22] Capacity-building activities to prepare the judiciary for the implementation of the new regulations were implemented with the assistance of Germany.[23]

The ratifications also significantly affected substantive family law. The Hague Convention on Intercountry Adoption eventually persuaded the Government to propose a complete revision of the regulation of adoption – national and international. Chapter Six of the Family Code (FC) was fully re-drafted in 2003, which constituted the first change in family law since 1985.[24] Similar changes of the FC not only in the area of adoption but also in parent–child relations were proposed by experts and NGOs long before the start of the accession process and after the Child Protection Act was passed but they attracted little attention from the authorities.[25] It was the 'top down' pressure in the accession framework that provoked the Government to react by making the necessary legislative and institutional changes.

---

18 Ratification Law promulgated in State Gazette 78 of 13.08.2002.

19 Ratification Law promulgated in State Gazette 82 of 16.09.2003.

20 Ratification Law promulgated in State Gazette 104 of 28.11.2003.

21 Not yet promulgated in State Gazette.

22 Amendments were introduced also in the Law of Legal Advisers, Law on State Taxation and Law on the Supreme Administrative Court.

23 It was a project between the Bulgarian Ministry of Justice and the German Foundation for International Legal Cooperation. See more in: Protection of Children. International conventions in the area of civil law. Sofia, 2004. Ministry of Justice.

24 The Law for Changes and Amendments of the Family Code, promulgated in State Gazette 84 of 23.09.2003. More about the changes in: TODOROVA, V., 'The new Legislation on International Adoption in Bulgaria: in the Interests of Children?', in: BAINHAM, A., (ed.), The International Survey of Family Law, 2005 edition, Jordan Publishing, Bristol, 2005, p. 119 ff.

25 TODOROVA, V., 'Adoption and the legal protection of children placed in residential institutions in Bulgaria', *4 Savremenno pravo*, (1994).

The transformative and harmonising effect on Bulgarian family legislation was not driven only by the requirement to ratify the Hague Conventions as part of the pre-accession strategy for Bulgaria. The 'top down' pressure worked through other accession instruments, such as the Accession Partnerships (AP), Regular reports (RR) and Twinnings.[26] For example, the revised AP for Bulgaria (1999) defines as a priority in the JHA *acquis inter alia* – "to strengthen the efficiency of the court system, including case management and alternative dispute resolution mechanisms; and to strengthen the enforcement of civil and penal judgments".[27] In order to meet the conditions for EU membership, in 2001 the Government passed a Strategy for Reform of the Judiciary.[28] Following its priorities a drafting of new penal procedural legislation started and new laws were passed – the Mediation Act[29] and a Code on Private International Law.[30] These laws provided another impetus for changes in family legislation.

The Strategy for Judicial Reform was twice updated in 2003 and 2004 in order to incorporate the accumulation of growing demands of the Commission.[31] It was the new AP of 2003, for instance, that made unsatisfactory assessment that Bulgaria "does not fully meet the *acquis* criteria...".[32] Based on that the AP has proposed to the Government to "take further measures to ensure the implementation of Community instruments in the area of judicial cooperation in civil matters ...". Two years later the Government started drafting a new Civil Procedure Code. The adoption of a new Family Code was planned in the revised Strategy for Judicial Reform of 2003. The relevant part of the Strategy was motivated by the need to *harmonise* Bulgarian legislation with EU law and bring it into compliance with the best standards and practices of the EU. Irrespective of this formula, the working group charged with the task of drafting a new Family Code did not receive any specific instructions or political

---

26 The Accession Partnership (AP) is an instrument created at the Luxemburg European Council (December, 1997) to establish the single framework for the pre accession of each candidate country (see Council Regulation (EC) No. 622/98). The APs for Bulgaria were decided in 1998 (revised in 1999, 2001 and 2002) and in 2003 (Council Decision 2003/396/EC). The Annual Progress reports (since 1998) of the Commission are very efficient instruments for screening a country's progress towards accession. The Twinning programme launched by the Commission in 1998 is an instrument for institutional capacity building.

27 Bulgaria: 1999 Accession Partnership, available at: http://ec.europa.eu/enlargement/archives/dwn/ap_02_00/en/ap_bg_99.pdf.

28 Governmental Decision No. 672/1.10.2001. A National Programme for the Implementation of the Strategy was passed in 2002 that contained short, mid- and long term priorities. At: www.mjeli.government.bg/strategy.aspx.

29 Promulgated, State Gazette No. 110/17.12.2004.

30 Promulgated, State Gazette No. 42 /17.05.2005.

31 Governmental Decision No. 260/21.04.2003. At: www.mjeli.government.bg/strategy.aspx.

32 Bulgaria Accession Partnership (2003), available at: http://ec.europa.eu/enlargement/bulgaria/pdf/apbg_0303_en.pdf.

direction.[33] Obviously, although the need of a new family law policy was politically acknowledged, there was not a concept on that matter at political level. A trust was put in the capacity of domestic academic thought to forge a law compatible with the best standards and practices within the EU. The opposite happened with the drafting of the Code on International Private Law and the Civil Procedure Code. A large amount of foreign expertise was involved within a Twinning project that provided for harmonising effect not only on civil procedure, but also in some areas of family legislation.[34]

A specific reference should be made to the Council Regulation of European Commission No. 2201/2003 concerning jurisdiction and the recognition and enforcement of judgments in matrimonial matters and matters of parental responsibility, repealing Regulation (EC) No. 1347/2000. The Regulation was the subject of particular activity in the frame of the same Twinning project. A list of concrete proposals was submitted by the pre accession Twinning experts to the Bulgarian authorities for them to discuss and revise the Family Code and the Child Protection Act in order to incorporate the concepts of the Regulation, especially those of 'parental responsibility', 'contact between parent and children' and 'exercise of parental responsibilities'. The extent to which these proposals were accepted and reflected to in the Draft FC is a matter of another discussion.

The developments described so far prove the potential of the enlargement process to produce transformative – harmonising effects in areas that are beyond the competence of the EU. The case of Bulgaria suggests that not only that the provisions of concern for the Union in the area of family law that were reflected at national level but also that the much broader transfer of legal ideas and regulations in related areas influenced family legislation as a whole. The literature on Europeanisation in the East explains these processes as the result of the asymmetry of power between the EU and the candidate countries. The latter are placed in a weaker position, which gives the European Union more coercive routes of influence in domestic policy making'.[35] The aspirant countries voluntarily applied for membership and were willing to adopt models offered following communism but, being out of the 'club', they were not involved in the development of the *acquis*, with the result that these countries were mainly "downloading" policies.[36] So it was mainly the power of coercion deriving

---

33 Apart from the instruction to incorporate the concepts and instruments of the Hague conventions.

34 A Twinning project was implemented by the Bulgarian Ministry of Justice and the Ministry of Justice of Spain and the Austrian Centre on Legal Competence: 'Reform of the Civil Procedures in Bulgaria', Twinning BG/03/IB/JH/01A. At: http://www.mjeli.government.bg/Gpk/docs/gpk-title.doc.

35 Grabbe, H., 'The EU's transformative power: Europeanisation through conditionality in Central and Eastern Europe' (2006), p. 51. Grabbe, H., 'The process of EU Accession: What will it bring to Southeast Europe?' (2003), p. 303.

36 Grabbe, H., 'The EU's transformative power: Europeanisation through conditionality in Central and Eastern Europe' (2006), p. 43–45.

from the asymmetrical position of Bulgaria as a candidate for membership that pushed the government to prioritise the harmonisation of its private international law, procedural rules and eventually family legislation, among many other issues. Without the enlargement of the EU, all these transformations would have happened much slower and inconsistently. Notwithstanding the forced nature of harmonisation, I would argue that it reflects the legal expectations of the citizens of Bulgaria. The next chapter will analyse the legitimating of already existing social norms in family behaviour, supported by Europeanisation.

2.2. DEMOCRATIC CONDITIONALITY

'Democratic conditionality' was the next framework to exert a harmonising impact on family law within the Bulgaria's process of accession, although there was no such explicit statement. At the pre-accession stage, the Commission stated of Bulgaria that "Shortcomings remain on respect for fundamental rights ... considerable efforts must be made to combat corruption, improve administration of justice and provide fuller protection for individual freedoms...".[37] The Accession Partnerships, notwithstanding their legally non-binding nature,[38] expanded the scope of 'democratic conditionality' making the EU requirements more explicit.[39] The commentators note that the purpose of 'conditionality' was not only to prepare the candidates for membership but to respond to the 'anxieties of the old members about the impact that enlargement might have on EU institutions and policies.[40] The first AP (revised in 1999), for instance, mentions only the efforts needed to respect and protect the rights of the Roma people.[41] The AP of 2003 identified more than 20 problem areas and made a specific recommendations to the Government, including the need to "continue to implement

37 Commission Opinion on Bulgaria's Application for Membership of the European Union, p.8. DOC/97/11 Brussels, 15.07.1997.

38 Throughout the monitoring process established by the regular reports on the country's progress and the pre-accession financial aid, the AP made the Copenhagen conditionality a quasi – legal instrument. See: GRABBE, H., 'The EU's transformative power: Europeanisation through conditionality in Central and Eastern Europe' (2006), p. 15.

39 In monitoring Bulgaria's progress in meeting the conditionality, the Commission has obtained a wealth of information on Bulgaria's situation from the Bulgarian authorities, and has utilized many other sources of information, including the member states and numerous international organizations and local NGOs. That has helped for a better identification of problematic areas and for the formulation of recommendations. Commission Opinion on Bulgaria's Application for Membership of the European Union, p.8. DOC/97/11 Brussels, 15.07.1997.

40 GRABBE, H., 'The EU's transformative power: Europeanisation through conditionality in Central and Eastern Europe' (2006), p. 11.

41 In fact Bulgaria ratified the European Convention for the Protection of Human Rights and Fundamental Freedoms and its main additional protocols in 1992. Under Article F of the EU Treaty, this set of provisions forms part of the *acquis*: any State wishing to join the European Union must first have ratified the said texts.

the national reform strategy for the judicial system, adopt and start to effectively implement comprehensive anti-discrimination legislation transposing the Community anti-discrimination *acquis*, ensure implementation and sufficient budgetary resources to ensure access to justice and legal aid…".[42]

In line with this pressure, new legislation was passed aimed at providing protection of human rights and access to justice: the Act for Protection against Discrimination,[43] the Legal Aid Act,[44] the Ombudsman Act,[45] and Act for Protection against Domestic Violence.[46] Apart from the Legal Aid Act, each of these pieces of legislation was initially drafted and debated by civil society organisations, which well illustrates the 'bottom up' pressure on the legislature by 'empowered' domestic actors dealing with the defence of human rights and gender issues. Once they reached the Parliamentary commissions and the plenary, all these bills went through dramatic debates and partial or total rejection. The Anti-Discrimination Act and the Act against Domestic Violence, for example, were debated by two legislatures prior to their adoption, mainly under the pressure of the accession process.[47] A further noteworthy circumstance is the fact that the most adamant resistance against this legislation was shown by the academic lawyers and magistrates (*against the two procedural laws*). It is exactly these laws however, which best illustrate the modernisation of legislation under the 'top-down' pressure. For instance, the reluctantly adopted Act for Protection against Discrimination has already fostered a practice, which is very favourable for the adoption of modern matrimonial law. The Commission for Protection against Discrimination was the first agency to articulate the need for regulating *cohabitation de facto* on the grounds of non-discrimination. By contrast the Government simply removed from the Draft the chapter discussing the new family life styles from the recently adopted Strategy for Demographic Policy.[48] We can take another example with the extensive case law under the very much debated Act against Domestic Violence, which was even rejected by one legislature.

In summary, the parallel processes of judicial reform and the adoption of legislation corresponding to European human rights standards put pressure on the authorities that allowed for some areas of Bulgarian family law to be subjected to consistency remodelling, leading towards harmonisation.

---

42 AP of 2003 at: Bulgaria Accession Partnership (2003), available at: http://ec.europa.eu/enlargement/bulgaria/pdf/apbg_0303_en.pdf.

43 State Gazette No. 86 /30.09.2003.

44 State Gazette No. 79 /4.10.2005.

45 State Gazette No. 48 /23.05.2003.

46 State Gazette No. 27 /29.03.2005.

47 The shorthand records are available in Bulgarian at: http://www.parliament.bg/?page=plSt&SType=browse&lng=bg&SYear=2005&SMonth=7.

48 The Governmental strategy at: http://www.mlsp.government.bg/bg/docs/demography/STRATEGY-%20FINAL.pdf.

3. THE 'BOTTOM UP' PRESSURES FOR CONVERGENCE OF FAMILY LAW: THE NEW 'OLD' FAMILY IN BULGARIA

As Martiny[49] states, unification is also facilitated by the common features of the changing character of family structure and values which can be observed in European countries. These features can be perceived in Bulgaria too.

There is a consensus between experts and politicians that Bulgaria is facing a serious demographic crisis.[50] This is the context of the statistical and sociological surveys, though they are small in number, which outline the changing family model in Bulgaria: a growing number of de facto cohabitation and single parent families, late marriages and delayed/postponed child birth, a growing share of children born out of wedlock (almost 50% of all children).[51] The divorce rate is increasing and the division between fault-based and consensual divorce remains 50 percent.[52] The dominant for the last 60 years 'dual-earner' family model remains untouched. These details suggest for a growing individualisation in family life however, the autonomy of family members is hampered by the low standard of living in Bulgaria. The solidarity between generations not only in the upbringing of children but also in the care of elderly family members is another preserved feature of the family life in Bulgaria. The significance of this model is increasing within the context of the growing emigration of the younger generations and the serious ageing of the population.[53]

In parallel, psychologists and social researchers comment on the preserved conservative model of parent – child relationship, supported by a hierarchy arrangement of family relations, a patriarchal outlook and a fixed pattern of interdependency.[54] By contrast, public policy for children focuses on their rights and participation in the society and within the family as well as on responsible parenthood. Meanwhile, there is a factual abandonment of parenthood, by which economic

---

49 Martiny, D.,'Unification of Family Law Feasible or even Desirable?' (2004), p. 317–318.

50 National Strategy for Demographic Development of Bulgaria – 2006–2020, at http://www.mlsp.government.bg/bg/docs/demography/STRATEGY-%20FINAL.pdf.

51 Atanasov, A., Ivanov M., (eds.), Demographic Development of Bulgaria. Sofia, Bulgarian Academy of Sciences, UNDP. (2005).

52 Statistical Reference Book of the Republic of Bulgaria. 2006.

Year	1998	1999	2000	2001	2002	2003	2004	2005
Crude marriage rate	4.3	4.3	4.3	4.0	3.7	3.7	4.0	4.3
Crude divorce rate	1.3	1.3	1.3	1.3	1.3	1.5	1.9	1.9

53 Atanasov, A., Ivanov M., (eds.), Demographic Development of Bulgaria (2005).

54 The Foster Care and Public Attitudes towards Fostering. Sociological survey, Alpha research, 2005, commissioned by the Agency for Social Assistance, unpublished. Banova, V., Interview at www.zdrave.net

emigrants assign parental responsibilities to third parties through private agreements. This affects mainly adolescent children and is becoming a new challenge for childcare reform. Increased mobility has generated a new dimension to the problem of contact between parents and children.

The development of a free market economy also became a pressure factor on some of the established family law institutions, such as the common ownership of property of spouses as a single imperative legal regime.[55] There is an increasing demand to liberalise that regulation in order to provide options to spouses to choose among preserving individual ownership or concluding a premarital agreement as well as an imperative regime of common ownership.[56]

In conclusion, the economic and social changes in Bulgaria result in new family values (in the insightful comment of a politician: the state (during the communism) managed to separate the church from the family and now the market is separating the family from the state). Contracting comes to parallel the rigid institutionalism of the effective Family Code. The defence of human rights and child protection actually question the understanding that the family is a private domain, protected from external intervention. Parenthood is conceptualised as responsibility rather than rights. Whether the legislator, however, is predisposed to reflect these changes in the new Family Code is a question which will find its answer only after the opening of the parliamentary debates on the Draft Code.

4. POLITICAL FACTORS 'FOR' OR 'AGAINST' CONVERGENCE OF FAMILY LAW IN BULGARIA

It is difficult to predict the political platforms that will inform the debate around the new family legislation in Bulgaria. The Code is on the agenda of Parliament but not yet submitted for discussion. The sporadic debates on issues related to marriage,

55 Art. 19 of the Family Code reads: Matrimonial Community Property (1)The properties and rights in properties, and also the bank deposits, acquired by the spouses during the marriage as a result of their common contributions, belong jointly to them irrespective in whose name they have been acquired. (2)The mutual contribution of the spouses may be expressed by the investment of means and labour, by care for the children and work in the household. (3)The mutual contribution is presumed until proved otherwise.

56 The Draft Code introduces three alternative regimes, which allow the spouses a choice – separate property, common ownership of real property and pre marital contract. The following values were preferred by the experts: defence of separate property where the established family model is for both spouses to be employed, freedom in negotiating property relations, protection of the market. Common ownership has narrowed its scope: it now applies only to real property acquired during the marriage as a result of joint contribution. All other rights become separate by law. A protective regime for disposing dealing with a family home which is the separate property of one spouse has been preserved.

family property and parenthood prove the support for traditional family values rather than for the emerging new values and social norms in family behaviour. Thus one could assume that the conservative stance will prevail.

There is evidence that demographic concerns will inspire the debate on the matrimonial law. For instance, the Government (a tripartite coalition dominated by the Socialist Party) and the Anti Discrimination Commission (which is a parliamentary body) have already conceptualised de-facto families in a conflicting way. The academic version of the Demographic Strategy identifies cohabitation as a problem for society or as a crisis in the family[57] on a par with the decreasing birth rate. As it was already noted, the Government fully deleted that paragraph of the document presumably because the mere mention of de facto families would legitimate the new family styles. By contrast, in the context of anti-discrimination policies, changes are being asserted in matrimonial law against the discrimination against couples living together and of the children born in such families.[58] It is worth noting also that the Chamber of Notaries also voiced the need for legitimation of de facto families, providing evidence that their clients want to make family arrangements on a contractual basis.[59] The discourse of same-sex cohabitation or marriages is rather inconsistent and biased and has no impact on politicians.[60] A reinstatement of religious marriage was proposed in an attempt to invoke religion as a remedy for preserving family stability. The idea has so far been definitely rejected by the drafters of the Family Code but the politicians maintain an ambiguous stance on it.[61]

The Draft Family Code supports a model of matrimonial law that preserves and reinforces the spirit of the present law. The Draft maintains the secular nature of marriage whilst simultaneously maintaining the marriage impediments that stem from religion: monogamy, heterosexuality, and prohibited degree of affinity – banning marriage to relations up to the 4th degree, including relations to the second degree by adoption. The prohibition of marriage between persons suffering from illnesses potentially dangerous to the other spouse and their offspring is also preserved. The procedures for contracting marriage become less rigorous in order to respond to the varying practices with regard to the place of marriage, which is an attempt to make the marriage more accessible and attractive for those who hesitate.

---

57 A group of parliamentarians initiated a discussion within the Parliament and executive power on the institutionalization of the religious marriage in 2006. The concept paper was sent to the Expert Group drafting the new Family Code.

58 A letter sent to the Experts group drafting the Family Code by the Chair of the Commission.

59 *Dnevnik*, daily, 27.03.05, at www.dnevnik.bg.

60 TOPALOVA, N., 'The same sex couples are looking for political support to regulate the cohabitation', *Sega daily*, 16 May 2005, www.segabg.com.

61 Marriage was secularized in Bulgaria in 1945 by the Constitution and by the Marriage Law. The secular nature of the marriage is a principle of the Constitution of 1991 (art. 46) and of the Family Code of 1985 (art. 6).

The Draft introduces a very sparse set of regulatory provisions for cohabitation de facto between a man and a woman and does not equalise it to the marriage in terms of legal consequences. The leading idea is that account is to be taken of the will of those who do not want to marry. No barriers are posed to entering cohabitation de facto, except for the sex of partners. The cohabitation becomes a fact by the act of registration of the place of residence by the two partners pursuant to the Civil Registration Act. The termination of such cohabitation can be effected at the request of one of the partners only. The following consequences are attached to the cohabitation: the presumption of paternity, obligation of the partner to assist the parent in exercising parental responsibilities. Other pieces of legislation also attach some legal consequences to cohabitation such as the Social Assistance Act, the Act against Domestic Violence, etc.

On the other hand, the multidirectional social processes described previously place the social system, including public childcare, under strong pressure: both in economic and value terms. As a response, social support and social security, tax and labour legislation have been changed, providing grounds for an emerging family policy. The focus is (again) on pro-natalism (to encourage the 'two children' family model) as well as to support the reconciliation between work and family life.[62] Financial incentives are secured to the reproductive function of the family, such as: increased amount and duration of the maternity leave compensation (90% of the salary on which social security had been paid for 350 days against 135 days before),[63] a new system of parental leave (up to six months, unpaid, till the child reaches 8 years of age) to be used by both parents.[64]

The increased public cost of 'family policy' based on the 'social *acquis*' but not family or child law, gave rise to the notions of "responsible parenthood" and „shared parenthood".[65] The Act on Family Benefits for Children underwent multiple revisions and is currently providing a clear expression of the policy of paying benefits conditionally on bringing up the child within the family and the child's attendance at school. Also along these lines, tax relief was introduced for bringing up children as well as a partial subsidy for private day childcare (if such care service is used during the paid maternity leave and the mother returns to work).

Against this background one may assume that the debate on the Draft Family Code will be inspired by social and economic concerns rather than by the emerging autonomous family behaviour of Bulgarians. As far as the parents-children law is

---

62 Some of the changes in legislation resulted from the approximation with the 'social *acquis*'- EU Directives 96/34/EC, 86/613/EC

63 Art. 9 of the Code on Social Security.

64 Art. 167a of the Labour Code amended in 2004.

65 Interview of the Minister of Labour and Social Policy, 10.11.2006, Sega, daily, www.segabg.com.

concerned, the possibly prevailing patriarchal values have already been challenged by the new legislation and its implementation.

5. THE CHILD CARE REFORM AND THE NEW FAMILY LAW

Childcare reform in Bulgaria is a case worth analysing in the context of the Europeanisation of the East.[66] First, it proved to be a channel for exerting a 'top-down' pressure for the harmonisation of family law. Second, it illustrates well how domestic actors find opportunities to influence domestic policies using the accession process. Child care reform is not subject to this analysis but should be mentioned as an example of 'bottom up' pressures resulting in the convergence of family legislation.

Unlike the position in Romania, where child care reform was conditionality for the opening of accession negotiations, child care reform in Bulgaria gained significance in the course of negotiations and the monitoring of the country's progress.[67] In the context of Romania's accession the Commission highlighted the fact that childcare is a matter of human rights, and they would not initiate negotiations until this issue was dealt with.[68] The first AP for Bulgaria (revised in 1999), for instance, does not make any mention of children's rights. The revised AP of 2001 however, has brought to light the problems of child care reform, requiring Bulgaria to: "adopt and implement secondary legislation necessary for the effective functioning of the Child Protection Act,..., ensure the full implementation of the UN CRC."[69] The AP of 2003 repeats the same demand, thus expressing the dissatisfaction of the Commission with Bulgaria's progress in this field. Therefore it could be argued that the key factor for the start of reform was the aspiration of Bulgaria to join the EU and the process of negotiation that followed thereafter.[70]

The role of domestic actors should not be underestimated though. Prior to the start of negotiations the Child Protection Act was passed in Bulgaria (May, 2000) and

---

66 See: PEEVA, S., *Childcare Reform in Bulgaria – a Case of Europeanization?* (2006).

67 One of the two principal conditions for the opening of negotiations for Romania in 2000 was: "... *that the ... government have taken effective action.... to provide adequate budgetary resources and to implement structural reform of child care institutions before the end of 1999.*" European Commission: A Composite paper: Reports on progress towards accession of the candidate countries. 1998.

68 See: EU Commission: Composite paper. Reports on progress towards accession by each of the candidate countries, 1998, p. 5. At: http://ec.europa.eu/enlargement/archives/pdf/key_documents/1998/composite_en.pdf.

69 Bulgaria Accession Partnership (2001), available at: http://ec.europa.eu/enlargement/key_documents/ pdf/2001/apbg_en.pdf.

70 More in: TODOROVA, V., 'Organisation of Youth Care: New Trends and Experiences in Bulgaria and Romania after the fall of the 'Iron Curtain'', in: Jansen, S., Meuwese, S., et. al, (eds.), *100 Years of Child Protection*, 2007, Wolf Legal Publishers, Nijmegen, 2007, forthcoming.

a new administration was to be created. The Act was made possible only because of the strong pressure of experts and civil society organisations that overcame the obstructions of the Government and parliamentarians.[71] The community of NGOs contributed a lot to childcare reform becoming part of the agenda for accession[72] and eventually being to some extent prioritised by the Government.

The key concepts of the Act such as: the consideration of the best interests of the child, child participation, judicial control over placement of the child outside family were influential first on courts' practices in dealing with family cases and consequently for the modification of the related provisions in family law. The policy for developing public child protection has made further contribution to the modification of family law. For instance, the effort to strengthen foster care has been a channel through which public awareness of children's rights and parental responsibilities has been raised.[73] Not only the legislation but the previously established expertise and confidence within the administration and NGOs in managing child protection cases, in representing children in the court process, in developing new services have become pressure factors encouraging the drafters to accept and introduce new concepts in the Draft Code. As a result, the Draft Family Code suggests rules which have not been broadly discussed so far for both family-law doctrine and judicial practice in Bulgaria such as: rights of the child within the family, a ban on corporal punishment, assigning parental responsibilities to third parties and even to a public body, which was previously unthinkable. Again, the civil law arguments against the adoption of the term 'parental responsibilities' dominated over the family-law arguments, though the latter received direct support from Western experts.[74] The key objection was based on the lack of a contextually faithful Bulgarian translation of the term 'responsibility' – in Bulgarian law the term 'responsibility' has the meaning of "liability".

The old term 'parental rights and obligations' remains functional but the drafters make an attempt to delineate its contents: (1) *The parent has the right and the duty to take care of the physical, mental, moral and social development of the child, his/her education, personal and property interests. (2) The parent takes care of the child, forms his/her views and provides for his/her education according to needs of the child as a person with evolving capacities. The parent has no right to use violence or methods of upbringing, which breach the child's dignity. (3)The parent shall determine a minor child's attitude towards religion and assist an underage child to form their religious convictions. (4) The*

---

71 See more in: TODOROVA, V., 'Bulgarian Children Act – Battlefield for Adult Policies or a Genuine Commitment to Children', in: MACLEAN, M., (ed.), *Making Law for Families*, Hart Publishing, Oxford, 2001.

72 For example the successful advocacy and lobbying of Save the Children, analysed by PEEVA, S., in her *Childcare Reform in Bulgaria – a Case of Europeanization?* (2006).

73 Amendments in this direction were introduced into the Child Protection Act and a Regulation on professional Foster Care was passed – State Gazette, 38, 82 and 100 of 2006.

74 Report of Spanish experts under the Twinning BG/03/IB/JH/01A.

parent provides permanent supervision over minor child and a suitable control over the conduct of adolescent child (Art. 136).

The holders of parental rights and obligations are the parents, based on proven biological origin or adoption. In both cases, the rights and obligations derive directly from the law. The new regulations introduce a general rule that persons with whom the child has been placed as a measure of public protection under a court decision[75] exercise parental rights and obligations, but do not acquire them. The exercise of parental rights and obligations originates from the court decision, and may not stem from agreement between third parties and the parents. It is proposed also that persons entitled to exercise of parental rights and obligations could include a public organisation – the Department for Social Assistance, though temporarily. The exercise of parental rights and obligations comprises both factual and legal actions, but with no legal mechanism for representing the child.

For the first time since 1949, the exercise of parental rights and obligations is restricted by the interests of the child.[76] The term is used to mean "in the child's interest" and not "in the best interests of the child", again due to the resistance of the majority of experts. Also for the first time, the law formulates rights for children in their relations with their parents. The child is entitled to adequate care for his/her normal development. The child is entitled to express his/her opinion on all matters affecting him/her. The views, wishes and opinions of the child are being accounted for by the parent with regard to the child's age, maturity and interests. In a case of disagreement between a parent and a child who has attained the age of 14, the child may, via the Social Assistance Directorate, refer to the regional court of their area of residence for resolution of the dispute. The law incorporates a provision that all proceedings shall allow the child to be heard under the regulations of Article 15 of the Child Protection Act.

6. CONCLUSION

The Europeanisation of Bulgaria attracted the political attention to the family legislation that resulted in a conscious harmonisation of the family law, but only in the areas already unified through the Conventions on Private International Law or where the EU has the relevant capacity. These are the areas in which judicial

---

75 Mainly relatives, close to the family persons or foster parents. The placement is under the Child Protection Act.

76 The Law for Persons and the Family passed in 1949 was the only piece of law stating that the parental rights and duties are to be exercised only in the interests of children (Art. 85). This provision was abolished by the Family Code of 1968 and never appeared again.

cooperation is needed in order to respond to the social needs – in adjudication of parental responsibility, contact with children, child abduction, and adoption of children. In fact, the contribution of Europeanisation was unification to abridged deadlines – under pressure. On the other hand, the new legislation passed under 'democratic conditionality' supported the national actors in articulating their legitimate interests and lobbying for their expression in the law. Still, the Draft Family Code does not depart from interventionist and protective approaches particularly in matrimonial and divorce law. The fear of new family styles that politicians translate in economic and demographic terms hampers the convergence of Bulgarian family law with the modern family legislation of some EU member states.

FAMILY LAW IN THE FORMER SOVIET UNION: MORE DIFFERENCES OR MORE IN COMMON?

Olga A. Khazova

A simple answer to this question would be: many differences and much in common.[1]

1. THE BACKGROUND

There were 15 republics in the Soviet Union before its dissolution in 1991; today all of them are independent states. Eight of the former Soviet republics are found in geographical Europe: Belarus, Estonia, Georgia, Latvia, Lithuania, Moldova, Russia, and Ukraine. Nine former Soviet republics are Member States in the Council of Europe: Armenia, Azerbaijan, Estonia, Georgia, Latvia, Lithuania, Moldova, Russia, and Ukraine. Three former Soviet republics – Estonia, Latvia, and Lithuania – are in the European Union.

To understand the current state of family law in the European post-Soviet countries and the main trends in its development within the European context, we need to be aware of the origins of family law in these countries. It is important to note that it came, to a lesser or greater extent, from the family law of the USSR. Putting aside an overall critique of the Soviet political regime, I would state that family law in the Soviet Union was relatively liberal and at a certain stage it significantly outstripped Western family law. In this regard, it is important to point out that in the aftermath of the 1917 October revolution a new family law was created that was entirely different from the Western family law of the same period.

Before the 1917 Revolution, family law in the Russian Empire did not differ considerably from Western law: spouses' relationships were based on the subordinate

1 It is hardly possible in a short article to cover in detail all the aspects of post-Soviet family law in ten countries and to discuss all the issues that fall within the topic. I see my task rather in focusing on some common trends and peculiarities that, in my opinion, characterize the post-Soviet family law.

position of a married woman; the husband was the head of the family; marriage, as well as divorce, fell within the jurisdiction of ecclesiastical courts; and the dissolution of marriage was either forbidden or permitted only on a fault basis; and the law discriminated against illegitimate children.

One of the main tasks of the new Soviet power with respect to marriage and family was to break down completely, as quickly as possible, the old family law rules.[2] The *Bolshevik's* new legislation on marriage and the family enacted in 1917–18 withdrew marriage from the jurisdiction of the ecclesiastical courts, introduced civil (secular) marriage, declared women equal to men, gave children born out of a wedlock equal rights with those born within a wedlock, abolished fault-based divorce, introduced divorce by consent, and later, in 1926, even recognized the validity of *de facto* cohabitation.[3] At that time it was the most liberal and progressive family law in the West and could be seen, to quote M. Antokolskaia, "as an early herald of the pan-European 'family law revolution.'"[4] It would take the West nearly 50 years to pass similar reforms.

Slightly digressing from the main theme of this paper, I need, nevertheless, to state that during the subsequent Stalinist period most of the liberal provisions of the first post-revolutionary legislation were turned upside down, especially when the infamous Act of 8 July 1944 abolished most of the liberal rules as defined in earlier, post-revolutionary family law.[5] The liberal provisions were restored only in late 1960s with one exception: *de facto* marriage or cohabitation has not been recognized since being abolished in 1944.

Soviet family law was designed to meet the Soviet society's demands. This was a society with no market economy where the overwhelming majority of population earned low salaries. The Soviet regime did not allow spouses to freely make their own property arrangements; and the legal rules on property and financial relations between spouses were imperative and very restrictive. The Soviet regime recognized just one legal matrimonial regime – the regime of common joint property; it considered the

---

2 The Bolsheviks understood that to establish a new social order it was necessary first to reorganize the family, to free women from their husbands' 'tyranny', and to break the old stereotypes.

3 For more details see: KHAZOVA, O., 'The New Codification of Russian Family Law', in: EEKELAAR, J., NHLAPO, T., (eds.), *The Changing Family: International Perspectives on the Family and Family Law*, Hart Publishing, Oxford, 1998, p. 73 ff.

4 ANTOKOLSKAIA, M., *Harmonisation of Family Law in Europe: A Historical Perspective*, Intersentia, Antwerpen-Oxford, 2006, p. 238.

5 Particularly it abolished all the *de facto* marriages, made divorce very difficult and put it under strict control of the courts. It abolished also the institution of establishing paternity outside legal marriage, and went to the opposite extreme, since it became impossible for a man to recognize his child born out of a wedlock and for an unmarried mother to institute paternity proceedings.

marriage contract as a 'bourgeois survival from the past' and did not permit spouses to deviate from the statutory rules. Both spouses were supposed to work. Provision of alimony occurred only in rare cases: if a wife was pregnant or had a newborn child, or one of the spouses had reached pension age, or in some other specifically delimited situations.

Formally speaking, according to the federal structure of the Soviet state, the Soviet Republics were granted, at least in theory, the right to have their own family law. However, in reality, the Republics did not have any freedom in designing these laws. Instead, they were obliged to follow the federal law – the Fundamentals of the Legislation of the USSR and Soviet Republics on Marriage and the Family of 1968, which established the main family law principles. Apart from that, the imperial nature of the Soviet state presupposed not the independence of the republics but on the contrary, was determined that they would copy the legislation of the Russian Soviet Federal Socialist Republic (RSFSR)[6] – the 'main' Soviet Republic considered to be 'the first among equals.' The result was that differences between the republican Family Codes (the Codes on Marriage and the Family), if any, were slight; and they all had the RSFSR Code on Marriage and the Family of 1969 as a common, in fact, compulsory model.

2. NEW LAWS – POST-SOVIET REFORMS – GENERAL OVERVIEW

One of the immediate results of the breakdown of the Soviet Union in 1991 and the formation of the new independent states was significant law reform in these countries. Family law reform was a constituent part of this revision. Family law had to be adapted to the new social and economic realities, which came to these countries together with tremendous political change. It is not surprising, therefore, that after these countries became independent and released from the pressure of the Soviet state, a completely different picture of family law emerged. All the countries under consideration adopted new family legislation. In chronological order, they are as follows:

1990 – the Civil Code of Latvia (Part One on Family Law);[7]

1994 – the Family Law Act of Estonia (included as a separate book into the Civil Code);[8]

1995 – the Family Code of Russian Federation (Russia);

6 After the USSR breakdown – the Russian Federation.

7 The English version of the Code may be found at: http://www.ttc.lv/lv/publikacijas/civillikums.pdf.

8 The English version of the Act may be found at: http://www.legaltext.ee/en/andmebaas/ava.asp?m=022.

1997 – the Civil Code of Georgia (Book Five on Family Law);[9]
1999 – the Code on Marriage and the Family of Belarus;
2000 – the Civil Code of Lithuania (Book Three on Family Law);[10]
2000 – the Family Code of Azerbaijan;
2001 – the Family Code of Moldova;
2005 – the Family Code of Ukraine;[11]
2004 – the Family Code of Armenia.

Family law on the post-Soviet European territory currently presents a mixed bag of new and old laws and rules. Recent reforms were carried out in different forms. They introduced both liberal and what have been traditionally considered as conservative provisions into the post-Soviet family law. The Latvian and Lithuanian family law reforms represent the most significant departure from the Soviet family law model. The most innovative law, in my opinion, is the Ukrainian Family Code.[12] The diversity of approaches is so significant that at first it seems impossible to systemize the reforms to family law carried out in the post-Soviet countries. However, notwithstanding all the differences between these laws, the drafters of new family law in post-Soviet countries seemed to have been guided by three underlying motivations. These motivations revealed themselves, though to a different extent, in all or nearly all of the post-Soviet family law reforms, the differences being explained by divergent political, historical and cultural circumstances.

Firstly, for what were most likely purely political reasons, the drafters of the new family laws tended to reject the old Soviet legislation, regardless of its value, good or bad. There were also objective reasons for the re-consideration of Soviet family law: many of the old rules were outdated and did not correspond to the new order that was being established in the countries released from the restraints of ideological pressure emanating from a totalitarian regime and socialist planned economy. It concerned, first of all, the rules that governed property issues.

A remarkable feature of the development of post-Soviet family law in this regard is the departure of some of the countries from differentiation between civil and family law as a theoretical concept that was traditional for the Soviet law. The Soviet theory

9 The English version of the Code may be found at: http://www.g-p.ge/code_civil.pdf.

10 The English version of the Code may be found at: http://www.tm.lt/default.aspx?item=aktual &id=4536.

11 The English version of the Code may be found at: http://www.mfa.gov.ua/data/upload/publication/usa/en/7148/family_kideks_engl.pdf.

12 See also ZHILINKOVA, L., 'Property Relations of Spouses in Slavonic Post-Soviet Countries (Ukraine, Russia, Belarus)', in: BAINHAM, A., (ed.), *The International Survey of Family Law*, Jordan Publishing Limited, Bristol, 2004, p. 483.

of law divided socialist law into branches[13] and saw family law as a separate branch, and accordingly, family law was regulated by a legal act[14] that dealt exclusively with matrimonial and family issues and was not included into the Civil Code. This separation of family law had a historical explanation; it initially occurred in the post-revolutionary legislation for reasons of legal technique only. At that time, while the country urgently needed a radical reform of family law, it did not, on the contrary, need any civil law at all, as all private property, which exceeded the 'bare need of consumption',[15] was abolished as an attribute of capitalism.[16]

However, later, by the end of the 1920s – beginning of the 1930s the separate existence of family law acquired a strong ideological basis. It helped to substantiate the differences between the Soviet and the bourgeois family, where the former was free from mercantile considerations and based on love and the latter had a pragmatic, mercenary basis, which was alien to the official Soviet vision of marriage and the family. The Soviet state had always defended vigorously the 'separate existence' of family law; and this concept is still very strong, at least in Russian legal doctrine, though in the post-Soviet era it has lost its spirits of confrontation with the West.

In post-Soviet Latvia, Lithuania, Estonia, and Georgia family law has been included in the Civil Codes, thus becoming an integral part of civil law,[17] a position that has been traditional in continental law since the Napoleonic Code of 1804.

The Lithuanian drafters also conceptualised the transfer of family law provisions from the Code on Marriage and the Family into the Civil Code by emphasizing the contractual element of marriage. It influenced significantly and in some way even determined the way certain issues were solved in the Code (particularly, engagement, property relations, separation, and divorce).[18]

Nevertheless, many of the Soviet family law concepts did outlast their creator, the USSR, and have since been transferred to the post-Soviet family laws. Kai Kullerkupp,

---

13 Division of public and private law was abolished during the Soviet regime as a 'bourgeois' concept.

14 Each republic had its own Code on Marriage and the Family.

15 GSOVSKI, V., 'Soviet Civil Law', *Michigan Legal Studies*, University of Michigan Law School, Ann Arbor, 1948, p. 10.

16 By 1922 when, as a result of the New Economic Policy (NEP), the first Civil Code was adopted, the 1918 Family Code (the full title – RSFSR Code on Acts of Civil Status, Marriage, Family, and Guardianship) had been successfully functioning for almost four years; and its revision had not become necessary yet.

17 KESERAUSKAS, S., 'Moving in the Same Direction? Presentation of Family Law Reforms in Lithuania', in: BAINHAM, A., (ed.), *The International Survey of Family Law*, Jordan Publishing Limited, Bristol, 2004, p. 315, 317.

18 For a detailed discussion see: ibid, p. 315 ff.

for instance, admits that 'regulation method and prevalent ideology' of the Estonian Family Law Act 'largely rely' on the Code that was in force on territory of Estonia during the Soviet period.[19] Commentators on the Russian family law in the post-Soviet period noted that it underwent 'surprisingly few changes';[20] and that the Family Code could not be called 'a revolutionary document'.[21]

The second motivation that can be said to have guided legal drafters – at least those in the former Soviet Republics that became part of the Soviet Union in 1940 – was to consider fully or partially restoring the law that was in force before their annexation, as far as it made sense. A good example is Latvia,[22] which re-enacted the Civil Code of 1937, the drafting of which, in the opinion of the Latvian Minister of Justice, 'was guided by the latest trends in the civil law of the time in continental Europe.'[23]

A third motivation can be traced to the need to follow recent European trends in family law. The scale of globalisation and the extent of the internationalisation of family law require European drafters of national law to make it consistent with international instruments and international practice and, in particular, to be in line with the UN Convention on the Rights of the Child,[24] and to meet the European standards established in the European Convention of Human Rights and Fundamental Freedoms. For those countries that planned to join the European Union, conformity with EU law was of particular importance. Also many of the French, Dutch, German, Italian, Swedish, and even English family law provisions served as examples for the new, post-Soviet family laws.[25] Most of the new provisions seemed to fit in well with

---

19 KULLERKUPP, K., 'Statutory Marital Property Law de lege lata and de lege ferenda', 4 *Juridica International* (2001), p. 78.

20 BUTLER, W.E., 'The Russian Family Code', in *Russian Family Law*, Simmonds & Hill, London, 1998, p. xxiii.

21 KRASHENINNIKOV, P.V., 'Introductory', in: *Family Code of the Russian Federation with the Clause-By-Clause Comments*, Spark, Moscow, 1996, p. 5. See also: DAMIRCHIEVA, M., 'Family Law in the Republic of Azernaijan', in: BAINHAM, A., (ed.), *The International Survey of Family Law*, Jordan Publishing Limited, Bristol, 2005, p. 69 ff.

22 In Estonia restoration of some of the concepts and ideas of the draft Civil Code 1940 has been widely discussed in connection with the 'next round' revision of the Family law. See: KULLERKUPP, K., 'Statutory Marital Property Law de lege lata and de lege ferenda' (2001), p. 82.

23 Expressed in the Preface to the English translation to the Code. See: The Civil Code of Latvia. T&TC, 2001.

24 *See*, for instance: BUROVA, S., 'Regulation of Marriage and Family Relations in Belarus', in: BAINHAM, A., (ed.), *The International Survey of Family Law* 1997, Kluwer Law International, The Hague, 1999, p. 48.

25 See for instance: KESERAUSKAS, S., 'Moving in the Same Direction? Presentation of Family Law Reforms in Lithuania' (2004), p. 316–317; CHANTURIA, L., Foreword to the English translation of the Civil Code of Georgia, 2001, p. 2.

the national legislations, notwithstanding some transplantation difficulties in practice.[26]

Perhaps it may sound ambitious, but I will risk stating that it is also evident that many of those family laws that were adopted after the enactment of the Russian Family Code of 1995 were based on the Russian model, or at least the Russian Family Code was thoroughly reviewed.[27] There are many provisions in some of the post-Soviet family codes that repeat verbatim the wording of the Russian FC sections.

Looking for similarities among the family law reforms on post-Soviet territory, I emphasize just two common distinguishing features that undoubtedly characterize all the laws under consideration:

- All the laws govern spousal property relations in greater detail and provide the spouses with much more freedom than before in making their own arrangements regarding their property and finances through marriage contracts or agreements.
- All the laws expressly forbid same-sex marriages and do not contain any rules that would allow registered partnerships or similar unions designed for same-sex couples.

3. PECULIARITIES OF SOME OF THE LAWS

As I have stated before, today family law in the former Soviet Union is a mixed bag. Each of the national systems of family law has its peculiarities, distinguishing it both from the previous Soviet legislation, and from the laws of other post-Soviet countries. Below I will emphasize the peculiarities of a particular country or countries as applied to the main family law institutions: marriage, divorce, family property, and spousal maintenance.

3.1. MARRIAGE

One of the most significant reforms with regard to marriage law is the restoration of the religious form of marriage in Latvia, Lithuania, and Estonia as an alternative to

---

26 Particularly, there was resistance from the Russian court to apply a Family Code provision, borrowed from English law, which required the court on its motion to resolve child-related consequence before issuing a divorce order (provided the parents were silent on this matter). See: KHAZOVA, O., 'Five Years of the Russian Family Code: The First Results', in: BAINHAM, A., (ed.), *The International Survey of Family Law*, Jordan Publishing Limited, Bristol, 2002, p. 349.

27 It proves that there were undoubtedly good reasons for strong reception of the Russian Family Code.

civil (secular) marriage. Perhaps one could interpret this as a conservative phenomenon. However, taking into account the Soviet background, it seems, rather, a natural reaction to the suppression of the Church during the Soviet regime, which deprived people of the opportunity to choose the form of marriage ceremony that was the most appropriate to their tastes and beliefs.

Section 53 of the Latvian Civil Code states that 'a marriage shall be solemnized by the registrar of a General Registry office or a minister from the denominations set out in Section 51 if the provisions regarding the entering into of marriage have been complied with.' The denominations specified in s. 51 are the following: Evangelical Lutheran, Roman Catholic, Orthodox, Old Believers, Methodist, Baptist, Seventh Day Adventist or believers in Moses (Judaism), provided the minister of the respective denomination has the relevant permission from the leaders of the denomination. The Civil Code requires that the ministers of denominations, for each solemnized marriage, within a period of forty days, send to the General Register Office, in which territory the marriage has taken place, the necessary information required for the Marriage Register. If the minister fails to perform this duty, he or she may be held administratively liable (s. 58).

The Estonian Family Law Act of 1994 initially did not provide for a religious form of marriage. The amendments to the Act made in 2004 entitled the Minister of Regional Affairs to grant a minister of religion of a church, congregation or association of congregations, who has received appropriate training, the right to perform the functions of a vital statistics officer related to the conclusion of marriages. Provided the minister of religion has been properly authorized, he or she has the right to register marriages and issue marriage certificates (§130^1 (1), (2)).

There is much more uncertainty with regard to Lithuanian version of religious marriage. The Lithuanian Civil Code permits formation of religious marriage in the procedure established by the church (confessions) (art. 3.24). Further, in the same article the Civil Code laid down the conditions under which religious marriage would 'entail the same legal consequences as those entailed by the formation of a marriage in the Register Office.' Among them there is a requirement that the formation of a marriage in the procedure established by the Church (confessions) be 'recorded at the Register Office in the procedure provided for herein'.[28] The person authorized by the respective religious organization is obliged to present to the local Register Office notification of the religious marriage solemnized in the procedure set by the church

[28] For this purpose, the Code also requires that: 1) the conditions for concluding a marriage laid down in the Civil Code be satisfied; and 2) the marriage be formed according to the procedures established by the canons of a religious organization registered in and recognized by the Republic of Lithuania.

(confession) within ten days of the marriage ceremony (art. 3.304 (1)). If this requirement has been fulfilled, and the Register Office received the notification on time, a marriage is considered to be concluded on the day of the religious ceremony. However, if the notification requirement has not been fulfilled on time, 'the marriage shall be held to have been contracted on the day when it was registered in the Register Office.'

In such a case, the question reasonably arises whether the Lithuanian version of religious marriage is a 'true' religious marriage or just a marriage ceremony that acquires all the requisites of lawful marriage and entails the legal consequences of a lawful marriage only after its registration in the state administrative bodies. If it is not a 'true' religious marriage but a religious marriage that 'transcends into a civil one'[29] – and such a conclusion suggests itself from the wording of the Civil Code – then the Civil Code in this part is not quite in line with the 1992 Lithuanian Constitution, which 'provides for an unconditional recognition of religious marriage'.[30] A practical question that could be raised in this regard is whether a person who died within the ten-days period after a religious marriage ceremony without having his or her marriage registered in the Register Office, will be considered by law as married or not with all the legal consequences thereof. There is no answer to this question in the Civil Code of Lithuania, though it could help to clarify the situation and to define whether the religious ceremony, under the Lithuanian law, is an investitive fact or not.[31]

Restoration of the religious form of marriage was accompanied by restoration of 'publication' for civil and religious marriage, a contemporary version of the ancient institution of the publication of banns. 'Before a marriage is solemnized, it shall be published,' the Latvian Civil Code declares (s. 40). The Lithuanian Civil Code also provides for 'public announcement of an application for the registration of marriage' (art. 3.302). It aims, as it did long ago, to announce a forthcoming marriage ceremony and to let those who have objections or knowledge of legal impediments against the marriage to raise them.

Another institution that relates to the conclusion of marriage, which was abolished in the USSR and restored as a result of recent reforms in some of the countries, is betrothal (Latvia) or engagement (Georgia, Lithuania, and Ukraine). The betrothal or engagement provisions do not aim to force a person to marry somebody to whom

---

29 KESERAUSKAS, S.,'Moving in the Same Direction? Presentation of Family Law Reforms in Lithuania' (2004), p. 323.

30 For more detail on this matter see: KESERAUSKAS, S., 'Moving in the Same Direction? Presentation of Family Law Reforms in Lithuania' (2004), p. 322–323.

31 *I.e.* the fact that gives rise to one's rights and duties.

he or she gave prior consent to marry. 'The engagement does not create the obligation to marry,' article 31 (2) of the Ukrainian Family Code states. Instead, generally speaking and putting aside the peculiarities of the respective national laws, the purpose of these provisions is twofold. First, it aims to protect the property rights of the betrothed (engaged), especially when he or she is not responsible for the cancellation of the betrothal. Second, it aims to increase the responsibility for promising to marry by imposing sanctions on the person who refused the marriage without good cause. Ukrainian Code declares that 'persons that have filed an application for marriage registration are deemed to be engaged' (art. 31 (1)). Lithuanian family law, in particular, differentiates between private and public agreements to marry (engagement) made in private and in public (arts. 3.7–3.11); and in the latter case it allows for compensation claims for non-pecuniary damage.

In accordance with the 'civil law ideology' underlying some of the Lithuanian family law institutions and, particularly, conceptualising marriage as 'a voluntary agreement' (art. 3.7), family law scholars interpret engagement as a 'preliminary agreement,' – a kind of 'agreement-marriage' and an act that gives rise to 'pre-contractual obligations.'[32]

It is interesting to note here, in the context of the restored 'old' family law institutions, that the Latvian Civil Code also introduced the concept of the dowry, with which 'parents, kin or other persons have endowed a woman' in the event of marriage, and which 'shall be the property of the wife even if it has been given to the husband' (s. 111).

3.2. DIVORCE AND SEPARATION

Divorce. The introduction of fault-based divorce and the abolition of administrative divorce for cases, where there is mutual consent between the spouses, and where there are no common children, marked a complete departure from the Soviet model of divorce law. It took its most comprehensive form in the Latvian and Lithuanian laws.

Apart from other grounds for divorce, the Civil Code of Latvia stipulates that a spouse may request the dissolution of a marriage: 1) if his or her life or health is endangered by the other spouse; 2) if the other spouse deserts him or her, and the absence continues for not less than one year; and 3) if the other spouse committed a criminal offence ('such as to tarnish reputation') or lives so dishonourably or immorally that marital cohabitation with him or her cannot be required to continue (ss. 71–74).

---

[32] KESERAUSKAS, S., 'Moving in the Same Direction? Presentation of Family Law Reforms in Lithuania' (2004), p. 318.

The Code also provides for possibilities to dissolve a marriage that do not fit into the fault-based divorce concept but relate to what in the theory of divorce law is called a 'divorce-remède':[33] one spouse may request a dissolution of the marriage if the other spouse becomes ill 'with a protracted, difficult-to-cure mental illness or contracts a contagious disease of a similar nature' (s. 73). Another ground for divorce not directly linked to the fault of one of the spouse (but which under certain circumstances may have fault-related divorce consequences) is the deterioration of marital life to the extent 'that further cohabitation of the spouses and preservation of the family is not possible' (s. 75). Finally, the Latvian Civil Code permits divorce in the event of the spouses' 'continuous, sustained living separate and apart... for three years' (s. 76), as well as divorce by mutual consent of the spouses but only after the expiration of a one-year period from the conclusion of the marriage (s. 77).

In accordance with the fault-based divorce logic, Latvian law says that a former spouse who by his or her actions 'has promoted the disintegration of the marriage' looses the right to get support from the other spouse' (s. 82).[34]

Lithuanian divorce law represents a more sophisticated approach. It differentiates between divorce by mutual consent of the spouses, divorce on the application of one of the spouses, and divorce through the fault of one of the spouses. In this respect, it resembles the French divorce reform of 1975, which was described as establishing 'divorce *à la carte*'.[35]

The Code permits divorce by mutual consent under a simplified procedure provided one year has elapsed from the moment of the marriage, the spouses made a contract regarding all the consequences of the divorce (both property and child-related), and both of the spouses have full legal capacity (s. 3.51). However, there is still no 'automatic' divorce even if there is mutual consent between the spouses regarding the divorce itself and all divorce-related issues. The spouses must indicate in their mutual application for divorce the reasons for the breakdown of their marriage. The court will issue a divorce order 'if it is satisfied that the marriage has been broken down irretrievably' (s. 3.53). Separation 'from board and bed' for over a year makes divorce much easier as it serves as a statutory presumption that a marriage has irretrievably broken down.

Divorce on the application of one of the spouses is designed for those cases when there are no fault-based grounds for divorce and the spouses do not apply for divorce by

---

33 Ancel, M., *Le divorce à l'étranger*, La Documentaion française, Paris, 1975, p. 16.

34 The duty to support also ceases if a former spouse claiming support has entered into a new marriage.

35 See: Glendon, M.A., *The Transformation of Family Law: State, Law, and Family in the United States and Western Europe*, The University of Chicago Press, Chicago, 1989, p. 162.

mutual consent. These are as follows: 1) the spouses have been separated for over one year; 2) one of the spouses, after the conclusion of the marriage, has been declared legally incapacitated by the court; 3) one of the spouses has been declared missing by the court; or 4) one of the spouses has been imprisoned for over a year for a non-premeditated crime (s. 3.55). The Code establishes a simplified procedure for this type of divorce too. However, it also sets out what may be called 'a hardship clause,' which may prevent the spouses from getting divorced even after one year of separation: the court, taking into consideration the age of one of the spouses, the length of marriage, and the interests of minor children may refuse to grant a divorce decree 'if the divorce may cause significant harm to the property and non-property interests of one of the spouses or their children' (s. 3.57 (3)).

The fault-based grounds for divorce are traditional; a serious breach of family or matrimonial duties must occur, namely: if a spouse committed adultery, or has been violent towards the other spouse or family members, or has deserted the family for over one year, or has been convicted of a pre-meditated crime (s. 3.60). The court may find that both spouses are at fault for the breakdown of their marriage. In such a case, the same consequences as in divorce for mutual consent will follow.

In accordance with the fault-based approach to divorce, a spouse who was at fault is not entitled to receive support from another spouse after divorce, or the amount of support may be significantly reduced. Thus, the Latvian law says that 'the duty to support a former spouse ceases, if the latter by his or her actions has promoted the disintegration of the marriage' (s. 82). Similarly, in Lithuania in case of divorce granted on the fault basis a spouse at fault looses the right of a divorcee under the law or even under the marriage contract, including the right to maintenance (art. 3.70 (1)).

The Family Code of Moldova, though not having any provisions on fault-based divorce, nevertheless did introduce the fault idea into the rules on divorce-related consequences. It says that if the court established that a marriage had been broken down because of fault of one of the spouses, the court may release the other spouse from paying the former maintenance or restrict this duty by a certain period of time (even if a spouse claiming maintenance is in need) (s. 95-d). In addition, a spouse 'not guilty' in divorce may ask the court to declare the property acquired by him or her when they lived separately to be his or her personal property (s. 20 (5)). The rule itself is not harsh, but the very fact of using the term 'fault' is noteworthy.

Finally, in Ukrainian law where there is no fault-based divorce concept either and where the term 'fault' is not used, the idea if guiltiness, nonetheless, exists. The Family

Code says that a spouse who behaved badly in the marriage does not have the right to maintenance (s. 75 (5)).

Thus, the concept of fault, in this or that form, turned out to be returned into the family law of some of the countries under consideration.

Commentators on Lithuanian divorce law reform interpret the introduction of fault-based divorce and of the consequences for fault-based divorce as the logical continuation of the marriage=agreement concept.[36] If marriage is a contract, then, as the logic suggests, a contract termination analogy is applicable. In other words, marriage, like any contract, may be terminated either by the parties' consent or because of a breach of the contract's obligations by one of the parties. In such a case the party at fault should be held liable and bear the negative consequences of the breach; while the non-guilty party is entitled to some compensation. Thus, we see here the conceptual transformation of fault-based divorce from matrimonial offence into the 'breach of contract' theory.

Among the drafters of the Russian Family Code, there were also those who considered the contractual nature of marriage as one of the key points in family law reform, for instance, drawing a parallel between the dissolution of a marriage without mutual consent to divorce and the 'unilateral repudiation of a contract.'[37]

However, I would not go so far as to equate marriage with a contract. It is true that these days women are no longer subordinate to men at least under the law, as in the time of fault-based divorce. Spouses are now considered autonomous individuals with equal rights; and their relationships in a contemporary egalitarian family more closely resembles a partnership rather than a marital unity as was interpreted in the time of W. Blackstone.[38] Indeed, emancipation of women brings more civil law components into the family relations. Nevertheless, it does not, in my opinion, transform marriage into a contract. Leaving aside a detailed analysis I would just state that marriage is still a *sui generis* institution in which the parties' consent (undoubtedly, a contractual element) is one of the crucial points.

---

36 Ibid. p. 331.

37 Particularly I mean my friend and colleague Masha Antokolskaia. *See:* ANTOKOLSKAIA, M., *Semeinoe pravo (Family Law)*, Urist, Moscow, 2004, p. 133.

38 Expressed in his well-known definition of the husband and wife as 'one person in law'. *See:* Blackstone's Commentaries on the Law. From the Abridged Edition of Wm. Hardcastle Browne... Washington Law Book Co., Washington, D.C., 1941, p. 189. A similar concept of the old Russian law was embodied in a statement: 'Husband and wife are one body. Husband is the head of the wife'. *See*, for instance: POBEDONOSTSEV, K.P., *Kurs grazhdanskogo prava (The Course of Civil Law)*, Vol. 2, Garant, Moscow, 2003 (Reprint version of 1896 edition), p. 110.

It is evident that the aim of divorce reform was not only to bring back the fault grounds to divorce law, but also to make the divorce procedure itself more complicated. It aimed to produce a 'preventive and educative effect on society'. Particularly, it was one of the goals that the drafters of the Lithuanian Code set by both making divorce more difficult to achieve and the consequences for the guilty party harsher. However, as to whether it may prevent people from divorcing and promote stability in the family, I share the scepticism expressed by Lithuanian scholars.[39]

Separation. The introduction oflegal separation in Lithuania and Ukraine proves the Russian saying that roughly translates as, "new things are old things long forgotten." Fifteen years ago I could not have imagined that the institution of separation as an alternative to divorce for couples who do not want to live together any longer would become topical again and would be included in active law on post-Soviet territory.

One probably would agree that if the divorce procedure had not become more difficult, for instance as is the case in Lithuania, there would be no need for legal separation as an institution complementary to the dissolution of marriage by divorce.[40] Probably that is true as far as it concerns Lithuania. Nevertheless, the Ukrainian example does not support this as a general thesis; here, along with a relatively simple divorce procedure and no fault-based grounds, the Family Code stipulated the possibility for spouses to establish a regime of separation. If a legal separation was established by the court, under art. 120 of the Ukrainian law, property subsequently acquired by each of the spouses "is not deemed to be property acquired in the marriage"; "a child born by the wife after ten months is not deemed to be affiliated to her husband"; and "the wife and the husband may adopt a child without the consent of each other."

Legal separation seems to be a good option for those who for different reasons (in particular, religious) do not consider divorce acceptable.

3.3. PROPERTY ISSUES AND SPOUSAL MAINTENANCE

Property Issues. As I have already mentioned, one of the distinguishing features of the post-Soviet family legislation common to all the countries under consideration without any exception is the detailed regulation of property relations between the spouses, much more detailed in comparison with how property relations were

---

39 See: KESERAUSKAS, S., 'Moving in the Same Direction? Presentation of Family Law Reforms in Lithuania' (2004), p. 331–332.

40 Ibid., p. 338.

governed under Soviet law. Another distinguishing feature of all the post-Soviet family laws is the variety of opportunities given to the spouses or would-be spouses to settle their property and financial matters. All the laws without exception stipulate a contractual agreement, which allows the parties to deviate from the matrimonial regime that operates under the law.

In all post-Soviet jurisdictions, the legal regime that operates by default, *i.e.* in the absence of a contract or an agreement, is a regime of joint ownership. Of course, there are some variations in the national property regimes; and each country has its peculiarities in what kind of property the legal regime includes, how it operates while the marriage lasts and upon its dissolution, etc.[41] Although these issues are important, I have to leave them aside.[42] For the purposes of this paper, another issue calls for close consideration.

Most post-Soviet laws do not provide any special protection for the family home and other assets that a family uses in the household. At this time in the majority of jurisdictions no particular property, such as the family home has a special status.

In this regard, Lithuanian law is of interest. A signal achievement is a legal rule that separates the part of the property called 'family assets' or 'family property' from all the other property that the spouses own jointly or separately. According to art. 3.84 of the Lithuanian Family Code, family assets are defined as property owned by either spouse before or during marriage, which include: 1) the family dwelling; and 2) the movables intended for household use, including furniture. These types of property acquire 'the legal status of family assets on the date of registration of marriage' and may be used only to meet the needs of the family. Even if just one of the spouses is the sole owner of the family dwelling he or she may not, without the written consent of the other spouse, 'alienate, pledge or lease this dwelling'. The premises must be registered in the public register as a family asset in order to let a non-consenting spouse claim annulment of the other spouse's act (art. 3.36 (2)). Moreover, in order to protect the family assets the law does not allow the spouses to change the legal regime of family assets in the marriage contract. If the dwelling space is rented by one of the spouses, similar restrictive rules are applied to the tenant-spouse's right

41 For instance, with regard to the Latvian scheme of matrimonial property, a more appropriate term would be 'the limited acquisition regime'. Here, the law stipulates that each spouse retains, apart from the property, 'which belonged to him or her before the marriage', also 'the property he or she acquires during the marriage'; joint property constitutes everything that spouses acquired together or one of them, but from resources of both spouses or 'with the assistance of the actions of the other spouse' (art. 89).

42 These issues require special in depth analysis. See, e.g.. ZHILINKOVA, L., 'Property Relations of Spouses in Slavonic Post-Soviet Countries (Ukraine, Russia, Belarus)' (2004), p. 483 ff, KULLERKUPP, K., 'Statutory Marital Property Law de lege lata and de lege ferenda' (2001), p. 78 ff.

'to terminate the lease agreement, to sublease it or to transfer the rights under the lease agreement' (art. 3.36 (1)).

The Lithuanian rule on family home and household goods appears to be more than just a peculiarity of the family law of a particular country; rather it may be seen as a sign of a trend that is only emerging now in family law on the post-Soviet territory. Ukrainian law, for instance, states that the spouse who is the sole owner of the property (for example, if he or she acquired the house or the apartment before the marriage), 'when administering his/her property... should take into account the interest of the child, other family members that, in accordance with law, have the right to use it' (s. 59 (2)). We can expect that court practice will show how the judges will interpret this provision and how it will function in the future. In Estonia, there is a draft law that suggests restrictions on the sole owner's right to dispose his or her property if it belongs within the sphere of the family's 'joint and primary interests'.[43] More specifically, it says that the owner of the property may not dispose of it without the consent of his or her spouse if: a) that property constitutes the whole of his/her property or the majority of it; and b) that property constitutes the dwelling in which the family jointly resides, as well as substantial property belonging with the dwelling.[44] Among drafters of the Russian Family Code, there were those who also suggested including similar provisions into the Code aiming to protect the 'family home', but this idea was rejected.

The purpose of such legal provisions is clear: to protect the interests of the family as a social unit and the interests of an economically weaker spouse and children, especially in case of a conflict.

Spousal Maintenance. Another noteworthy feature of post-Soviet law that also only few legislative acts stipulate is to give more financial protection to the spouse who stayed at home looking after children and running the household. Here again the Lithuanian and Ukrainian laws are good examples.

Here, some preliminary explanations are necessary. As I noted before, the Soviet family model 'knew no "housewife marriage"'.[45] Since both spouses worked and neither was a homemaker spouse, neither one required the right to claim maintenance if a marriage broke down. Spousal duty to provide support to each other was rather a moral one, because spousal maintenance as a legal concept although existing in

---

43 KULLERKUPP, K., 'Statutory Marital Property Law de lege lata and de lege ferenda' (2001), p. 84.

44 Ibid, p. 84–85.

45 KULLERKUPP, K., 'Family Law in Estonia', in: BAINHAM, A., (ed.), *The International Survey of Family Law,* Jordan Publishing, Bristol, 2001, p. 102. These issues are discussed in greater detail in KHAZOVA, O.A., 'Equality Within The Family: A View From Russia', in: L?DRUP, P., MODVAR, E., *Family Life and Human Rights,* Gyldendal Norsk Forlag AS, Oslo, 2004, p. 337–346.

principle, was limited to exceptional circumstances when the spouse claiming support was not able to work either due to serious health reasons or due to old age.

The origin of this rule goes to the post-revolutionary period, when the 1917–1918 legislation declared women equal to men. To achieve economic freedom in reality, and not only in word, to become free from economic dependency on their husbands, the women had to work themselves however. The State, in ruins after the turbulence of the revolution and the civil war, badly needed women's participation in the labour market. To improve the economy of the country it was necessary to release as many 'human resources' as possible. The female workforce was a great contribution in this respect, and pushing women out of their homes to the labour market became the family policy of the State. The concept of marriage as a union free from any mercenary spirit and based only on love fit perfectly into both the post-revolutionary mood and ideas of freedom, including the freedom of love, and the new strategy towards the family. According to the new social order, everybody, irrespective of their sex, was supposed to work; and the right of a woman to claim maintenance from her husband merely because of her status as a wife was abolished as 'a bourgeois survival of the past.' Alimony was declared to be 'not a charity', it could not allow one spouse 'to parasitise' at the expense of another one[46] – otherwise it would be incompatible with the ideology of the proletarian State. This ideology survived through decades of Soviet power, though very soon it entirely lost its flavour of freedom.

Surprisingly, despite all the recent changes in the post-Soviet countries and particularly the revival of a 'housewife marriage,' the presumption that both spouses necessarily work and each of them can support him or herself still dominates within the public. Probably most of those who were involved in the elaboration of the new laws turned out to be under the influence of this assumption too; as most of the laws under discussion did not introduce any significant changes in the rules on spousal support. The Russian Family Code provisions are very typical in this regard. The Code states that in order to be entitled to maintenance a spouse shall satisfy certain requirements that are enlisted in ss. 89–90. Putting aside the details and nuances that are not important in the present context, the list includes: a needy and unable to work (ex)spouse; a (ex)wife during pregnancy and three years after the birth of a common child; and a needy (ex)spouses looking after a common disabled child; a (ex)spouse who attained pension age. In practice it means that in the overwhelming majority of cases, if the spouses are not too old or disabled, if they do not have a disabled child in the family, or the wife is not pregnant and etc., *i.e.* if they are young enough and able to work (even if they have five common children!) to get alimony for a

46 GENKIN, D.M., NOVITSKYI, I.B., RABINOVITCH, N.V., *Istoria sovetskogo grazhdaskogo prava (History of Soviet Civil Law)*, VIYUN, Moscow, 1949, p. 440.

spouse's maintenance by a court order is impossible.[47] Therefore, it also means that if a married woman has decided to stay at home and 'to devote herself to her family,' she will not acquire the right to claim alimony from her husband during the marriage or after its dissolution only on the ground of her 'wife's status.' She is not entitled to any payments even on a temporary basis, as compensatory or 'rehabilitation' alimony, which would allow her to adjust to the new financial situation. The same is true as to the husband if he is a homemaker spouse and has no income due to his work at home.

We find a significant departure from such an approach in the Lithuanian and Ukrainian laws, and that is why they attract particular attention. Thus, the Lithuanian Civil Code says that 'maintenance shall be presumed to be necessary' if a spouse is bringing up a minor child of the marriage or is incapacitated for employment because of age or state of health (art. 3.72 (2)). It may seem that this provision does not differ significantly from what other post-Soviet family laws set out and what was established in the former Soviet law. However, the main difference between Lithuanian law in this respect and most of the others is that the former speaks about a minor child, *i.e.*, a child not having reached majority,[48] while the latter restrict the spouse's right to maintenance until the child reaches 3 years of age. The next paragraph of this article is a breakthrough in legal regulation of spousal maintenance indeed. It states:

> 'A spouse that was not able to obtain any qualifications for work (complete his or her studies) because of the marriage, the common interests of the family or the need to care for the children, shall have the right to demand that the former spouse cover the costs related to the completion of his or her studies or retraining'.

The Ukrainian Family Code provisions on spousal maintenance deserve similar appraisal, as it sets out a similar rule (s. 76 (4)):

> 'Whenever one of the spouses was unable to obtain an education, be employed or hold an appropriate position because of bringing up a child, keeping house, caring for family members, being ill, or owning to any other circumstances that are of vital importance, he/she is entitled to a maintenance if the marriage dissolves even if he/she is employable, on condition that he/she needs material support and that the former husband or the former wife is able to provide such material support.
>
> In such a case, the duration of the right to maintenance is for three years after the date of marriage dissolution'.

---

47 The law regulated the parental duty to maintain their children separately; child support payments have no connection with maintenance of a spouse.

48 A minor child is 'a person who has not reached full legal age'. *See:* Merriam-Webster Dictionary and Black's Law Dictionary.

Thus, these laws demonstrate a clear example of a concept that in American law acquired the name of 'rehabilitative' alimony. It aims to help the spouses, in particular, an economically weaker spouse, to adjust to new post-divorce social and economic realities. Drafters of the family law in Lithuania and Ukraine achieved what we, in Russia, did not.

4. COHABITATION

Concerning one of today's most topical family law issues – extramarital cohabitation, timid attempts have been made towards legal recognition in a just a few countries, particularly Ukraine and Lithuania. Family law in the majority of the post-Soviet jurisdictions clearly says that only lawful marriage, i.e. officially registered in the order established in a respective country, shall give rise to marital rights and duties.[49]

The Ukrainian Family Code provisions may look misleading at first, as in one of the sections the Code states that 'a woman and a man's living as a family without being married does not constitute a ground for them to have the rights and responsibilities of a married couple' (s. 21 (2)). However, in fact, the Code does recognize that living together as a family may produce legal consequences with regard to property rights and spousal support. To confirm that fact one just needs to read the Code further. Thus, in accordance with s. 74, if a man and a woman live together as a family but without being legally married, the property they acquire during the period of cohabitation 'belongs to them as a common joint property,' unless a written contract made between them states otherwise. As a reminder, the matrimonial regime of common joint property is the one that is available only for married couples and it operates by law only after the conclusion of marriage. The cohabitees' property rights with regard to the common joint property are governed by the Code's provisions that relate to property rights of the spouses.

In the same way, the Ukrainian Code deals with spousal support between cohabitating couples. If a man and a woman, who are not married to each other, have been living together for a prolonged period of time, – as section 91 says, – the one of them that became unable to work during the period of their living together has the right to maintenance on the same terms as a spouse in the case of divorce. The Code also extends the right to maintenance granted to a spouse with whom a child under 3 years of age or a disabled child resides, to a cohabitee who is in the same situation.

---

[49] *See, e.g.:* the Russian Family Code, art. 10 (2); the Family Code of Moldova, art. 2 (2), 9 (2); the Code on Marriage and the Family of Belarus, art. 15; the Civil Code of Georgia, art. 1151; the Family Code of Armenia, art. 9 (2).

The Civil Code of Lithuania dedicated a whole chapter to the property rights of cohabiting but not legally married couples (Chapter XV). However, it conditioned recognition of the rights and duties of cohabitees with regard to their property on a requirement to register their cohabitation. Chapter XV covers only those couples who 'having been cohabiting at least for a year with the aim of creating family relations' registered their cohabitation 'in a procedure laid down by the law' (art. 3.229). If the parties have registered their cohabitation, their property rights are similar to those that married couple enjoy. Special protection is given to the dwelling house or flat the cohabitees use for their life together. If the assets are to be divided, a dwelling space may be awarded to the cohabitee who is in greater need, all the circumstances being taken into account (age, health, the interests of minor children, etc.).

Estonian law did not introduce any provisions on cohabitation into the law, though the Estonian family law scholars noted that there was a wide range of cohabitational relationships in the society already ten years ago.[50] However, depending on the circumstances, the courts have been recognizing the legal consequences of factual cohabitation for some time now when a property dispute between cohabiting couples came to their attention.[51]

Thus, though there is still no wide recognition of cohabitation in the post-Soviet jurisdictions, in some of the countries the first steps in this direction have been taken; and this is, undoubtedly, a remarkable feature of new law.

5. CONCLUDING REMARKS

After having looked at the great variety on display in the post-Soviet family laws and the departure of some of them from what has been generally interpreted as liberal family law concepts, one may argue that Harry Willekens's statement that 'when change occurs the direction is always the same'[52] does not work for post-Soviet family law. However, despite this variety and the distinctly conservative tone of some of the laws, movement towards European models is evident. Most of the national post-Soviet laws were undoubtedly influenced by European laws or were created with their conformity with the European standards in mind. Perhaps this movement is not as fast as one might expect nor does it necessarily look like movements in other areas of law. It is also not straightforward – due to the peculiarities of mostly political, but

50 SALUMAA, E., 'The Family Law Act', *Juridica International* (1996), p. 94.

51 See: KESERAUSKAS, S., 'Moving in the Same Direction? Presentation of Family Law Reforms in Lithuania' (2004), p. 333.

52 WILLEKENS, H., 'Long Term Developments in Family Law in Western Europe: An Explanation', in: EEKELAAR, J., NHLAPO, T., *The Changing Family: International Perspectives on the Family and Family Law*, Hart Publishing, Oxford, 1998, p. 48.

also social and economic conditions, but the movement does indeed exist, and the direction is obvious. To move their family law forward some of the jurisdictions under consideration had to start from where their development was 'interrupted'. It is unlikely that it will take a long time. The time seems already ripe for some of them 'to go on a second round'.[53]

[53] KULLERKUPP, K., 'Statutory Marital Property Law de lege lata and de lege ferenda' (2001), p. 79. In this regard it is enough just to have a look at the hot debate on recognition of same-sex marriages in Estonia in 2005–2006. See, for instance, at: http://en.wikipedia.org/wiki/Same-sex_marriage_in_Estonia.

PART III
CONVERGENCE AND DIVERGENCE IN SPECIFIC FIELDS OF FAMILY LAW

O TEMPORA, O MORES! THE EVOLVING MARRIAGE CONCEPT AND THE IMPEDIMENTS TO MARRIAGE

FREDERIK SWENNEN

1. PREVIOUSLY IN FAMILY LAW

'*[Du mariage] doivent naître des fruits dont la vie (...) ne commencera que par les douleurs de leur mère, ne sera conservée que par ses soins pénibles, et ne pourra être soutenue que par les travaux et la protection du père. (...) Le lien du mariage est doublé par celui de la naissance.*'[1]

From a socio-biological point of view, family law is concerned with biosocial reproduction.[2]

The family originated from the need to provide for the survival and socialisation of children during their (prolonged) maturation; the basic function of a family is childbearing and –rearing. Family *law* originated from the need to provide a legal framework for this *parental investment*, supplied in the first instance by the mother.[3]

During the process of hominisation, the necessary parental investment intensified to such a degree that mothers could no longer provide for themselves (during and after childrearing) and for the child(ren). Fathers needed to be mobilised to support the mothers and their children. Hereto, qualities such as sense of responsibility, love, constant sexual receptivity and fidelity developed. Having arisen as a supporting

1 *Rapport* by GILLET before the *Tribunat*, in: FENET, P.A., *Recueil complet des Travaux Préparatoires du Code civil*, t. IX, Réimpression, Otto Zeller, Osnabrück, 1968, p. 182.

2 CLIQUET, R., 'Sociobiologie van het gezin', *1 Recht der Werkelijkheid* (1997), p. 25, 26–27 and 36.

3 CLIQUET, R., *ibid*, p. 29 ff; CLIQUET, R., AVRAMOV, D., 'The future of the family: A sociobiological approach', in: MATTHIJS, M., (ed.), *The Family*, Leuven University Press, 1998, p. 159, 161 ff; WILLEKENS, H., 'Het gezinsrecht in de sociale wetenschappen', *1 Recht der Werkelijkheid* (1997), p. 1, 9; WILLEKENS, H., 'De liefde, het kind en de institutionalisering van persoonlijke relaties', in: RAES, K., (ed.), *Liefde's onrecht: het onmogel?ke huwel?k tussen liefde en recht*, Mys & Breesch, Gent, 1998, p. 1, 8 ff.

mechanism, socio-biologists consider *enduring partnership* (between the parents) as the second basic function of the family, subservient to the first.[4]]

Parenthood and partnership, being interwoven, were consequently dealt with in a sole (legal) institution: marriage. The etymology of the word marriage (*mater* (mother) + *monium* (condition)) clearly refers to its original basic function. Beside the above-mentioned functions, marriage also fulfilled several secondary functions.

On the ground of that briefly described origin of family (law), families were considered the "orchard of the State".[5] Families were formed by marriage; marriage therefore was "the source for reproduction, the community between spouses being the first of communities".[6] It is interesting to see how the cited high-flown declarations during the drawing-up of the *Code napoléon* were almost literally copied into the post-WWII human rights instruments confirming the importance of (the family and) marriage as the basic unit of society.[7]

The communal function of marriage and the interest of families and society at large therein, allowed the States to institutionalise it by binding rules on its content.[8] In function of that content, and in function of policy considerations, States also enacted rules on formation and dissolution of marriage.[9]

In regard to the formation of marriage, States may lay down substantive and procedural conditions. These conditions must not injure the essence of the right to marry,[10] so as to deprive a person or category of persons of that right. They must be based on generally recognised considerations of public interest, in connection with the nature and functions of marriage.[11]

---

4 CLIQUET, R., 'Sociobiologie van het gezin', (1997), p. 29 ff; WILLEKENS, H., 'Het gezinsrecht in de sociale wetenschappen'(1997), p. 10–13; WILLEKENS, H., 'De liefde, het kind en de institutionalisering van persoonlijke relaties'(1998), p. 8 ff.

5 *Exposé des Motifs* by PORTALIS before the *Corps Législatif*, FENET, P.A., *Recueil complet des Travaux Préparatoires du Code civil*, t. IX, Réimpression (1968), p. 138.

6 *Rapport* by GILLET before the *Tribunal* (1968), p. 182.

7 Art. 16.3 Universal Declaration of Human Rights; art. 23.1 International Covenant on Civil and Political Rights; art. 10.1 International Covenant on Economic, Social and Cultural Rights; art. 16 European Social Charter.

8 **Belgium:** SENAEVE, P., *Compendium van het personen- en familierecht*, Part 3, 9th ed., Acco, Leuven, 2006, p. 1488.

9 COESTER-WALTJEN, D., COESTER, M., 'Formation of marriage', in: *International Encyclopaedia of Comparative Law*, Vol. IV *Persons and Family*, GLENDON, M-A, (ed.), Mohr, Tübingen, 1997, p. 1, 162. **Germany:** BVerfG 14th November 1973, *BVerfGE* 31, nr. 17, 161. *Adde* STAUDINGER/STRÄTZ (2000), *Vorbem zu §§ 1303 ff*, 1.

10 As guaranteed in art. 16.1 Universal Declaration of Human Rights; art. 23.2 International Covenant on Civil and Political Rights; art. 12 ECHR; art. 9 Charter of Fundamental Rights of the European Union.

11 **Declaration of Human Rights:** LAGOUTTE, S., ÁRNASON, A.T., 'article 16', in: ALFREDSSON, G., EIDE, A., *The Universal Declaration of Human Rights. A Common Standard of Achievement*, Martinus Nijhoff, The Hague, 1999, p. 325, 329, 334. **Covenant on Civil and Political Rights:** NOWAK, M., *U.N. Covenant on Civil and Political Rights. CCPR Commentary*, Engel, Kehl am Rein, 1993, p. 19.

Due to scientific, economic[12] and ideological liberalising trends,[13] the functions of marriage and of the family have changed dramatically over the last decades. These trends have liberated women sexually, economically and culturally, making them less dependent upon a husband and thus ruling out asymmetrical partner roles.[14]

Most of the secondary functions of marriage and of the family have been taken over by other public or private social structures. More importantly, parenthood and partnership have been formally unlinked from each other[15] and from marriage. Marriage is no longer the exclusive legitimising framework for parenthood and partnership. The communal function of marriage being on the decline, the emphasis is now on its "private" function of partnership based on love and serving self-fulfilment of the spouses.[16] As a consequence, the considerations of public interest on which State intervention in marriage may be based, have also changed. Logically, the private interest of (future) spouses will gradually outweigh the weakening public interest in marriage so as to make State intervention by binding rules less acceptable. The emphasis is now on the spouses' fundamental right to marry; the legitimation of the limitation thereof must meet higher requirements.[17]

ECHR: ECtHR, *Rees v. United Kingdom*, 17th October 1986, http://cmiskp.echr.coe.int, §50; ECtHR, *F. v. Switzerland*, 18th December 1987, http://cmiskp.echr.coe.int, §32; ECtHR, *Goodwin v. United Kingdom*, 11th July 2002, http://cmiskp.echr.coe.int, §99; ECtHR, *I. v. United Kingdom*, 11th July 2002, http://cmiskp.echr.coe.int/, §79; ECtHR, *B and L. v. United Kingdom*, 13th December 2005, http://cmiskp.echr.coe.int/, §34; ECHR, *Hamer v. United Kingdom*, No. 7114/75, 13th December 1979, *D.R.* 24, 5, §§60–62; ECHR, *Draper v. United Kingdom*, No. 8186/78, 10th July 1980, *D.R.* 24, 72, §§47–49; ECHR, *X. and Y. v. United Kingdom*, No. 7229/75, 15th December 1977, *D.R.* 12, 32, §56. *Adde* GEHUCHTE, A., VAN DE, HAECK, Y., and STAELENS, V., 'Artikel 12', in: VANDE LANOTTE, J., HAECK, Y., (eds.), *Handboek EVRM*, II, vol. 2, Intersentia, Antwerpen, 2004, 41, 44–45; GRUNDERBEECK, D. VAN, *Beginselen van personen- en familierecht. Een mensenrechtelijke benadering*, Antwerpen, Intersentia, 2003, p. 265; VERSCHRAEGEN, B., 'Right to private life and family life, the right to marry and to found a family, and the prohibition of discrimination', in: BOELE-WOELKI, K., FUCHS, A., (eds.), *Legal Recognition of Same-sex Couples in Europe*, Intersentia, Antwerpen-Oxford, 2003, p. 194, 204–205. **Germany**: BVerfG 14th November 1973, *BVerfGE* 31, nr. 17, 162. *Adde* SCHWAB, D., *Familierecht*, München, Beck, 2005, p. 78; STAUDINGER/STRÄTZ (2000), *Einl. zu §§ 1303 ff*, 55–56.

12 GLENDON, M.A., *The New Family and the New Property*, Toronto, Butterworths, 1981, p. 2, 6.

13 RENCHON, J.-L., 'Indisponibilité, ordre public et autonomie de la volonté dans le droit des personnes et de la famille', in: WIJFFELS, A., (ed.), *Le Code civil entre ius commune et droit privé européen*, Bruylant, Brussel, 2005, p. 269, 19 and 24 ff.

14 CLIQUET, R., AVRAMOV, D., 'The future of the family: A sociobiological approach' (1998), p. 169.

15 Hereto e.g. CARILLON, A., 'L'influence des arrêts *Christine Goodwin* et *I* sur le consentement au mariage en droit français', *Rev. trim. dr. homme* (2005), p. 350, 351–356.

16 COESTER-WALTJEN, D., COESTER, M., 'Formation of marriage' (1997), p.160–161. From a socio-biological point of view: CLIQUET, R., 'Sociobiologie van het gezin' (1997), p. 26 ff and 39; CLIQUET, R., AVRAMOV, D., 'The future of the family: A sociobiological approach' (1998), p.165, 169, 170. **Belgium**: RENCHON, J.-L., 'Indisponibilité, ordre public et autonomie de la volonté dans le droit des personnes et de la famille' (2005), p. 2.

17 COESTER-WALTJEN, D., COESTER, M., 'Formation of marriage' (1997), p. 2, 9, 19 and 160.

This pendulum from institutionalisation toward privatisation has been discussed extensively,[18] e.g. by Meulders-Klein[19] and Renchon.[20] Glendon[21] refers to deregulation of marriage (formation) law as an important convergence trend. Notwithstanding official declarations in that sense,[22] the remaining public interest of marriage will probably prevent it from becoming a purely private contract.[23]

In regard to the impediments to marriage, the liberalising trend can be summarised with Renchon as "*la levée des interdits*" (withdrawal of bans).[24] As mentioned above, every impediment to marriage must, as a limitation of the right to marry, be justified by considerations of public interest, in connection with the nature and functions of marriage. In the light of the changing functions of marriage, to reserve marriage for *two, non-related,* persons of the *opposite gender* is questionable.[25] In this contribution, the evolution of three substantive impediments to marriage is therefore addressed: kinship and affinity (Ch. 2), polygamy (Ch. 3), and gender (Ch. 4). In addition to the relevant international instruments, the law of four States where the Supreme or Constitutional Courts have had to explore the marriage concept is examined: Belgium,

---

18 In general COESTER-WALTJEN, D., COESTER, M., 'Formation of marriage' (1997), p. 5; DEWAR, J., 'Family Law and its Discontents', *14 Int'l J. L. Pol. & Fam.* (2000), p. 59, 65 and 70–73. **Belgium:** LELEU, Y.-H., *Droit des personnes et des familles*, Brussel, Larcier, 2005, p. 311 (approving); RIGAUX, F., 'L'évolution du droit de la famille en Belgique, in: SCHWARZ-LIEBERMANN VON WAHLENDORF, H.A., *Mariage et famille en question*, (ed.), du C.N.R.S., Paris, 1980, p. 87, 2; SWENNEN, F., *Gezins- en familierecht in kort bestek*, Intersentia, Antwerpen, 2005, p. 395/1. **Germany:** STAUDINGER/STRÄTZ (2000), *Einl. zu §§ 1303 ff*, 48–50; STRÄTZ, H.-W., 'Ehe und Familie als Institute des bürgerlichen Rechts', in: *Ehe und Familie unter veränderten gesellschaftlichen Rahmenbedingungen*, Aschendorff, Münster, 2001, p. 13, 19.

19 MEULDERS-KLEIN, M.-T., 'L'évolution du mariage: de l'institution au contrat, et au-delà', in : MEULDERS-KLEIN, M.-T., *La personne, la famille et le droit. Trois décennies de mutations en Occident*, Bruylant- L.G.D.J Brussel- Paris, 1999, p. 35.

20 RENCHON, J.-L., 'Indisponibilité, ordre public et autonomie de la volonté dans le droit des personnes et de la famille' (2005).

21 GLENDON, M.-A., 'Introduction: Family Law at a time of turbulence', in: *International Encyclopaedia of Comparative Law*, Vol. IV *Persons and Family*, GLENDON, M.-A., (ed.), Mohr, Tübingen, 2006, p. 1, 2, 6 and 9–10; GLENDON, M.-A., *The New Family and the New Property* (1981), p. 4, 28 ff.

22 E.g. by the Belgian Minister of Justice on the occasion of a proposed divorce reform: "*marriage is not considered a rigid and indissoluble institution any more, but a sui generis pact that needs to be renewed on a day-by-day basis*". *Parl. St.* Kamer 2005–06, nr. 51–2341, p. 6. Adde: WILLEKENS, H., 'Het gezinsrecht in de sociale wetenschappen'(1997), p. 1.

23 COESTER-WALTJEN, D., COESTER, M., 'Formation of marriage' (1997), p. 160. Cf. LÉVI-STRAUSS, C., *Het gezin*, SUN, Nijmegen, 1983, p. 27: marriage is not, has never been and cannot be a private matter.

24 RENCHON, J.-L., 'Indisponibilité, ordre public et autonomie de la volonté dans le droit des personnes et de la famille' (2005), p. 51 ff. *Adde* COESTER-WALTJEN, D., COESTER, M., 'Formation of marriage' (1997), p. 1 and 161; BRADLEY, D., 'Convergence in Family Law: Mirrors, Transplants and Political Economy', 6 *MJ* 2 (1999), p. 127, 130. **France:** RAYMOND, G., 'Mariage. Conditions à réunir dans la personne des époux', *J.-Cl. Civ.*, art. 144–147, Fasc. 10, 16. **Germany:** SCHWAB, D., *Familierecht* (2005), p. 78.

25 COESTER-WALTJEN, D., COESTER, M., 'Formation of marriage' (1997), p. 9 and 19. Comp. for **the Netherlands:** D'ONORIO, J.-B., 'La protection constitutionnelle du mariage et de la famille en Europe', *RTDCiv.* (1988), p. 1, 4.

France, Germany and the Netherlands. Whether or not this evolution marks a new era of divergence[26] or of convergence[27] will be assessed in the conclusion.

Each impediment to marriage is – or should be – justifiable separately, so a separate analysis is necessary. One should be cautious not to be misled by slippery slope arguments,[28] such as "if one allows same-gender marriage, one should also allow polygamy".[29] Nonetheless, the impediments to marriage reflect a certain marriage concept. Should this concept change fundamentally, this logically could influence all impediments – albeit not necessarily to the same extent or in the same direction.

2. CONVERGENCE WITH INTERVALS: THE IMPEDIMENTS TO MARRIAGE ON THE GROUND OF KINSHIP AND AFFINITY (BY ADOPTION)

'Öffentliche Interessen, die über das individuelle Interesse des Verlobten an sich selbst hinausreichen, spielen bei der Eheschließung keine Rolle mehr.'[30]

2.1. ANALYSIS

As a substantive condition to marriage, States may lay down rules concerning prohibited degrees of kinship, affinity or adoption.[31] Lévi-Strauss stresses the universal character of such prohibitions.[32]

---

26 This is the opinion of, amongst others, S. SANCHEZ LORENZO, 'Case note in Spanish Dir. Gen. des Régistres et du Notariat 24th January 2005', *94 Rev. crit. DIP 4* (2005), p. 618, I.

27 BRADLEY, D., 'Convergence in Family Law: Mirrors, Transplants and Political Economy', 6 *MJ* 2 (1999), p. 135: the convergent trend of liberalisation does however not erase some significant differences.

28 Hereto MCKNORRIE, K., 'Marriage is for heterosexuals – may the rest of us be saved from it', *12 Child Fam. L. Q.* 4 (2000), p. 363, 364–365. E.g. ENDRÉO, G., 'Bigamie et double ménage', *RTDCiv* (1991), p. 263, 267: *"une fois la limite franchie, il n'en existe aucune autre"*.

29 E.g. the brief preceding Arbitragehof nr. 159/2004 of 20th October 2004, www.arbitrage.be.

30 STRÄTZ, H.-W., 'Ehe und Familie als Institute des bürgerlichen Rechts' (2001), p. 23.

31 PALM-RISSE, M., *Der völkerrechtliche Schutz von Ehe und Familie*, Duncker & Humblot, Berlin, 1990, p. 158–159 and 161–162. **Declaration of Human Rights:** LAGOUTTE, S., ÁRNASON, A.T., 'article 16' (1999), p. 329, 334 and 335. **Covenant on Civil and Political Rights:** NOWAK, M., *U.N. Covenant on Civil and Political Rights* (1993), p. 20. **ECHR:** ECHR, *Hamer v. United Kingdom*, No. 7114/75, 13th December 1979, *D.R.* 24, 5, §62; ECHR, *Draper v. United Kingdom*, No. 8186/78, 10th July 1980, *D.R.* 24, 72, §49. NOWAK, M., *U.N. Covenant on Civil and Political Rights* (1993), p. 20 is however of the opinion that adoption is not an acceptable impediment to marriage under the Covenant of Civil and Political Rights.

32 LÉVI-STRAUSS, C., *Het gezin* (1983), p. 42 ff.

Whereas a common core of prohibited degrees exists in Europe, the range of the prohibitions differs from country to country. As will be shown in para. 2, there is however a convergent trend of erosion of impediments to marriage between relatives, their four rationales being undermined.

The first rationale for the prohibited degrees was the need for exogamy so as to create community life (and thereby progress) by making families interdependent for marriage.[33] The survival chances of isolated endogamous families would be limited.[34] Later on, exogamy was useful so as to avoid accrual of land, capital or power in one family.[35]

Already the draftsmen of the *Code civil* however questioned the interest of the State to promote exogamy by binding rules, the (economic) significance of the extended family diminishing anyhow.[36]

A second rationale for these impediments was to promote eugenic marriages.[37]

The rationale of avoiding genetic defects however only applies to opposite-gender marriages between next-of-kin – less one would adhere to the Christian view that man and woman become one flesh so are related and not affiliated to the other spouses' next-of-kin.[38] Moreover, modern eugenics disaffirms the risk of eugenic defects as a consequence of procreation by related persons[39] – on the contrary this risk would accrue in groups where impediments do exist.[40] Most importantly, the impediment would not be very effective in legal systems where sexual relations between next-of-kin are not prohibited and where the parent-child relationship could be established on both sides outside marriage.

---

33 Hereto PORTALIS in the *Discussion du Conseil d'Etat* (1968), p. 21–22 and *Exposé des Motifs* by PORTALIS before the *Corps Législatif*, in: FENET, P. A., *Recueil complet des Travaux Préparatoires du Code civil*, t. IX, Réimpression (1968), p. 151–152. **France:** BATTEUR, A., 'L'Interdit de l'inceste. Principe fondateur du droit de la famille', *RTDCiv* (2000), p. 759, 761.

34 LÉVI-STRAUSS, C., *Het gezin* (1983), p. 42 ff.

35 COESTER-WALTJEN, D., COESTER, M., 'Formation of marriage' (1997), p. 85. **Belgium:** VAN GYSEL, A.-C., (ed.), *Précis de droit de la famille*, Brussel, Bruylant, 2004, p. 177.

36 *Exposé des Motifs* by PORTALIS before the *Corps Législatif*, in: FENET, P.A., *Recueil complet des Travaux Préparatoires du Code civil*, t. IX, Réimpression (1968), p. 151–152.

37 PORTALIS in the *Discussion du Conseil d'Etat*, in: FENET, P.A., *Recueil complet des Travaux Préparatoires du Code civil*, t. IX, Réimpression *l'Etat*' (1968), p. 21 ; COESTER-WALTJEN, D., COESTER, M., 'Formation of marriage' (1997), p. 86. **Belgium:** SENAEVE, P., 'La prohibition du mariage en raison de la parenté et de l'alliance', *Rev. trim. dr. fam.* (1978), p. 321, 1; SWENNEN, F., *Gezins- en familierecht in kort bestek* (2005), p. 419 VAN GYSEL, A.-C., (ed.), *Précis de droit de la famille* (2004), p.177.

38 BATTEUR, A., 'L'Interdit de l'inceste. Principe fondateur du droit de la famille' (2000), p. 762 and 765.

39 COESTER-WALTJEN, D., COESTER, M., 'Formation of marriage' (1997), p. 86.

40 LÉVI-STRAUSS, C., *Het gezin* (1983), p. 44.

The third rationale to keep natural and legal families separate by prohibited degrees would be to avoid confusion of or over their different legal consequences.[41] This confusion would be greater in the case of vertical endogamy, e.g. combination of roles of grand- and stepfather or of ex-husband and son-in-law, than in the case of horizontal endogamy, more legal consequences existing in vertical family relations.[42] However, the legal ties between extended family members are weakening. Moreover, a hierarchy in the case of overlap of legal ties does exist.

Social and moral considerations seem to be the foremost rationale for prohibited degrees.[43] Family ties in the basic unit of society should be well organised so as to prepare the family members for society at large. Thereto, confusion of roles should be avoided. Firstly, *educational and sexual roles* should not be confused. Thereto, an impediment exists between ascendants and descendants, including in-laws and stepfamily members. On the same ground, an impediment applies between (great-) aunt or -uncle and (grand-) niece or -nephew, given the motherly or fatherly role (possibly) taken up by the former.[44] Secondly, the draftsmen of the *Code civil* were of the opinion that an impediment to marriage should exist between other *members of the same household* whose ties of affection should not be troubled by other expectations.[45] It seems that forced exogamy was the real rationale. The existing impediment between *cousins* was indeed abandoned since households were no longer composed of extended families, so that exogamy did not need to be imposed any

41 ECtHR, *B and L. v. United Kingdom*, 13th December 2005, http://cmiskp.echr.coe.int/, §§37–39 and J.M. SCHERPE, 'Should there be degrees in prohibited degrees? Case note in B. and L. / UK', 65 *CLJ* 2006, 32. **Belgium**: SWENNEN, F., *Gezins- en familierecht in kort bestek* (2005), p. 419. **Germany**: BVerfG 14th November 1973, *BVerfGE* 31, nr. 17, 167.

42 VAN GYSEL, A.-C., 'Abrogation de la prohibition du mariage entre beau-frère et belle-soeur', *Div. Act.* (2001), p. 106, 107.

43 PORTALIS in the *Discussion du Conseil d'Etat*, in : FENET, P.A., *Recueil complet des Travaux Préparatoires du Code civil*, t. IX, Réimpression *l'Etat'* (1968), p. 21 ; COESTER-WALTJEN, D., COESTER, M., 'Formation of marriage' (1997), p. 86. **Belgium**: LELEU, Y.-H., *Droit des personnes et des familles* (2005), p. 329; MAHILLON, P., 'Beaux-frères et belles-soeurs', *A.N.E.* (1958), p. 124, 1; SENAEVE, P., 'La prohibition du mariage en raison de la parenté et de l'alliance' (1978), p. 1; SWENNEN, F., *Gezins- en familierecht in kort bestek* (2005), p. 419; VAN GYSEL, A.-C., (ed.), *Précis de droit de la famille* (2004), p. 177. **France:** HAUSER, J., LEMOULAND, J-J., 'Mariage', *Rep. Dalloz* (2002) p. 510–511; LAMBOLEY, A., 'Mariage. Prohibition du mariage entre parents et alliés', *J.-Cl. Civ.*, art. 161–164, 1–13. **Germany**: STAUDINGER/STRÄTZ (2000), *§ 1307*, 5.

44 PORTALIS in the *Discussion du Conseil d'Etat*, FENET, P. A., *Recueil complet des Travaux Préparatoires du Code civil*, t. IX, Réimpression (1968), p. 22 and FENET, P.A., *Recueil complet des Travaux Préparatoires du Code civil*, t. IX, Réimpression (1968), p. 149 ff.

45 *Exposé des Motifs* by PORTALIS before the *Corps Législatif*, FENET, P.A., *Recueil complet des Travaux Préparatoires du Code civil*, t. IX, Réimpression (1968), p. 149 ff; *Rapport* by GILLET before the *Tribunat*, FENET, P.A., *Recueil complet des Travaux Préparatoires du Code civil*, t. IX, Réimpression (1968), p. 185–186.

more.[46] Finally, *sexual rivalry* between family members had to be prevented. Divorce rates had increased since marriages between brothers-in-law and sisters-in-law were no longer forbidden under Revolutionary Legislation. To prevent brothers and sisters from breaking into their siblings' marriages, the impediment was reintroduced in the *Code civil*.[47] It seems to me that the rationale for the impediments to marriage between stepparents and – children and between parents-in-law and children-in-law now falls under this rationale rather than the need to avoid confusion of sexual and educational roles.

There is a convergent trend of liberalisation with regard to the impediments to marriage in the "Old Family".[48] The interest of the individual('s fundamental right to marry) outweighs the weakening family interest. It is clear from the foregoing sketch that, with the loosening of the (legal) ties within the extended family and the nuclear family alike, impediments to marriage are now mainly based on social and moral views. These views have always been in motion. Probably as a consequence of the decreasing legal importance of family and marriage, marriages between related or affiliated persons are considered less morally reprehensible.[49] In the absence of a social consensus, impediments to marriage would be ineffective.[50] The draftsmen of the consecutive law reforms have systematically adhered to the descriptive rather than prescriptive function of (family) law.[51] Impediments on moral grounds have therefore

---

46 *Exposé des Motifs* by PORTALIS before the *Corps Législatif*, in: FENET, P.A., *Recueil complet des Travaux Préparatoires du Code civil*, t. IX, Réimpression' (1968), p. 152.

47 PORTALIS in the *Discussion du Conseil d'Etat*, in: FENET, P.A., *Recueil complet des Travaux Préparatoires du Code civil*, t. IX, Réimpression' (1968), p. 23–25.

48 COESTER-WALTJEN, D., COESTER, M., 'Formation of marriage' (1997), p. 86. France: BATTEUR, A., 'L'Interdit de l'inceste. Principe fondateur du droit de la famille' (2000), p. 760 and 762; HAUSER, J., LEMOULAND, J.-J., 'Mariage' (2002), p. 513; LEMOULAND, J.-J., VIGNEAU, D., 'Mariage-Concubinage-PaCS', *D.* (2006), *Pan.*, 1414, 1418. Germany: STRÄTZ, H.-W., 'Ehe und Familie als Institute des bürgerlichen Rechts' (2001), p. 21. The Netherlands: BOER, J., DE, *C. Assers' Handeling tot beoefening van het Nederlands burgerlijk recht. Personen- en familierecht*, Kluwer, Deventer, 2004, p. 123; PITLO, A., BURGHT, G., VAN DER, DOEK, J.E., *Personen- en familierecht*, Kluwer, Deventer, 2002, p. 143.

49 COESTER-WALTJEN, D., COESTER, M., 'Formation of marriage' (1997), p. 86. **The Netherlands:** PITLO/VAN DER BURGHT, DOEK, *Personen- en familierecht* (2002), p. 143; MEIJER-VAN DER AA, J.M., 'Het huwelijksverbod tussen aanverwanten in de opgaande en de neerdalende lijn', *FJR* (1982), p. 146, 147.

50 ECtHR, *B and L. v. United Kingdom*, 13th December 2005, http://cmiskp.echr.coe.int/, §39. **Germany:** BVerfG 14th November 1973, *BVerfGE* 31, nr. 17, 165 ff. **The Netherlands:** VAN ZEBEN, C.J., et al., *Parlementaire Geschiedenis van het nieuwe BW*, Boek 1, Kluwer, Deventer, 1961, p. 155; PITLO/VAN DER BURGHT, DOEK, *Personen- en familierecht* (2002), p. 143; MEIJER-VAN DER AA, J.M., 'Het huwelijksverbod tussen aanverwanten in de opgaande en de neerdalende lijn' (1982), p. 146. Comp. for **France** in another context: CALAIS-AULOY, M.-T., 'Pour un mariage aux effets limités', *RTDCiv* (1988), p. 255, 11: "*Si l'individu a besoin d'une règle de conduite ce n'est pas au législateur qu'il doit s'adresser, c'est à la morale et à la réligion*".

51 **The Netherlands:** VAN ZEBEN, C.J., et al., *Parlementaire Geschiedenis van het nieuwe BW*, Boek 1 (1961), p. 184.

been repealed, at the least when no rational justification existed.[52] Moreover, in Germany the sanctions to the remaining impediments have been relaxed.[53]

Impediments to marriage in fact have never held back family members in a forbidden degree to start a relationship.[54] In one view, these relations should not be rewarded by the prospect of a marriage. In another view, (mostly) men must not be allowed to escape their responsibility by forbidding formalising the relationship by marriage. Moreover, the 'risk' of a marriage could hold them back from starting a relationship in the first place. An impediment to marriage would also (undesirably) promote them living as concubines.[55]

Proponents of the prescriptive, moralising, function of (family) law at least wanted to hold on to relative impediments, with a possibility of dispensation. Opponents however considered dispensations a pure formality by which the legislator would not give the right signal.[56]

In some cases, the interest of the children was put forward to justify the abolition of an impediment.[57] This justification of course only applies to cases where no alternative to legitimise[58] or support[59] the children is available.

However, I do not yet find the "New Family" – to speak in Glendon's words – systematically back in the impediments to marriage or other registered relations. As

---

52 ECtHR, *B and L. v. United Kingdom*, 13th December 2005, http://cmiskp.echr.coe.int/, §39. **Germany:** BVerfG 14th November 1973, *BVerfGE* 31, nr. 17, 149–151 and 162–163.

53 SCHWAB, D., *Familierecht* (2005), p. 87; STRÄTZ, H.-W., 'Ehe und Familie als Institute des bürgerlichen Rechts' (2001), p. 23.

54 ECtHR, *B and L. v. United Kingdom*, 13th December 2005, http://cmiskp.echr.coe.int/, §37. **Germany:** STAUDINGER/STRÄTZ (2000), *Vorbem zu §§ 1303 ff*, 7. **The Netherlands:** VAN ZEBEN, C.J., et al., *Parlementaire Geschiedenis van het nieuwe BW*, Boek 1 (1961), p. 163: "Zou het jongere zusje, dat ten tonele wordt gevoerd in stukken als indringster in het huwelijk van haar oudere zuster ooit gedacht hebben: laat ik dat niet doen, want ik kan toch niet met die zwager trouwen?"

55 **Germany:** BVerfG 14th November 1973, *BVerfGE* 31, nr. 17, 165. **The Netherlands** VAN ZEBEN, C.J., et al., *Parlementaire Geschiedenis van het nieuwe BW*, Boek 1 (1961), p. 157 ff; MEIJER-VAN DER AA, J.M., 'Het huwelijksverbod tussen aanverwanten in de opgaande en de neerdalende lijn' (1982), p. 146.

56 **Germany:** STAUDINGER/STRÄTZ (2000), *Einl. zu §§ 1303 ff*, 7; BOSCH, F, 'Die geplante Neuregelung des Eheschließungsrecht' *FamRZ* (1997), p. 65, 75. **The Netherlands:** VAN ZEBEN, C.J., et al., *Parlementaire Geschiedenis van het nieuwe BW*, Boek 1 (1961), p. 158, 159 and 161.

57 E.g. on the occasion of the abolition of the impediment between brothers-in-law and sisters-in-law in France or between parents-in-law and children-in-law and stepparents and stepchildren in the Netherlands. Also see BVerfG 14th November 1973, *BVerfGE* 31, nr. 17, 165 with regard to the impediment of *Geschlechtsgemeinschaft*. Furthermore, PORTALIS in the *Discussion du Conseil d'Etat*, in: FENET, P.A., *Recueil complet des Travaux Préparatoires du Code civil*, t. IX, Réimpression' (1968), p. 23.

58 E.g. in **Belgium**: Arbitragehof, nr. 169/2003, 17th December 2003, www.arbitrage.be with regard to the establishment of the parent-child relationship on both sides of an incestuous child (stepfather-stepdaughter).

59 E.g. art. **Belgian** art. 336 B.W., **Dutch** art. 1:394 N.BW and **French** art. 342–1 C.c.

far as the foregoing rationales for the impediments to marriage still apply, their legal translation should take into account the fact that marriage is no longer the (exclusive) legal framework for family ties. The justifiable impediments to marriage should therefore be systematically applied to other legal structures fulfilling the same function, e.g. by broadening the concept of affinity.[60] The piecemeal approach in this regard is a convergent characteristic of the examined legal systems.

The traditional impediments to marriage have generally been copied into the Dutch *geregistreerd partnerschap*,[61] the French *PaCS*[62] and the German *Lebenspartnerschaft*,[63] yet not into the Belgian *wettelijke samenwoning*[64] – albeit that the latter institution has a remarkable genesis. In regard to the impediment between parents and children, a parent may not marry his or her child or adopted child. The educational rationale applies to both cases. Why shouldn't the impediment apply to the different categories of 'nursing parents',[65] e.g. in the case of the Dutch *gezamenlijk gezag* or application of the German *§9 LPartG*? The difference could of course be justified *de lege lata* by the weaker legal consequences of 'nursing parenthood'. In countries where the impediment to marriage between stepparents and stepchildren still applies, a person may not marry the ex-spouse of a parent. In France he may neither *PaCS* him. Under Belgian law however, a child may marry, or cohabit legally with, the ex-legal cohabitant or ex-factual cohabitant of his parent. One could again justify a different treatment by the weaker legal consequences than marriage (towards the (step) child) of legal or factual cohabitation or even sexual relations, and by the risk of legal uncertainty. Nevertheless, an adopted child under the Belgian 'weak adoption' (*adoption simple*)[66] may marry neither the ex-spouse, nor the ex-legal cohabitant nor even the ex-factual cohabitant of his adopter. The Belgian ecologist party opposed to the impediment between the adopted child and the *factual* cohabitant of a parent, on the ground that nowadays one would not always know whether a factual affinity exists. This amendment was rejected on ethical grounds.[67] Legal uncertainty however was referred to by the *Bundesverfassungsgericht* as one of the grounds to assess as unconstitutional the marriage impediment of *Geslechtsgemeinschaft*.[68] A similar impediment was also abolished under English

---

60 HAUSER, J., LEMOULAND, J-J., 'Mariage', p. 532.

61 Art. 1:80a para. 6 BW.

62 Art. 515–2 C.c. Though not with regard to weak adoption (art. 366 C.c.).

63 § 1 LPartG.

64 Art. 1475 B.W.

65 With regard to impediments to marriage between children and nursing parents: COESTER-WALTJEN, D., COESTER, M., 'Formation of marriage' (1997), p. 1–13.

66 The impediment illogically does not apply in the case of 'strong adoption' (*adoption plénière*).

67 *Parl. St.* Kamer 2001–2002, nr. 50–1366/11, 52–53, www.dekamer.be.

68 BVerfG 14th November 1973, *BVerfGE* 31, nr. 17, 169. With regard to the impediment: STAUDINGER/STRÄTZ (2000), § *1307*, 2.

law.[69] Anyhow, one should be cautious not to return to the situation before the introduction of the *Code civil*, where there was a multiplicity of impediments that '*mettait des entraves trop multipliés à la liberté des mariages et imposait un joug trop incommode à la société*'.[70]

In conclusion, on the one hand, weakening 'traditional' family ties result in convergent trends of liberalisation of the impediments to marriage between relatives. On the other hand, the rising of 'new' family forms has not yet resulted in a global set of 'functional' impediments. The new impediments that are introduced here and there do not in my opinion mark internal divergence in relation to the abolition of other impediments,[71] but reflect the same trend of modernisation of family law.

2.2. OVERVIEW

In all examined legal systems, an absolute impediment to marriage applies between (adoptive) *parents and* (adoptive) *children*. The impediment does not apply after dissolution of the adoption. It applies to the original family after adoption.[72] The parent – (adult) child relationship has patrimonial and extra-patrimonial legal consequences in accordance with its nature, which seem to exclude the need to abolish the impediment to marriage.[73]

This impediment is in line with the abovementioned rationales; it could even be extended to the New Family forms.

All examined legal systems contain an absolute impediment to marriage between *brothers and sisters*, on ethical grounds.[74] The impediment applies to half-brothers and -sisters, but not to stepbrothers and -sisters. An impediment exists between adoptive brothers and sisters; dispensation is then possible (in the case of a weak adoption).[75]

---

69 COESTER-WALTJEN, D., COESTER, M., 'Formation of marriage' (1997), p. 85.

70 *Exposé des Motifs* by PORTALIS before the *Corps Législatif*, in: FENET, P.A., *Recueil complet des Travaux Préparatoires du Code civil*, t. IX, Réimpression' (1968), p. 151.

71 **France**: LAMBOLEY, A., 'Mariage. Prohibition du mariage entre parents et alliés', p. 20–25.

72 **Belgium**: art. 161, art. 353–13, art. 356–1 B.W. **France**: art. 161, art. 356, art. 364, art. 366 C.c. HAUSER, J., LEMOULAND, J-J., 'Mariage' (2002), p. 51–63; LAMBOLEY, A., 'Mariage. Prohibition du mariage entre parents et alliés', p. 45–50. **Germany**: § 1307, § 1308 BGB SCHWAB, D., *Familierecht* (2005), p. 87. **The Netherlands**: art. 1:41 BW.

73 Comp. for **Germany** BVerfG 17th July 2002, www.bundesverfassungsgericht.de, §110 and para. 0 above. Only in **Belgium** can parent and child register in a 'partnership'.

74 **The Netherlands**: ASSER-DE BOER (2004), 123.

75 **Belgium**: art. 162, art. 353–13, art. 356–1 B.W. LELEU, Y.-H., *Droit des personnes et des familles* (2005), p. 330 B; SENAEVE, P., 'La prohibition du mariage en raison de la parenté et de l'alliance' (1978), p. 3. **France**: art. 162, art. 356, art. 364, art. 366 C.c. HAUSER, J., LEMOULAND, J-J., 'Mariage'

In the light of the abovementioned rationales, one could question the existence of an impediment to marriage between (half-)brothers and sisters who are not raised in the same household. Already Portalis considered that these brothers are sometimes more strangers to each other than cousins were before. Under Swedish law, only a relative impediment exists between half-brothers and –sisters, because they are not raised in the same household.[76]

On the other hand, should one not introduce impediments to marriage between stepbrothers and –sisters sharing the same roof? And how should one then define the stepfamily?

The range of impediments to marriage between *other collaterals* differs from system to system.

In Germany, no impediments between collaterals other than brothers and sisters were enacted in the BGB.

In the Netherlands, all impediments between collaterals other than brothers and sisters have been abolished at the occasion of the new Civil Code, since dispensation was almost always awarded before.[77] In Belgium marriage is relatively prohibited between collaterals to the third degree, i.e. uncle or aunt and nephew or niece.[78] The extension to uncles/aunts and nephews/nieces to the 4th degree is contested on formal grounds.[79] An isolated proposal to repeal this impediment has been made.[80] In France, the same impediments exist as in Belgium. The *Cour de cassation* however has interpreted the terms uncle/aunt and nephew/niece so as to include great-uncles/-aunts and grand-nephews/-nieces.[81]

Only in Belgium and France is marriage still prohibited between *stepparents and stepchildren* and between *parents-in-law and children-in-law.*[82] The impediment is absolute in Belgium. In France, dispensation has been possible since 1938 only where the person who created the relationship is dead and not in the case of divorce, so as

(2002), p. 517; LAMBOLEY, A., 'Mariage. Prohibition du mariage entre parents et alliés', p. 41 and 45–50. **Germany:** § 1307, § 1308 BGB **the Netherlands:** art. 1:41 BW ASSER-DE BOER (2004), 123.

76 COESTER-WALTJEN, D., COESTER, M., 'Formation of marriage' (1997), p. 86.

77 VAN ZEBEN, C.J., et al., *Parlementaire Geschiedenis van het nieuwe BW*, Boek 1 (1961), p. 152–153 and 157–158.

78 Art. 163, art. 164 B.W.

79 SENAEVE, P., 'La prohibition du mariage en raison de la parenté et de l'alliance' (1978), p. 3.

80 *Ibid*, p. 8.

81 Art. 163, art. 164 C.c. Cass. req. 28th November 1877, *D.P.* 1878, I, 209 and hereto HAUSER, J., LEMOULAND, J-J., 'Mariage' (2002), p. 521; LAMBOLEY, A., 'Mariage. Prohibition du mariage entre parents et alliés', p. 72.

82 **Belgium:** art. 161 B.W. GERLO, J., *Personen- en familierecht*, Die Keure, Brugge, 2003, p. 421; SENAEVE, P., *o.c.*, 1529. **France:** art. 161 C.c. Hereto BATTEUR, A., 'L'Interdit de l'inceste. Principe fondateur du droit de la famille' (2000), p. 765.

to avoid rewarding adultery.[83] Amendments to generalise the possibility of dispensation were rejected.[84] It is questionable whether the Belgian and French impediments can be upheld after the *B. and L. v United Kingdom* judgment of the ECtHR The Court found that the English relative impediment between parents-in-law and children-in-law violated article 12 ECHR for it was based on tradition and neither factually nor legally achieved its legitimate aims.[85] The same applies to Belgium and France.[86] In Belgium, several amendments have been proposed to repeal the (absolute) impediment.[87] In the Netherlands, the impediment to marriage between stepparents and stepchildren and between parents-in-law and children-in-law was abolished in 1983 on the ground of a change in moral views and of the interest of the children.[88] In Germany, the impediment was abolished in 1998. A possibility of dispensation had existed since 1938 and dispensation had been mostly granted. The moral background therefore didn't outweigh the freedom to marry any more.[89] However, the *Bundesverfassungsgericht* seemed at least not to disapprove of this impediment.[90]

In none of the examined systems has the impediment between *brothers-in-law and sisters-in-law* survived.

In Germany, such an impediment was not even introduced in the BGB. In the Netherlands, the impediment between brothers-in-law and sisters-in-law was repealed in 1970, on the occasion of the abolition of adultery as an impediment, the former being based on the latter. A vivid discussion on the risk of younger sisters breaking up their older sisters' marriages preceded the abolition.[91] The impediment was already abolished in the case of death in 1939 and dispensation was possible in the case of divorce. After reintroduction of the impediment in the French *Code civil* in 1804, a possibility of dispensation in the case of the death of the person who created the relationship was introduced in 1832. Dispensation mostly being granted, the prohibition was repealed in 1914. The legislator considered children would be better off with an uncle or aunt as stepparent than with a third person. In 1938, a possibility of dispensation was introduced in the case of divorce. Again, dispensation was granted most of the time. In 1975, the moral views had changed to a degree so as to allow

---

83 Art. 164 C.c. BATTEUR, A., 'L'Interdit de l'inceste. Principe fondateur du droit de la famille' (2000), p. 764.

84 LAMBOLEY, A., 'Mariage. Prohibition du mariage entre parents et alliés', p. 83–87.

85 ECtHR, *B and L. v. United Kingdom*, 13th December 2005, http://cmiskp.echr.coe.int/, §§ 37–39.

86 LEMOULAND, J.-J., VIGNEAU, D., 'Mariage-Concubinage-PaCS' (2006), p. 1418; MARGUÉNAUD, J.-P., 'Vers la liberté du mariage entre alliés en ligne directe', *RTDCiv* (2005), p. 735, 736.

87 SENAEVE, P., 'La prohibition du mariage en raison de la parenté et de l'alliance' (1978), p. 7; SENAEVE, P. 'De wet van 27 maart 2001 tot afschaffing van het huwelijksverbod tussen schoonbroer en schoonzus', *E.J.* (2001), p. 86, 10.

88 ASSER-DE BOER (2004), p. 124.

89 STAUDINGER/STRÄTZ (2000), *Vorbem zu §§ 1303 ff*, 7.

90 Cf. BVerfG 14th November 1973, *BVerfGE* 31, nr. 17, 165 and 167.

91 VAN ZEBEN, C.J., et al., *Parlementaire Geschiedenis van het nieuwe BW*, Boek 1 (1961), p. 157 ff.

complete abolition of the impediment between brothers-in-law and sisters-in-law.[92] As in the Netherlands, the abolition of adultery as an impediment to marriage and as a conclusive ground for divorce was relevant in this regard.[93]

The Belgian evolution is in line with the French. A possibility of dispensation in the case of death was introduced in 1831. Dispensation mostly being granted, the prohibition was abolished in 1920. From 1957 on, dispensation was possible in the case of divorce.[94] The impediment was repealed completely in 2001, since dispensation was only a formality and moral views had changed.[95] Adultery as an impediment to marriage had already been abolished in 1972.

In Belgium and France, the foregoing impediments to marriage also apply to the ties between a child('s family) and the (family of the) man who had sexual intercourse with the mother of the child during the statutory period of conception, in the case that subsidies are awarded on that ground.[96] The impediments to marriage apply to the 'natural family' in Germany[97] and the Netherlands,[98] albeit that the absence of a formal reference point leads to legal uncertainty.[99]

---

92 BATTEUR, A., 'L'Interdit de l'inceste. Principe fondateur du droit de la famille' (2000), p. 762; LAMBOLEY, A., 'Mariage. Prohibition du mariage entre parents et alliés', p. 80–82.

93 BUFFELAN-LANORE, Y., 'Cas de divorce. Divorce pour faute. Faits imputables à un époux : principales applications', *J.-Cl. Civ.*, 21–22; HAUSER, J., LEMOULAND, J-J., 'Mariage' (2002), p. 461; MAYAUD, Y., 'L'adultère, cause de divorce depuis la loi du 11 juillet 1975', *RTDCiv* (1980), 494, 8.

94 MAHILLON, P., *l.c.*; SENAEVE, P., 'La prohibition du mariage en raison de la parenté et de l'alliance' (1978).

95 SENAEVE, P., 'De wet van 27 maart 2001 tot afschaffing van het huwelijksverbod tussen schoonbroer en schoonzus', *E.J.* (2001); VAN GYSEL, A.-C., 'Abrogation de la prohibition du mariage entre beau-frère et belle-soeur' (2001).

96 **Belgium**: art. 341 B.W. **France**: art. 342–7 C.c. and hereto BATTEUR, A., 'L'Interdit de l'inceste. Principe fondateur du droit de la famille' (2000), p. 763.

97 STAUDINGER/STRÄTZ (2000), *§ 1307*, 6.

98 ASSER-DE BOER (2004), p. 123. Also see VAN ZEBEN, C.J., et al., *Parlementaire Geschiedenis van het nieuwe BW*, Boek 1 (1961), p. 18 and 157. Cf. art. 1:394 BW.

99 Comp. to the abolished German impediment of *Geschlechtsgemeinschaft*: BVerfG 14th November 1973, *BVerfGE* 31, nr. 17, 149–151.

3. CONVERGENCE IN DISGUISE: A SHORT INTERMEZZO ON POLYGAMY

'La conception monogamique du mariage est éclipsée par la question du mariage lui-même.'[100]

All examined legal systems are convergent in prohibiting polygamous – both polygynous and polyandrous – marriages.[101] Monogamy is considered a fundamental of marriage (in Western societies) so that it is a considered an admissible substantive condition to marriage under the relevant international instruments.[102] From an anthropological point of view, monogamy is self-evident in regard to the natural one-to-one balance of men and women.[103] Usually, other rationales are however put forward. A first rationale is the equality of sexes. Polygamy is traditionally opposed to because it would violate the equal treatment and the dignity of women.[104] This argument only applies to exclusively polygynous systems. Would the equal treatment requirement be met if both polygyny and polyandry – or combined forms of polygamy – are possible?[105] A second, socio-biological, rationale therefore seems to be more relevant. Mostly, polygamous relations would create feelings of jealousy and hatred which would undermine the stability of the relationship.[106] The stability of marriage should however be protected in view of its social and economic functions with regard

100 ENDRÉO, G., 'Bigamie et double ménage' (1991), p. 267.

101 **Belgium**: art. 147 B.W. SWENNEN, F., *Familierecht in kort bestek* (2007), p. 198–199. **France**: art. 147 C.c. RAYMOND, G., 'Mariage. Conditions à réunir dans la personne des époux', 32. **Germany**: §1306 BGB. BVerfG 4th May 1971, *BVerfGE* 31, nr. 7, 69; BVerfG 7th October 1970, *BVerfGE* 29, nr. 21, 176; BVerfG 29th July 1959, *BVerfGE* 10, nr. 5, 66. SCHWAB, D., *Familienrecht* (2005), p. 12, 14 and 50; STAUDINGER/STRÄTZ (2000), *Einl. zu §§ 1303ff*, 45 and 52. **The Netherlands**: art. 1:33 BW H.R. 1st July 1993, *NJ* 94, 105, case note WH-S; ASSER-DE BOER (2004), p. 103; VLAARDINGERBROEK, P., et al., *Het hedendaagse personen- en familierecht,* Kluwer, Deventer, 2004, p. 83.

102 **Declaration of Human Rights**: LAGOUTTE, S., ÁRNASON, A.T., 'Article 16' (1999), p. 329. **Covenant on Civil and Political Rights** NOWAK, M., *U.N. Covenant on Civil and Political Rights. CCPR Commentary* (1993), p. 20; PALM-RISSE, M., *Der völkerrechtliche Schutz von Ehe und Familie* (1990), p. 91 ff. **ECHR**: ECtHR, *Johnston v. Ireland*, 18th December 1986, http://cmiskp.echr.coe.int/, § 52; ECHR, *X. v. United Kingdom*, No. 3998/68, 22th July 1970, *Yearbook XIII*, 674, 686; PALM-RISSE, M., *Der völkerrechtliche Schutz von Ehe und Familie* (1990), p. 82, 159 and 161; GEHUCHTE, A., VAN DE, HAECK, Y., and STAELENS, V., 'Artikel 12' (2004),p. 8; DIJK P., VAN, HOOF, G.J.H., VAN, *Theory and Practice of the European Convention on Human Rights*, 2nd ed., Kluwer, Deventer, 1990, p. 441.

103 LÉVI-STRAUSS, C., *Het gezin* (1983), p. 22.

104 **Covenant on Civil and Political Rights**: *H.R.C.*, General Comment 28, § 24; *CEDAW*, General Recommendation 21, § 14. **ECHR**: GRUNDERBEECK, D., VAN, *Beginselen van personen- en familierecht* (2003), p. 293. **France**: GUILHO, P., 'Case note in C.E. 24th January and 11th February 1994 (2 judgments)', *D.* (1995), *Jur.*, p. 108, 110; HAUSER, J., LEMOULAND, J-J., 'Mariage' (2002), p. 466; SÉRIAUX, A., 'Une définition civile du mariage (prière d'insérer)', *D.* (2005), *Chron.*, p. 1966, 1966–1967.

105 Comp. LAGOUTTE, S., ÁRNASON, A.T., 'Article 16' (1999), p. 335.

106 In this regard: *Exposé des Motifs* by PORTALIS before the Corps *Législatif*, in: FENET, P.A., *Recueil complet des Travaux Préparatoires du Code civil*, t. IX, Réimpression' (1968), p. 148–149.

to parenthood and partnership. The same social considerations of familial peace underlying the prohibited degrees therefore justify the principle of monogamy. However, the need for the State to guarantee the stability of marriage gradually decreases as marriage loses its (exclusive) social and economic functions.[107] The more marriage evolves to contractual regulation of the patrimonial aspects of a household, the less does the number of parties to this contract matter. The principle of monogamy is therefore questioned;[108] in Germany, the sanction on polygamy has been relaxed.[109]

Be that as it may, the convergent formal condition of monogamy is disguising another convergent trend of factual polygamy.[110] Both with regard to parenthood as with regard to partnership, the original idea of prohibition of both simultaneous and successive relations[111] has disappeared. With regard to parenthood, extramarital and therefore potentially multiple procreation and childrearing is now legitimate in all examined legal systems. With regard to partnership, the obstacles to successive marriages have first been lifted. More importantly, legal consequences have been attached to factual relations coexisting with a marriage (or registered partnership). The discussion of the monogamous conception of marriage is indeed outshined by the discussion of marriage *tout court*.[112]

There are no socio-economic reasons to enter into polygamous relations.[113] There being no such external pressure, most love-based relations still seem to be monogamous.[114] Such monogamous relations fulfil a biosocial function in marriage, e.g. with regard to stable childrearing. The functions of marriage are now assumed by other structures. One should be cautious not to lose sight of the function of the

---

107 ENDRÉO, G., 'Bigamie et double ménage' (1991), p. 268–270 and 282, with references to FOUCAULT and ENGELS.

108 E.g. for **Germany**: SCHWAB, D., *Familienrecht* (2005), p. 80; for **the Netherlands**: D'ONORIO, J.B., *l.c.*, 4.

109 STRÄTZ, H.-W., 'Ehe und Familie als Institute des bürgerlichen Rechts' (2001), p. 23.

110 COESTER-WALTJEN, D., COESTER, M., 'Formation of marriage' (1997), p. 45; WILLEKENS, H., 'Explaining Two Hundred Years of Family Law in Western Europe', *1 Recht der Werkelijkheid* 1997, p. 59, 71. **Belgium**: HEYVAERT, A., 'De Belgische polygamie in de jaren '90', *Journ. Proc.* No. 252 (1994), p. 18; MEULDERS-KLEIN, M.-T., 'L'évolution du mariage: de l'institution au contrat, et au-delà' (1999). **France**: ENDRÉO, G., 'Bigamie et double ménage' (1991), p. 264, 266–267 and 271–275; HAUSER, J., LEMOULAND, J-J., 'Mariage' (2002), p. 468. **The Netherlands**: Vragen van het lid Van der Staaij aan de Minister van Justitie over een samenlevingscontract tussen twee vrouwen en een man (nr. 219). Antwoord, *Tweede Kamer*, 2005–2006, Aanhangsel, 469.

111 *Exposé des Motifs* by PORTALIS before the *Corps Législatif*, in: FENET, P.A., *Recueil complet des Travaux Préparatoires du Code civil*, t. IX, Réimpression' (1968), p. 149.

112 ENDRÉO, G., 'Bigamie et double ménage' (1991), p. 267.

113 To such reasons COESTER-WALTJEN, D., COESTER, M., 'Formation of marriage' (1997), p. 41.

114 COESTER-WALTJEN, D., COESTER, M., 'Formation of marriage' (1997), p. 45.

underlying relationship,[115] e.g. so as to introduce forms of simultaneous and successive 'poly-parenthood'.[116] In other substituting structures, such as registered partnerships, a mono-relational conception of the family is however adhered to.[117]

4. TEMPORARY DIVERGENCE: SAME-GENDER MARRIAGE

'La notion sexuée de mari et femme est l'écho de la notion sexuée de père et mère.'[118]

The relevant provisions in the applicable international instruments, as well as the relevant provisions in the French and German civil codes, are interpreted so as to consider the opposite gender of the spouses a self-evident substantive condition to marriage, even though gender is no longer determined by purely biological criteria.

This interpretation is based on the argument of tradition, on scattered provisions referring to husband and wife or man and woman, but foremost on the linking of marriage and procreation, e.g. in the right to marry *and to found a family* (by natural procreation).[119]

---

115 ENDRÉO, G., 'Bigamie et double ménage' (1991), p. 270 and 282.

116 Apart from stepparent adoption, see in **Germany**: §9 LPartG and in **the Netherlands**: art. 1:253a ff BW In **Belgium** several amendments have been proposed in view of introducing forms of 'nursing parentship'.

117 **Belgium**: art. 1475 para 2, 1° B.W. **France**: art. 515–1 and art. 515–2, 2° and 3° C.c. **Germany**: §1306 BGB and §1(1) and (2)1 LPartG. **The Netherlands**: art. 1:42 and 80a para 1 BW Only in Germany and the Netherlands does a registered partnership exclude the registered partners from marriage. In Belgium and France, the partnership is dissolved automatically by a subsequent marriage.

118 Bordeaux 19th April 2005, *D.* 2005, *Jur.*, 1687, case note E. AGOSTINI, 'Où le couple "redevient" paire'.

119 COESTER-WALTJEN, D., COESTER, M., 'Formation of marriage' (1997), p. 75–78. **Declaration of Human Rights:** LAGOUTTE, S., ÁRNASON, A.T., 'Article 16' (1999), p. 328; GRUNDERBEECK, D., VAN, *Beginselen van personen- en familierecht* (2003), p. 241. **Covenant on Civil and Political Rights:** *H.R.C., Juliet Joslin et al. v. New Zealand*, 902/1999, http://sim.law.uu.nl, 8.2. NOWAK, M., *U.N. Covenant on Civil and Political Rights. CCPR Commentary* (1993), p. 13 and 21. **ECHR**: ECtHR, *Rees v. United Kingdom*, 17th October 1986, http://cmiskp.echr.coe.int/, §§49–50; ECtHR, *Cossey v. United Kingdom*, 27th September 1990, http://cmiskp.echr.coe.int/, §46; ECtHR, *Sheffield and Horsham v. United Kingdom*, 30th July 1998, http://cmiskp.echr.coe.int/, §66; ECtHR, *Goodwin v. United Kingdom*, 11th July 2002, http://cmiskp.echr.coe.int/, §§98 and 100; ECtHR, *I. v. United Kingdom*, 11th July 2002, http://cmiskp.echr.coe.int/, §§78 and 80; ECHR, *X. and Y. v. United Kingdom*, No. 7229/75, 15th December 1977, *D.R.* 12, 32, §57; ECHR, *W. v. United Kingdom*, No. 11095/84, 7th March 1989, *D.R.* 63, 34, §40. PALM-RISSE, M., *Der völkerrechtliche Schutz von Ehe und Familie* (1990), p. 80–82; GEHUCHTE, A., VAN DE, HAECK, Y., and STAELENS, V., 'Artikel 12' (2004), p. 8 and 18. **France:** HAUSER, J., LEMOULAND, J-J., 'Mariage' (2002), p. 44–45; LEMOULAND, J.-J., VIGNEAU, D., 'Mariage-Concubinage-PaCS' (2006), p. 1414; RAYMOND, G., 'Mariage. Conditions à réunir dans la personne des époux', 17. **Germany**: BVerfG 4th October 1993, *FamRZ* 1993, 1419 and on this case RADLOFF, 'Case note in BVerfG 4th October 1993', *FamRZ* 1994, 21 and S. GRÜLL, 'Eheverbot für gleichgeschlechtiche Paare', *ZRP* 1994, 40; BVerfG 17th July 2002,

States *may* nevertheless extend the right to marry to same-gender couples.[120]

Whereas neither tradition nor existing legal provisions would suffice to oppose such an extension by amending or interpreting the law,[121] proponents of same-gender marriages have concentrated on the latter argument.

Successive law reforms in all examined legal systems, after the (in)famous *Marckx*-case, have increasingly neutralised legitimate procreation and education of children from marriage or other relations between the parents. Marriage is now at the most a sufficient but not indispensable condition for the (unconditional) establishment of paternity[122] and for (unconditional) joint custody.[123] There is in other words no more exclusive legal link between marriage and procreation.[124] Isn't it significant that only months after the Court of Appeal of Bordeaux confirmed the heterosexual concept of marriage with reference to its function of founding a legitimate family,[125] the French legislator abolished the distinction between legitimate and illegitimate families?[126] Marriage thus losing its vertical legal function, the accent is now more on its horizontal function of the regulation of the patrimonial and extra-patrimonial aspects of the love and affection between the partners.[127] In regard to the horizontal function of marriage, same-gender couples are not pertinently different from

---

www.bundesverfassungsgericht.de, §79. *Adde* STAUDINGER/STRÄTZ (2000), *Einl. zu §§ 1303ff*, 44, 46 and 52; TETTINGER, P.J., 'Grundgesetzlich gewährleistete besondere Schutz von Ehe und Familie', in: *Ehe und Familie unter veränderten gesellschaftlichen Rahmenbedingungen*, Aschendorff, Münster, 2001, p. 117, 133–134. Comp. before the opening of marriage for **Belgium**: DELVA, J., 'Homohuwelijk en homo-ouderschap onder het kijkglas van de wetgever', *T.B.P.* (1998), p. 463, 465 and for **the Netherlands**: H.R. 19th October 1990, *NJ* 1992, 129, concl. adv.-gen. MOLTMAKER and case notes EAAL and EAA, 3.3.

120 LAGOUTTE, S., ÁRNASON, A.T., 'Article 16' (1999), p. 328; PALM-RISSE, M., *Der völkerrechtliche Schutz von Ehe und Familie* (1990), p. 91.

121 FORDER, C., 'Artikel 23 IVBPR: een mondiaal familierecht in een notedop', *NJCM-Bulletin* (1994), p. 907, 912; MAERTENS, P., 'Egalité et transcendance', (case note in ECtHR, *Fretté v. France*, 26th February 2002), *J.L.M.B.* (2002), p. 775, 782–783.

122 **Belgium**: art. 315–317 B.W. **France**: art. 312 C.c. **Germany**: § 1592 BGB. **The Netherlands**: art. 1:199 BW.

123 Only in **Germany** (§1626a BGB) and in **the Netherlands** (art. 1:252 para 1 BW). In **Belgium** (art. 373–374 B.W.) and **France** (art. 372 C.c.), joint custody does not depend on marital status at all.

124 On the link with opening marriage for **the Netherlands**: ASSER-DE BOER (2004), p. 104 and for **Belgium**: Wetsvoorstel tot openstelling van het huwelijk (...), *Parl. St.* Senaat 2001–02, nr. 2–1173/1 and LELEU, Y.-H., *Droit des personnes et des familles* (2005), p. 324. *Adde* VAN GYSEL, A.-C. (ed.), *Précis de droit de la famille* (2004), p. 169 ff.

125 Bordeaux 19th April 2005, *D.* 2005, *Jur.*, 1687, case note AGOSTINI, E., 'Où le couple "redevient" paire'.

126 Ord. no 2005–759 of 4th July 2005; came into force on 1st July 2006.

127 GLENDON, M.-A., 'Introduction: Family Law at a time of turbulence' (2006), p. 27. **Belgium**: SWENNEN, F., *Familierecht in kort bestek* (2007), p. 191; VAN GYSEL, A.-C. (ed.), *Précis de droit de la famille* (2004), p. 169–172.

opposite-gender couples – the similarity is actually confirmed by the copying of the horizontal marriage provisions into registered partnerships in some countries.[128] In that regard, it is not discriminatory to open marriage.[129]

On that ground, Belgium and the Netherlands[130] have opened marriage to same-gender couples. The Netherlands[131] seems to have considered the question more profoundly than Belgium, where a political compromise existed.[132]

In both legal systems, the remaining vertical marriage provisions do not apply to same-gender marriages. As legal parentage is primarily based on biological ties, it would be inappropriate to do so.[133] Some scholars therefore uphold the fact that marriage is not open to same-gender couples but that a new institution of registered partnerships was introduced beside marriage, albeit with the same name.[134] In my opinion, the logical inapplicability of biology-based rules on paternity however does not justify this distinction.[135]

The reference to 'men and women' has also been left out of art. 9 of the Charter of Fundamental Rights of the European Union. Moreover, the (single) right to marry and to found a family has been divided into two separate rights. Even though there was no agreement on the opening of marriage,[136] neither was there on the preservation of the traditional definition. It is for the Member States to decide on the matter.[137] The interpretation of article 12 ECHR is moving in the same direction. Even though the Court clearly confirmed the traditional view on marriage as a bond between two

---

128 Albeit that the creation of registered partnerships is also interpreted as confirmation of the heterosexual definition of marriage. E.g. for **France** TGI Bordeaux 27th July 2004, *D.* 2004, *Jur.*, 2392 case note AGOSTINI, E., 'Le mariage homosexuel? "Peut-être jamais, peut-être demain, mais aujourd'hui c'est certain"' and RAYMOND, G., 'Mariage. Conditions à réunir dans la personne des époux', 17. Also see Conseil Constitutionnel, D. n° 99–419 of 9th November 1999, www.conseil-constitutionnel.fr.

129 For **Belgium:** Arbitragehof, nr. 159/2004, 20th October 2004, www.arbitrage.be, B.4.7.

130 And some five other countries or states that were not included in this research.

131 See the conclusions of the KORTMANN commission in ASSER-DE BOER (2004), 110 and VLAARDINGERBROEK, P., et al., *Het hedendaagse personen- en familierecht,* Kluwer, Deventer, 2004, p. 84–85.

132 Verslag namens de Commissie voor de Justitie, *Parl. St.* Senaat 2002–2003, nr. 2–1173/3, 4 and hereto RENCHON, J.-L., 'L'avènement du mariage homosexuel dans le Code civil belge', *Rev. trim. dr. fam.* (2003), p. 439.

133 **Belgium:** Wetsvoorstel tot openstelling van het huwelijk (...), *Parl. St.* Senaat 2001–02, nr. 2–1173/1, 1. **The Netherlands:** ASSER-DE BOER (2004), p. 110.

134 **Belgium:** P. SENAEVE, *o.c.*, 1489–2. **The Netherlands:** WORTMANN, S.F.M., DUIJVENDIJK-BRAND, J., VAN, *Compendium van het personen- en familierecht,* Deventer, Kluwer, 2005, nr. 28.

135 SWENNEN, F., 'Het "homohuwelijk" bestaat niet anno 2005', *EJ* (2005), p. 66.

136 Cf. VERSCHRAEGEN, B., 'Right to private life and family life, the right to marry and to found a family, and the prohibition of discrimination'(2003), p. 210.

137 Declaration concerning explanations relating to the Charter of Fundamental Rights, Final Act to the Treaty establishing a Constitution for Europe, *OJ* 2004, C 310/432.

persons of the opposite gender,[138] it considered on the ground of major social changes in the institution of marriage that the ability to found a family is not a condition to the enjoyment of the (separate?) right to marry.[139] The interpretation of article 12 ECHR so as to include the right to marry for same-gender couples is advocated by some scholars.[140]

Be that as it may, the opposition to same-gender marriages is not solely based on the vertical *legal function* of marriage. Another counter-argument can be summarised as follows. Even though the vertical legal function of marriage is on the decline and even though neither the wish nor the ability to procreate is a condition to a valid marriage, marriage still fulfils an important biosocial function. It does so both through its remaining vertical and horizontal dimensions by offering a socio-legal framework (between the partners) that serves the stable procreation and education of children.[141] This function is important, since the preservation of the human species depends on procreation. Access to marriage should therefore be organised in regard to this social interest. As procreation biologically is a heterosexual affair, marriage should be reserved for opposite-gender couples, who at least in theory are able to procreate.[142] Same-gender couples are not naturally able to procreate. Their relationship has no intergenerational interest in regard to procreation and education, so should not be protected by marriage. As a familial institution, marriage should not be directed towards self-realisation and self-development of the partners, but towards realisation

---

138 GRUNDERBEECK, D., VAN, *Beginselen van personen- en familierecht* (2003), p. 406; VERSCHRAEGEN, B., 'Right to private life and family life, the right to marry and to found a family, and the prohibition of discrimination'(2003), p. 210.

139 ECtHR, *Goodwin v. United Kingdom*, 11th July 2002, http://cmiskp.echr.coe.int/, §§ 98 and 100; ECtHR, *I. v. United Kingdom*, 11th July 2002, http://cmiskp.echr.coe.int/, §§78 and 80. Comp. ECHR, *Van Oosterwijck v. Belgium*, No. 7654/76, 1st March 1979, *Série B*, 36, 10, §59. The right to found a family however still depends on marriage. GEHUCHTE, A., VAN DE, HAECK, Y., and STAELENS, V., 'Artikel 12' (2004), p. 6 and 30. Comp. for **Germany**: BVerfG 11th October 1978, *BVerfGE* 49, nr. 18, 300 (right to marry for transsexuals).

140 DIJK, P., VAN, HOOF, G.J.H., VAN, *Theory and Practice of the European Convention on Human Rights* (1990), p. 442.

141 **Belgium** : Arbitragehof, nr. 128/98, 8th December 1998, www.arbitrage.be. **France**: FULCHIRON, H., 'Couples, mariage et différence des sexes', in: *Des concubinages: droit interne, droit international, droit comparé: études offertes à Jacqueline Rubellin-Devichi*, Litec, Paris, 2002, p. 29, 47; SÉRIAUX, A., 'Une définition civile du mariage (prière d'insérer)' (2005), p. 1968. **Germany**: BVerfG 4th October 1993, *FamRZ* 1993, 1419. Comp. LÉVI-STRAUSS, C., *Het gezin* (1983), p. 42 and 44 in regard of the division of labour between the sexes. Comp. BRADLEY, D., 'Convergence in Family Law: Mirrors, Transplants and Political Economy', 6 *MJ* 2 (1999), p. 133.

142 Their concrete ability to procreate would not be relevant. PALM-RISSE, M., *Der völkerrechtliche Schutz von Ehe und Familie* (1990), p. 84–85; LAGOUTTE, S., ÁRNASON, A.T., 'article 16' (1999), p. 336; NOWAK, M., *U.N. Covenant on Civil and Political Rights. CCPR Commentary* (1993), p. 20. Comp. DIJK, P., VAN, HOOF, G.J.H., VAN, *Theory and Practice of the European Convention on Human Rights* (1990), p. 443–444.

and development of a(n intergenerational) family.[143] In regard to this social justification, it would not be discriminatory to exclude from marriage couples who cannot found a(n intergenerational) family by marrying.[144]

Firstly, it is of course disputable that the horizontal relation between partners only needs a legal framework in regard to children. Partners are worthy of protection on other grounds than parental investment too, e.g. in the case that one partner is involved in the professional activities of the other or in the care of parents(-in-law). It is questionable whether or not it is relevant that the partners are of the same gender.[145] It is yet another question whether marriage is the appropriate structure to offer protection.

More relevant with regard to the familial function of marriage is that parenting by same-gender couples is possible legally or at least factually in a growing number of situations.[146] The opposition to same-gender marriages on the ground that it would pave the way for (undesirable) same-gender parenting[147] has therefore partly been superseded.

These same-gender partners would then be worthy of protection as parents too.[148]

---

143 AGELL, A., 'The legal status of same-sex couples in Europe – a critical analysis', in: BOELE-WOELKI, K., FUCHS A., (eds.), *Legal Recognition of Same-sex Couples in Europe*, Intersentia, Antwerpen, Oxford, 2003, p.122, 131 and 133–134; GLENDON, M.-A., 'Introduction: Family Law at a time of turbulence' (2006), p. 15. **Belgium**: DELVA, J., 'Homohuwelijk en homo-ouderschap onder het kijkglas van de wetgever' (1998), p. 465 ff.; RENCHON, J.-L., 'L'avènement du mariage homosexuel dans le Code civil belge' (2003), n° 11; RENCHON, J.-L., 'Indisponibilité, ordre public et autonomie de la volonté dans le droit des personnes et de la famille' (2005), p. 29. Also see Advies van de Raad van State, *Parl. St.* Kamer 2001–02, nr. 50–1692/1, 19–20. Very interesting parliamentary debates were devoted to this point: Verslag namens de Commissie voor de Justitie, *Parl. St.* Senaat 2002–03, nr. 2–1173/3, 8, 17–19, 50–52; *Hand.*, Senaat 2002–03, 28th November 2002, nr. 2–46, 3; *Hand.*, Kamer 2002–03, 30th January 2003, CRIV 50 PLEN 318, 14–15, 30, 33. **France:** FULCHIRON, H., 'Couples, mariage et différence des sexes' (2002), p. 50–51.

144 **France:** TGI Bordeaux 27th July 2004, *D.* 2004, *Jur.*, 2392 nota AGOSTINI, E., 'Le mariage homosexuel? "Peut-être jamais, peut-être demain, mais aujourd'hui c'est certain"'. Comp. for **Germany:** BVerfG 17th July 2002, www.bundesverfassungsgericht.de, §109.

145 No: SWENNEN, F., *Het huwelijk afschaffen?*, Intersentia, Antwerpen, 2003, p. 19. Yes: MCKNORRIE, K., 'Marriage is for heterosexuals – may the rest of us be saved from it'(2000); VERBEKE, A., 'Homohuwelijksvermogensrecht', *in Liber amicorum Paul Delnoy*, Larcier, Brussel, 2005, p. 513. Comp. for **Germany**: IDEL, S.W., *Der Familienbegriff grund- und einfachrechtlicher Normen*, Peter Lang, Frankfurt, 2005, p. 22.

146 Comp. for **the Netherlands**: Concl. adv.-gen. MOLTMAKER IN H.R. 19th October 1990, *NJ* 1992, 129, 6.2, 6.3 and 6.6.

147 E.g. FULCHIRON, H., 'Couples, mariage et différence des sexes' (2002), p. 50–52; SÉRIAUX, A., 'Une définition civile du mariage (prière d'insérer)' (2005), p. 1966.

148 YTTERBERG, H., 'All human beings are equal, but some are more equal than others – equality in dignity without equality in rights?', in: BOELE-WOELKI, K., FUCHS, A., (eds.), *Legal Recognition of Same-sex Couples in Europe*, Intersentia, Antwerpen-Oxford, 2003, p. 1, 9.

Even more important is that a growing number of opposite-gender couples are having and raising children outside marriage.[149] Since marriage is no longer the only legal framework for procreation and education of children,[150] the protection of parenting partners should not be limited to marriage.[151]

In conclusion, spouses are increasingly independent economically from each other and thus from marriage. Moreover (and as a consequence thereof), children are increasingly born and educated outside marriage. On the one hand, marriage therefore has lost its vertical legal function to a large extent. As a consequence thereof, there is a decreasing need to regulate the horizontal relationship between the spouses in regard to the stable procreation and education of children on the other hand. The intergenerational function of marriage being neutralised, a logic consequence would be to open marriage to couples who will not found a(n intergenerational) family. Other legal systems will therefore follow the opening of marriage. Be that as it may, there is yet no other (legal) structure than the family to organise procreation and education of children.[152] A legal framework for parental investment, including rules on the relationship between the parents, should therefore be maintained. As marriage actually does no longer suffice in this regard, a new framework that links the horizontal to the vertical family should be developed. In theory, that framework does not need to be reserved for heterosexual couples and their natural offspring, but can be extended to any small group of adults raising children.[153] Not the least scholars however stress the need for the legislator to offer a family type model of heterosexual partnership and parenthood. The influence of atypical family forms (in regard to procreation) on family law would endanger the original function thereof.[154] Whereas family law should not be purely descriptive, one should however not overestimate its prescriptive, moralising, power.

---

149 This was considered irrelevant in BVerfG 4th October 1993, *FamRZ* 1993, 1419.

150 As admitted by FULCHIRON, H., 'Couples, mariage et différence des sexes' (2002), p. 50.

151 VERBEKE, A., 'Weg met huwelijk en echtscheiding', *T.P.R.* (2004), p. 969, 13 and more elaborated FORDER, C., VERBEKE, A., 'Geen woorden maar daden. Algemene rechtsvergelijkende conclusies en aanbevelingen', in: FORDER, C., VERBEKE, A., (eds.), *Gehuwd of niet: maakt het iets uit?*, Intersentia, Antwerpen, 2005, p. 489 ff.

152 CALAIS-AULOY, M.-T., 'Pour un mariage aux effets limités' (1988), p. 10; COESTER-WALTJEN, D., COESTER, M., 'Formation of marriage' (1997), p.162; CLIQUET, R., 'Sociobiologie van het gezin' (1997), p. 39 and 48; ENDRÉO, G., 'Bigamie et double ménage' (1991), p. 270.

153 Cf. *Ibid*, 26–27.

154 AGELL, A., 'The legal status of same-sex couples in Europe – a critical analysis' (2003), p. 133–134; GLENDON, M.-A., 'Introduction: Family Law at a time of turbulence' (2006), p. 15 and 27. **France:** FULCHIRON, H., 'Couples, mariage et différence des sexes' (2002), p. 50; SÉRIAUX, A., 'Une définition civile du mariage (prière d'insérer)' (2005), p. 1966.

5. THE WEAKEST LINK

'La famille fondée sur le mariage n'occupe plus dans notre société un rôle central, elle n'est plus le modèle type offert aux citoyens.'[155]

Until recently pivotal of family law, civil marriage has become its weakest link. The '*conjugal family*'[156] is on the decline.[157] In the first instance, family law is neutralised in regard to marriage so as to refer to any partnership. Subsequently, family law is neutralised in regard to any partnership whatsoever, so as to individualise rights and duties.[158] The preceding analysis has shown how the decreasing significance of marriage for the different circles of family members has resulted in the abolition of the impediments to marriage that were organised in regard to that interest. "*Die Hurden auf dem Weg zum Standesamt wurden ständig abgebaut, heute gibt es nahezu keine Hindernisse mehr*".[159] The vanishing of the extended family resulted in the abolition of the impediments to marriage on the ground of kinship or affinity regarding extended family members. The decreasing socio-economic significance for the spouses themselves and for the children has resulted in an evolution towards factual polygamy at the least. Finally has the loss of its vertical legal function led marriage to become a horizontal relationship that no longer needs to be reserved for couples who might found a(n intergenerational) family. Whereas the actual degree of convergence differs from one impediment to another, the general trend of convergence is one of advancing liberalisation. The declining legal significance of marriage is more a consequence than a cause of the changing marriage concept.[160] The abolition of impediments therefore only translates a foregoing evolution.

That being said, the preceding analysis has also shown that the examined impediments to marriage to some extent still fulfil a function, in particular with regard to the link between partnership and parenthood. The family can still be considered a basic unity of society, there being no alternative (yet) for the family with regard to procreation and education of children. In that regard, one should more generally not underestimate the social or collective dimension of the family in which society at large has an interest.[161] To some extent, the family still is the orchard of the State that can

155 MASSIP, J., 'Le nouveau droit de la filiation', *Defrénois* (2006), p. 6, n° 2.

156 GLENDON, M.-A., 'Introduction: Family Law at a time of turbulence' (2006), p. 1.

157 GLENDON, M.A., *The New Family and the New Property* (1981), p. 28 ff ; RENCHON, J.-L., 'Indisponibilité, ordre public et autonomie de la volonté dans le droit des personnes et de la famille' (2005), p. 51–54.

158 To this double evolution: SWENNEN, F., *Het huwelijk afschaffen?* (2003), p. 5–11. On the atomism in family law: GLENDON, M.A., *The New Family and the New Property* (1981), p. 35.

159 STRÄTZ, H.-W., 'Ehe und Familie als Institute des bürgerlichen Rechts' (2001), p. 21.

160 GLENDON, M.A., *The New Family and the New Property* (1981), p. 65.

161 COESTER-WALTJEN, D., COESTER, M., 'Formation of marriage' (1997), p. 162; ENDRÉO, G., 'Bigamie et double ménage' (1991), p. 270; FULCHIRON, H., 'Couples, mariage et différence des sexes' (2002),

counterbalance the negative effects of increasing individualisation. Family law still has a future. The linking of partnership and parenthood through the remaining functional impediments should therefore be modernised.

It is questionable whether marriage is the appropriate structure for this modernisation. On the one hand, the biological, economic and cultural foundations of the 'traditional' marriage no longer exist.[162] On the other hand, marriage is being modernised towards a horizontal relationship in a growing number of countries. The origin of this modernisation is the unlinking of marriage and parentage after the *Marckx*-case. Civil marriage will probably further evolve towards a bond regulating horizontal households rather than vertical families. In that regard, the number and gender of the parties and their relatedness is no longer relevant.[163] The advanced phase of the evolution would hamper its inversion. Inversion is easier in countries where 'horizontal' families have been directed towards a registered partnership and marriage is still reserved for 'vertical' families.[164]

If the future of family law lies outside marriage, the new challenge will be to find an appropriate alternative legal framework to link parenthood and partnership, beside other family supporting measures to prevent sustained low fertility.[165] Marriage will be reinvented,[166] taking into account the actual bio(techno)logical, economic and cultural foundations of modern society. Several proposals have already been presented in this regard.[167] My conclusion is the same as in my inaugural speech some years ago: marriage is dead, long live marriage.[168]

---

p. 50; RENCHON, J.-L., 'Indisponibilité, ordre public et autonomie de la volonté dans le droit des personnes et de la famille' (2005), p. 29 and 77.

162 CLIQUET, R., AVRAMOV, D., 'The future of the family: A sociobiological approach' (1998), p. 169; CALAIS-AULOY, M.-T., 'Pour un mariage aux effets limités' (1988), p. 5.

163 SWENNEN, F., *Het huwelijk afschaffen?* (2003), p. 22.

164 Which is proposed as the desirable evolution e.g. by AGELL, A., 'The legal status of same-sex couples in Europe – a critical analysis' (2003), p. 131 and LAGOUTTE, S., ÁRNASON, A.T., 'Article 16' (1999), p. 356.

165 CLIQUET, R., AVRAMOV, D., 'The future of the family: A sociobiological approach' (1998), p. 169; SWENNEN, F., *Het huwelijk afschaffen?* (2003), p. 16 and 22.

166 Comp. to the American covenant marriages, 'Developments in the Law – The Law of Marriage and Family', *116 Harv. L. Rev.* (2003), p. 1996, 2090–2091.

167 E.g. CALAIS-AULOY, M.-T., 'Pour un mariage aux effets limités' (1988), p. 7 ff; FORDER, C., VERBEKE, A., 'Geen woorden maar daden. Algemene rechtsvergelijkende conclusies en aanbevelingen' (2005), VERBEKE, A., 'Weg met huwelijk en echtscheiding' (2004), p. 13; WILLEKENS, H., 'De liefde, het kind en de institutionalisering van persoonlijke relaties' (1998), p. 20 ff; Hoger Instituut voor de Gezinswetenschappen, *Van huwelijkscontract naar opvoedingsbelofte*, 2006.

168 SWENNEN, F., *Het huwelijk afschaffen?* (2003). The conclusion I reached there, was the reinvention of marriage as a horizontal institution. The other functions can be reinvented in another familial institution.

CONVERGENCE AND DIVERGENCE IN THE LAW ON SAME-SEX PARTNERSHIPS

INGEBORG SCHWENZER*

1. INTRODUCTION

Not too long ago, homosexuality was still criminally prosecuted in many countries; at the very least, it was not socially accepted. Beginning in Denmark in 1989,[1] a gradual change took place, with more and more states initially granting legal recognition of same-sex relationships in the form of a registered partnership. Whereas at first, many legislators still sought to meticulously distinguish between registered partnerships on the one hand, and marriages on the other hand, in the early 2000s, a gradual rapprochement between registered partnerships and marriages took place. In 2001, the Netherlands were the first country to open up marriage to same-sex couples,[2] with other countries subsequently following suit.[3]

---

* I am greatly indebted to my assistants lic. iur. Anne-Florence Bods and Mariel Dimsey LLM, Lawyer (NSW) for their most valuable contributions throughout our research.

1 Act No. 372 of 7 June 1989 on registered partnership with effect from 1 October 1989. On the Danish Act on registered Partnership see: LUND-ANDERSEN, I., 'The Danish Registered Partnership Act', in: BOELE-WOELKI, K., FURCHS, A., (eds.), *Legal Recognition of Same-Sex Couples in Europe*, Intersentia, Antwerp, 2003, p. 13 ff.; see also: DOPFFEL, P., SCHERPE, J.M., 'Gleichgeschlechtliche Lebensgemeinschaften im Recht der nordischen Länder', in: BASEDOW, J., HOPT, K.J., KÖTZ, H., DOPFFEL, P., *Die Rechtsstellung gleichgeschlechtlicher Lebensgemeinschaften*, Mohr Siebeck, Tübingen, 2000, p. 7, 10.

2 Art. 1:30(1) Dutch Civil Code, inserted by the Act Opening Marriage to Same-Sex Couples of 21 December 2000, in force as of 1 April 2001, Staatsblad 2001, No. 9. See: WÖLFL, T., *Gleichgeschlechtliche Lebensgemeinschaft – Das Recht in Deutschland und im europäischen Ausland*, Thesis, Hamburg, 2005, p. 628.

3 *South Africa*: In LESBIAN AND GAY EQUALITY PROJECT AND EIGHTEEN OTHERS V. MINISTER OF HOME AFFAIRS AND OTHERS, Constitutional Court of South Africa, CCT 10/05, 1 December 2005 and in MINISTER OF HOME AFFAIRS AND ANOTHER V. FOURIE AND ANOTHER, Constitutional Court of South Africa, CCT 60/04, 1 December 2005, the court has declared s 30(1) Marriage Act 25 of 1961 and the common law definition of marriage inconsistent with the Constitution. It has, however, suspended the declaration of invalidity for twelve months in order to allow the parliament to correct the defects by assigning to same-sex couples the same status, entitlements and responsibilities as marriage law accords to heterosexual couples. The Chair of the South African Parliamentary

Currently in Europe, we can discern five groups of legal systems. The most advanced are those countries that have opened marriage to same-sex couples, namely the Netherlands[4] and Belgium,[5] as well as Spain.[6] In the second group, registered partnership, an institution more or less akin to marriage, has been created, encompassing the Scandinavian countries in particular,[7] but also Germany,[8] Great Britain,[9] the Czech Republic,[10] Slovenia[11] and, as of 2007, Switzerland.[12] In the third group, although some kind of institution for same-sex partners has been created, there are only a few legal consequences attached to this form of partnership, however, as a whole, it does not resemble the institution of marriage. Countries in this group comprise France, with its *pacte civil de solidarité*,[13] Portugal[14] and Luxembourg.[15] In the fourth group, comprising Austria, Greece, Ireland, and Liechtenstein, the introduction of a registered partnership for same-sex couples is currently under discussion. Finally, there are the countries that are yet to undertake steps to recognize same-sex partnerships or utterly discriminate against them, as the Baltic states and Poland.

Although much convergence can be found in the change of the general attitude towards the legal recognition of same-sex couples, the main area of divergence is still present with respect to children in same-sex parent families. To this very day, the

---

Committee on Home Affairs has recently announced, that same-sex marriage will be legalized by way of amendments to the marriage act 1961 rather than a constitutional amendment, see: British Institute of International and Comparative Law, 16 BLD 2006. *Canada*: Art. 2 Civil Marriage Act, in force as of 20 July 2005; see also: note 2, 5 and 6.

4 See: note 2.

5 Art. 143 Code civil.

6 Art. 44 Código civil, Ley 13/2005, de 1 de julio, por la que se modificó el Código civil en materia de derecho a contraer matrimonio (BOE núm. 157 de 2 de julio de 2005), see also: BEILFUSS, G., 'Gleichgeschlechtliche Ehen und Blitzscheidung im neuen spanischen Familienrecht', *Die Praxis des Familienrechts* 2006, p. 878-884.

7 *Denmark*: see: note 1; *Sweden*: Lag om registerat partnerskap (Registered Partnership Act), Act 1994:1117 of 23 June 1994, in force as of 1 January 1995; *Finland*: Registered Partnership Act, Act 950/2001, in force as of 1 March 2002; *Norway*: Lov om registreret partnerskap, No. 40/1993 of 20 April 1993, in force as of 1 August 1003; *Iceland*: Act on registered Partnership, No. 87 of 12 June 1996, in force as of 27 June 1996.

8 Lebenspartnerschaftsgesetz (LPartG) of 16 February 2001, BGBl I 266, in force as of 1 August 2001, modified by the Law of 6 February 2005, BGBl I 203 with effect from 1 January 2005.

9 Civil Partnership Act 2004, in force as of 5 December 2005.

10 Civil Partnership Law, in force as of 1 July 2006.

11 Law on Registered Partnership, in force as of 23 July 2006.

12 Partnerschaftsgesetz (PartG) of 18 June 2004, SR 211.231, in force as of 1 January 2006.

13 Loi relative au pacte civil de solidarité, loi No. 99–944 of 15 November 1999, inserting Arts. 515–1 to 515–7 in the Code civil.

14 Lei No. 7/01 of 11 May 2005, Adopta medidas de protecção das uniões de facto, DR Série I-A, 2797.

15 Loi du 9 juillet 2004 relative aux effets légaux de certains partenariats, published in Mémorial A, No. 143 on 6 August 2004, 2020, in force as of 1 November 2004.

opinion still prevails in many jurisdictions that a child must have a father and a mother. Thus, parenting in same-sex relationships is usually treated differently from that in heterosexual relationships, regardless of whether these relationships are based on marriage or not.

However, ample psychological research has been conducted in recent decades concerning children in same-sex partnerships. All research reveals that there are no significant differences regarding intellectual, emotional and social development between children brought up in same-sex families and those in heterosexual ones.[16] With respect to sexual orientation, behaviour defined by gender roles, psychological well-being, social integration and competence, these children resemble those from heterosexual families.[17] There is but one significant difference: children from same-sex families display more tolerance and empathy towards other persons and are more likely to enter into egalitarian relationships, which may be ascribed to the fact that they experience a family model that is more oriented towards equal rights and capabilities of their parents.[18]

Keeping these considerations in mind, this presentation will now focus on the breadth of approaches to the issue of same-sex parenting from a comparative law perspective. In general, as will be shown, there is a world of difference between the approach of the Anglo-American systems and that of most of the Continental legal systems. Whereas the former have adjusted their legal norms to better reflect reality in recent years, the latter are still stuck on the image of the two-heterosexual-parent-nuclear-family of the late nineteenth century. This anachronistic approach is not only found in the attitude towards same-sex families, but also with respect to parentage in heterosexual patchwork families.

---

16 STACEY, J., BIBLARZ, T., '(How) does the Sexual Orientation of Parents Matter?', *66 American Sociological Review* (2001), p. 159, 176; RAUCHFLEISCH, U., 'Gleichgeschlechtliche Partnerschaften aus psychologischer Sicht', *Die Praxis des Familienrechts* (2004), p. 507, 516; DITTBERNER, M., *Lebenspartnerschaft und Kindschaftsrecht*, Thesis, Frankfurt a.M. 2004, p. 160 ff; AMERICAN PSYCHOLOGICAL ASSOCIATION,'Lesbian and Gay Parenting: A Resource for Psychologists', Washington D.C. (1995), 8, http://www.apa.org/pi/parent.html; cf. also MURRAY, C., 'Same-Sex Families: Outcomes for Children and Parents', *34 Family Law* (2004), p. 136 ff. For an overview of studies analysing the situation of children in same-sex partnerships see: RAUCHFLEISCH, U., *Alternative Familienformen. Eineltern, gleichgeschlechtliche Paare, Hausmänner*, Vandenhoeck & Ruprecht, Göttingen, 1997, p. 70 ff.

17 FTHENAKIS, W.E., 'Gleichgeschlechtliche Lebensgemeinschaften und kindliche Entwicklung', in: BASEDOW, J., HOPT, K.J., KÖTZ, H., DOPFFEL, P., *Die Rechtsstellung gleichgeschlechtlicher Lebensgemeinschaften* (2000), p. 251, 382 ff.; STACEY, J., 'Legal Recognition of Same-Sex Couples: The Impact on Children and Families', *23 Quinnipiac Law Review* (2004), p. 529, 531 ff.

18 MUSCHELER, K., *Das Recht der eingetragenen Lebenspartnerschaft*, Erich Schmidt, Berlin, 2004, p. 335; RAUCHFLEISCH, U., 'Gleichgeschlechtliche Partnerschaften aus psychologischer Sicht', (2004), p. 516 ff.

In addressing same-sex parentage, I will first turn to the widest approach, whereby same-sex partners can be granted legal parentage of a child regardless of biological parentage. I will then deal with questions of adoption in the context of same-sex partnerships, then with the possibility, at the very least, of recognizing the factual relationship by granting parental responsibility without parentage.

2. LEGAL PARENTAGE AND MEDICALLY-ASSISTED PROCREATION

In heterosexual relationships, it has long been an established principle that, on the basis of the *pater est quem nuptiae demonstrant* presumption,[19] the husband of the mother was automatically regarded as the father of the child. Since the advent of medically-assisted procreation, in many legal systems, this presumption has been extended to the husband who gives consent to the insemination of his wife with donor sperm.[20] However, only in very recent times has the issue of applying this presumption in the context of lesbian partnerships even arisen for consideration.

At the outset, the first question is whether lesbian women are allowed access to medically-assisted procreation measures at all. According to the general positive trend towards medically-assisted procreation, most Anglo-American legal systems do not confine this possibility to heterosexual couples, thus allowing lesbian women to undergo such treatment.[21] Indeed, in Canada, discrimination on the basis of sexual orientation or marital status is expressly prohibited by federal law.[22] Closely affiliated with the Anglo-American approach are the Scandinavian countries, with the exception of Norway, as well as a new wave of modern continental legal systems, such as the

19 See e.g. *Austria*: Art. 138(1) ABGB; *Belgium*: Art. 315 Code civil; *Croatia*: Art. 54 Family Act; *Germany*: § 1592 BGB; *Greece*: Art. 1465 Civil Code; *Japan*: Art. 772(1) Civil Code; *Switzerland*: Art. 225(1) ZGB.

20 See e.g. *Canada*: Art. 538.3 Code civil du Qébec; *Great Britain*: sec. 28(2)(a) Human Fertilisation and Embryology Act 1990 (c. 37); *France*: Art. 312(1) Code civil; cf. *Germany*, § 1592(1) and § 1600(4) BGB, here, however, the child can challenge the paternity of the father; *Switzerland*: Art. 23(1) FMedG (SR 810.11).

21 For *Australia* cf. BEEM, P., 'Where Does a Man Stand on Issues of Assisted Reproduction, Surrogacy, Artificial Insemination within Lesbian Relationships and Posthumous Conception?', *18 Australian Journal of Family Law* (2004), p. 41, 45 ff.; *England and Wales*: cf. ALMACK, K., 'Seeking Sperm: Accounts of lesbian couples' reproductive decision making and understandings of the needs of the child', *20 International Journal of Law, Policy and the Family* (2006), p. 1, 3 ff.; *USA*: CHAMBERS, D.L., 'What if – The Legal Consequences of Marriage and the Legal Needs of Lesbian and Gay Male Couples', *95 Michigan Law Review* (1996), p. 447, 466.

22 Art. 2(e) Assisted Human Reproduction Act 2004, c. 2.

Netherlands,[23] Belgium and, now, under the socialist government, Spain.[24] In contrast, quite a few continental systems, in a truly conservative approach, still limit medically-assisted procreation with donor sperm to married, heterosexual couples, or at least couples living in a stable heterosexual relationship.[25]

In those systems that now allow lesbian women to undergo medically-assisted procreation treatment, most of them have not gone so far as to enable the consenting lesbian partner's parentage to be recognized. As yet, this possibility is only allowed in Sweden,[26] New Zealand,[27] South Africa,[28] select US states,[29] Canadian provinces,[30] and Australian states and territories.[31] Interestingly, Great Britain has not yet amended

---

23 DETHLOFF, N., 'Registrierte Partnerschaften in Europa', *Zeitschrift für Europäisches Privatrecht* (2004), p. 59, 64.

24 Art. 6 Ley 14/2006 de 26 mayo sobre técnicas de reproducción humana asistida, BOE núm 126, 19950, expressly states that any woman, regardless of her sexual orientation, shall have access to artificial reproduction technique.

25 *Germany*: Guidelines of the federal chamber of the medical profession regarding assisted reproduction (Richtlinie der Bundesärztekammer zur Durchführung der assistierten Reproduktion), Art. 3.1.1.; cf. also Deutsches Ärzteblatt 2006, A 1319, A 1400; see also: MUSCHELER, K., *Das Recht der eingetragenen Lebenspartnerschaft* (2004), p. 428; *France*: Art. L2141–2 Code de la santé publique; *Switzerland*: Art. 28 PartG, see: note 12.

26 Prop. 2004/05:137, Asisterad befruktning och föraldraskap (= Governmental Bill on Artificial Fertilisation and Parenthood); see also: BURRELL, R., *Assisted Reproduction in the Nordic Countries – a Comparative Study of Policies and Regulation*, Nordic Council of Ministers, Copenhagen 2006, p. 15.

27 Sec. 18 Status of Children Act 1969, modified by sec. 14 Status of Children Amendment Act 2004.

28 In *J AND B V. DIRECTOR GENERAL: DEPARTMENT OF HOME AFFAIRS AND OTHERS*, Constitutional Court of South Africa, CCT 46/02, 28 March 2003, the court held that sec. 5 Children's Status Act was inconsistent with the Constitution and ordered that it should be read to provide the same status to children born from artificial insemination to same-sex permanent life partners as it currently provides to such children born to heterosexual married couples.

29 E.g. *Massachusetts*: Mass. Gen. Laws Ann. 46 § 4B; *California*: Cal. Fam. Code § 297.5(d) and § 7613(a), cf. also the UPA-Provision on presumed parents in Cal. Fam. Code § 7611(d); *Vermont*: 15 V.S.A. § 1204(f) (2006) and 15 V.S.A. § 308(4); *Conneticut*: Conn. Gen. Stat. § 46b-38nn (2006) and Conn. Gen. Stat. § 45a-774 (2006); *New Jersey*: *IN THE MATTER OF THE PARENTAGE OF THE CHILD OF KIMBERLY ROBINSON*, Superior Court of New Jersey, Chancery Division 2005, 383 N.J. Super. 165, 890 A.2d 1036; see also: JOSLIN, C.G., 'The Legal Parentage of Children Born to Same-Sex Couples: Developments in the Law', *39 Family Law Quarterly* (2005), p. 683, 684 ff.; ELROD, L.D., SPECTOR, G., 'A Review of the Year in Family Law: Parentage and Assisted Reproduction Problems Take Center Stage', *39 Family Law Quarterly* (2006), p. 879, 887 ff.; FRELICH APPLETON, S., 'The Public and Private Faces of Family Law: Adoption in the Age of Reproductive Technology', *The University of Chicago Legal Forum* (2004), p. 393, 414 ff.; FORMAN, D.L., 'Married with Kids and Moving: Achieving Recognition for Same-Sex Parents under the Uniform Parentage Act', *4 Whittier Journal of Child and Family Advocacy* (2005), p. 241, 252 ff.

30 *Alberta*: *FRAESS V. ALBERTA*, Alberta Court of Queen's Bench, [2005] A.J. No. 1665 Q.B.; *British Columbia*: *GILL AND MAHER, MURRAY AND POPOFF V. MINISTRY OF HEALTH*, British Columbia Human Rights Tribunal, 2001 BCHRT 34; *Ontario*: *M.D.R. v. ONTARIO*, Ontario Superior Court of Justice, [2006] O.J. No. 2268; *Québec*: Art. 538.1 Code civil du Québec.

31 *Australian Capital Territory*: sec. 11(4) Parentage Act 2004; *Northern Territory*: sec. 15DA Status of Children Act; *Tasmania*: sec. 10C(1) Status of Children Act 1974; *Western Australia*: sec. 6A Artificial Conception Act 1985.

its Human Fertilisation and Embryology Act to reflect the changes made by the enactment of the Civil Partnership Act 2004, thus not yet opening up the presumption of parentage to the consenting lesbian partner.[32] More expansive are the rules in some US states that automatically attribute parentage to the married or registered lesbian partner of the birth-giving mother.[33]

Owing to purely biological considerations, these legal rules cannot apply in the case of gay men, who are dependent on surrogacy arrangements. To my knowledge, only South Africa in its new Children's Act 2005 adopts a clear, even revolutionary stance in this respect, where a valid surrogate motherhood has the effect that, for all purposes, the commissioning parents are the child's legal parents, thus including two gay men.[34] In all other legal systems, if surrogacy is allowed at all, a change of parentage may only be effected by way of adoption.

3. ADOPTION

Whereas the initial position was that adoption was strictly limited to married, heterosexual couples, there have since been two trends that ultimately lead to a broader recognition of adoption by same-sex persons.

The first trend, again mostly found in common law states, has been to do away with adoption requirements dependent on status, i.e. the prerequisite of marriage, and to extend the right to jointly adopt to two persons living in a non-marital relationship. This is in line with the greater importance given to factual relationships in many common law systems, together with the emphasis on the best interests of the child. On this basis, it was easier to allow same-sex partners to adopt, taking into account the facts of the individual case. However, particularly in federal states such as the US, Canada and Australia, to the very day still, a very diverse picture can be discerned.

Within the US, there are currently several states allowing for same-sex couples to adopt jointly.[35] Almost all other states, at the very least, recognize so-called "co-

---

32 In 2004, the UK Government announced, that it would review the HFEA and for this purpose held a public consultation. The government consultation is available online at http://www.dh.gov.uk/ assetRoot/04/11/78/72/04117872.pdf; the results of the consultation (published 29 March 2006) are available at http://www.peoplescienceandpolicy.com/downloads/ DH_consultation.pdf; cf. also BIRK, D., 'The Reform of the Human Fertilisation and Embryology Act 1990', *39 Family Law* (2005), p. 563 ff.

33 See: note 29.

34 § 297(1)(a) Children Act 2005 (No. 38 of 2005), not yet in force.

35 California, Connecticut, District of Columbia, Illinois, Massachusetts, New Jersey, New Mexico, New York, Oregon, Vermont. See: Liberty Counsel, Same-Sex Adoption Laws by State, available online at: http://www.lc.org/ProFamily/samesex_adoption_by_state.pdf; http://www.nclrights.org/ publications/adptn0204.htm.

parent" or stepchild adoption, either allowing a same-sex partner to adopt the biological, or even previously adopted child of his or her partner.[36] Florida is the only state that expressly prohibits adoption by homosexuals in general;[37] other states such as Mississippi[38] and Utah[39] make adoption virtually impossible by still strictly adhering to the requirement of marriage.

In Canada[40] and Australia,[41] the situation is comparable. The law differs between each state, province, or territory, with a clear trend towards a more liberal approach. Interestingly, in New Zealand, although initial parentage of the lesbian partner of the

---

36 *California*: Cal. Fam. Code § 9000(b); *Connecticut*: Conn. Gen. Stat. § 45a-724(3); *District of Columbia*: In re M.M.D. v. B.H.M., District of Columbia Court of Appeals 1995, 662 A.2d 837 (D.C. 1995); *Illinois*: In re PETITION OF K.M. & D.M. to adopt Olivia M., Appellate Court of Illinois 1995, 274 Ill. App. 3d 189, 653 N.E.2d 888; *Indiana*: IN THE MATTER OF THE ADOPTION OF INFANT K.S.P. AND INFANT J.P., Court fo Appeals of Indiana 2004, 804 N.E.2d 1253; IN RE THE ADOPTION OF M.M.G.C., H.H.C., AND K.E.A.C., Court of Appeals of Indiana 2003, 785 N.E.2d 267; *Massachusetts*: Adoption of Tammy, Supreme Judicial Court of Massachusetts 1993, 416 Mass. 205, 619 N.E.2d 315; *New York*: IN THE MATTER OF JACOB, AN INFANT. IN THE MATTER OF DANA., Court of Appeals of New York 1995, 86 N.Y.2d 651, 660 N.E.2d 397, 636 N.Y.S.2d 716; *New Jersey*: IN THE MATTER OF THE ADOPTION OF TWO CHILDREN BY H.N.R., Superior Court of New Jersey 1995, 285 N.J. Super. 1, 666 A.2d 535; *Pennsylvania*: In Re ADOPTION OF R.B.F. AND R.C.F., Supreme Court of Pennsylvania 2002, 569 Pa. 269, 803 A.2d 1195; *Vermont*: ADOPTIONS OF B.L.V.B. AND E.L.V.B., Supreme Court of Vermont 1993, 160 Vt. 368, 628 A.2d 1271 and 15A V.S.A. § 1–102; FORMAN, D.L., 'Same-Sex Partners: Strangers, Third Parties, or Parents? The Changing Legal Landscape and the Struggle for Parental Equality', *40 Family Law Quarterly* (2006), p. 23, 43; JOSLIN, C.G., 'The Legal Parentage of Children Born to Same-Sex Couples: Developments in the Law' (2005), p. 691; DETHLOFF, N., 'Same-Sex Parents in a Comparative Perspective', *7 Forum du droit international* (2005), p. 195, 196.

37 Fla. Stat. § 63.042(3).

38 Miss. Code Ann. § 93–17–3.

39 Utah Code Ann. § 78–30–1 (3)(b).

40 Joint and step-parent adoption possible in *British Columbia*: sec. 5 Adoption Act [R.S.B.C. 1996] ch. 5; *Manitoba*: The Charter Compliance Act [S.M. 2002], c. 24; *Newfoundland & Labrador*: sec. 20 Adoption Act [S.N.L. 1999] c. A-2.1 as amended by sec. 10 An Act to amend the Adoption Act [S.N.L. 2002] c. 13; *Northwest Territories*: sec. 1(1), 5(1)(b) and 5(1)(c) Adoption Act [S.N.W.T. 1998] c. 9 as amended by sec. 1 [S.N.W.T. 2002] c. 6; *Nova Scotia*: Re M (S.C.) (2001), 194 N.S.R. (2d) 362, 202 D.L.R. (4th) 172 [S.C.(Fam.Div.)]; *Ontario*: sec. 146 Child and Family Services Act [R.S.O. 1990] c. 11 and sec 10(1) Human Rights Code [R.S.O. 1990] c. H19; *Québec*: Art. 546 Code civil du Québec; *Saskatchewan*: sec. 16(2)(c) Adoption Act [S.S.) ch. 5.2; see also: FISHER, J., 'Outlaws or In-laws?: Successes and Challenges in the Struggle for LGBT Equality', *49 McGill Law Journal* (2004), p. 1183, para. 14; WINTEMUTE, R., 'Sexual Orientation and the Charter: The Achievement of Formal Legal Equality (1985–2005) and Its Limits', *29 McGill Law Journal* (2004), p. 1143, para. 28; CASSWELL, D.G., 'Any two Persons in Canada's Lotusland, British Columbia', in: WINTEMUTE, R., ANDENÆS, M., *Legal Recognition of Same-Sex Partnerships, A Study of National, European and International Law*, Hart, Oxford, 2001, p. 215, 228.

41 Joint Adoption: e.g. *Australian Capital Territory*: sec. 18(1)(b) Adoption Act 1993; *Western Australia*: sec. 39(1)(d) Adoption Act 1994; step-parent Adoption: *Tasmania*: sec. 20(2A)(a) Adoption Act 1988; see also: COOPER, D.M., 'For Richer for Poorer, in Sickness and in Health: Should Australia Embrace Same-Sex Marriage?', *19 Australian Journal of Family Law* (2005), p. 153, 161.

birth mother is possible, the issue of adoption by same-sex partners has only been raised recently,[42] with an adoption law reform still to come.[43]

Out of the European countries, England and Wales also follow this trend. The Adoption and Children Act 2002 now simply states that an adoption order may be made on the application of a couple without any reference to status or sex.[44] The same holds true for South Africa.[45]

The second trend is derived from the question of status. This is the one predominantly followed in continental Europe. As has already been mentioned, Denmark was the first legal system to introduce the possibility of a registered partnership.[46] Whereas in the early days, registered partnership did not confer a right to joint adoption or even to stepchild adoption, nowadays, especially in the aftermath of opening up marriage, the winds have changed.

It comes as no great surprise that those states that have opened marriage to same-sex partners no longer distinguish between heterosexual and same-sex marriages regarding the issue of adoption, thus allowing for both joint and stepchild adoption by married, same-sex couples. However, even here, change sometimes occurred gradually, as is evidenced by Belgium,[47] which, until recently, did not permit adoption by same-sex spouses at all, as well as by the Netherlands,[48] where at least international adoption

---

42 New Zealand Parliamentary Debates (Hansard) Vol. 622, 17423, 7 December 2004.

43 Cf. *Law Commission of New Zealand*, Report 65, Adoption and its Alternatives, A Different Approach and a New Framework, Wellington 2000, para. 350 ff; *Law Commission of New Zealand*, Preliminary Paper 38, Adoption: Options for Reform, Wellington 1999, para. 179 ff.

44 Sec. 49(1)(a) Adoption and Children Act 2002. The term "couple" is defined in sec. 144 (4)(aa) and (b) as "two people who are civil partners of each other" (aa) or as "two people (whether of different sexes of the same sex) living as partners in an enduring family relationship". HARPER, M., LANDELLS, K., 'The Civil Partnership Act 2004 in Force', *39 Family Law* (2005), p. 963, 969; WASHINGTON, J., ALEXANDER, S., 'Civil Partnership Made Easy', *39 Family Law* (2005), p. 243, 245.

45 Du *Toit and Another v. The Minister for Welfare and Population Development and Others*, South Africa Constitutional Court, CCT 40/01, 10 September 2002.

46 See: note 1.

47 Loi du 18 mai 2006 modifiant certaines dispositions du Code civil en vue de permettre l'adoption par des personnes de même sexe, published on 20 June 2006 in the Moniteur Belge/Belgisch Staatsblad, modifying Art. 343 Code civil.

48 Art. 1:227 Dutch Civil Code (Burgerlijk Wetboek); MAXWELL, N.G., FORDER, C., 'The Inadequacies in U.S. and Dutch Adoption Law to Establish Same-Sex Couples as Legal Parents: A Call for Recognizing Intentional Parenthood', *38 Family Law Quartely* (2004), p. 623, 638 ff.; VONK, M., 'One, Two or Three Parents? Lesbian Co-Mothers and a Known Donor with "Family Life" under Dutch Law', *18 International Journal of Law Policy and the Family* (2004), p. 103, 105; BOELE-WOELKI, K., SCHRAMA, W.M., 'Die Rechtsstellung von Menschen mit homosexueller Veranlagung im niederländischen Recht', in: BASEDOW, J., HOPT, K.J., KÖTZ, H., DOPFFEL, P., *Die Rechtsstellung gleichgeschlechtlicher Lebensgemeinschaften* (2000), p. 51, 94.

by same-sex spouses was initially not allowed but will soon be made possible.[49] By contrast, in Spain, in 2005 same-sex marriage and adoption were made legal simultaneously.[50]

With respect to the countries that have not opened up marriage to same-sex couples, but nevertheless allow some kind of registered partnership, three different approaches can be observed.

A true equalization with heterosexual married couples regarding the issue of adoption can nowadays be found in Sweden,[51] as well as in Iceland as of June 2006.[52] Both countries recognize both joint and stepchild adoption by same-sex registered partners.

Under the second approach, at least stepchild adoption has been made available in recent times. This possibility was introduced in the last five years in Denmark,[53] Norway[54] and Germany.[55] In French case law, it is unresolved whether "adoption simple" is open to same-sex partners who have entered into a *pacte civil de solidarité*.[56]

---

49 Bill pending, see the press release of the Dutch Ministry of Justice of 4 May 2006, available online at: http://english.justitie.nl/currenttopics/pressreleases/archives2006/adoption-by-same-sex-spouses.aspx?cp=35&cs=1578.

50 Joint adoption: Art. 176(4) Código Civil; step-parent Adoption Art. 176 and 178(1) Código Civil; GARCÍA CANTERO, G., 'Family Law Reform in Differing Directions', in: BAINHAM, A., (ed.), *The International Survey of Family Law,* Jordan Publishing, Bristol, 2006, p. 435, 437; BEILFUSS, G., 'Gleichgeschlechtliche Ehen und Blitzscheidung im neuen spanischen Familienrecht' (2006) p. 878–88.

51 On 1 February 2003, ch. 3 § 2 of the Law on Registered Partnership has been rescinded (SFS 2002:603), thus registered couples have the same right to adopt as married couples. See: JÄNTERA-JAREBORG, M., SÖRGJERD, C., 'The Experiences with Registered Partnership in Scandinavia', *Die Praxis des Familienrechts* (2004), p. 577, 581; SALDEEN, Å., 'The Children's Ombudsman, Adoption by Homosexual Partners and Assisted Reproduction', in: BAINHAM, A., (ed.), *The International Survey of Family Law,* Jordan Publishing, Bristol, 2004, p. 439 ff; SAVOLAINEN, M., 'The Finish and the Swedish Partnership Acts – Similarities and Divergences', in: BOELE-WOELKI, K., FURCHS, A., (eds.), *Legal Recognition of Same-Sex Couples in Europe,* Intersentia, Antwerp, 2003, p. 24, 39.

52 GUNNARSDOTTIR, H., 'Important Improvements in Gay and Lesbian Rights in Iceland', available online at: http://www.ilga-europe.org/europe/guide/country_by_country/iceland/important_improvements_in_gay_and_lesbian_rights_in_iceland.

53 § 4(1) Act on Registered Partnership, inserted by Lov 360/1999; LUND-ANDERSEN, I., 'The Danish Registered Partnership Act'(2003), p. 17.

54 § 5a(2) Act on Adoption (Adoptionsloven).

55 § 9(7) LPartG, BGBl 2001 I, 3396, in force as of 1 January 2005; DETHLOFF, N., KROLL, K., 'The Constitutional Court as Driver of Reforms in German Family Law', in: BAINHAM, A., (ed.), *The International Survey of Family Law* (2006), p. 217, 223; SIEGFRIED, D., 'Kinder vom anderen Ufer', *Familie Partnerschaft Recht* (2005), p. 120, 121; WELLENHOFER, M., 'Das neue Recht für eingetragene Lebenspartnerschaften', *Neue Juristische Wochenschrift* (2005), p. 705, 706; PÄTZOLD, J., 'Die gemeinschaftliche Adoption Minderjähriger durch eingetragene Lebenspartner', *Familie Partnerschaft Recht* (2005), p. 269 ff.

56 Art. 360 Code civil ff. Affirming: Tribunal de grande instance de Paris, 7 July 2004; Tribunal de grande instance de Clermont-Ferrand, 24 March 2006, (1st instance); overturned by Cour d'appel de Riom, 27 June 2006 (2nd instance).

The most restrictive approach can still be found in the Czech Republic, Slovenia, Finland[57] and Switzerland,[58] which do not allow any form of adoption. Switzerland even discriminates against registered partners to the extent that registered partners are not even permitted to adopt individually; however, every non-registered person, regardless of sexual orientation, may adopt a child alone if it is in the best interests of the child.

4. PARENTAL RESPONSIBILITY

If the non-genetic social parent in a same-sex partnership is denied any possibility of attaining legal parentage, either initially or by adoption, it is crucial to examine whether he or she may be vested with parental responsibility or another similar legal concept of care for the child. The answer to this question is closely linked to the position the legal systems take in addressing the issue of parental responsibility in stepfamilies in general. Again, several layers of development can be distinguished here.

The most advanced, and probably most appropriate approach to same-sex families can be found in the Netherlands. Whenever a child is born during a marriage or registered partnership, provided that the mother is the only legal parent, the partner of the mother automatically attains joint parental responsibility.[59] If there is a second legal parent, parental responsibility may be attributed by the court upon joint application.[60]

The second approach recognizes a generous attribution of comprehensive parental responsibility to third parties in general, regardless of sexual orientation. Many common law countries belong to this group.[61] Finland also follows this approach. As

---

57 Art. 9(2) Registered Partnership Act.

58 Art. 28 PartG; COTTIER, M., 'Registered Partnerships for Same-Sex Couples in Switzerland: Constructing a New Model of Family Relationships', in: MACLEAN, M., (ed.), *Family Law and Family Values*, Hart, Oxford, 2005, p. 181, 195; SCHWENZER, I., 'Registrierte Partnerschaft: Der Schweizer Weg', *Die Praxis des Familienrechts* (2002), p. 223, 231 ff.

59 Art. 253aa Dutch Civil Code (Burgerlijk Wetboek); BOELE-WOELKI, K., 'Registered Partnership and Same-Sex Marriage in the Netherlands', in: BOELE-WOELKI, K., FURCHS, A., (eds.), *Legal Recognition of Same-Sex Couples in Europe*, (2003), p 46.

60 Art. 253t Dutch Civil Code (Burgerlijk Wetboek).

61 E.g. *Australia*: sec. 65C Family Law Act 1975, according to which parental responsibility can be attained by a parenting order and sec. 63A FLA 1975, regarding parenting plans. In *RE MARK: AN APPLICATION RELATING TO PARENTAL RESPONSIBILITIES*, [2003] FamCA 822, 23 August 2003, the Australian Family court issued a parenting order to the male same-sex partner of the biological father of a child conceived pursuant to a surrogacy agreement; cf. also DICKEY, A., Family Law, Law Book Co, Sydney, 2002, p. 362 ff. *New Zealand*: According to sec. 23 Care of Children Act 2004, step parents (by civil union or de facto partners) can be appointed as additional guardians by

in the case of a married heterosexual stepparent, parental responsibility can be attributed to the same-sex partner either by agreement,[62] or by court order.[63]

Where the partner has already been vested with parental responsibility during the ongoing relationship, it goes without saying that, in case of dissolution, in the same way as in case of divorce, the partners either keep joint parental responsibility or it is allocated in accordance with the best interests of the child. Similar results are achieved in many US states where, although parental responsibility is not an issue during the ongoing, amicable relationship, in case of separation or divorce, parental responsibility can be attributed according to concepts of de facto, psychological or functional parenthood.[64]

"Mini-custody" is perhaps the best way of describing the approach that grants the least recognition to the social parentage of the same-sex partner, a concept found in Germany and Switzerland, albeit with a different scope in the two countries, respectively. In Germany, "mini-custody" comprises a right to participate in decisions concerning the child;[65] in Switzerland, the partner has an obligation to support the

---

consent of the child's parents; ATKIN, B., 'New Zealand, Landmark Legislation', in: BAINHAM, A., (ed.), *The International Survey of Family Law* (2006), p. 305, 311.

62 Art. 9(1)(4) Child Custody and the Right of Access Act; BOELE-WOELKI, K., BRAAT, B., SUMNER I., (eds.), *European Family Law in Action*, Volume III: Parental Responsibilities, European Family Law Series No. 9, Intersentia, Antwerp, 2005, p. 393.

63 Art. 14(1) Child Custody and the Right of Access Act.

64 E.g. *Colorado*: *IN THE INTEREST OF E.L.M.C., A CHILD, AND CONCERNING CHERYL ANN CLARK, APPELLANT, AND ELSEY MAXWELL MCLEOD, APPELLEE*, Court of Appeals of Colorado 2004, 100 P.3d 546; *Maine*: C.E.W. v. D.E.W., Supreme Judicial Court of Maine 2004, 2004 ME 43, 845 A.2d 1146; *Maryland*: Donna Gestl v. Lisa M. Frederick, et al., Court of Special Appeals of Maryland 2000, 133 Md. App. 216, 754 A.2d 1087; *Massachusetts*: E.N.O. v. L.M.M., Supreme Judicial Court of Massachusetts 1999, 429 Mass. 824, 711 N.E.2d 886; *Minnesota*: *LACHAPELLE V. MITTEN*, Court of Appeals of Minnesota 2000, 607 N.W.2d 151; *New Jersey*: V.C. v. M.J.B., Supreme Court of New Jersey, 2000, 163 N.J. 200, 748 A.2d 539; *New Mexico*: *BARNAE V. BARNAE*, Court of Appeals of New Mexico 1997, 123 N.M. 583, 1997 NMCA 77, 943 P.2d 1036; *Washington*: *IN THE MATTER OF THE PARENTAGE OF L.B., SUE ELLEN ("MIAN") CARVIN V. PAGE BRITAIN*, Supreme Court of Washington 2005, 155 Wn.2d 679, 122 P.3d 161; *Wisconsin*: *IN RE THE CUSTODY OF H.S.H-K., HOLTZMAN V. KNOTT*, Supreme Court of Wisconsin 1995, 193 Wis. 2d 649. 533 N.W.2d 419; see also: MAXWELL, N.G., FORDER, C., 'The Inadequacies in U.S. and Dutch Adoption Law to Establish Same-Sex Couples as Legal Parents: A Call for Recognizing Intentional Parenthood' (2004), p. 633; FORMAN, D.L., 'Same-Sex Partners: Strangers, Third Parties, or Parents? The Changing Legal Landscape and the Struggle for Parental Equality' (2006), p. 23, 32 ff. Cf. also in the UK: *RE G*, EWCA Civ 372, Court of Appeal, Thorpe, Laws and Hallett LJJ, 6 April 2006, [2006] FLR (forthcoming); CLARKE, S., 'Residence Applications – Does Biology Matter?', *40 Family Law* (2006), p. 679, 681 ff., referring to the concept of the "psychological parent". In Canada, cf. *RICHARDSON V. LAFRANCE*, Ontario Court of Justice, [2005] O.J. No. 5186, 2005 ONCJ 229.

65 § 9(1) LPartG; DETHLOFF, N., 'Parental Rights and Responsibilities in Germany', *39 Family Law Quarterly* (2005), p. 315–325; DITTBERNER, M., *Lebenspartnerschaft und Kindschaftsrecht* (2004), p. 109 ff.; SCHWAB, D., *Die eingetragene Lebenspartnerschaft*, Gieseking, Bielefeld, 2002, 171 ff.; WÖLFL, T., *Gleichgeschlechtliche Lebensgemeinschaft – Das Recht in Deutschland und im europäischen Ausland* (2005), p. 262 ff.

parent in his or her custodial role.[66] Recently in France, the *Cour de Cassation* allowed a partial delegation of parental responsibility to the same-sex partner of the mother of the children, where a stable relationship was present and social parentage existed.[67]

However, the rights and duties of the partner under these systems are restricted to the ongoing relationship; in case of dissolution, they cease in their entirety without the possibility of granting parental responsibility, even if the interests of the child so require.

5. CONTACT

In the same way as separation or divorce of heterosexual legal parents, it is still important in cases of separation of same-sex partners that the child maintain ongoing contact with the partner who has acted as social parent. It goes without saying that in cases of initial legal parentage or adoption, there is no need for special rules regarding contact. The same holds true where comprehensive parental responsibility has been attributed. However, contact is an important issue in those legal systems that, up to now, do not recognize any possibility of attributing comprehensive parental responsibility to the same-sex partner. At least here, these legal systems are increasingly recognizing the possibility of contact with third parties that have a significant relationship with the child, thus easily encompassing the same-sex social parent.[68]

---

66 Art. 27(1) PartG; GRÜTTER, M., SUMMERMATTER, D., 'Das Partnerschaftsgesetz', *Die Praxis des Familienrechts* (2004), p. 449, 463 ff.

67 Cour de Cassation, Arrêt No. 652 of 24 February 2006.

68 E.g. *Germany*, § 1685 BGB; PLÖTZGEN, S., *Das Umgangsrecht von „Nicht-Eltern", Ein Vergleich des deutschen Rechts mit den Umgangsrechtlichen Regelungen in England und in der Schweiz*, Thesis, Berlin, 2005, p. 153; BÜTE, D., 'Elterliche Sorge und Umgangsrecht', Teil 3, *Familie und Recht* (2006), p. 170, 174; *Switzerland*: Art. 274a ZGB; *Australia*: sec. 60B(2)(b) Family Law Act 1975; DICKEY, A., Family Law (2002), p. 441 ff; *New Zealand*: cf. ATKIN, B., 'New Zealand, Landmark Legislation', in: BAINHAM, A., (ed.), *The International Survey of Family Law* (2006); *USA*: e.g. *Conneticut*: *LISA LASPINA-WILLIAMS V. CHERYL LASPINA-WILLIAMS*, Superior Court of Conneticut 1999, 46 Conn. Supp. 165, 742 A.2d 840; *Maryland*: Donna Gestl v. Lisa M. Frederick, et al., Court of Special Appeals of Maryland 2000, 133 Md. App. 216, 754 A.2d 1087; *Massachusetts*: E.N.O. vs. L.M.M., Supreme Judicial Court of Massachusetts 1999, 429 Mass. 824, 711 N.E.2d 886; *New Jersey*: V.C. v. M.J.B., Supreme Court of New Jersey, 2000, 163 N.J. 200, 748 A.2d 539; *Pennsylvanina*: T.B. v. L.R.M., Supreme Court of Pennsylvania 2001, 567 Pa. 222, 786 A.2d 913; *Rhode Island*: *MAUREEN V. RUBANO V. CONCETTA A. DICENZO*, Supreme Court of Rhode Island 2000, 759 A.2d 959; *West Virginia*: *CLIFFORD K. AND TINA B. V. PAUL S.*, Supreme Court of Appeals of West Virginia 2005, 217 W. Va. 625, 619 S.E.2d 138.

6. SUMMARY

In summary, although in the area of general recognition of same-sex partnerships, certain convergence can be discerned, this presentation has shown that significant divergence still exists when it comes to the question of parent-child relationships in these families. At one end of the scale, we have legal systems that place same-sex parentage on totally equal footing with that of heterosexual parentage. The other extreme is represented by legal systems that still simply ignore the social phenomenon of this form of parentage.

If we examine the more modern solutions described here closely, two different situations become apparent. For many legal systems, same-sex families still only seem to be conceivable on the basis that one of the partners brings a child from a previous heterosexual relationship to the new relationship. However, more and more same-sex families are founded on the common intention of the partners to conceive and raise a child together. Indeed, the desire to have children is at least as prevalent in same-sex relationships as in heterosexual ones. Legal rules have to deal with these two distinct forms of same-sex families. As has been shown by the psychological studies at the outset of this presentation, there are no viable grounds for distinguishing between heterosexual and same-sex families in this respect.

This leads to the following conclusions. First, current legal issues concerning children conceived within the partnership should be addressed under the topic of legal parentage, which ultimately leads to a new concept of intentional parentage. Furthermore, joint adoption should certainly be made available. The second group of – reconstituted – families should be dealt with in the same way as heterosexual patchwork families, whereby stepchild adoption is increasingly viewed sceptically, the better approach being to depart from a restricted notion of parental responsibility and to acknowledge social parentage. As I have shown to you today, inspiration in this regard can be taken from the approaches adopted in many common law legal systems, especially those outside Europe. Many continental legal systems are still very-much status oriented and, thus, have a long way to go in grappling the modern family constellations as we find them in twenty-first-century societies.

MOVING TO THE SAME DESTINATION? RECENT TRENDS IN THE LAW OF DIVORCE

Bea Verschraegen

1. INTRODUCTION

Trends in the law of divorce[1] can be similar or different; this depends of the parameters applied in the countries at stake. These parameters can e.g. be: the *rapidity* with which divorce can be obtained, the degree of *judicial supervision*, and the *tension* between the principles of a "clean-break" versus continuing responsibility. This contribution focuses on these parameters and the degree to which they influence one another.

2. RAPID DIVORCE, JUDICIAL SUPERVISION AND CLEAN-BREAK VERSUS CONTINUING RESPONSIBILITY

Basically, legislators still consider marriage as a long-term commitment, whereas divorce rates or factual separation of the parties demonstrate, that one or both parties do have a quite different view. But also legal provisions within one and the same country are not necessarily coherent: marriage usually is not regulated as a simple contract which can be departed from once one party does not comply with his/her contractual obligations. Quite to the contrary, although marriage is considered as a contract, many countries require a specific procedure in which grounds for divorce must be examined and proved and in which usually a judge pronounces divorce. Yet,

---

1 This contribution is based on Verschraegen, B., 'Divorce', in: Glendon, M.A., (ed.), *International Encyclopedia of Comparative Law,* Volume IV *Persons and Family,* Chapter 5, 2004, p. 1–87. For summary information see the internet site of the European Commission, European Judicial Network: http://ec.europa.eu/civiljustice/divorce.

this picture is misleading. Secular legal systems show various characteristics.[2] Where breakdown of the marriage, accompanied by faulty behaviour of one or both spouses (e.g. France and Austria), is a valid ground for divorce, an immediate dissolution of marriage is possible. How rapidly divorce is pronounced, depends of the seriousness of the facts and the degree of judicial supervision. The decreasing supervision in this context has, in many countries, been the reason for introducing a no-fault divorce and/or a divorce by mutual consent. Where parties agree on divorce (and the consequences), the power of the court to examine breakdown of the marriage seems superfluous, especially when certain periods of separation are required before the divorce can be pronounced. In addition, some countries provide for what is called a "paper divorce" (e.g. Denmark, England and Wales, the Netherlands, Norway and Sweden). This means that the procedure is written by nature, and no hearing is required. Hence, divorce is more or less an act of registration. The tendency of western European secular systems is rather to decrease and partly eliminate judicial supervision.[3]

Parties are given an increasing contractual freedom to agree upon the consequences of divorce, their equal bargaining power is assumed and the agreement can only in very harsh cases be set aside. This is true for the financial consequences of divorce, whereas judicial supervision is increased with respect to child related issues, because welfare of the child is, at least theoretically, paramount. Although very few states deny a divorce for reason of hardship to the children, custody, visitation and child support are always reviewable in the best interest of the child.

The real battlefield is, therefore, not so much how to "get" a divorce, but how to obtain a "good" divorce. This implies for most parties the economic conditions of their divorce.[4] From a substantial point of view, the clear tendency is to reduce matrimonial support after divorce, whereas support claims against third parties seem to be reclassified as a type of "new property". These "property rights", e.g. pension benefits, are divided because equal treatment or fairness so demands. The result is, that divorce itself is relatively easy to obtain, and in many cases quickly available, but that some notion of continuing responsibility of one spouse towards the other is present.

A clean break with regard to the consequences cannot and should not be realized if there are minor children in custody of one parent. Statistically, this is so in the majority of cases. From an economic point of view, this responsibility may also

---

2 Verschraegen, B., Divorce (2004), 1 (72 f) with further references.

3 Verschraegen, B., Divorce (2004), 1 (72 f) with references.

4 For spousal support upon divorce see: Martiny, D., 'Ehescheidung und nachehelicher Unterhalt in Europa,' *8.3 Electronic Journal of Comparative Law* (2005), http://www.ejcl.org/.

function as a bar to divorce. However, even in countries where rules on the division of property and pension benefits have been enacted, the parties may deviate from the law by agreeing differently before or on the occasion of divorce (e.g. in the Netherlands, Germany and Sweden). Due to their contractual freedom the parties may waive substantial rights.[5]

3. ASSESSMENT

It seems that the *different patterns of divergence* are, in some cases, rather a matter of degree than of substance. Strictly speaking, non-consensual divorce always represents some sort of "repudiation". The question then is, whether and to what extent the "repudiated spouse" is protected, when dealing with the consequences of divorce. By contrast, the "clean-break" principle has been a reaction to situations in which marriages, although they had broken down in fact, were maintained on paper, because divorce was legally impossible or difficult to obtain. This pattern has changed dramatically. A clean break is urged nowadays with regard to the consequences of divorce. Obviously, an economic clean break in the sense that no protection is due to the other spouse may cause poverty of the economically weaker party. The reaction of some legislators and courts has been to cut short post-divorce support, but to look for new sources, such as the "new property". The message, therefore, seems to be that breakdown of the marriage allows for a "clean break" of that marriage, i.e. for a divorce, so that each party has the possibility to remarry. As to the consequences of divorce, the "clean break" principle is gradually eroding the notion of spousal support upon divorce. Instead, compensation payments and/or divisions of "new property" based on some notion of continuing responsibility are emerging. Consequently, a further marriage may become too costly.

From a *comparative* point of view, Western European countries would seem to be increasingly adopting no-fault grounds for divorce, including divorce by mutual consent. On the other hand, many legal systems do not want to entirely exclude fault and retain it in limited situations, such as when the "reason" for the breakdown is deemed to be relevant, or when the concept of hardship comes into play. Some legal systems (like France and Austria) have openly retained fault to some degree by combining no-fault and fault grounds for divorce.

There seem to be mainly *three factors influencing parties to assert grounds other than the real grounds for divorce*:[6] namely, the *discretionary power* of the judge, the possibility

---

5 VERSCHRAEGEN, B., Divorce (2004), 1 (80 f) with further references.

6 VERSCHRAEGEN, B., Divorce (2004), 1 (76) with further references.

of *paper divorces* (so-called summary procedures), and the *bargaining* for the consequences of divorce in in-of-court or out-of-court mediation procedures. Obviously, the discrepancy between asserted and real grounds for divorce only arises when a ground is needed in order to obtain a divorce or when the ground for divorce has some impact on the consequences. It also seems to be quite clear that paper divorces are more susceptible to the assertion of false reasons when the law provides for an immediate divorce if certain circumstances, such as e.g. adultery or cruelty have occurred, and the "defendant" does not defend him-/herself (e.g. England and Wales). However, as was a widespread phenomenon of the true fault-era in the different laws of divorce, the problem of asserted grounds for divorce has, in practice, not been resolved. If parties want an immediate divorce, they will usually be successful in convincing the court that serious misconduct has taken place.

Public policy in divorce cases is to save marriages that can be saved, to prevent repudiation, to grant divorce where the marriage has irretrievably broken down, and not to force a spouse to continue marital life with a spouse who is at fault for marital misconduct. For this reason, immediate divorces should not be abolished, even if they are abuse-prone. It then all depends on the standard of proof and the inquisitional powers of the court. Yet, abuses cannot be excluded. Just one look at the French system with its various grounds for divorce shows that also very sophisticated systems are prone to abuses: both divorce by mutual agreement applied for by one spouse and accepted by the other, as well as divorce based on fault under (former) French law seem to virtually invite the parties to advance reasons which do not reflect reality, because in the former case facts must be admitted, without the necessity of evaluating the behaviour of the other party and without the judge examining too thoroughly the reasons advanced; in the latter case divorce is granted immediately, and some say automatically.

Many parties, practitioners and legal scholars advocate a "quick divorce", and indeed there is a high rate of quick divorces.[7] The reasons for this are manifold: either the law allows for a quick divorce as a form of more friendly dispute resolution and especially a cheaper way to dissolve marriages, or a fault ground – e.g. adultery or misbehaviour – is used as a vehicle to obtain a quick divorce, or the inquisitional powers of the court remain unused, or, finally, a (judicial) separation has preceded and facilitates an immediate divorce. Divorce based on faulty behaviour usually leads to a quick divorce, provided the parties both want the divorce and obviously agree upon its terms. Divorce based on fault under French law for example proves to be both quick and popular, although e.g. marital duties must have been seriously or

---

[7] VERSCHRAEGEN, B., Divorce (2004), 1 (76 f) with further references.

repeatedly violated and marital life must, therefore, be unbearable. The success of this ground for divorce may be explained by the fact that judges merely take note of the statements. Under Spanish law for example it seems that judicial separation is regularly sought, because it speeds up the procedure. Such a separation may be applied for by both or either party, and the grounds for separation are manifold. The length as well as the reason for separation may lead to an immediate divorce.

Also *paper divorces* allow for a quick divorce, because no hearings will delay the proceedings. Standard forms are examined in a restrained way and judges know they are dealing with an undefended divorce – e.g. England and Wales, where the so-called "special procedure" as described above has, in practice, been transformed into a very common procedure.

Under Dutch law for example, courts are satisfied that the marriage has broken down, if either spouse has assumed cohabitation with a third person or has lived separately from the other spouse. Lacking a waiting period for the divorce, Dutch law has reduced all the divorce requirements to compliance with the few procedural conditions. In addition, the parties may jointly request that no oral hearing shall take place. Written divorce procedures are well known in Scandinavian countries too, such as Norway and Sweden, where parties can even choose between a judicial and an administrative procedure.

4. POLICY MATTERS

But, many parties, judges and legal scholars are also unhappy with the state of law and the consequences of divorce for families and society. Therefore, some have sought for *explicit and implicit bars* to divorce.[8] Existing laws offer an interesting and varied picture. Several substantive and procedural aspects may constitute bars: (1) strict grounds for divorce coupled with inquisitorial powers of the court (e.g. under German and Spanish law the question of responsibility of a spouse), (2) hardship-clauses (e.g. England and Wales, Germany and France), (3) waiting or separation periods (as in Sweden, Germany and France), (4) mandatory or non-mandatory conciliation or mediation (as in Austria, Norway and Denmark), (5) the need to meet a whole set of procedural requirements (e.g. under French law for a divorce by mutual consent upon joint application, or Swiss law, when the parties seek for divorce by mutual consent), and last, but not least (6) the consequences of divorce in general.

---

8 VERSCHRAEGEN, B., Divorce (2004), 1 (78 f) with further references.

Undefended cases *functionally* are divorces by mutual consent, and so are divorces based on fault, where courts accept the facts alleged by the parties.[9] In reality, practice seems to indicate that spouses who agree on divorce are not likely to opt for grounds for divorce that imply a waiting period. Irretrievable breakdown of the marriage as evidenced by mutual consent to the divorce and its consequences is one of the alternatives offered by German law. In court practice, parties do conclude agreements upon divorce, when they also advance other reasons. This is not necessarily contrary to public policy, as long as all the legal requirements are met. By contrast, spouses may agree upon a divorce and petition for it after a one-year separation period without presenting an agreement. It is questionable, whether this was the objective of the German legislator. Also in Austrian practice, parties may leave the asserted fault grounds undefended and end up with a divorce by mutual consent in the guise of a court decision, leaving it up to the court to decide on the property issues upon application of one party, or, as the case may be, to reach a friendly settlement with regard to the financial aspects.

Public policy which once regarded *agreements* on divorce as a threat to marriage and an example of collusion of the parties has changed radically.[10] Agreements may relate to divorce itself and/or to all or part of the consequences. In the latter case courts in some countries will fill the gaps (e.g. in Spain, the Netherlands, Switzerland and France). Legislators also distinguish between agreements made before marriage, during marriage, on the occasion of divorce or after divorce. A lot could be said about those different types of contracts, but fact is, that there seems to be growing frustration with long-term agreements, because of unforeseeability of changing facts and assumed responsibility related to the time at which the contract was concluded. Some laws provide for an incorporation of the agreement in the decision decree, with the consequence, that the incorporated agreement can only be reviewed under the same conditions as a court decision, which may make it more difficult to achieve modifications in view of the rules on judicial review (e.g. France, Switzerland). Contracts entailing total waivers (regarding spousal support, property, equalization of benefits, inter partes also child support) may at the end of the day not be upheld by the courts – important court decisions e.g. in Germany and Austria illustrate this. But also here, the tendency is, that any agreement resulting in burdening society will not be accepted, this also applies e.g. to the Netherlands.

There is some *divergence* with regard to the fact, that the *"clean-break" principle* is hardly ever observed, for the simple reason that people need support and some

9 VERSCHRAEGEN, B., Divorce (2004), 1 (79 f) with further references.
10 VERSCHRAEGEN, B., Divorce (2004), 1 (80 f) with further references.

valuable on which to subsist.[11] Spousal support upon divorce has in some countries been limited in extent and time (e.g. in the Netherlands, Sweden, Denmark), but at the same time was relabelled compensation payments. The notion of property to be divided has been widened and it has become necessary to take into account equitable standards in order to modify the harsh sanctions of a clear-cut equal division of community property (e.g. under Belgian, Danish, Dutch, German Norwegian and Swedish law).

Further, there seems to be some *divergence* with regard to the *limited adequacy of judicial proceedings in divorce cases.* Mainly for this and for financial reasons mediation and other forms of alternative dispute resolution methods have been developed in different countries. Due to lacking legal quality standards this form of deregulation gradually is turning into a regulated in- or outdoor ADR-procedure, in which it is tried to make the bridge between equality of the parties and equity of the result achieved.

There also is a *growing discussion* on the need of *marriage and divorce counselling,* including *pre-marital education,* on the need of *conciliation periods,* on the need of introducing *legal separation* besides marriage (e.g. in Poland[12]), and to some extent on the need to *restrict divorce when there are children* (USA), because especially in such cases, family members end up poorer than ever before. Statistics show that this concerns mothers and children, but also divorced parties without children. Whether this is due no-fault divorces seems hard to say, same would say yes, others would deny. In Germany for example, fault-based divorce was abolished in 1977 and replaced by the break-down principle, which apparently did not influence divorce statistics, but lead to an increase of proceedings concerning the consequences of divorce, child matters included. Comparative analysis has shown, that parties concerned find ways to get their divorce, if they so wish, with or without consent of the other party. This will probably also be the case in states which have introduced the so-called covenant marriage, such as Louisiana and Arizona, albeit more difficult.

In Western Europe, besides the efforts to *enhance mediation,* there is a certain tendency to *simplify divorce procedures.* France for example modified its law of divorce in 2005;[13] the law reform considers itself as technical support in cases in which

11 VERSCHRAEGEN, B., Divorce (2004), 1 (82 f) with further references.

12 See e.g. KWAK, A., 'Divorce law Reform and public Opinion in Poland: the case of legal Separation', *13 International Journal of Law, Policy and the Family 2* (1999), p. 213–224.

13 E.g. Ch. 'Butruille-Cardew, Reform and European prospects', Eurojuris, Sorrento – April 2004, ED/CBC.

marriage has irretrievably broken down. Child matters are – as in other European countries – regarded as a separate matter. Reform projects also exist in Germany.[14]

Although many European legislators have tried to separate the divorce issue from the consequences of divorce and thus drastically limited the impact of faulty behaviour in the context of the consequences, those parties who loose most on the occasion of divorce claim that serious misconduct in marriage should influence the settlement of the consequences of divorce. Some American and Australian scholars for example would like to counter unilateralism in divorce by empowering both spouses through the requirement of consensual application and consensual settlement agreements, or by recourse to a fault-based settlement in specific cases. This would lead to a system, which only provides for divorce by mutual consent and for faulty divorce, and thus presupposes, basically, equality of the parties concerned. This assumption is not self-evident.

Well, a divorce is more than a divorce and each divorce is different. This also applies to marriage. There are long-term marriages and many marriages are short-term of nature. Even those legislators, like the German one, who really distinguish these various cases, are reviewing their divorce law and more concretely the provisions on spousal support upon divorce and the divorce procedure. Divorce by mutual consent is said to be simplified by providing i.a. a notarial deed, thus excluding a judicial procedure, if the couple has no children. This corresponds to the general trend in Europe, to make divorce proceedings easier, quicker and more efficient.

Having said this, *divergence* prevails with regard to spousal support upon divorce, which is characterized by equity-principles, post-divorce solidarity and elements of compensation or, as the case may be, by a mixture of these guiding principles.[15] The same seems to apply to the division of property, because the property regimes differ from country to country, divorce philosophies differ and exemptions from property division vary. Few European countries provide for the division of pension benefits.

5. SUMMARY

Summarizing, the various ideal models of a family as well as the individual wishes of the parties differ during marriage; legislators leave the couples to a wide extent the freedom to shape their marriage as they wish. However, upon divorce dependent

[14] E.g. Bundesministerium der Justiz – Pressemitteilung vom 15.2.2006 – Familienrecht.

[15] VERSCHRAEGEN, B., Divorce (2004), 1 (83 f) with further references.

parties claim full protection and at the same time their independency is a goal of most legislators and – usually – of all parties who are better off than others.

Although the main trends in Europe, such as rising divorce rates, rising number of single parents, rising frustration about the post-divorce situation as well as growing poorness upon divorce, show considerable *convergence*, substantive and procedural law of divorce and their underlying principles as a reaction to these developments *differ* to a great extent. *Harmonisation* within the European Union may prove to be very difficult, as the legislative reactions and policies in Western European countries do not coincide with those in Middle and Eastern European countries, where the traditional concept of marriage and divorce seems to prevail over the more western-like individualistic approach.[16]

---

16 The Academic Colloquium on Marriage, which took place in Vienna from October 6 until October 7, 2006, organised by L.D. *Wardl* (USA), R. G. *Wilkins* (USA) and myself dealt with "Developments in Marriage and Marital Law in Central and Eastern Europe: Reports, Prospects and Analysis". Selected contributions will be published in Volume 2007 "The Family in the new Millenium", sponsored by The Doha International Institute for Family Studies and Development (FSD).

THE ESTABLISHMENT OF PARENTHOOD: A STORY OF SUCCESSFUL CONVERGENCE?

CAROLINE FORDER AND KEES SAARLOOS

INTRODUCTION

The law on legal affiliation or parentage determines who the legal parents of a child are and how legal parenthood is established and annulled. The law on legal affiliation does not deal with the consequences of the existence of legal affiliation, such as parental responsibility, inheritance and maintenance. Together with the law on marriage, the law on legal affiliation is at the heart of family law in European legal systems, since broadly speaking, marriage and affiliation define the legal family.

Since the national rules on legal affiliation influence the family life of the individuals involved, they have to withstand the scrutiny of Article 8 of the European Convention on Human Rights (hereafter: ECHR) which guarantees the respect for private and family life. In the field of legal affiliation, landmark cases of the European Court of Human Rights (hereafter: the European Court) on Article 8 ECHR, like *Marckx*[1] and *Keegan*,[2] are generally understood to have had a converging effect on the law on legal affiliation in Europe. In this paper we will explore exactly in which matters the European Court has been active and to what extent the European Court's case law leaves room for divergent national laws on legal affiliation.

Our starting-point is the assumption that in order to determine the harmonising effect of the case law of the European Court, one has to analyse to what extent the supranational legal order, in this case Article 8 ECHR as interpreted by the European Court, allows for differences among the national legal systems. The degree of convergence of national laws on legal affiliation is determined by the leeway for which the legal order of the ECHR allows. In order to examine this leeway we will first

1 *Marckx v Belgium*, ECtHR, 13th June 1979, Series A No. 31.
2 *Keegan v Ireland*, ECtHR, 26th May 1995, Series A No. 291.

analyse the differences between national laws regarding legal affiliation. This will involve setting out the whole scope of the law of affiliation. This part draws extensively upon the doctoral thesis currently being prepared by Kees Saarloos, under the working title "Towards European Private International Law on Affiliation". After that, it will be examined which parts of the national laws on legal affiliation are affected by the European Court's case law and which parts are not. In the third part, a conclusion will be drawn regarding the tendency in the law on legal affiliation towards harmonisation or divergence.

1. NATIONAL LAWS ON LEGAL AFFILIATION: HOW DO THEY DIFFER?

1.1. A MODEL FOR THE COMPARISON OF NATIONAL LAWS ON LEGAL AFFILIATION

In this part it will be examined how the national laws on legal affiliation differ in relation to each other. It is submitted on the basis of a study of the national laws on legal affiliation in England and Wales, France, Germany, the Netherlands and Sweden, that the national legal systems in Europe can be analysed with a general model which consists of three layers. The three layers represent the steps a hypothetical legislator would have to take were it to legislate for the first time on the question of legal parenthood. First of all, the hypothetical legislator would have to ask who, in the abstract, should be the parents of the child. At this stage, the ground for legal affiliation is formulated. The reply to the question would probably be something like: in case of natural reproduction the child ideally should be affiliated with his or her genetic parents *but* some interests might require that in a concrete case that this is not the case. The formulation of these interests is the second step. The interests are reflected in the system of establishment and annulment of legal parenthood. Therefore, the second stage is concerned with establishment and annulment of legal parenthood. If the hypothetical legislator has determined the starting-point for a regulation on legal affiliation and if it has determined the interests which, in a concrete case, allow for a deviation from that starting-point, the legislator has to come up with a system to translate the legal reality into tangible evidence, which will probably be a piece of paper (birth certificate, instrument of civil status, judgement and so on) explaining the legal situation. Hence, the third step our hypothetical legislator would have to take is to come up with a system for providing evidence of legal parenthood.

Based on these steps, the first layer of the model is the starting-point or *ground* which a national legislator has taken in its national law on legal affiliation. It will be explained below that most national legal systems have two or three grounds for legal affiliation which apply in carefully-defined circumstances. The second layer is the establishment and the annulment of legal affiliation in a concrete case. It will be explained that there are various methods to establish legal parenthood and that some of these methods allow for a certain possibility that legal parenthood is not established in conformity with the starting-point for legal affiliation in a national legal system. This result can, in certain circumstances, be remedied by an action for annulment of parenthood. The extent to which the mode of establishment of legal parenthood together with the action for annulment of legal parenthood allow for a deviation from the starting-point in a national legal system, reveals the additional interests which the legislature chooses to honour. The legislature can choose to honour public interests such as stability of personal status or the preservation of the traditional family and private interests such as the child's interests or the biological or social parents' interest. The third layer concerns the system of evidence of (legal) affiliation in and out of court. 'Legal' is put between brackets here, because it will be shown that, depending on the relationship between the first and the second layer in a national legal system, one may or may not have to prove legal affiliation or some other kind of affiliation (*e.g.* genetic affiliation).

In the following section, the model will be explained separately for legal maternity and legal paternity. Legal paternity should be understood broadly as the second parent additional to the mother, since for example in Sweden the lesbian partner of the mother can become the child's second mother by means of the Swedish rules on legal affiliation.

It is submitted that the difference between legal systems at the first level results in the most profound differences between national laws on the establishment of parenthood. After all, a difference at the first level means that legal systems differ as to who should be the legal parent of the child *in abstracto*. It will appear that legal systems differ regarding the starting-point of their laws on legal affiliation. Since these differences have been maintained or even reinforced in the course of recent national modifications, it seems that at a national level we are diverging, especially when it comes to the consequences of assisted reproduction.

1.2. GROUNDS FOR LEGAL AFFILIATION

The ground or grounds for legal affiliation in a national legal system are the central idea or ideas around which the rules on legal affiliation are built. It concerns central ideas on who should be the parent of a child for legal purposes. An obvious question is how one finds the ground for legal affiliation in a certain national legal system. Unfortunately no legislator works as systematically as the hypothetical legislator described above. The answer is therefore that it depends on the legal system involved. Sometimes the grounds are stated expressly in the law of the legal system involved, as is done in Sweden for cases involving assisted reproduction. Sometimes the grounds have to be derived from the provisions on judicial establishment of legal parenthood and annulment of legal parenthood, as is the case in France, Germany and the Netherlands. In that case, it is submitted that the fact that has to be proved (*e.g.* genetic affiliation or consent to fertility treatment) in order to establish or annul legal parenthood is the central idea for the purpose of the proposed model. This point needs some further explanation.

How do we know that the central idea of a legal system is found by peeling away the provisions on judicial establishment and annulment of legal parenthood? The answer is that we don't. Concepts like 'starting point' or 'ground' are not used by the respective legislators. The fact that most legislators did not work according to the model which has been described above already indicates that they were probably not aware of something like a ground for legal affiliation and additional interests on the basis of which one can deviate from that ground. They were simply craftsmen taking up their task employing the tools which had been handed down by previous legislators. The central idea or the ground for legal affiliation are concepts which have been invented in order to be able to create a model which fits all the national laws into the present comparison. Consequently, the model only presents a certain perspective on what is out there in the different legal systems on legal affiliation. Although the model does not represent the absolute truth, its formulation is not at all gratuitous. On the one hand, it should fit all the legal systems in order to facilitate the comparison, but, on the other hand, it should give a fair impression of the actual content of the legal systems considered.

1.2.1. Grounds for Legal Maternity

A study of the laws on legal affiliation in England and Wales, France, Germany, the Netherlands and Sweden reveals that there are two grounds for the establishment of legal maternity: childbirth and social affiliation (apparent status or *possession d'état*). Legal systems differ as to which grounds they use and to which situations a certain ground applies.

1.2.1.1. Childbirth

Childbirth is the ground for legal maternity in the case of natural reproduction and assisted reproduction in all legal systems involved. Under Dutch and German law this ground follows directly from the Civil Code itself, which states that the woman who gives birth to the child shall be the child's legal mother.[3] The same holds true for English[4] and Swedish law.[5]

The French Civil Code does not expressly provide who should be the legal mother of the child. It only provides how legal maternity can be established and annulled: legal maternity under French law is defined formally, not substantively. However, it is apparent from the provisions of the Civil Code that the legislative aim is to establish the legal maternity of the woman who gave birth to the child. First, Article 332 French Civil Code states that legal maternity can be annulled if it is proved that the legal mother did not give birth to the child. Second, Article 55 French Civil Code states that the birth has to be declared within three days after the birth of the child, which indicates that the woman who gives birth to the child should be mentioned in the birth register as the child's mother. However, it should be mentioned immediately that the birthmother will not in all cases indeed be the legal mother of the child, as will explained below, at 1.3.

It could be argued that childbirth in fact is not really the essence of the law on legal affiliation. One could argue that in case of natural reproduction legal maternity is based on genetic affiliation and that in case of differentiated maternity, *i.e.* the case where the woman who carries the child is not the child's genetic mother, the legislator based legal maternity on the intention of the birthmother to get the child. However, it turns out that in the legal systems under consideration legal maternity is only based on intention if the birthmother is not the genetic mother of the child. The intention of the genetic mother in such a case is not honoured in any of the legal systems involved, at least not immediately.[6] From the parliamentary history of legislation on parenthood in the last few years in, for example, the Netherlands and Germany, it appears that the rule that the birth mother is always the legal mother is meant to

---

3 Art. 1:198 Dutch Civil Code; Art. 1591 German Civil Code.

4 In case of natural reproduction, or, more specifically, in cases to which the Human Fertilisation and Embryology Act 1990 does not apply, childbirth as a ground for legal maternity follows from the *Ampthill Peerage Case* [1977] A.C. 547, at 577. See also CRETNEY, S.M., et al, *Principles of Family Law* (2003), p. 523. In case of assisted reproduction section 27 Human Fertilisation and Embryology Act 1990 also provides that the woman who gives birth to the child shall be the child's legal mother.

5 Swedish law has no specific provisions on legal maternity in the situation of natural reproduction. It was considered self-evident that the woman who gives birth to the child was the child's mother. The fact that the woman who gives birth to the child is the child's legal mother has to be derived from the Registration Act (*Folkbokföringslag (1991:481)*), which links the registration of parents directly to the birth of the child (Socialstyrelsen, *Att fastställa faderskap*, Stockholm: Elanders Gotab (2005), p. 105). Nowadays Art. 1:7 of the *Föräldrabalk* (1949:381) (Children and Parents Code) provides that if a woman gives birth to a child who has been created with the ovum of another woman, the woman who gives birth to the child shall be considered to be the child's mother.

6 Under English law the genetic mother can acquire parental rights under certain circumstances, but even under English law the guiding rule is that the birth mother is the child's mother (*cf.* Human Fertilisation and Embryology Act 1990, section 27 and 30*ff*).

discourage or ban surrogacy constructions.[7] It seems that the act of giving birth is strongly connected with the idea of maternity and therefore intention is probably not an essential concept in case of legal maternity and assisted reproduction.

1.2.1.2. Apparent Status or Possession d'État

The second ground for legal affiliation is apparent status.[8] The concept of apparent status or *possession d'état* is typical for French law on legal affiliation, but it also exists in other legal systems, such as the Dutch legal system, which have been influenced by French law. *Possession d'état* literally means possession of status. One possesses a certain status by exercising the rights and performing the duties associated with a certain personal status. Here *possession d'état* has been translated as apparent status, since the personal status one possesses is determined by apparent facts. If a child has a certain apparent status, it means that from apparent facts it appears that a certain man or woman is the (legal) father or mother of the child. Such facts are that the child is being raised and supported by the man and the woman, that the child bears their name and that society in general and the administration considers the man and the woman to be the child's legal parents.[9] This is not the place to explain the ins and outs of the concept of apparent status.[10] What is important is that apparent status is not dependent on genetic affiliation: one can have the apparent status of being a certain person's child, without being the genetic child of that person.[11]

Apparent status is only a qualification of a certain fact-pattern and as such the concept is universal. However, the function it has differs among the countries that use the concept. For example, under Dutch law the concept is only used to prevent actions for annulment of legal affiliation.[12] The rationale behind that Dutch rule is that if apparent status indicates that a certain person is the child's legal mother or father, apparently a certain social reality has crystallised and it is deemed undesirable to disrupt that social reality.[13] Under French law apparent status even has the function

---

7 Germany: BR Drucks. 180/96, p. 92 and BT Drucks. 13/4899, p. 82. The Netherlands: Second Chamber, 1995/96, 24 649, nr. 3 (explanatory report), p. 7.

8 Also BÉNABENT, A., *Droit civil la famille*, Litec, Paris, 2001, nr. 580.

9 *Cf.* Art. 311–1 French Civil Code.

10 For an exhaustive explanation of apparent status under French law: MORGAND-CANTEGRIT, V., *La possession d'état d'enfant*, Thèse Université de Lille II Droit et Santé (1993). See also HUET-WEILER, D., 'L'établissment de la filiation par la possession d'état', *Recueil Dalloz Sirey* (1982), 185–192;. RÈMOND-GOUILLOUD, M., 'La possession d'état d'enfant', *Revue Trimestrelle de Droit Civil* (1975), 459–481.

11 *Cf.* MALAURIE, P., FULCHIRON, H., *Droit civil: La famille*, Défrenois, Paris, 2006, p. 387.

12 Art. 1:209 Dutch Civil Code.

13 On apparent status under Dutch law see SAARLOOS, K., 'Bezit van staat of het wormvormige aanhangsel van het Nederlandse afstammingsrecht?' *Weekblad voor privaatrecht, notariaat en registratie* (2006), p. 123–129.

of a ground for establishment of legal affiliation for the same reason; according to the French legislator social reality should be clearly reflected in the legal situation.[14] Therefore, if under French law the apparent status of a child is that he or she is the legal child of a certain woman, that woman is *by dint of that very fact* the child's legal mother, provided that the apparent status has been recorded in an affidavit.[15] On the basis of this assertion it would still be possible to argue that apparent status is only a means of establishing legal maternity. However, legal maternity based on the existence of apparent status cannot be annulled by proving that the legal mother did not give birth to the child: the applicant has to prove that the child's apparent status at the moment legal maternity was established did not indicate that the woman in question was the child's legal mother.[16]

1.2.1.3. The Relationship Between Genetic Affiliation and Apparent Status Under French Law

The fact of coexistence of two grounds for legal maternity under French law, raises the question as to when apparent status is a ground for legal affiliation and when childbirth is such a ground. There is no distinctive fact-pattern for genetic affiliation and apparent status; both can apply in the same case, but not together. This follows from the system of French law on affiliation. Article 310–1 French Civil Code provides that legal affiliation is established by registration, acknowledgement, apparent status or judicial establishment. Apparent status can only serve as a means to establish legal affiliation if the existence of apparent status has been recorded either in an affidavit (Art. 310–1 in conjunction with Art. 317 French Civil Code) or in a judgment (Art. 330 French Civil Code). Legal affiliation based on apparent status can be annulled on the basis of Article 335 French Civil Code, if it has been recorded in an affidavit. According to Article 320 French Civil Code, the establishment of legal affiliation is not possible if legal affiliation with another person already exists. In that case, the first relationship has to be annulled before a new relationship can be established. In other words, it is not possible to establish legal maternity by means of apparent status if the child has been acknowledged by another woman and if

---

14 On the role of apparent status and the importance of 'social affiliation' in French law see Dekeuwer-Defossez, F., et al, *Rénover le droit de la famille: propositions pour un droit adapté aux réalités et aux aspirations de notre temps*, La documentation française, Paris, 1999 and Théry, I., Couple, *filiation et parenté aujourd'hui: le droit face aux mutations de la famille et de la vie privée*, La documentation française, Paris, 1998.

15 Art. 310–1 French Civil Code.

16 Art. 335 French Civil Code. See also Granet-Lambrechts, F., Hauser, J., 'Le nouveau droit de la filiation', *Recueil Dalloz* (2006), p 17–28, at p. 23. However, Massip states that legal affiliation on the basis of apparent status can also be annulled by proving the absence of genetic affiliation (J. Massip, *Le nouveau droit de la filiation*, Défrenois, Paris (2006), p. 57). *Cf.* Malaurie, P., Fulchiron, H., *Droit civil: La famille* (2006), p. 571.

that acknowledgment has not been annulled. This does not mean that apparent status as such cannot exist in such a case. On the contrary, it is possible that woman X first acknowledged the child, but that the child later on develops apparent status with woman Y. In that case, the apparent status does not establish the legal maternity of woman Y. The only consequence is that the acknowledgment of the child by woman X is easier to annul: if the acknowledgment is not in conformity with the apparent status everyone with an interest can apply for annulment of the acknowledgment within ten years of the date of the acknowledgment (Art. 334 French Civil Code). If the acknowledgment is in conformity with the child's apparent status, the acknowledgment can only be annulled upon application by the child, the legal parents or the person who claims to be the child's biological parent. These persons have to apply before the acknowledgment and the apparent status have been in conformity for five years (Art. 333 French Civil Code).

1.2.2. Grounds for Legal Paternity

The grounds for legal paternity are far more complicated to describe than the grounds for legal maternity. First, it is submitted that, in the legal systems which have been examined in this study, there are three grounds for legal affiliation: genetic affiliation, intention and apparent status. However, not only do legal systems differ according to whether or not these grounds are used at all in the laws on legal affiliation, but they also differ as to the situations in which the grounds apply. For example, under most legal systems intention is a ground for legal affiliation if the child has been born as a result of fertility treatment. However, not all legal systems define the scope of application of the rules on legal affiliation in case of fertility treatment in the same way. Moreover, in a model which aims to fit all the legal systems under consideration, it is formally not correct to speak of legal *paternity*. After all, as explained above, under Swedish law the second parent (apart from the mother) can, under certain circumstances, also be female if she is the mother's consenting partner and if the fertility treatment took place within the framework of Swedish law.[17] This paragraph will discuss genetic affiliation and intention as a ground for legal parenthood. Apparent status as a ground for legal paternity will not be discussed here. It is only a ground for legal paternity under French law and the discussion on apparent status as a ground for legal maternity applies equally to legal paternity.

[17] Art. 1:9 Children and Parents Code (1949:381). The possibility for the lesbian partner of the mother to become the child's legal mother has been inserted by Act SFS 2005:434 and entered into force on the 1st of July 2005. On the Swedish law see i.a. JÄNTERÄ-JAREBORG, M., 'Sweden: Lesbian couples are entitled to assisted fertilisation and to equal rights of parentage', *Zeitschrift für das gesamte Familienrecht* (2006), p. 1329–1330.

1.2.2.1. Genetic Affiliation

In the case of natural reproduction, genetic affiliation is the ground for legal paternity in all the five legal systems under consideration. Under English law this proposition follows from the unwritten rules of common law.[18] In the other legal systems the proposition has to be derived from the grounds for judicial establishment and annulment of legal paternity: in case of natural reproduction, all legal systems provide that one has to prove either the existence or the absence (depending on the action) of genetic affiliation.[19]

1.2.2.2. Intention

Intention as a ground for legal affiliation is less straightforward than genetic affiliation. The deployment of intention as a ground implies that intention as such to become the parent of a child is sufficient to actually become the legal parent, without it being possible to annul the legal parenthood on the basis of another ground. Therefore voluntary acknowledgment of paternity in case of natural reproduction in this model is not based on intention, although in most legal systems acknowledgment of paternity only requires that the acknowledger has full legal capacity (as for all legal acts) in order for the acknowledgement to be effective; the validity of the acknowledgment does not depend on the genetic reality. However, it is important that it is at least presumed that the acknowledger is the child's genetic father.[20] This presumption is evidenced by the fact that, apart from cases of assisted reproduction, the acknowledgment can be annulled if it is not in conformity with genetic reality.[21] The fact that the action

---

18 CRETNEY, S.M., et al, *Principles of Family Law* (2003), p. 524; *Halsbury's Laws of England, Children and Young Persons*, Butterworths, London, 2001, par. 93, p. 54.

19 Art. 327 and 332 French Civil Code, Art. 1599 (1) German Civil Code (German law does not specify the ground for judicial establishment of paternity, but it is generally accepted that in case of judicial establishment of paternity under German law, it has to be proved that the respondent is the child's genetic father (Staudinger's Kommentar zum BGB, Part IV/Rauscher, Berlin: Sellier – de Gruyter (2004), p. 474; Münchener Kommentar zum BGB Volume 8/Seidel (2002), p. 224), Art. 1:200 (1), 1:205 (1) and Art. 1:207 Dutch Civil Code and Art. 1:2, 1:4 (3) and 1:5 Swedish Children and Parents Code (1949:381).

20 For the Netherlands see: *Kamerstukken* II 2004/05, 28 457 and 26 672, nr. 23, p. 3; NUYTINCK, A.J.M., 'Het gezag over minderjarige kinderen en de andere levensgezel' *Weekblad voor Privaatrecht, Notariaat en Registratie* (2006), p. 885–888, p. 887; BOER, J. DE, *Asser's Personen en Familierecht*, Kluwer, Deventer, 2002, p. 632; WORTMANN, S., 'Sekseneutraal afstammingsrecht?' *Tijdschrift voor familie- en jeugdrecht* (2001), p. 231–236, p. 235; WILLEMS, A., 'Adoptie door homo-ouders en de positie van de spermadonor' *Tijdschrift voor familie- en jeugdrecht* (2000), p. 226–229, p. 228; VLAARDINGERBROEK, P., 'Adoptie door paren van gelijk geslacht' *Tijdschrift voor familie- en jeugdrecht* (2000), p. 198–202; Rapport Commissie inzake openstelling van het burgerlijk huwelijk voor personen van hetzelfde geslacht, Den Haag, October 1997, p. 7.

21 Germany: Art. 1599 German Civil Code; France: Art. 332 French Civil Code; the Netherlands: Art. 1:205 Dutch Civil Code; Sweden: Art. 1:4 Children and Parents Code (1949:381). In English law acknowledgment of paternity does not exist as such since legal parenthood always exists *ex lege* (see below).

for annulment of acknowledgment is severely restricted under some legal systems does not weaken the point now being made. After all, it is submitted that the restrictions on an action for annulment of acknowledgment are imposed by the fact that in that legal system genetic affiliation is not a goal in itself but merely a starting-point. The establishment of legal affiliation by means of the acknowledgment of parenthood will be explained in more detail below.

Intention within the meaning of this model is the ground for the establishment of legal paternity in case of assisted reproduction in all legal systems under consideration except under Dutch and German law.

Under English[22] and Swedish law[23] the law provides explicitly that intention is a ground for legal affiliation. The fact that intention is a ground for legal paternity under French law has to be inferred from the law on legal affiliation. In particular, it can be inferred from Article 311–20 French Civil Code which explicitly provides that legal paternity cannot be annulled if the legal father consented to the assisted reproduction even if he is not the child's genetic father. Moreover, that article also provides that the man who consented to the assisted reproduction is obliged to acknowledge paternity.

Under Dutch and German law intention as such is not a ground for legal paternity, since the child is able to annul legal paternity if the man is not the child's genetic father, even if the man consented to the fertility treatment. Under these rules only the legal mother and father are barred from applying for annulment of legal paternity if the legal father consented to the assisted reproduction.[24] The reason given for this rule under German law is that the child has a constitutionally protected right to know his or her genetic origins.[25] Under Dutch law it is possible to obtain information regarding one's genetic ancestors without it being necessary to establish legal affiliation with the genetic parents.[26]

There are further indications that intention is not a ground for legal affiliation under Dutch and German law. Under Dutch law, the fact that the acknowledger consented

22 Section 27 Human Fertilisation and Embryology Act 1990.
23 Art. 1:6 and 1:8 Children and Parents Code (1949:381).
24 Art. 1600 (4) German Civil Code; Art. 1:200 (3) and 1: 205 (1) Dutch Civil Code.
25 GERNHUBER, J., COESTER-WALTJEN, D., *Familienrecht*, Verlag C.H. Beck, München, 2006, p. 627.
26 On the right to know one's genetic affiliation under Dutch law: BOER, J. DE, *Asser's Personen en Familierecht* (2002), p. 496; FORDER, C. J., *Legal Establishment of the Parent-Child Relationship: Constitutional Principles in Dutch, English and German Law, having Regard to the European Convention for the Protection of Human Rights and Fundamental Freedoms and Other Applicable Instruments*, Maastricht, 1995, p. 126–139. Independent of the legal affiliation status of the child, the child can obtain information about his or her genetic affiliation under the Donor Information Act 2002 (*Wet donorgegevens kunstmatige bevruchting*, Stb. 2002, 240).

to the assisted reproduction is not, as such, a bar to an application by the child's legal parents for annulment of the acknowledgment. The only ground for annulment of acknowledgment under Dutch law is that the acknowledger is not the child's biological father.[27] This submission should, however, be refined. First, the child's legal parents are only allowed to apply for annulment of acknowledgment if they can show that, at the moment of the acknowledgment, they lacked capacity either to acknowledge or to consent.[28] Moreover, should an applicant actually pass this hurdle, the annulment of acknowledgment against the mother's or child's will would be without effect, since the mother and child have the possibility of reversing the annulment by exercising their right to apply for judicial establishment of legal paternity on the basis of Article 1:207 Dutch Civil Code. So, although the parent's right to apply for annulment of acknowledgment exists if the acknowledger, although not the genetic father of the child, consented to the assisted reproduction, this right is certainly not unconditional.

The fact that intention is not a ground for legal affiliation under German law is furthermore demonstrated by the fact that judicial establishment of paternity on the basis that the man consented to the assisted reproduction is not possible. Only the paternity of the genetic father can be judicially established.[29]

So far we have seen that, under Dutch and German law, intention is not a ground for the establishment of legal affiliation. However, even among the legal systems according to which intention is a ground for legal affiliation, the application of the ground is not the same. Legal systems which use intention as a ground for legal affiliation use it differently. Firstly, the field of application of intention as a ground for legal affiliation differs between countries involved. Secondly, the elements which are required to constitute a valid expression of the intention differ. These differences will be explored in more detail.

A. Definition of the Field of Application of Intention As a Ground for Legal Affiliation

In order to determine the field of application of intention as a ground for legal affiliation the field of application of the rules on the consequences of assisted reproduction for the legal affiliation status of the child must be defined. The reason is that intention as a ground for legal affiliation only exists in cases where the child has been born as a result of assisted reproduction. However, not all the provisions

27 Art. 1:205 (1) Dutch Civil Code.
28 Art. 1:205 (1) under b and c Dutch Civil Code.
29 See note 19.

which have been enacted to regulate the consequences of assisted reproduction can be taken to signify that intention has been accepted as a ground for legal affiliation. We have already shown that under Dutch and German law this is not the case. Accordingly, a definition of the field of application of the national provisions regarding the consequences of assisted reproduction in all the countries under consideration is, strictly spoken, not necessary. However, the scope of application of the Dutch and German provisions on assisted reproduction will be discussed nonetheless, for the sake of completeness.

Under Dutch law, the rule that the consenting husband cannot annul marital paternity (Art. 1:200 (3) Dutch Civil Code) and the rule that the paternity of the consenting partner can be judicially established (Art. 1:207 Dutch Civil Code) applies in all cases where the mother's partner consented to the conception of the child, even if the conception took place naturally. It should be stressed that the provisions are not confined to consent to assisted reproduction. This follows from Article 1:200 Dutch Civil Code which provides that the legal paternity of the mother's husband cannot be annulled if he consented to the act which could have resulted in the procreation of the child and Article 1:207 Dutch Civil Code, which provides that legal paternity can be established on the same basis if the man was the partner of the child's mother at the moment at which he consented.[30]

Under French law, the field of application of intention as ground for legal affiliation is narrower than under Dutch law. It applies to all cases where the child has been born as a result of medically-assisted fertility treatment with donor semen (*procréation médicalement assistée avec tiers donneur*).[31] If the child is not born as a result of fertility treatment with donor semen, genetic affiliation is the ground for legal paternity under French law. Hence, if the child is born after private insemination, *i.e.* without medical assistance, intention will not be a ground for legal affiliation under French law. This does not mean, however, that the private donor cannot, in a concrete case, become the child's legal parent, but it means that the establishment of him as the child's father will be susceptible to annulment.

Although German law does not recognise intention as a ground for legal affiliation, a specific consequence is nevertheless attached to the fact that a child has been born

---

30 'The act which could have resulted in the conception of the child' should be correctly understood. In a decision of the 7th of February 2003 (NJ 2003/358), the Dutch Supreme Court held that the husband who consented to and encouraged his wife to commit acts of prostitution could not annul the relationship of legal paternity between himself and the child born as a result of the prostitution. According to the Supreme Court, the husband consented to an act which could have resulted in the conception of the child.

31 Art. 311–20 French Code Civil.

as a result of assisted reproduction. Article 1600(4) German Civil Code provides that the child's legal father and mother are not allowed to apply for annulment of legal paternity if the legal father consented to the fertility treatment. However, since it is not possible to judicially establish that the consenting partner is the child's father, the field of application is limited to the situation in which the child is born to a married couple or to the situation in which the consenting partner became the legal parent through voluntary acknowledgement of paternity.

English law, moreover, has its own peculiar definition of the scope of application for intention as a ground for legal affiliation. The provisions on the consequences of assisted reproduction on the legal affiliation of the child, contained in the Human Fertilisation and Embryology Act 1990, only apply if the child is born as a result of the placement of an embryo or of sperm and ova in the woman's uterus or as a result of artificial insemination.[32] Moreover, if the treatment is provided to an unmarried couple the rule only applies if the treatment took place in a licenced hospital within the meaning of the Human Fertilisation and Embryology Act 1990.[33] Hence, if the treatment took place abroad and was provided to an unmarried couple, intention cannot provide a ground for legal affiliation. In fact, it will be impossible to establish that the male consenting partner was the father of the child born in consequence of the treatment. Whether genetic affiliation is a ground for legal affiliation in such a case depends on who provided the sperm which was used for the treatment. If the sperm comes from a sperm donor within the meaning of 28(6) Human Fertilisation and Embryology Act 1990 or if the sperm of a deceased person has been used,[34] genetic affiliation is not a ground for legal affiliation and the genetic father cannot be established to be the child's father. As a consequence, the child remains fatherless.[35]

Finally under Swedish law, the demarcation of the scope of application of intention as a ground for legal affiliation depends on whether the consenting partner is male or female. If the consenting partner is male, intention is a ground for legal affiliation if the child is born in consequence of insemination (*insemination*) or fertilisation of the mother's ovum outside her body (*befruktning av moderns ägg utförts utanför hennes*

---

32 Sections 27 and 28 Human Fertilisation and Embryology Act 1990.

33 Section 28 (3) (a) Human Fertilisation and Embryology Act 1990.

34 Post-mortem registration of paternity is only symbolic and does not confer any rights on the child. On the question of post-mortem registration of paternity see Sections 28 (5A) to (5D) and (5I) Human Fertilisation and Embryology Act 1990. On the background of the provisions and the consequence of the registration for the status of the child see the explanatory notes to the Human Fertilisation and Embryology (Deceased Fathers) Act 2003, par. 4. See also LOWE, N., DOUGLAS, G., *Bromley's Family Law*, Oxford University Press, Oxford, 2007, p. 311.

35 See also CRETNEY, S.M., et al, *Principles of Family Law* (2003), p. 526; Lee, R.G., Morgan, D., *Human Fertilisation and Embryology. Regulating the reproductive revolution*, Blackstone, London, 2001.

kropp).[36] However, if the consenting partner is female the treatment must take place within the Swedish legal framework for this kind of treatment if intention is to be treated as a ground for legal affiliation according to Swedish law. As a consequence of the structure of Swedish affiliation law, the female consenting partner can never become the legal parent if the treatment took place outwith the Swedish legal framework.[37]

B. Differences Between National Provisions on the Consequences of Assisted Reproduction

The contents of the provisions on the consequences of assisted reproduction differ considerably. The provisions in the legal systems studied on the consequences of assisted reproduction for legal affiliation are typically built on four variables. These variables are: the partner's consent to the fertility treatment; the relationship between the mother and the consenting partner; the object of the consent; and the causal relationship between the approved treatment and the conception of the child and the spatial reach of the provisions on the consequences of assisted reproduction.

The first variable is the consent. A person who is not the child's genetic parent will only be considered to be the parent if he or she consented to the treatment. However, systems differ as to the formal requirements of the consent and as to events which render the consent ineffective. Most countries do not require any formalities for the consent to be effective. This is the case in England and Wales,[38] Germany[39] and the Netherlands. In Sweden this is only the case in so far as it concerns the mother's male partner.[40] If the consenting partner is female, her consent has to be in writing in order for her to be considered the child's parent.[41] In France, the requirements for a valid consent are more demanding. According to Article 311–20 Code Civil the consenting partner will only be the legal father if his consent has been given before a judge or a civil law notary who has to inform the couple of the legal consequences of the consent.

---

36 Art. 1:6 and 1:8 Children and Parents Code (1949:381).

37 Art. 1:9 Children and Parents Code (1949:381). See also prop. 2004/05:137, p. 44.

38 Cretney, S.M., et al, *Principles of Family Law* (2003), p. 525.

39 Gernhuber, J., Coester-Waltjen, D., *Familienrecht* (2006), p. 628; Staudinger's Kommentar zum BGB, Part IV/Rauscher, Berlin: Sellier – de Gruyter (2004), p. 390.

40 A valid consent only requires that the man is able to determine his will (*e.g.* that he is not mentally ill), Walin, G., *Föräldrabalken och internationell föräldrarätt*, Norstedt, Stockholm, 1996, p. 81.

41 Art. 1:9 Children and Parents Code (1949:381) provides that the female partner of the child's mother is only the child's legal parent if the fertility treatment took place within the framework of the *Lag (2006:351) om genetisk integritet m.m.*. Art. 6:1 and 7:3 *Lag (2006:351) om genetisk integritet m.m.* provides that the consent to the fertility treatment has to be in writing.

Another important aspect of consent concerns the circumstances under which the consent is deemed to be ineffective. Some legal systems have legal provisions which render the consent automatically ineffective. Other legal systems have formal requirements as to how the consent should be withdrawn and before which time. French law provides an example. The consent of one of the partners becomes ineffective if the consenting person dies or if the couple applies for divorce or any other comparable action. Under French law, a person can also withdraw his or her consent, but the withdrawal has to be in writing in order to be valid and the doctor in attendance has to be notified of the withdrawal. Moreover, it follows from Article 311–20 French Civil Code that consent can only be invalidated *before* the treatment takes place. However, Dutch and German law do not contain provisions on these issues.

The second variable is the relationship between the consenting person and the mother. The question is whether there has to be a certain relationship (marriage, partnership etc.) between the mother and the consenting person before the consent of that person can serve as a basis for legal affiliation. All legal systems require that there is a certain relationship between the mother and the consenting person, although English law is ambiguous in this matter. English law provides that, if the treatment takes place out of wedlock, the consenting partner is only the child's legal father if he and the mother received treatment together. 'Receiving treatment together' does not mean that the persons should be married or living together. What it does mean is not entirely clear.[42] In France the couple has to be married or the man and the woman have to live together.[43] The same holds true under the legal system of the Netherlands[44] and Sweden.[45]

The third variable is the object of the consent and the causal relationship between the treatment and the conception of the child. Regarding the object, Dutch law is the only exception to the rule that the man should have consented to fertility treatment. Under Dutch law, consent is a basis for legal affiliation if the husband or the partner consented to the act which could have resulted in the begetting of the child.[46] Under the laws of England and Wales, France, Germany and Sweden the partner has to consent to the fertility treatment.

---

42 There is some case law on the meaning of 'receiving treatment together'. See: LOWE, N., DOUGLAS, G., *Bromley's Family Law* (2007), p. 313. See also CRETNEY, S.M., et al, *Principles of Family Law* (2003), p. 525.

43 Art. 311–20 French Civil Code.

44 Art. 1:200 and 1:207 Dutch Civil Code.

45 Art. 1:6, 1:7 and 1:8 Children and Parents Code (1949:381).

46 See also note 30.

As to the causal relationship between the fertility treatment and the birth of the child in question there is more diversity. Dutch[47] and Swedish law[48] provide that it must be likely that the child was born as a result of the fertility treatment. Neither legal system specifies whether it is possible to prove that the child was not born in consequence of the treatment. English and German law is stricter; the consenting partner is only the child's father if the child was born as a result of fertility treatment to which the father consented. Hence it is possible to prove that the child was not conceived as a result of the agreed treatment.[49] French law provides explicitly that it is possible to prove that the child is not the result of the fertility treatment to which the husband consented.

The fourth variable is probably the most exciting one. It concerns the spatial reach of the provisions regarding the consequences for legal affiliation in the context of assisted reproduction. In most legal systems the rules on the consequences for legal affiliation apply notwithstanding the place where the treatment took place. This is only different for parts of the English and Swedish legal system. It has been pointed out above that under Swedish law the consent of the mother's female partner has to be in writing in order for the provisions on the consequences of assisted reproduction to apply. In fact, Article 1:9 Children and Parents Code (1949:381) provides that the whole treatment has to take place within the framework of the Swedish law on assisted reproduction (*Lag om genetisk integritet m.m.* (2006:351)) for the female partner to be able to become the child's parent. Swedish law even specifies the kind of hospital where the treatment has to take place.[50] It follows that if two Swedish women receive treatment abroad and if the child is born in Sweden, the mother's female partner will not be considered to be the child's mother. A similar provision is found in the English Human Fertilisation and Embryology Act 1990 in relation to the consequences

---

47 Art. 1:200 and 1:207 Dutch Civil Code provide that the man must have consented to the act which *could* have resulted in the conception of the child.

48 Art. 1:6, 1:7 and 1:8 Children and Parents Code (1949:381) provide that it must have been *sannolikt* that the mother's child has been created as a result of the fertility treatment to which the man (or woman) consented. *Sannolikt* more or less means 'likely'. However, the term should be understood in its context. *Sannoligt* is an adjective which indicates the second highest burden of proof. The highest burden of proof is that the one has to prove that something is *utrett* (proven). On the different burdens of proof in Swedish law on legal affiliation see SALDEEN, Å., *Faststellende av faderskap*, Norstedts Stockholm, 1980, p. 55.

49 For English law: *Leeds Teaching Hospital NHS Trust v. A* [2003] EWHC 259 (QB), [2003] 1 FLR 1091. The court held that the husband was not the father, since he could not be taken to have consented to the treatment of his wife, who was – accidentally – impregnated by someone else's sperm. Cited in LOWE, N., DOUGLAS, G., *Bromley's Family Law* (2007), p. 313. For German law see MÜLLER, L., in: HOPPENZ, R., (ed.), *Familiensachen*, C.F. Müller Verlag, Heidelberg, 2005, p. 537. Staudinger's Kommentar zum BGB, Part IV/Rauscher, Berlin: Sellier – de Gruyter (2004), p. 392.

50 Art. 6:2 and 7:4 *Lag (2006:351) om genetisk integritet m.m.*

of assisted reproduction out of wedlock. Section 28(3) of the Act provides that the consenting partner who is not the child's genetic father shall only be the legal father if the fertility treatment was provided for him and the mother together 'by a person to whom the licence applies'. Only institutions established in the United Kingdom can obtain a licence. If the treatment took place abroad, the consenting partner will not be considered to be the child's legal father if he is not the genetic father.[51]

1.2.3. Grounds for Legal Parenthood – Overview

So far we have discussed the grounds for legal affiliation under the laws of England and Wales, France, Germany, the Netherlands and Sweden. For the sake of clarity the following table gives an overview of this examination.

	Legal maternity		Legal paternity (or second mother)	
	Natural reproduction	Assisted reproduction	Natural reproduction	Assisted reproduction[52]
England and Wales	Childbirth	Childbirth	Genetic affiliation	Intention
France	Childbirth Apparent status	Childbirth Apparent status	Genetic affiliation	Intention
Germany	Childbirth	Childbirth	Genetic affiliation	Genetic affiliation
the Netherlands	Childbirth	Childbirth	Genetic affiliation	Genetic affiliation
Sweden	Childbirth	Childbirth	Genetic affiliation	Intention

1.3. ESTABLISHMENT AND ANNULMENT OF LEGAL PARENTHOOD

The previous paragraph has shown what is at the heart of a national system of legal affiliation. It has not shown how a person becomes the child's legal parent. The establishment of legal affiliation is therefore the subject of this third paragraph. The establishment of legal affiliation is also the second layer in the model which we deploy to describe and compare the national laws on legal affiliation. This paragraph aims to describe two things. First, there are four ways of establishing legal parenthood: automatically or *ex lege*; as a result of apparent status; by acknowledgement or by judicial establishment of paternity. Legal systems differ as to which methods they use

---

51 Lowe, N., Douglas, G., *Bromley's Family Law* (2007), p. 314; Lee, R.G., Morgan, D., *Human Fertilisation and Embryology* (2001), p. 221.

52 If the provisions on the consequences of assisted reproduction apply.

and how they use them and it is the aim of this paragraph to analyse these differences. One important difference between *ex lege* establishment of legal affiliation and the other methods has to be mentioned in advance. In case of *ex lege* establishment of legal affiliation the legal affiliation will (almost) always be in conformity with the ground for legal affiliation (the only exception is the *ex lege* establishment of the legal paternity of the mother's husband). For this reason, legal systems provide for systems for annulment of legal affiliation. However, the possibility of applying for annulment of legal parenthood is often not unconditional. Hence, there are two moments in the law on establishment of legal affiliation at which the legislator has to make policy considerations. The first is at the moment at which the legislator has to choose between *ex lege* establishment of legal affiliation, with the certainty that legal parenthood will always be in conformity with the ground for legal affiliation, and any other method of establishment of legal affiliation which does not offer this guarantee. The second important moment for policy considerations is when the legislator has to come up with a system for annulment of legal parenthood. The legislator has to determine to what extent it is acceptable to annul an existing legal relationship which has such a profound impact on the private life of the individuals involved.

The second aim of this paragraph is therefore to give insight into the reasons for deviating from the starting-point for establishing legal affiliation in a national legal system. It will turn out that there are not always very clear policy considerations for a certain regulation. Tradition and the system of law have played an important role in the establishment and annulment of legal parenthood.

Hereafter, the four methods of establishing legal parenthood will be described. It will be explained how they work and how they are applied in the various legal systems. After that, a comparative overview of the legal regulations on annulment of legal parenthood will be presented.

1.3.1. Establishment of Parenthood – Four Methods

1.3.1.1. Ex Lege Existence of Parenthood

Ex lege existence of parenthood means that legal parenthood exists automatically, without any legal action being required to be taken once the requirements are fulfilled as laid down in the law. Characteristic for the existence of parenthood *ex lege* is that the existence of parenthood does not depend on action by one of the persons involved. An example of *ex lege* existence of parenthood is the existence of parenthood under English law. Under English law, the genetic father is the legal father *by dint of being* the genetic father of the child. It is not necessary to establish his paternity. This is also why legal maternity under French law never exists *ex lege*. After all, under French law one must at least mention the mother's name on the birth certificate before she will be considered to be the child's legal mother, which requires an official action (Art. 311–25 French Civil Code). Legal maternity does not exist by dint of birth. The fact that Article 310–1 French Civil Code states that legal affiliation is established by operation of law (*par l'effet de la loi*) does not alter this proposition.[53]

In the case of existence of parenthood *ex lege*, action is only required in order to create proof of the legal situation which has come about automatically; persons involved have to register the child as their own. However, in case of *ex lege* existence of parenthood, the legal parenthood does not depend on the registration; it also exists without the registration.

The consequence of *ex lege* existence of parenthood is that legal parenthood usually corresponds with the national ground of legal affiliation. In the typical case the law will state something like: X is the parent of the child (*e.g.* the woman who gives birth to the child is the child's mother, the man who consents to the artificial insemination is the child's father *etc.*). The consequence of such a system of *ex lege* attribution of parenthood is that a legal system does not provide for a procedure for annulment of parenthood, since there is nothing to annul. This is only different in case of marital paternity, *i.e.* paternity which exists on the basis of marriage of the man with the child's legal mother (see below).

In the countries under consideration we find *ex lege* existence of parenthood at various places in the law. First of all, existence of parenthood under English law is, as has been

---

53 It must be realised that under French law registration is not considered to be a constitutive element of the establishment of legal maternity. In the French perspective legal maternity therefore does not follow from the registration of the mother's name on the birth certificate. It follows from the law, since the law provides explicitly that legal maternity follows from registration (Art. 311–25 French Civil Code). Without that provision, the registration of the mother's name would – according to French law – have no consequence for the legal affiliation of the child. Registration of maternity is therefore from the French perspective not the same as acknowledgment of maternity. In case of acknowledgment of maternity, the legal maternity follows directly from the acknowledgment.
From a comparative perspective however registration and acknowledgment under French law are the same. It does not matter very much whether one says that legal maternity follows from the law, but the law requires registration, or whether one states that the law provides for a possibility of acknowledgment of maternity as a result of which legal maternity is established. In both cases, the existence of legal maternity depends on legal action being taken. However, there is a fundamental difference between the French idea that legal maternity is established by operation of the law if the mother's name is registered as such, and, for example, the Dutch or German idea that even if the mother is not registered, she will be the child's legal mother. This is especially so if one realises that under French law, the registration of the mother's name is at her discretion; it is up to the mother whether or not she wants her name to be mentioned on the birth certificate (Art. 326 French Civil Code).

stated above, always *ex lege*, also if it concerns paternity out of wedlock. Thus under English law the birthmother is automatically the child's legal mother and the genetic father is automatically the child's legal father in cases where the Human Fertilisation and Embryology Act does not apply. If the Human Fertilisation and Embryology Act applies and if the conditions of section 28 of that Act are fulfilled, the consenting partner will automatically be the child's legal father.

How do we know this? It should be noted that under English law parenthood in case of natural reproduction is a matter of common law and as such it has not been codified. Thus, there is no statute which says something like 'the genetic father of the child is his or her legal father'. Moreover, the proposition that parenthood exists *ex lege* is a typical continental way of stating the law. An English lawyer will not use this terminology, because the fact that, for example, legal paternity exists *ex lege*, does not have the consequence that the genetic father will have parental responsibility. Outside of marriage, the fact that the man is the child's genetic father at least has to be registered before he has parental responsibility.[54]

The reason why it is still important to consider the alleged *ex lege* existence of paternity under English law is because continental law makes a clear distinction between, on the one hand, establishment of parenthood and, on the other hand, the consequences of parenthood. The method of establishing legal parenthood is a *big issue* in continental legal systems, judging from the huge piles of legal writing which are dedicated to this issue. The argument for *ex lege* existence under English law goes as follows. Let us take for example section 10 Births and Deaths Registration Act 1953. It provides:

> *Notwithstanding anything in the foregoing provisions of this Act [and subject to section 10ZA of this Act], in the case of a child whose father and mother were not married to each other at the time of his birth, no person shall as father of the child be required to give information concerning the birth of the child, and the registrar shall not enter in the register the name of any person as father of the child except [...].*

The provision provides that the unmarried 'father' of the child will not be registered, unless certain conditions are fulfilled. Obviously one wants to know who is meant with the 'father'. Under legal systems like the French or the German, the word would mean legal father and on the basis of the provisions in the Civil Code one would investigate who is the child's legal father. In case of an unmarried father one will find that there is no legal father, unless someone acknowledged paternity. It follows that continental legal systems put forward a formal concept of legal parenthood: parenthood does not depend on a material fact such as genetic affiliation or intention,

---

[54] Section 4 Children Act 1989 (inserted by section 11 Adoption and Children Act 2002).

but on a formality such as marriage or a formal procedure such as acknowledgment. However, English law does not have such rules.[55] Under English law, parenthood is defined substantively, *i.e.* with reference to material facts. The first sentences in the part on fatherhood from a leading textbook on family law state:

> *With four exceptions, the law recognises the child's biological father as his legal father. First, if the parents are married any child born to the wife is presumed to be the child of the couple.*[56]

The presumption of legitimacy which is mentioned in the citation is only a rule of evidence which is used in court proceedings on legal affiliation. And even in such proceedings it is a very weak presumption. In *Re F (a minor)* it was formulated as follows:

> *That means that the presumption of legitimacy now merely determines the onus of proof. Once evidence has been led it must be weighed without using the presumption as a make-weight in the scale for legitimacy. So even weak evidence against legitimacy must prevail if there is no other evidence to counterbalance it. The presumption will only come in at that stage in the very rare case of the evidence being so evenly balanced that the court is unable to reach a decision on it.*[57]

Formally the presumption of legitimacy also exists in case of registration of paternity, but it is easily rebutted. The Handbook for Registration Officers instructs registration officers as follows:

> *In space 4 the registrar must enter the name and surname (in block capitals) of the father where he is married to the child's mother at the time of the birth. The registrar should ask: 'What was the full name and surname of the child's father at the date of the birth?' When the informant is the mother particular care should be taken to avoid asking for the information by a question such as 'What is your husband's name?'.*[58]

It turns out that if there is a father who has to be registered, it is the genetic father of the child. This becomes very clear if we continue reading the instructions for the registration officer:

> *Under the Perjury Act 1911, a person is guilty of an offence if he/she wilfully gives a false answer to any question put by a registrar of births and deaths relating to the particulars required to*

---

55 For certain specified areas of law, such as nationality law (section 50 (9) British Nationality Act 1981), English law provides for a definition of paternity.

56 CRETNEY, S.M., et al, *Principles of Family Law* (2003), p. 524. See also LOWE, N., DOUGLAS, G., *Bromley's Family Law* (2007), p. 321.

57 [1993] 3 WLR 369, (1993) 143 NLJ 472, [1993] Fam. Law 407.

58 *Handbook for Registration Officers*, p. B2.20–23c, par. 21, 22 (last update 1/1994/P1).

> *be registered, or deliberately gives to the registrar false information about a birth or death, or makes a false statement with the intent to have it inserted in a register of births or deaths. In these circumstances the informant should state the facts which he/she considers to be true, and should not state that the mother's husband is the father of the child if it is known that he could not have been (e.g. by reason of his death or continuous absence from her over a long period). The informant would be committing an offence if he/she gave information for the registration of the birth as that of the child of the mother and her husband knowing that in fact, her husband was not the child's father. But see also para 31a.*[59]

It follows that the presumption of legitimacy has hardly any relevance any more under English law. The above also shows that references to father or mother are apparently references to the father and mother at common law or under the Human Fertilisation and Embryology Act. Hence, at common law and under the Human Fertilisation and Embryology Act, the father and mother are defined substantively (*i.e.* with reference to material facts on which parenthood is based) and not formally (*i.e.* with reference to a certain procedure which has conferred the status of legal parent on the person involved) as is the case under continental law. Consequently, if the method of establishing parenthood under English law has to be qualified, it has to be qualified as existence of legal parenthood *ex lege*.

The consequence of the fact that parenthood exists *ex lege* under English law is that English law does not have a procedure equivalent to the continental procedure of acknowledgment. The registration of paternity under English law strongly resembles acknowledgment of paternity, but it does not create legal affiliation, as continental law acknowledgment does. Moreover, English law also does not have a judicial procedure for establishment or annulment of legal affiliation, since obviously there is nothing to establish or to annul. English law only provides for a procedure to obtain a declaration of parentage, which is enough.[60] Functionally a declaration of parentage is the same as a continental judicial procedure for establishment or annulment of parenthood but again, the big difference is that under continental law those procedures affect the legal reality, while under English law the legal reality remains the same, but its appearance changes. It follows that English law on legal affiliation is based almost exclusively on evidence. This will be discussed more in detail below under 'evidence'.

Parenthood also exists *ex lege* under continental legal systems. Legal maternity under Dutch and German law exists *ex lege*. Under both legal systems, the birthmother is

---

59 *Handbook for Registration Officers*, p. B23-d-31, par. 28 (last update unknown).

60 Section 55A Family Law Act 1986 (inserted by the Child Support, Pensions and Social Security Act 2000).

the legal mother of the child solely by dint of the fact that she gave birth to the child.[61] Under Swedish law it is uncertain whether legal maternity exists *ex lege* or whether it depends on registration. The Children and Parents Code (1949:381) does not give an answer and neither does Swedish literature.[62] Legal maternity under French law does not exist *ex lege*, but depends on the registration of the mother's name on the child's birth certificate.[63]

Another part in the law on legal affiliation where we find *ex lege* existence of parenthood is the rule that the mother's husband is the child's legal father. This rule exists under all legal systems under consideration, except under English law.[64] The reason why the existence of the legal paternity of the mother's husband is *ex lege* is because his paternity does not arise from any action. It only arises from the existence of the legal maternity of the man's spouse and his marriage to her.

From a systematic point of view it is important to realise that a legal system which provides for parenthood existing *ex lege* has one major problem and that is evidence. Although the parents and the child involved acquire their status immediately, they do not immediately have a means to prove their status in society. A registration system generally does not guarantee that the evidence of a legal affiliation (the birth certificate) represents the legal reality. This introduces legal uncertainty in the registers of civil status, something of which especially continental lawyers are not fond. A solution to this problem is to make legal parenthood dependant on an administrative action which produces tangible evidence of the legal relationship it creates. In that case there will be greater certainty that the birth certificate (or any other document meant to prove legal affiliation) correctly represents the legal situation.

1.3.1.2. Establishment of Parenthood by Means of Administrative Action

It is submitted that in every case in which the existence of legal parenthood depends on an official action taken by the persons involved and thus does not exist *ex lege*, it has to be established. Establishment of parenthood can be done by an administrative authority or by a court (judicial establishment of parenthood). Judicial establishment of parenthood will be discussed in the next paragraph.

---

61 Germany: Art. 1591 German Civil Code; the Netherlands: Art. 1:198 Dutch Civil Code.

62 For a discussion of legal maternity in Swedish law see: TOLSTOY KONGSTAD, T., *Mater simper certa est? En discussion kring moderskappresumtionen i svensk rätt och behovet av lagreglering rörande rättsligt moderskap*, Examsarbete Juridiska Fakulteten vid Lunds Universitet, Lund, 2003.

63 Art. 311–25 French Civil Code.

64 Art. 312 French Civil Code; Art. 1592 (1) German Civil Code; Art. 1:199 Dutch Civil Code; Art. 1:1 Swedish Children and Parents Code (1949:381). On the presumption of legitimacy under English law see *supra*.

From the national legal systems under consideration we can derive three kinds of administrative action which establish legal parenthood or which are at least mandatory in order to establish legal parenthood: registration of the parents on the child's birth certificate, acknowledgment of parenthood and the procedure to obtain an affidavit recording to apparent status of the child.

Establishment of parenthood through an administrative action has three important characteristics. First of all, the existence of legal affiliation depends upon the action of the persons involved; no legal relationship exists before the registration or the acknowledgment, unlike in case of parenthood which arises *ex lege*. Secondly, and contrary to *ex lege* existence of legal parenthood, the establishment of legal parenthood through an administrative action immediately creates proof of legal parenthood. It has already been explained above that a system in which the establishment of legal parenthood immediately produces the document which is meant to prove the legal parenthood enhances legal certainty. The final characteristic is the registrar's role in case of registration or acknowledgment. Although the precise function and powers of the registrar vary from country to country, the main task of a registrar is to register the facts declared to him by the persons involved. Unlike a judge, a registrar usually has little power to investigate the truth of the declarations of the persons before him. Notwithstanding the similarities between administrative actions for establishment of legal parenthood, it is important to keep them apart because the rules on annulment of legal parenthood are usually different.

A separate consequence of a system which obliges persons to establish legal affiliation is that such a system allows for more flexibility. By disconnecting the grounds for legal affiliation from the process of establishment of affiliation, a legal system has the possibility to create rules which allow deviation from the grounds of legal affiliation. Under French law for example, legal maternity does not exist *ex lege*, but it depends on the registration of the mother's name on the child's birth certificate.[65] The mother is however not obliged to register her name; she has the right to give birth anonymously (*accouchement sous X*).[66] Since the whole idea of anonymous birth is that the birthmother does not become the child's legal mother, it makes sense that a legal system does not provide for *ex lege* existence of legal maternity, if it wants to grant women the right of anonymous birth and thus wants to allow a certain flexibility as to the ground for legal affiliation (*i.e.* childbirth).

In the legal systems under consideration, only French law requires registration in order to establish the existence of parenthood. Also the procedure to obtain an affidavit

65 Art. 311–25 French Civil Code.
66 Art. 326 French Civil Code.

which records the apparent status of the child only exists in France,[67] and therefore it will not be discussed extensively here.

The third administrative procedure to establish legal parenthood is acknowledgment. Acknowledgment of parenthood exists under all legal systems under consideration, except under English law.[68] The English functional equivalent of acknowledgment – registration of the unmarried father – will be discussed under the heading of evidence. The common ground in the institutions of *Anerkennung*, *reconnaissance*, *erkenning* and *bekräftelse* is that they are considered a legal act within their legal system (*Rechtsgeschäft*, *acte juridique*, *rechtshandeling*, *rättshandling*), meaning that legal parenthood is established by virtue of an expression of the acknowledger's will, manifest in a legal act. The fact that the validity of the acknowledgment depends on the acknowledger's will does not mean that intention is the ground for legal parenthood that follows from the acknowledgment. An acknowledgment raises a presumption that the acknowledger is the genetic father or – depending on the legal system involved – the consenting partner. This is shown by the fact that acknowledgment can be annulled if the acknowledger is not the genetic father or the consenting partner. The acknowledger's will has nothing to do with the substantive aspects of the acknowledgment; it is only a formal part of the acknowledgment. The importance of the acknowledger's will is the result of the systems of law in which the acknowledgment exists. Dutch, French, German and Swedish civil laws are built around the concept that legal consequences follow from a legal act, which, in order to be valid, has to be the expression of the will, which at its turn must have been formed freely. If the will is defective because of threat, mistake or deceit the legal act is null and void and if the legal act is valid it can be annulled in the way prescribed by law.[69] It is submitted that the importance of the acknowledger's will in civil law systems is a consequence of the nature of the legal system where it is used: the continent had a system of civil law which was built around the concept of legal act and the system to establish legal parenthood had to fit in that system.

An important consequence of acknowledgment as a system for attribution of legal parenthood is that legal parenthood can exist even if it is not in conformity with the ground for legal parenthood in the legal system involved, because the validity of the acknowledgment does not depend on the substantive truth, but on its formal validity. The degree to which this is considered to be a problem varies from country to country: in Sweden the discrepancy between the existence of legal parenthood and the ground

67 Art. 317 French Civil Code.

68 Art. 1594 – 1598 German Civil Code; Art. 316 French Civil Code; Art. 1:204 Dutch Civil Code; Art. 1:4 Swedish Children and Parents Code (1949:381).

69 Some legal systems provide that annulment of acknowledgment because of a defective will is not possible. However, that is then an exception to the general rule that legal acts can be annulled because of a defective will.

upon which it is founded was considered unacceptable and therefore Swedish law provides for a system in which an acknowledgment cannot be valid without the consent of the *Socialnämnd* (social welfare commission). The *Socialnämnd* will only consent to the acknowledgment if it is convinced that the acknowledger is the child's genetic father (or if he consented to the fertility treatment).[70] At the other side of the spectrum is French law which does not have any problems with substantive truth. Also under French law, acknowledgment of paternity raises the presumption that the man is the child's genetic father, but no one will check the truth. After a certain period of time it even becomes impossible to apply for annulment of acknowledgment.

1.3.1.3. Judicial Establishment of Parenthood

Judicial establishment of parenthood is a judicial procedure by which the court establishes legal parenthood upon proof of the existence of a ground for legal affiliation (genetic affiliation, intention or apparent status).[71] Judicial establishment of parenthood is only possible if the child does not yet have a parent from both sexes (or under Swedish law, if the lesbian partner did not acknowledge maternity). Therefore judicial establishment of legal maternity is not possible in countries in which legal maternity exists *ex lege*. Since judicial establishment of parenthood creates a legal relationship, a declaration of parentage under English law is not judicial establishment of parenthood although it is its functional equivalent. Declarations of parentage will be explained under the heading of evidence.

The characteristics of judicial establishment of parenthood are the inverse of establishment of parenthood by an administrative action. So, it is pretty sure that parenthood will only be attributed in conformity with the ground for legal parenthood. Moreover, the national authority involved has extensive competence to investigate whether the applicant or the respondent is the child's father or mother.

Legal systems on judicial establishment of parenthood differ in various respects. The most important difference concerns the rules on the use of DNA evidence. This will be discussed below under evidence. Other differences concern the exceptions to the ground of legal affiliation, the *locus standi* and the statutory periods of limitation.

A. Exceptions to the Grounds of Legal Affiliation

The general rule under the legal systems under consideration is that the court will establish legal parenthood if the existence of a ground for legal affiliation is proven. Hence, the establishment of the spermdonor as a parent is prohibited under all legal

---

[70] Art. 1:4 Swedish Children and Parents Code (1949:381).

[71] Art. 1600d German Civil Code; Art. 325 – 331 French Civil Code; 1:207 Dutch Civil Code; 1:5 Swedish Children and Parents Code (1949:381).

systems except under German law.[72] There are a couple of exceptions to this rule. First of all, regarding Dutch law it has been stated that only genetic affiliation is a ground for legal affiliation. However, according to Article 1:207 Dutch Civil Code, the man who consented to the act which could have resulted in the procreation of the child can also be established to be the child's father, if he was the mother's partner. This provision should be considered together with the provision that under Dutch law only the child and the mother can apply for judicial establishment of paternity. The reason for this rule is primarily to protect the mother's interest: it was deemed unacceptable that if the mother and her partner decided to obtain fertility treatment with donor semen, the partner could escape his responsibilities by not acknowledging paternity. Also the child's interest in having a legal father played an important role. The establishment of the legal paternity of the anonymous sperm donor is for the same reason prohibited under Dutch law.[73] While, on the one hand, the interests of the mother and child are honoured by giving them a possibility to apply for judicial establishment of paternity, the consenting partner's interest (*i.e.* his intention to become the legal parent) is, on the other hand, not protected, which indicates that intention is still not a ground for legal affiliation under Dutch law. After all, in case of marital paternity the legal presumption of paternity in favour of the mother's husband is susceptible to annulment on application by the child[74] and in case of assisted reproduction out of wedlock the consenting partner can only establish that he is the child's father with the mother's consent.[75]

---

72 English law: Section 28 (6) Human Fertilisation and Embryology Act; French law: Art. 311–19 French Civil Code; Swedish law: Art. 1:5 Swedish Children and Parents Code (1949:381). Dutch law see note 73 below. German law: BT Drucks. 12/2091, in which the government answers the question to what extent the anonymity of the sperm donor is protected. See also Münchener Kommentar zum BGB Volume 8/Seidel (2002), p. 69.

73 Under Dutch law one can only judicially establish the legal paternity of the consenting partner or the begetter. The anonymous sperm donor is neither of these two persons. See also BOER, J. DE, *Asser's Personen- en Familierecht* (2002), p. 499.

74 Art. 1:200 (1) Dutch Civil Code.

75 Under Dutch law, legal paternity of the consenting partner can be established by means of acknowledgment of paternity and by means of judicial establishment. The consenting partner has no standing to apply for judicial establishment of his legal paternity (Art. 1:207 Dutch Civil Code) and acknowledgment of paternity requires the mother's consent (and the child when the child has reached the age of twelve) (Art. 1:204 (1) under c and d Dutch Civil Code). If the man is the begetter of the child, he can apply for substitution of the mother's consent on the basis of art. 1:204 (3) Dutch Civil Code, if she refuses to consent to his acknowledgment. However, the consenting partner is usually not the begetter of the child, since the begetter is the man who begot the child via sexual intercourse. Consequently, the consenting partner has no direct right of action under the Civil Code to apply for substitution of the mother's consent. So far the Dutch Supreme Court has not had the opportunity to pass judgement upon the legality of this situation. In a case where a sperm donor (also not a begetter) applied for substitution of the mother's consent, the Dutch Supreme Court held that the mother's consent could only be substituted by judicial consent if the donor could show that the mother's refusal amounted to an abuse of her right to give consent (HR 24th January 2003, NJ 2003/386). An important difference between the sperm donor and the consenting partner is that the former, but not the latter, is the child's genetic father.

The second exception to the rule that legal parenthood will be judicially established if the existence of a ground for legal affiliation is proved is that under Dutch and French law the establishment of legal affiliation with both parents is not possible in case of an incestuous relationship between the father and the child's mother.[76] Under those legal systems it is deemed not to be in the child's interest to have the incestuous relationship recognised in law.[77]

B. LOCUS STANDI

The right to apply for judicial establishment of parenthood is restricted under all legal systems under consideration. The reason to restrict the *locus standi* of this action is its personal nature. Within the legal systems involved, there are two groups of persons who have standing: the persons directly involved (the child, the mother and the father) and their heirs.

With regard to the *locus standi* of the persons who are directly involved in the action, most legal systems provide an unrestricted right for the child and a restricted or dependant right for the mother. Only under German law do the child, the mother and the alleged father have the right to apply for judicial establishment of paternity on an equal footing.[78] Under Dutch law the child has an unrestricted right to apply for judicial establishment of paternity, but during the child's minority he or she is represented by a special representative (*bijzondere curator*).[79] The mother's right to apply for judicial establishment is restricted by a statutory period of limitation: she has to apply within five years from the child's birth or within five years from the moment at which she knows who the begetter of the child is.[80] Under French law, only the child has the right to apply for judicial establishment of maternity or paternity.[81] However, during the child's minority only a person established to be a legal parent of the child has the right to apply on the child behalf.[82] Swedish law provides more or less the same. The child has the right to apply for judicial establishment of paternity, but during the child's minority the *Socialnämnd* or the mother have the right to exercise the right.[83] Since it will be argued below that the English declaration of

---

[76] Art. 1:207 (2) under b Dutch Civil Code; Art. 310–2 French Civil Code.

[77] France: DEKEUWER-DEFOSSEZ, F., et al, *Rénover le droit de la famille: propositions pour un droit adapté aux réalités et aux aspirations de notre temps* (1999), p. 45. The Netherlands: Second Chamber, 1995–96, 24 649, nr. 3, p. 19 (explanatory notes).

[78] Art. 1600[e] German Civil Code. See also Staudinger's Kommentar zum BGB, Part IV/Rauscher, Berlin: Sellier – de Gruyter (2004), p. 525.

[79] Art. 1:212 Dutch Civil Code.

[80] Art. 1:207 (3) Dutch Civil Code.

[81] Art. 325 and 327 French Civil Code.

[82] Art. 328 French Civil Code.

[83] Art. 3:5 Swedish Children and Parents Code (1949:381).

parentage is the functional equivalent of judicial establishment of parenthood, it is worth mentioning that under English law everyone with sufficient personal interest can apply for a declaration of parentage.[84]

The second group which has *locus standi* to apply for judicial establishment of parenthood are the heirs of the persons who are directly involved and who have a right to apply. Under German and Swedish law the heirs or the descendants do not have a statutory right to apply for judicial establishment of paternity after the child's death. Under Dutch law however, the descendants in the first degree (*afstammelingen*) of the child (X) are allowed to apply for judicial establishment of the fact that a man (Y) is the father of their deceased parent (X). However, their right is restricted: they only have that right if the alleged father (Y) is still alive and on condition that the right is exercised within one year after learning of the death of their parent (X).[85] The mother's descendants have no such right. Under French law, more or less the same rule applies. Not, as in Dutch law, the descendants, but the broader group of heirs have the right to exercise the right to apply for judicial establishment of paternity if the deceased died before expiry of the statutory period of limitation.[86] For judicial establishment of parenthood this means that the X's heirs can apply for judicial establishment of Y as X's father, if X died before the ending of the statutory period of limitation, which is ten years after X has come of age in case of judicial establishment of parenthood.[87]

C. Statutory Periods of Limitation

In general the right to apply for judicial establishment of parenthood is not restricted in time, certainly not for the child. This is only different under French law where the child has to apply within ten years after he or she has come of age.[88] Moreover, under Dutch and Swedish law the mother's right (and the *Socialnämnd*) is restricted in time. Under Dutch law, the mother has to apply within five years after she becomes aware of the identity of the begetter[89] and under Swedish law the *Socialnämnd* and the mother can only apply during the child's minority.[90] Under German law, the right to apply for judicial establishment of paternity is not restricted in time for any of the applicants. Even after the child has come of age, the alleged father and the mother have a statutory right to apply for judicial establishment of paternity.[91]

84 Section 55a (3) Family Law Act 1986.
85 Art. 1:207 (4) Dutch Civil Code.
86 Art. 322 French Civil Code.
87 Art. 321 French Civil Code.
88 See note 87.
89 See note 80.
90 See note 83.
91 Staudinger's Kommentar zum BGB, Part IV/Rauscher, Berlin: Sellier – de Gruyter (2004), p. 530.

1.3.1.4. Annulment of Parenthood

Annulment of legal parenthood is a mechanism which provides for the possibility to bring legal parenthood in conformity with the grounds for legal affiliation.[92] Therefore, procedures for annulment of legal parenthood only exist in legal systems which have a system of attribution of parenthood which does not guarantee that legal parenthood is in conformity with the grounds for legal affiliation. Annulment of parenthood which exists *ex lege* is usually not possible. The only exception to this rule within the systems under consideration is the procedure for annulment of paternity arising from the presumption of paternity by dint of marriage with the child's mother.

Procedures for annulment of legal parenthood are always restricted and there are a lot of possible restrictions: *locus standi*, statutory periods of limitation and additional requirements such as lack of capacity at the moment of acknowledgment or the absence of apparent status. Also the rules on evidence restrict the possibility of annulling legal parenthood under certain legal systems. Reasons which have been advanced for these restrictions are: the protection of the legal family or the private life of the persons directly involved (restrictions on *locus standi*); stability of the legal affiliation status of the child (statutory periods of limitation, existence of a lack of capacity at the moment of acknowledgment) and preservation of *de facto* family or of social reality (requirement of the absence of apparent status). These reasons will be discussed in more detail below. Here, it should be noted, in the light of the discussion on Article 8 ECHR below, that these reasons or *interests* can be formulated as public and private interests. For example, the reason for statutory periods of limitation usually is to protect the stability of the legal affiliation status. Stability of affiliation status is in the state's interest, in particular in the maintenance of a reliable state administration, but it is also in the child's interest because the development of a close personal relationship is supported by the measure. It will be explained below that when, in a concrete case, certain restrictions do not protect any private interest any more – for example, all the parties directly involved agree that notwithstanding the expiration of the statutory period of limitation the legal paternity should be annulled – it is more likely that the restriction will violate Article 8 ECHR.

Before we embark on a detailed analysis on the provisions on annulment of legal parenthood, two preliminary remarks on the structure of these provisions have to be made. First, in most cases annulment of legal parenthood can only be done by a court; one needs to follow a judicial procedure. However, under certain circumstances some legal systems allow for administrative annulment of parenthood. Second, some

[92] This paragraph does not deal with the possibility which exists in France to declare an acknowledgment null and void because of a defective will.

legal systems have a provision for annulment of parenthood which applies to all forms of establishment of legal parenthood but there are also legal systems which have separate provisions for the annulment of legal parenthood according to the form of establishment. In the following analysis judicial procedures for annulment of parenthood will first be discussed, followed by the administrative procedures. The legal systems under consideration do not provide for a possibility to annul legal parenthood which is based on judicial establishment. The possibility to set aside judicially established legal parenthood in a revision procedure falls outside the scope of this article.

A. Judicial Annulment of Legal Parenthood

Judicial annulment of maternity is only possible in France. Under Dutch, English and German law legal maternity exists *ex lege* and therefore annulment of legal maternity is not possible. It is possible under these legal systems that another woman than the birthmother is registered on the birth certificate and there are procedures to change the birth certificate in such a case. However, those procedures are not procedures for annulment of legal maternity. They only concern the registration of legal maternity and therefore they will be discussed under the heading of evidence. The procedure for annulment of legal maternity in France is the same as for legal paternity, so no separate reference will be made as to whether the procedure concerns the mother or the father.

The ground for annulment of legal parenthood in all legal systems is that legal affiliation does not correspond with the ground for legal affiliation which applies in the situation at hand.[93] So, the ground for annulment of legal paternity in Germany and the Netherlands is that the legal father is not the genetic father of the child. In Sweden the grounds are that the man is not the genetic father or that the parent did not (validly) consent to the fertility treatment. In France, one adds the absence of apparent status.[94] This paragraph will mainly focus on the different restrictions which are imposed on the possibility to apply for judicial annulment of parenthood. They are discussed under the headings of apparent status, *locus standi* and statutory periods of limitation. However, we will start with a separate discussion of the list of additional restrictions on the possibility to apply for annulment of legal paternity which only exist under Dutch law.

---

93 See § 1.2. Grounds for legal affiliation. See note 19 for an overview of the national provisions on annulment of legal parenthood.

94 Art. 335 French Code Civil.

B. Restrictions on Judicial Annulment of Paternity Under Dutch Law

Apart from the restrictions on annulment of legal paternity which will be discussed under the following headings, Dutch law contains a set of restrictions which are not found in the other legal systems. It concerns restrictions on the possibility to annul marital paternity and paternity established by means of acknowledgment of paternity.

The legal parents cannot annul marital paternity under Dutch law if the man knew before the marriage that the woman was pregnant[95] or if the man consented to the act which could have resulted in the procreation of the child.[96] These exceptions do not apply if the woman has deceived the man as to who has conceived the child.[97] The *raison d'être* of the consent-exception has already been discussed above.[98] The reason behind the first exception is that, according to Dutch law, marriage with a pregnant woman is considered a tacit acknowledgment of paternity.[99] This somewhat archaic justification also explains the exception to the exception: if the woman deceived her husband as to the paternity of the child he would probably not have married her in the first place (continuing the archaic line of reasoning), so he should at least be allowed to annul his paternity. Although the justification does not sound ultra modern, one has to point to the similarity with acknowledgment of paternity, which is also very hard to annul.[100]

The deceit-exception also applies to the consent-exception. Therefore, if the married couple agrees that the woman will have sexual intercourse with X in order to get a child, but secretly the woman has intercourse with Y, the husband is allowed to apply for annulment of his paternity.[101]

Also with regard to annulment of acknowledgment of paternity Dutch law provides for additional requirements. First of all, Article 1:205 (1) Dutch Civil Code provides that the child can only apply for annulment of legal parenthood on the basis of

---

95 Art. 1:200 (2) Dutch Civil Code.

96 Art. 1:200 (3) Dutch Civil Code.

97 Art. 1:200 (4) Dutch Civil Code.

98 § 1.3.1.4. a. Exceptions to the grounds of legal affiliation.

99 Art. 1:200 (2) Dutch Civil Code is almost a literal copy of Art. 314 French Civil Code 1804. The reason for this article is formulated as follows: "*On présume alors qu'il n'a contracté le mariage que pour réparer sa faute personnelle ; on présume qu'un pareil hymen n'eut jamais été consenti, s'il n'eût persuadé que la femme portait dans son sein le fruit de leurs amours : et lorsqu'il a eu dans la conduite de cette femme une telle confiance qu'il a voulu que leurs destinées fusses unies, comment pourrait-on l'admettre à démentir un pareil témoignage?*" (Motifs des lois du code civil des français, promulguées en l'an XI et l'an XII, Tome Premier, De l'imprimerie nationale (Paris, an XII, 1804), p. 147).

100 Boer, J. de, *Asser's Personen- en Familierecht* (2002), p. 507.

101 *Cf.* Boer, J. de, *Asser's Personen- en Familierecht* (2002), p. 509.

acknowledgment if the acknowledgment took place during his or her minority. If the acknowledgment took place during the child's minority, the child can apply without further restrictions for annulment of legal parenthood within the prescribed period of limitation (see next paragraph). If the acknowledgment took place after the child has come of age, the child has no right to apply for annulment of legal paternity at all. The legal parents can only apply for annulment of legal parenthood based on acknowledgment if the acknowledgment or the consent to the acknowledgment has come about under the influence of threats, mistake, deceit or, if the acknowledgment was done during the minority of the acknowledger or the mother, undue influence (*bedreiging, dwaling, bedrog of misbruik van omstandigheden*). The reason is that the establishment of legal affiliation was not considered something which the persons involved should be able to dispose of at will.[102]

C. Judicial Annulment of Legal Parenthood and Apparent Status

The meaning of apparent status has already been explained briefly above.[103] It has also been explained that the function of apparent status is diverse. Under French law, it is, for example, a ground for legal affiliation, but the concept is also used for other purposes under French and Dutch law. Under both legal systems the existence of apparent status in conformity with the title of legal affiliation (*i.e.* the birth certificate or the instrument of acknowledgment of parenthood) limits the possibility of annulling legal affiliation. Thus under Dutch law legal affiliation can only be annulled if the child has apparent status with regard to the parent who is mentioned on the birth certificate.[104] This provision has potentially far-reaching consequences, although it is hardly used in practice. Article 1:209 Dutch Civil Code means for example that if a child develops apparent status with regard to the husband before the expiry of the statutory period of limitation in Article 1:200 Dutch Civil Code, the husband will not be able to apply for annulment of the paternity established by the presumption based on marriage to the child's mother. Even if the wrong mother is registered on the birth certificate and if the child develops apparent status with regard to her, it is not possible to correct the birth certificate! The reason for this provision is that established social relations should not be disrupted.[105]

Under French law the coexistence of apparent status with the title of legal affiliation has as a consequence that the statutory period to annul the legal affiliation which exists on the basis of the title shortens and that the *locus standi* is more limited. Thus, Article

---

102 Second Chamber, 1995/96, 24 649, nr. 3 (explanatory report), p. 10.
103 § 1.2.1.2. Apparent status or *possession d'état.*
104 Art. 1:209 Dutch Civil Code.
105 See note 13.

333 French Civil Code provides that if the apparent status is in conformity with the title of legal affiliation, only the child, the legal parents and the alleged parents are allowed to apply for annulment of legal parenthood which is based on that title (*i.e.* a registration or an acknowledgment). Moreover, the above-mentioned persons have to act within 5 years after the apparent status has ceased to exist and before the apparent status and the title have coexisted for 5 years. If the title is not supported by apparent status, everyone with an interest is allowed to apply for annulment of legal parenthood within ten years after the title has been established.[106]

D. Locus Standi

Another important restriction on the possibility of annulling legal parenthood is the presence or absence of *locus standi*. The main reason in all legal systems to provide for a restriction on the *locus standi* for annulment of legal parenthood is the protection of the legal family and the private life of the members of that family.[107] This common idea does not prevent the legal systems involved from coming up with different regulations. Especially the right of the biological parent who is not the child's legal parent to apply for annulment of legal parenthood differs considerably. A second issue regarding *locus standi* is the right of the heirs to apply for annulment on behalf or in the place of a deceased relative and the right of the public prosecutor to intervene on behalf of the public interest.

Under German law, the child and the legal parents have the right to apply for annulment of legal paternity.[108] As will be explained below, the applicants' rights are not unrestricted: they are limited in time and the legal parents are not allowed to apply for annulment of legal paternity if they have consented to the assisted reproduction treatment.[109] The latter reason has been inserted by the *Kinderrechtverbesserungsgesetz* 2002. Notwithstanding German reluctance to allow assisted reproduction, the legislator wanted to provide for a minimum regulation to protect the child who has been conceived following fertility treatment with donor semen.[110] Besides the members of the nuclear family also the alleged genetic father has a limited right to apply for annulment of legal paternity, following a decision of the German Constitutional Court in 2003.[111] The right of the alleged genetic father is restricted though,

---

106 Art. 334 French Civil Code.

107 Germany: Münchener Kommentar zum BGB Volume 8/Seidel (2002), p. 171; France: MASSIP, J., *Le nouveau droit de la filiation*, Defrénois, Paris, 2006, p. 64; The Netherlands: Second Chamber, 1995–1996, 24 649, nr. 3, p. 18 (explanatory notes); Sweden: SINGER, A., *Föräldraskap i rättslig belysning*, Iustus Förlag, Uppsala, 2000, p. 167.

108 Art. 1600 (1) German Civil Code.

109 Art. 1600 (4) German Civil Code.

110 BT Drucks. 14/2096, p. 7.

111 BVerfG, 1 BvR 1493/96 of 9.4.2003.

in order to protect legal certainty and the legal family.[112] Article 1600 (2) German Civil Code provides that the alleged genetic father is only allowed to apply for annulment of legal paternity if there is no social family relationship (*sozial-familiäre Beziehung*) between the legal father and the child. Such a relationship is presumed to exist if the legal father has brought the child up and if the legal father lived or lives together with the legal mother and child.[113]

French law has a separate regulation for annulment of legal affiliation which exists *ex lege* (*i.e.* marital paternity), either, on the one hand, on the basis of registration or acknowledgment, or, on the other hand, legal affiliation which exists on the basis of apparent status recorded in an affidavit. *Locus standi* for annulment of legal parenthood which exists *ex lege* or on the basis of registration or acknowledgment is more or less the same as under German law, but in French law there seem to be fewer problems in accepting the right of the alleged parent (father or mother) to apply for annulment of parenthood. Under French law the *locus standi* depends on whether the title for legal affiliation (*i.e.* the birth certificate or the instrument of acknowledgment) is supported by apparent status or not. If the title is supported by apparent status, which is usually the case, only the child, the legal parents and the alleged parents have the right to apply for annulment of parenthood.[114] If the legal affiliation which is based on registration or acknowledgment is not supported by apparent status, the legal affiliation can be annulled by everyone with sufficient interest.[115] *Locus standi* to annul legal affiliation which exists on the basis of apparent status recorded in an affidavit can be annulled by everyone with sufficient interest.[116]

Under Dutch and Swedish law the alleged parent is not allowed to apply for annulment of legal parenthood, although under Dutch law there is a possibility to circumvent this rule under certain circumstances. Under Dutch law, only the legal parents and the child have a statutory right to apply for annulment of marital paternity[117] or paternity which exists on the basis of acknowledgment.[118] Nonetheless, the biological father has a possibility to set aside the acknowledgment by another man under certain circumstances. In that respect one has to distinguish the case in which the biological father is the begetter of the child from the case in which he is the sperm

112 BT Drucks. 15/2253, p. 11.
113 Art. 1600 (3) German Civil Code.
114 Art. 333 French Code Civil.
115 Art. 334 French Code Civil.
116 Art. 335 French Code Civil.
117 Art. 1:200 (1) Dutch Civil Code. For limitations on the right of the legal parents to annul legal paternity see § 1.3.1.4.b. Restrictions on judicial annulment of paternity under Dutch law.
118 Art. 1:205 (1) Dutch Civil Code. For limitations on the right of the legal parents to annul legal paternity see § 1.3.1.4.b. Restrictions on judicial annulment of paternity under Dutch law.

donor. If the begetter wants to acknowledge paternity and if the mother refuses to consent, he can apply for judicial consent which will replace the consent of the mother.[119] He will obtain judicial consent, unless it is shown that the establishment of his paternity is detrimental to the child's interests. Emotional resistance on the mother's part is not enough to refuse the begetter judicial consent.[120] It is however possible that the mother consented to the acknowledgment of the child by another man. In that case the Dutch Supreme Court decided that the begetter's possibility to set aside the acknowledgment depends on whether the mother allowed the begetter the possibility to apply for judicial consent.[121] If that is the case, *i.e.* if the begetter had enough time to apply for judicial consent following the refusal of the mother to consent, the court will only set aside the acknowledgment of the other man if the begetter shows that the mother's consent was given with no other reason than to harm the begetter's interests. If the mother did not allow the begetter enough time, the court will set aside the acknowledgment if the begetter shows that the mother could not have reasonably consented to the acknowledgment, taking into account the begetter's interests. There is no case law on the question whether the biological father has a possibility to set aside an acknowledgment, in the situation that the genetic father is not the child's begetter but the sperm donor.[122]

Under Swedish law only the child and the legal father have the right to apply for annulment of marital paternity.[123] Swedish law does not have statutory provisions on *locus standi* for annulment of acknowledgment, but is generally accepted that only the legal father and the child have the right to apply for annulment of acknowledgment.[124]

Besides the persons who are directly involved in the issue of legal affiliation, the heirs and the public prosecutor also have standing to apply for annulment of legal

---

119 Art. 1:204 (3) Dutch Civil Code.

120 Dutch Supreme Court 13th April 2001, NJ 2001/464; Dutch Supreme Court 16th February 2001, NJ 2001/571.

121 Dutch Supreme Court 12th November 2004, NJ 2005/248.

122 The Dutch Supreme Court ruled on the question whether a sperm donor can apply for judicial consent to his acknowledgment, if the mother refuses consent and if there is no acknowledgment yet. In that case, the Court held that the statutory regulation in Art. 1:204 (3) Dutch Civil Code does not apply, since that provision only applies to the begetter. Accordingly the sperm donor can only obtain judicial consent if the mother has no other reason for her refusal than to harm the interests of the sperm donor (Hoge Raad 24th January 2003, NJ 2003/386).

123 Art. 3:1 and 3:2 Children and Parents Code (1949:381).

124 SALDEEN, Å., *Karnov, Svensk lagsamling med kommentarer* (tenth edition ed.), Thomson Fakta, Stockholm, 2005/06, p. 372f, note 17; SALDEEN, Å., *Barn- och föräldrarätt*, Iustus Förlag, Uppsala, 2005, p. 77; WALIN, G., S. Vängby *Föräldraskap. En Kommentar. Del I. 1–13 kap* (with supplements), Norstedts Juridik, Stockholm, 2001, p. 1:15; SINGER, A., *Föräldraskap i rättslig belysning* (2000), p. 196.

parenthood under certain circumstances. The applicant's heirs have standing to apply for annulment of legal parenthood, if the applicant died before the expiration of the period of limitation which applied to the applicant. They also have to bring their action within the period which applied to the decedent.[125] Under Dutch law Article 1:201 Dutch Civil Code provides for a regulation which applies equally to annulment of marital paternity (based on the presumption arising from marriage to the child's mother) and paternity based on acknowledgment. The descendants, and if there are none, the spouse, and if there is no spouse, the parents of the legal parent, have the right to apply for annulment of parenthood if the legal parent died before the expiration of the period of limitation which applies to the deceased legal parent. They have to apply within one year after they are informed of the death of the legal parent. In case of the child, only the descendants of the child have the right to apply for annulment of legal paternity if the child died before the expiration of the period of limitation which applies to the child. If the child died after he or she has come of age, the descendants have to apply within one year after they were informed of the child's death. If the child died during his minority, the descendants have to apply within one year after the moment the child would have come of age.

Finally, under French law the public prosecutor has the right to apply for annulment of legal parenthood if it appears from the register itself that the legal affiliation is not in conformity with the grounds for legal affiliation or in case of *fraus legis*.[126] In Dutch law, the power of the public prosecutor is limited to legal affiliation on the basis of acknowledgment, if the acknowledger is not the child's begetter and if his acknowledgment violates Dutch public policy.[127] A proposal is pending to introduce a similar possibility under German law.[128]

E. Statutory Periods of Limitation

As with the regulation on *locus standi*, the reasons why legal systems provide for statutory periods of limitation are usually the same, but that does not prevent considerable difference in outcome: we will see periods of limitation ranging from one to ten years. The main reason to provide for a time limit on the action for annulment of legal parenthood is to grant stability to the legal affiliation status of the child. Also the protection of family peace has been mentioned in this respect.[129]

---

125 Art. 322 French Civil Code.
126 Art. 336 French Civil Code.
127 Art. 1:205 (2) Dutch Civil Code.
128 Henrich, D., 'Zum Entwurf eines Gesetzes zur Ergänzung des Rechts zur Anfechtung der Vaterschaft', *Zeitschrift für das gesamte Familienrecht* (2006), p. 977–979.
129 Germany: BR Drucks. 180/96, p. 97; BT Drucks. 13/4899, p. 87; Second Chamber, 1995–96, 24 649, nr. 3, p. 17 (explanatory notes).

Only Sweden has taken the step of abolishing the periods of limitation, since the protection of legitimacy was not necessary any more and it was deemed in the interest of both the father and the child to able to clarify the genetic affiliation at any time.[130]

Legal systems which provide for a period of limitation for annulment of legal parenthood differ as to the length of the period, but also as to the moment at which the period starts running. Under German law, the period of limitation is two years for all applicants.[131] The period starts running at the moment the applicant is informed that the legal father is probably not the child's genetic father. For the alleged genetic father who is not the legal father this means that the period starts running against him as soon as he is informed that the legal father is not the child's genetic father. Whether he is also informed that he is probably the genetic father is irrelevant.[132] Moreover, the period for the alleged father runs, even if there is a social family relationship within the meaning of Article 1600 (2) German Civil Code during which he is precluded from applying for annulment on the basis of that same article. The provisions are less severe for the child. If the legal paternity has not been annulled during the child's minority, he or she can apply for annulment within two years after he or she has come of age or at a later moment if the child is informed later that the legal father is probably not the genetic father. Moreover, Article 1600 (5) German Civil Code provides for a possibility to renew the period of limitation applicable to the child if at any time the child is informed of facts which make the existence of legal paternity intolerable for the child, for example when the legal parents get divorced or when the legal mother marries the child's genetic father.[133]

Under Dutch law the period of limitation for annulment of legal paternity is one year for the legal parents and three years for the child. For annulment of marital paternity the period starts running for the mother at the moment of birth.[134] For the legal father and the child the period starts running at the moment at which they are informed that the legal father is probably not the child's genetic father.[135] If the child is informed during his minority, the period starts at the moment at which he or she comes of

130 Prop. 1975/76:170, p. 134; WALIN, G., S. Vängby *Föräldraskap. En Kommentar. Del I. 1–13 kap* (2001), p. 3:3 and 3:6.

131 Art. 1600b (1) German Civil Code.

132 HÖFELMANN, E., 'Das neue Gesetz zur Änderung der Vorschriften über die Anfechtung des Vaterschaft und das Umgangsrecht von Bezugpersonen des Kindes', *Zeitschrift für das gesamte Familienrecht* (2004), p. 745–751, at p. 749; WELLENHOFER-KLEIN, M., 'Das Vaterschafts-anfechtungsrecht des leiblichen Vaters – Vorslag zur Änderung von § 1600 BGB', *Zeitschrift für das gesamte Familienrecht* (2003), p. 1889–1894, at p. 1893.

133 Münchener Kommentar zum BGB Volume 8/Wellendorf-Klein (2002), p. 205.

134 Art. 1:200 (5) Dutch Civil Code.

135 Art. 1:200 (5) and (6) Dutch Civil Code.

age.[136] The rule is the same for annulment of legal paternity based on acknowledgment.[137] Regarding the moment at which the period starts to run against the legal parents, Article 1:205 (3) Dutch Civil Code provides that the period starts running at the moment at which the threats, mistake or deceit are discovered or when the undue influence has stopped.[138]

Finally, under French law the length of the statutory period depends on whether or not the child has a title (*e.g.* a birth certificate) which is confirmed by apparent status (*possession d'état*). If the title is not confirmed by apparent status the period starts running from the moment at which the child acquired the disputed status. Furthermore, the action must be brought within ten years.[139] If the title is confirmed by apparent status, there are two periods of limitation:[140] the first period starts running at the moment at which the title is confirmed by apparent status, after five years the status becomes inviolable. However, if the apparent status ceases to exist before the end of the fifth year the action for annulment of marital paternity must be brought within five years from the moment at which the apparent status has ceased to exist. In case of annulment of legal affiliation which exists on the basis of apparent status recorded in an affidavit, the period of limitation is five years from the moment at which the affidavit was drawn up.[141]

F. Administrative Annulment of Parenthood

Under Dutch, German and Swedish law it is possible to annul legal paternity which arises on the basis of marriage with the child's mother (the presumption of paternity) by an administrative procedure. The ground for annulment in such case is that it is unlikely that the husband is the child's genetic father, although the absence of genetic affiliation does not need to be proven.

Administrative annulment under Swedish and German law is only possible if at the same time another man acknowledges paternity. Swedish law offers the broadest possibility in that it is provided that marital paternity can always be annulled if someone else validly acknowledges parenthood.[142] Valid acknowledgment in this context means that the mother and the *Socialnämnd* have consented to the acknowl-

136 Art. 1:200 (6) Dutch Civil Code.
137 Art. 1:205 (3) and (4).
138 *Cf.* § 1.3.1.4.b. Restrictions on judicial annulment of paternity under Dutch law.
139 Art. 321 French Civil Code.
140 Art. 333 French Civil Code.
141 Art. 335 French Civil Code.
142 Art. 1:2 (2) Children and Parents Code.

edgment and, in case of annulment of marital paternity, also the legal father himself.[143] The consent of the *Socialnämnd* purports to guarantee that legal paternity will be in conformity with the genetic affiliation, since the *Socialnämnd* will only consent if it is convinced that the acknowledger is the child's parent according to the Swedish grounds for legal parenthood.[144]

Under Dutch and German law the possibilities of annulling marital paternity are much more limited than is the case under Swedish law. A possible explanation for the limitation is that, unlike under Swedish law, Dutch and German law do not have an institution similar to the Swedish *Socialnämnd*, which investigates whether the husband is indeed not the child's genetic father. Consequently, the possibility for administrative annulment is limited to only those situations where it is highly unlikely that the husband is the child's genetic father.[145] Accordingly, under Dutch law, the administrative annulment of marital paternity is only possible if the mother's husband died within 306 days before the birth of the child and if the husband and the wife lived separately from the 306th day before the birth of the child or if they were legally separated, but not divorced (*gescheiden van tafel en bed*).[146] If the mother was married at the moment of the child's birth, her new husband will be the child's legal father by dint of the presumption of paternity.[147] The Dutch provision should be seen in the light of the rule that normally, if the husband died within 306 days before the birth of the child, he will be considered to be the child's father, even if the mother was remarried at the moment of birth. If the marriage has been dissolved by other causes than death, the ex-husband will not be considered to be the child's legal father.[148]

According to German law, the administrative annulment of marital paternity has been introduced in order to avoid expensive judicial procedures in cases where everyone agrees and where it is already at the outset unlikely that the husband is the child's genetic father.[149] The administrative annulment is only possible if the child was born after the spouses have filed for divorce, but are not yet divorced. In such a case, another man can become the child's legal father by acknowledging paternity within one year after the divorce has become final and if the mother and her (ex)-husband consent to the acknowledgment.

143 Art. 1:2 (2) and 1:4 Children and Parents Code.

144 Art. 1:4 and chapter 2 Children and Parents Code.

145 Although this is certainly true for German law, the Dutch reason for an administrative procedure for annulment of legal paternity is less clear. The regulation was inserted in 1998 without any explanation (Second Chamber, 1996–97, 24 649, nr 28, p. 3 (letter from the State Secretary).

146 Art. 1:199 under b Dutch Civil Code.

147 Ibid.

148 Art. 1:199 under a and b Dutch Civil Code.

149 BR Drucks. 180/96, p. 63; BT Drucks. 13/4899, p. 53.

1.4. EVIDENCE AND LEGAL PARENTHOOD

The final step in the comparison of the laws on legal affiliation concerns evidence. Evidence is relevant to legal affiliation in two respects. First, a regulation which requires the production of tangible evidence of legal reality is the third step which our hypothetical legislator has to take. This step is less interesting in legal systems which use a method of attributing legal parenthood by means of administrative of judicial establishment, because the creation of evidence and the establishment of legal parenthood are basically the same thing. However, it becomes more important in a system which allows legal affiliation to arise in a given situation *ex lege*, such as is the case with legal parenthood under English law and legal maternity under Dutch and German law. In that case, it is interesting to see how the legislator tries to ensure that the evidence actually represents legal reality and to what extent the legislator creates the possibility of correcting that evidence if the legal parenthood thus established does not represent legal reality.

Secondly, evidence is an important issue in court proceedings on legal affiliation. It has been explained above that, in court proceedings concerning establishment or annulment of legal affiliation, it is necessary to prove the existence or absence of a ground for legal affiliation. Especially if genetic affiliation does has to be proven, the question of evidence becomes interesting because the legal systems under consideration give different answers to the question whether a DNA test is to be granted (depending on the circumstances) and to the question what should happen if one or more of the parties do not cooperate with a DNA test.

1.4.1. Evidence and Ex Lege Existence of Parenthood

When legal parenthood exists *ex lege*, the issue of registration is important. It has to be examined whether the registration provides for control mechanisms which enhance the chance that the registration is in conformity with legal reality. Under Dutch law, the registration of legal maternity is regulated in the Dutch Civil Code and in the Civil Status Degree 1994 (*Besluit Burgerlijke Stand 1994*).[150] Registration of the child's legal mother is mandatory.[151] According to Article 19e (9) Dutch Civil Code, the civil status registrar is authorised to require a written declaration given by a doctor or midwife that the woman mentioned as the child's mother indeed gave birth to that child.[152] The registrar is, however, not obliged to ask for such evidence. It happens as a result of fraud or mistake that the birth certificate does not mention the legal mother, but

---

150 Stb. 1994/160, last amendment Stb. 2004/190.

151 Art. 43 Civil Status Decree 1994. See also BOER, J. DE, *Asser's Personen en Familierecht* (2002), p. 69.

152 See also Art. 27 Civil Status Decree 1994.

another woman as the child's mother. In that case the birth certificate can be amended on the basis of Article 24 Dutch Civil Code, upon request by an interested party or the public prosecutor. There are neither statutory periods of limitation nor any special requirements with regard to evidence.[153] However, if the child has apparent status in conformity with the affiliation status as recorded in the register, only the child is allowed to apply for an amendment of his or her birth certificate.[154]

Under German law, the registration of civil status is regulated by the Civil Status Act 1937 (*Personenstandsgesetz* 1937). The procedure for registration of legal maternity under German law is more or less the same as under Dutch law. However, German law does not confer upon the registrar the possibility of requiring a written declaration by a doctor or midwife. In fact, there are no rules regulating how legal maternity should be proven.[155] If the wrong woman has been registered, for whatever reason, the registration can be changed following proof of the error in court.[156] The legal basis for such a procedure is either Article 47 Civil Status Act 1937 or Article 640 (2) German Code on Civil Procedure.

Under English law the registration of legal parenthood is regulated by the Births and Deaths Registration Act 1953 and the Registration of Births and Deaths Regulations 1987 (SI 1987/2088). As in the Netherlands and Germany, under English law, the registration of the mother's name and the legal father's name if he is married to the mother is mandatory[157] and as under German law there is no prescribed form for proving legal maternity. Under English law the registration of the unmarried father (*i.e.* the father who is not married to the mother of the child) is not mandatory and is regulated by Sections 10 and 10A Births and Deaths Registration Act.[158] These provisions in essence provide that if the child's parents apply to the civil status registrar's office together, or if either the mother or the father is able to produce written evidence of the consent of the other, the father will be registered as father on the birth certificate.[159] If the registration is disputed, either by one of the persons who has been registered as the child's parent or by someone else who claims to be the legal father, the person can apply for a declaration of parentage under Section 55A Family Law Act 1986. However, and otherwise than is the case a procedure for judicial

153 The general rules on evidence apply, Art. 149–207 Dutch Code on Civil Procedure.
154 Art. 1:209 Dutch Civil Code.
155 Staudinger's Kommentar zum BGB, Part IV/Rauscher, Berlin: Sellier – de Gruyter (2004), p. 188.
156 Art. 60 (2) Civil Status Act 1937.
157 Section 7 Registration of Births and Deaths Regulations 1987.
158 The meaning of 'father' has been explained above § 1.3.1.1. *Ex lege* existence of parenthood.
159 Section 10 Births and Deaths Registration Act applies to the registration of the unmarried father at the moment of the registration of the birth. Section 10A applies to the registration of the father after the birth has been registered.

establishment of parenthood in the above-mentioned continental systems, the court is allowed to refuse to hear an application under Section 55A Family Law Act, if the court considers that such application is not in the child's interests.[160] If the court finds that the registration is incorrect, the birth certificate will be changed accordingly.[161] The possibility of obtaining a declaration of parentage was introduced by the Child Support, Pensions and Social Security Act 2000 in order to satisfy the need to provide for a determination of legal affiliation which binds everyone. Findings by a court concerning legal affiliation of a child usually only bind the parties, but a decision on the basis of Section 55A Family Law Act 1986 binds everyone.[162] Pursuant to Section 55A (1) and (3) Family Law Act 1986, any person with a sufficient personal interest has the right to apply to the High Court, a county court or a magistrate's court for a declaration as to whether or not a person named in the application is or was the parent of another person so named. The notion of 'sufficient personal interest' is partly elucidated by Section 55A (4) Family Law Act 1986 and Section 27 of the Child Support Act 1991. On the basis of Section 55A (4) Family Law Act 1986 a child has always sufficient personal interest to apply for a declaration of paternity, just as a man does who wants to establish that he is the father of a child or the mother who wants to establish that a man is the father of her child. In a case in which a maintenance assessment has been made or is in force against a man who denies being the child's father or where the case does not fall within the scope of Section 26 (2) of the Child Support Act 1991, the person with care of the child shall be treated as having a sufficient personal interest for the purposes of Section 55A Family Law Act 1986. Outside the scope of Sections 55A (4) Family Law Act 1986 and Section 27 Child Support Act 1991 the criteria according to which it has to be established whether a person has 'sufficient personal interest' have not yet been decided. In its reaction to the consultation paper on paternity and parental responsibility[163] the Advisory Board on Family Law[164] stated in this respect:

> *Others should be able to make an application with leave, if they have a proper interest in the issue. The definition of 'proper interest' was considered in some detail. It would, for example, include siblings who wanted to establish a right to inheritance, and other family members*

---

[160] Section 55A (5) Family Law Act 1986.

[161] Section 14A Registration of Births and Deaths Regulations 1987. If a UK court or a foreign court has decided on the affiliation of the child in a procedure other than the procedure pursuant to Section 55A Family Law Act 1986, the birth certificate can be amended on the basis of Section 29A Births and Deaths Registration Act.

[162] Section 58 (2) Family Law Act 1986.

[163] Lord Chancellor's Department Consultation Paper, *Procedures for the determination of paternity and the law on parental responsibility for unmarried fathers* (1998).

[164] The Advisory Board on Family Law is a non-statutory, non-departmental public body which advises the Lord Chancellor.

such as grandchildren. It should not include merely public interest (for example newspapers making applications to establish the paternity of public figures).[165]

1.4.2. DNA Evidence in Court Proceedings on (Legal) Affiliation

The means of proving the absence or existence of genetic affiliation has been the subject of considerable debate and regulation in the legal systems under discussion. Nowadays all countries provide for the possibility of proving genetic affiliation by means of a DNA test; the use of legal presumptions is becoming rare.[166] However, the conditions under which a court or a private person can obtain a DNA test differ considerably between the legal systems, thus indicating that not all legal systems strive to get to the genetic truth at any price. This paragraph provides the legal framework of the national legal systems under consideration in the context of a request for the use of a DNA test. It will appear that, whereas under English, Dutch and Swedish law the use of DNA tests is not problematic (although not unrestricted either), under French and German law the legislator and the courts have restricted the use of paternity tests more severely than in the aforementioned systems, either to avoid embarrassing situations (*e.g.* the Yves Montand-affaire in France in 1998)[167] or to protect the legal family against 'fishing' exercises.

Under English law, the court will order a DNA test unless it is shown that the test is not in the child's interest. The leading cases for the use of a DNA test are *S v. S* and *W v. Official Solicitor*, in which the House of Lords considered the question whether a blood test should be ordered in a proceeding regarding the paternity and the legitimacy of a child.[168] The starting-point in the procedure is Section 20 of the Family Law Reform Act 1969, which grants the court the power to order blood tests in cases in which the parentage of a person falls to be determined. First, the court held that the presumption of legitimacy merely determines the onus of proof and that illegitimacy as such is not something from which the child ought in modern circumstances to be protected. Moreover, the general interests of justice require that all the evidence is presented and therefore, a blood test should be directed unless it is shown that the test would be contrary to the child's interest.

---

165 Second Annual Report of the Advisory Board on Family Law (1998/99), Annex C, par. IV.

166 *E.g.* For English law: *Re F (a minor)* [1993] 3 WLR 369, (1993) 143 NLJ 472, [1993] Fam. Law 407; for Sweden: SINGER, A., *Föräldraskap i rättslig belysning* (2000), p. 141.

167 In 1998 the French actor Yves Montand was exhumed in order to examine whether he was the father of a girl who claimed that she was his daughter. The affaire was one of the reasons to restrict the use of DNA tests after the death of the person whose DNA has to be examined.

168 [1970] 3 All ER 107, [1970] 3 WLR 366, (1970) 114 SJ 635.

The crucial question thus is: when it is in the child's interest not to direct a paternity test? There are hardly any cases in which the court found the direction of a paternity test not in the child's interests. The trend in English case law seems to be to emphasise the need to know the truth about a child's affiliation.[169] Thorpe LJ stated in this respect that "the paternity of a child is to be established by science and not by legal presumption or inference."[170] However, in two cases the court refused to order a paternity test: *Re F (a minor)* and *O. v L. (blood tests)*.[171] *In Re F (a minor)*[172] the applicant argued that he, instead of the mother's husband, was the child's father. The court refused to order a paternity test since, even were it to be established that the applicant was the child's biological father, his chances of obtaining parental responsibility and contact were remote. In *O. v L. (blood tests)*[173] the mother requested blood tests to prove that her lover, and not her husband, was the child's father. The child and the husband had had contact for three years when the mother told the husband that he was probably not the father. It appeared that the mother's reason for requesting the blood tests was to exclude contact between the child and the husband. However, such exclusion was not deemed in the child's interests and therefore the request was rejected. If a blood test is ordered and a party refuses to cooperate, the court can draw an adverse inference from the refusal to cooperate with a paternity test.[174] The person cannot be forced to submit to a blood test.[175]

Direct references to the child's interests as a criterion for an order for a DNA test are not found in Dutch and Swedish law.[176] Under Dutch and Swedish law, the emphasis is on the avoidance of unfounded or unnecessary DNA tests. Under Swedish law, the use of DNA tests in cases concerning affiliation is regulated by the Blood Examination

---

169 CRETNEY, S.M., et al, *Principles of Family Law* (2003), p. 528.

170 Re H and A (children) [2002] EWCA Civ 383, [2002] 2 FCR 469, par. 30.

171 In *Re CB (a minor) (blood tests)* [1994] 2 FLR 762 the applicant requested blood tests to ascertain whether he or the mother's husband was the child's father. However, the major reason for Wall J. not ordering blood tests seemed to be that he did not consider it relevant to order tests which could not be carried out anyway, since the mother, at that time still had the right to obstruct the taking of blood samples from the child. According to Wall J. the court's refusal to order a blood test does not affect the possibility to draw an inference against the mother who refuses to allow a child to be tested.

172 [1993] Fam 314.

173 [1995] 2 FLR 930.

174 Section 23 (1) Family Law Reform Act 1969. Also: *Re O; Re J (children)(blood tests: constraints)* [2000] Fam 139; *F. v Child Support Agency* [1999] 2 FCR 385; *Re G (parentage: blood sample)* [1997] 1 FLR 360; *Re H (a minor)(blood tests: parental rights)* [1997] Fam 89; *Re CB (a minor)(blood tests)* [1994] 2 FLR 762.

175 Section 21 (1) Family Law Reform Act 1969.

176 Compare also the absence of the 'child's interest criterion' in actions for judicial establishment under Dutch law and Swedish law with the possibility which an English court has allowed to refuse to hear an application for a determination of parentage on account of the child's interest (see § 1.4.1 Evidence and *ex lege* existence of parenthood, note 160).

Act.[177] Pursuant to this Act, the court can, on request of one of the parties or on its own motion, order any investigation to determine a person's genetic characteristics in order to determine the affiliation of the child.[178] However, in a proceeding for annulment of paternity based on acknowledgment or judicial establishment, the court can only order a paternity test if, *after* the acknowledgment or the judicial establishment, it turns out that the mother probably had sexual intercourse with another man.[179] If that is proved, the other man with whom the mother had sexual intercourse must be summoned and subjected to the necessary medical examination.[180] Moreover, if it was already known before the establishment of paternity that the mother had intercourse with another man, the court cannot order a paternity test. From the parliamentary history it is clear that it is the applicant's knowledge which determines whether the court can order a paternity test.[181] The reason for limiting the possibility of ordering a paternity test is to avoid unfounded interference by others in the private lives of the father and child.[182] The limitations on requesting a paternity test do not play a role in case of annulment of marital paternity. It is always possible to request a paternity test in a proceeding for annulment of marital paternity.[183]

If the parties do not co-operate with the court order to undergo medical tests, they can be fined and ultimately they can be forced by the police to undergo the necessary examinations.[184] The possibility of invoking enforcement by the police is, in the case of children under the age of 18, limited: samples cannot be taken from a child by means of police assistance if that would be detrimental to the child.[185]

In Dutch law, there are no specific provisions regarding the use of DNA tests. The evidence in a proceeding on affiliation is determined by the general rules of evidence of the Dutch Code on Civil Procedure.[186] In 2004, the Dutch Supreme Court held that the use of a DNA test in matters concerning legal affiliation is not mandatory.[187] The limits of that discretion were already determined in 2000, when the Dutch Supreme

---

177 *Lag (1958:642) om blodundersöking m.m. vid utreding av faderskap.* See also *Förordning (1969:624) om blodundersökning m.m. vid utredning.*

178 Art. 1 *Lag (1958:642) om blodundersöking m.m. vid utreding av faderskap.* See also SALDEEN, Å., *Karnov, Svensk lagsamling med kommentarer* (2005/06), p. 418, note 1; WALIN, G., S. Vängby *Föräldraskap. En Kommentar. Del I. 1–13 kap* (2001), p. 3:34.

179 Section 1a (1) Blood Examination Act.

180 Section 1, last sentence Blood Examination Act.

181 Prop. 1982/83:8, p. 12; Socialstyrelsen, *Att fastställa faderskap*, Stockholm: Elanders Gotab (2005), p. 66; WALIN, G., S. Vängby *Föräldraskap. En Kommentar. Del I. 1–13 kap* (2001), p. 3:36.

182 Prop. 1982/83:8, p. 7.

183 SINGER, A., *Föräldraskap i rättslig belysning* (2000), p. 221f.

184 Section 2a (1) Blood Examination Act. See also Prop. 1982/83:8, p. 9, 16.

185 Section 2a (2) Blood Examination Act.

186 Art. 149–207 Dutch Code on Civil Procedure.

187 Dutch Supreme Court, 11 June 2004, NJ 2005/116, RvdW 2004/84.

Court laid down the criteria for the use of a DNA test in matters concerning legal affiliation.[188] The court held that a DNA test can be ordered if, on the basis of facts and circumstances which have been established during the proceeding, it is plausible that the man is the begetter of the child. Whether it is possible to discharge this burden of proof by means of a privately arranged DNA test has not been decided. If the court orders a DNA test the judge can draw an adverse inference from the refusal to cooperate with the order.[189] The defence that the DNA test would constitute an infringement of the personal integrity of the person involved is not accepted under Dutch law, since the burden imposed on the individual by the provision of cell materials is negligible compared to the countervailing interests that are at stake.[190]

Under French and German law, the use of DNA tests is regulated more extensively. Under French law, Article 16–11 French Civil Code provides that the genetic identification of persons is only allowed pursuant to a court order. Private tests to determine genetic affiliation are not allowed. In civil proceedings, DNA identification is only allowed for the purpose of determining questions of affiliation and the person involved must consent beforehand to the execution of the tests. Hence, it is not possible to identify a deceased person with a DNA test if that person did not expressly consent to such test during his or her lifetime. In such case it is necessary to resort to other means of proving that the deceased person is the father of the applicant.[191] Furthermore, in French law a DNA test in a proceeding on legal affiliation is *de droit* (as of right),[192] meaning that, within the framework of Article 16–11 French Civil Code, the court is obliged to order medical examination on the request of either party, unless there are legitimate reasons not to do so.[193] The court order is essential, since

188 Dutch Supreme Court, 22 September 2000,NJ 2001/647, m.nt. JdB, RvdW 2000/184.

189 BLAUWHOFF, R.J., 'Procesrechtelijke kunstgrepen bij de gerechtelijke vaststelling van het vaderschap', *Tijdschrift voor Familie- en Jeugdrecht* (2006), p. 132–138, at p. 133; HEIDA, A., 'Vaderschaps-procedures en DNA-onderzoek', *Tijdschrift voor Familie- en Jeugdrecht* (2002), p. 122–129, at p. 127.

190 Advocate General Wesseling – van Gent in HR 9 December 2005, LJN AU3262, Advocate General Bakels in HR 22 September 2000, NJ 2001/647, BOER, J. DE, *Asser's Personen en Familierecht* (2002), nr. 738.

191 For examples see; PASCAL, A., TRAPERO, M.,'Vérité biologique et filiation dans la jurisprudence récente de la Cour de Cassation', in *La vérité. Rapport annuel 2004 de la Cour de Cassation*, La documentation Française, Paris, 2005.

192 Cass. 1er civ., 28 May 2000, 30 May 2000, Dalloz 2001, p. 1427; Cass. 1er civ., 17 September 2003 (01–03.408), Dalloz 2004, p. 659; S. LeGac-Pech, 'De Louis XVII à Z...' *Recueil Dalloz* (2001), 404–407.

193 The parties in a proceeding concerning legal affiliation only have the right to a DNA test if the child's genetic affiliation is relevant to the resolution of the dispute. If the applicant has to challenge the child's apparent status the genetic affiliation is irrelevant and neither party has a right to a DNA test (Cass. 1er civ., 6 December 2005, D. 2006, p. 99; GRANET-LAMBRECHTS, F., HAUSER, J., 'Le nouveau droit de la filiation', *Recueil Dalloz* (2006), p. 17–28, at p. 23; GRANET-LAMBRECHTS, F., 'Droit de filiation: panorama 2004', *Recueil Dalloz* (2005), p. 1748–1754, at p. 1751.

without the order it is not possible at all to execute a DNA test.[194] Legitimate reasons for rejecting a request for a DNA test are: that the request is only being made in order to delay the establishment of legal paternity,[195] that the test is requested in order to establish legal affiliation whereas the law prohibits such establishment,[196] or in case of fishing exercises or other abusive intentions.[197] Notwithstanding that an order for a DNA test is a matter of right, the *Cour de Cassation* held in 2003 that the refusal to cooperate with the court order for a paternity test is not enough to establish a presumption of paternity against that person.[198] The party who requested the test has to submit further evidence which supports the paternity of the alleged father.[199]

Under German law, the applicant has to present an *Anfangsverdacht* (ground for reasonable suspicion) before an application on legal affiliation will be heard at all.[200] According to the *Bundesgerichtshof* the applicant must

> *Umstände vortragen, die bei objectiever Betrachtung geeignet sind, Zweifel an der Abstammung des Kindes von dem als Vater geltenden Kläger zu wecken und die Möglichkeit der Abstammung des Kindes von einem anderen Mann als nicht ganz fernliegend erscheinen zu lassen.*[201] *(present circumstances which, when viewed objectively, raise doubt whether the applicant who is presumed to be the child's legal father actually is the father and the possibility that another man is the child's father is not entirely remote (tr. authors).*

The reason for the requirement of an *Anfangsverdacht* is to avoid paternity suits 'out of the blue'. One way to make an *Anfangsverdacht* is by establishing that it is probable that the mother has had sexual intercourse with another man. This is not readily

194 Art. 16–11 (1) French Civil Code.

195 Cass. 1er civ., 14 June 2005 (03–19.325), Dalloz 2005, p. 1804.

196 FERRAND, F., 'Verwertung heimlich eingeholter DNA-Vaterschaftstests', *Zeitschrift für Europäisches Privatrecht* (2006), p. 436–458, at p. 454.

197 GRANET-LAMBRECHTS, F., 'Droit de la filiation', *Recueil Dalloz* (2006), p. 1139–1148, at p. 1143.

198 Cass. 1er civ., 17 September 2003 (01–13.856), Dalloz 2004, p. 659. See also: Jacques Massip, Dalloz 2005, p. 660 ; Frédérique Granet-Lambrechts, Dalloz 2004, p. 1420.

199 See also Granet-Lambrechts, F., 'Droit de la filiation', *Recueil Dalloz* (2006), p. 1139–1148, at p. 1143; PASCAL, A., TRAPERO, M., 'Vérité biologique et filiation dans la jurisprudence récente de la Cour de Cassation' (2005).

200 BGH 22 April 1998 (nr. XII ZR 229/96), *FamRZ* 1998, p. 955; BGH 30 October 2002 (nr. XII ZR 345/00), *FamRZ* 2003, p. 155. See also FERRAND, F., 'Verwertung heimlich eingeholter DNA-Vaterschaftstests' (2006), p. 436–458, at p. 445*ff*; RITTNER, C., RITTNER, N.,'Rechtsdogma und Rechtswirklichkeit am Beispiel so genannter heimlicher Vaterschaftstests', *Neue Juristische Wochenschrift* (2005), 945–948, p. 945; WELLENHOFER, M., 'Die prozessuale Verwertbarkeit privater Abstammungsgutachten', *Zeitschrift für das gesamte Familienrecht* (2005), p. 665–668, p. 665; WOLF, A., 'Biologische Abstammung und rechtliche Zuordnung', *Neue Juristische Wochenschrift* (2005), p. 2417–2421, p. 2419; Staudinger's Kommentar zum BGB, Part IV/Rauscher, Berlin: Sellier – de Gruyter (2004), p. 318.

201 *BGH 12 January 2005 (nr. XII ZR227/03), FamRZ 2005, 342. Also* FERRAND, *F., 'Verwertung heimlich eingeholter DNA-Vaterschaftstests' (2006), at p. 446.*

established. In the case which came before the *Bundesgerichtshof* just mentioned, the fact that the child's mother had stated at various occasions that she loved the alleged father was not enough.[202] Also the fact that the mother refused to submit to a paternity test[203] or evidence of the limited fertility of the legal father[204] is, as such, not enough to make an *Anfangsverdacht*. Another way of presenting an *Anfangsverdacht* is by means of a privately-ordered paternity test.[205] However, in case of a paternity test it is important that all the parties involved consent to the test. In two decisions in 2005, the *Bundesgerichtshof* held that the use of paternity tests without the consent of the persons involved in order to make an *Anfangsverdacht*, is not permitted.[206] The court gave various reasons for its decision. First of all, in the absence of consent there can be no absolute certainty that the material used for the DNA-test is actually from the party involved. Moreover, removal of the material without consent of the party involved violates that person's right to personal integrity as enshrined in Article 2 (1) of the German Constitution.

If the applicant has raised an *Anfangsverdacht* the court will examine the application for annulment of paternity. In examining the application the court is obliged to collect all the evidence which is necessary for the determination of the question. The court can order a medical test *ex officio* or at the request of the parties.[207] The persons involved are obliged to cooperate with the medical test if the testing method is effective and if the medical examination is harmless to the person's health.[208] A refusal to cooperate without a good reason or without any reason at all can ultimately be sanctioned with imprisonment for the duration of the proceedings[209] and the unwilling person can be physically forced to undergo medical tests for the purpose of judicial establishment of paternity.[210]

---

202 BGH 30 October 2002 (nr. XII ZR 345/00), FamRZ 2003, p. 155.

203 BGH 12 January 2005 (nr. XII ZR60/03), *NJW* 2005, 497; *FamRZ* 2005, 665.

204 BGH 12 January 2005 (nr. XII ZR227/03), *FamRZ* 2005, 342.

205 Staudinger's Kommentar zum BGB, Part IV/Rauscher, Berlin: Sellier – de Gruyter (2004), p. 321, nr. 21.

206 BGH 12 January 2005 (nr. XII ZR60/03), *NJW* 2005, 497; *FamRZ* 2005, 665 and BGH 12 January 2005 (nr. XII ZR227/03), *FamRZ* 2005, 342. On these decisions see i.a. FERRAND, F., 'Verwertung heimlich eingeholter DNA-Vaterschaftstests' (2006), p. 436–458; Wellenhofer, M., 'Die prozessuale Verwertbarkeit privater Abstammungsgutachten', *Zeitschrift für das gesamte Familienrecht* (2005), p. 665–668, p. 666.

207 Art. 640 in conjunction with 616 ZPO.

208 Art. 372a (1) ZPO. See also: FRANK, R., 'Die zwangsweise körperliche Untersuchung zur Feststellung der Abstammung' *Zeitschrift für das gesamte Familienrecht* (1995), p. 975–981.

209 Art. 390 (1) ZPO.

210 Art. 372a (2) ZPO, see also Staudinger's Kommentar zum BGB, Part IV/Rauscher, Berlin: Sellier – de Gruyter (2004), p. 114, 118; Münchener Kommentar zum BGB Volume 8/Seidel (2002), p. 230; LÜDERITZ, A., *Familienrecht*, München, Beck'she Verlagsbuchhandlung, 1999, p. 270.

2. THE EUROPEAN COURT OF HUMAN RIGHTS AND NATIONAL LAWS OF PARENTHOOD

In the first part we have reviewed the breadth of scope of the law of parenthood in its totality and have observed considerable differences between the national laws on legal parenthood in England and Wales, France, Germany, the Netherlands and Sweden. In this part the case law of the European Court in the field of legal parenthood will be examined. The main question is what, according to the case law of the European Court, are the constitutive elements of family or private life and what is the degree of respect which the states are required to observe in relation to that particular dimension of family or private life, under Article 8 ECHR on the basis of which the national legal systems are obliged to allow for the establishment of legal parenthood. To the extent to which the European Court insists upon compliance by the Member States with a minimum assortment of rules, it is will be possible to speak of a trend by which Member States are obliged to bring their rules closer together. We will now examine whether such is the case, and, if so, to what extent.

2.1. PARENTHOOD: NATURAL REPRODUCTION AND ASSISTED REPRODUCTION

In the foregoing sections we have seen that a distinction is made in the national legal systems regarding the establishment of natural parenthood and the establishment of parenthood in consequence of assisted reproduction. We have shown that, in most legal systems, the ground for legal paternity is genetic affiliation in case of natural reproduction and intention in case of assisted reproduction. Even in legal systems such as Germany and the Netherlands where it has been submitted that intention is not the ground for legal affiliation, the requirement of consent to assisted reproduction has the effect that different rules apply than in the case of natural reproduction.

In the international setting this distinction can also be made. The distinction is found in the documents prepared under the auspices of the Council of Europe. For example, parenthood in consequence of natural reproduction is covered by the European Convention on the Legal Status of Children Born Outside Wedlock.[211] The Committee of Experts on Family Law of the Council of Europe is still working on a new convention which will try to improve the Luxembourg Convention. Pursuant to this project the White Paper on Principles Concerning the Establishment and Legal

[211] Opened for signature at Luxembourg, European Treaty Series nr. 85, in force 11th August 1978.

Consequences of Parenthood was published in 2002.[212] However, the distinction between natural parenthood and assisted reproduction is not a matter of principle and is therefore not water-tight. In the White Paper the first seventeen principles, which deal with the establishment of parenthood, include principles relating to 'low-technology' assisted reproduction techniques such as surrogacy and sperm donors.

Parentage in consequence of assisted reproduction is addressed by the work of the Ad Hoc Committee of Experts on the Developments in Bio-Medical Sciences (CAHBI), which in 1989 presented 21 principles to the Committee of Ministers. Those principles were not accepted. Since 1992 the work of CAHBI on assisted reproduction continues as part of the work of the steering committee on bio-ethics. That committee produced the Oviedo Convention for the Protection of Human Rights and Dignity of the Human Being with Regard to the Application of Biology and Medicine.[213] The First Protocol to that convention, containing a prohibition on cloning of human beings, came into force in 2001.[214] A further protocol dealing with the ethical aspects of the human genome and the development of new technology such as DNA chips is currently being prepared. This new protocol will deal, in a first part, with issues of individual genetic tests, screening programmes, gene therapy and genetics research. Issues of consent and quality of genetic services will be addressed, as well as, in a second part, the use of genetic tests in connection with employment and insurance.[215] The point here is that in the international context, a distinction is made between the different activities of the Council of Europe regarding, on the one hand, the principles applicable to natural reproduction and, on the other hand, the principles in the context of assisted reproduction. The same distinction can be found in the case law of the European Court, regarding establishment of parenthood. Accordingly the situations are distinguished in the discussion which follows.

2.2. NATURAL REPRODUCTION AND LEGAL PARENTHOOD

In this section a distinction is made between the establishment of the mother-child relationship and the child-father relationship.

212 Published at Strasbourg, 15th January 2002, CJ-FA (1001) 16 rev.

213 Signed on 4th April 1997, and in force 1st December 1999.

214 Additional Protocol to the Convention for the Protection of Human Rights and Dignity of the Human Being with regard to the Application of Biology and Medicine, on the prohibition of the Cloning of Human Beings, European Treaty Series nr. 168, signed on 12th January 1998; in force 1st March 2001.

215 The first meeting on the new protocol was in September 1997. The steering committee on Bio-Ethics considered the first part of the protocol in March 2004 (26th meeting of the steering Committee 16th-19th March 2004). The second part is currently under consideration.

2.2.1. *The Child-Mother Relationship*

In *Marckx v Belgium* the European Court held that the absence in Belgian law of the possibility for the unmarried mother Paula Marckx to establish, without serious disadvantages in matters such as inheritance law, a legal affiliation link between herself and her daughter Alexandra Marckx, violated Article 8 ECHR (lack of respect for private and family life), Article 14 in conjunction with the First Protocol, Article 1 ECHR (discrimination regarding quiet enjoyment of possessions) and Article 14 in conjunction with Article 8 ECHR (discrimination regarding respect for family life). The state's obligation imposed by Article 8 ECHR to respect family life

> *'means, amongst other things, that when the State determines in its domestic legal system the régime applicable to certain family ties such as those between an unmarried mother and her child, it must act in a manner calculated to allow those concerned to lead a normal family life. As envisaged by Article 8, respect for family life implies in particular, in the European Court's view, the existence in domestic law of legal safeguards that render possible as from the moment of birth the child's integration in his family. In this connection, the State has a choice of various means, but a law that fails to satisfy this requirement violates paragraph 1 without there being any call to examine it under paragraph 2.'*[216]

In considering the rules of the national systems above, it has been seen that only French law takes account of social factors which can influence whether a woman is or is not the child's mother (part. 1.2.1.2); in all other systems the decisive fact is that of giving birth to the child (part. 1.2.1). It will be seen below that, in relation to the father-child relationship, the European Court attaches considerable importance to the presence of social elements in the relationship between the parents or failing that between the child and the person regarding whom the legal affiliation link to the child is at issue. Regarding the European Court's judgment in the *Marckx case*, it is not entirely clear whether the European Court intended that the state's duty to provide for the establishment of the mother-child relationship arises purely by dint of birth or whether social elements were also considered relevant. In the *Marckx case* this matter was not put at issue since Paula and Alexandra did have a close social, as well as a biological, link to one another. The European Court remarks:

> *'Besides, it is not disputed that Paula Marckx assumed responsibility for her daughter Alexandra from the moment of her birth and has continuously cared for her, with the result that a real family life existed and still exists between them.'*[217]

---

216 ECtHR 13th June 1979, Series A vol. 31, § 31.
217 ECtHR 13th June 1979, Series A No. 31, § 31.

It is not certain that the European Court intended with this statement to imply that social facts regarding the mother-child relationship were needed to be established before the principles stated above requiring the establishment of parenthood could be activated. The fact that the requirement applies unconditionally and from the moment of birth suggests the contrary. In Principle 1 of the White Paper on Parenthood it is stressed that the bare fact of the birth determines legal maternal affiliation. Social aspects, such as the quality of the mother-child relationship are not relevant to the determination of the legal affiliation link. The Explanatory Notes to the White Paper state 'all previous circumstances concerning the conception and pregnancy (e.g. cases of surrogacy) and any subsequent modification of the legal parentage (e.g adoption by another person) will not affect the legal maternal affiliation at the moment of birth.'[218] By contrast, when the establishment of the father-child relationship is at issue, it will be seen below that the social character of the relationship between the mother and the man claiming to be the father or the relationship between the man and the child are of great importance.

2.2.2. The Child-Father Relationship

It has been seen above, in the consideration of the national systems, that the national systems allow for certain social circumstances, public and private interests which have an impact upon the possibility of establishing or annulling legal parenthood by a man (part. 1.3 above). One example are the restrictions applying to sperm donors on establishing parenthood at all (part 1.3.1.3(a)), the rules on locus standi regarding the establishment of parenthood (part. 1.3.1.3(b)), the restrictions on judicial annulment of paternity, (part. 1.3.1.4(b)) and the impact of apparent status and locus standi on the possibility of obtaining judicial annulment (part. 1.3.1.4(c) and (d)), and the use of statutory periods to restrict annulment of paternity (part. 1.3.1.3(e)). In various ways these rules take account of social elements in the relationship between the mother, legal father, putative father and the child. It will be seen below that, in relation to the father-child relationship, the European Court attaches importance to the presence of social elements in the relationship between the parents or failing that between the child and the person regarding whom the legal affiliation link to the child is at issue. However it will be seen that the European Court's main instrument is an instrument which does not appear within the scheme of our review of national laws at all: the presence or absence of a conflict of interest between the parties.

In the case law of the European Court regarding the establishment of the relationship between the child and the man claiming to be father there are three features which the European Court finds important:

---

218 Published at Strasbourg, 15th January 2002, CJ-FA (1001) 16 rev., page. 5.

(i) the presence or absence of a biological link between the man and the child;
(ii) the social relationship between the mother and father or between the father and the child;
(iii) the presence or absence of a conflict of interest regarding the establishment of parenthood.

2.2.2.1. The Presence or Absence of a Biological Link Between the Man and the Child

In many of the cases there was no dispute regarding the biological link between the man and the child. However, the presence of a biological link was disputed in the admissibility decision of the European Court in *Nylund v Denmark.*[219] The male applicant had had a brief relationship – lasting nine months, with cohabitation lasting seven months – with a woman. In the last two months of that period of cohabitation the woman became pregnant. Before the child was born the woman broke off the relationship with the applicant and married another man. The applicant, who had no right under Danish law to challenge the legal presumption of paternity arising by dint of marriage in favour of the mother's husband, brought his complaint to the European Court, alleging that Article 8 ECHR should give him the right to prove with DNA-testing that he was the child's father. The European Court stated:

> *'The Court notes that the instant case differs from the Rasmussen v Denmark*[220] *case in two respects. Firstly, in the Rasmussen case a husband wished to institute proceedings contesting his own paternity. Secondly, in that case the action aimed at the determination of the legal relations between the man and the child. In the instant case, the applicant's action is aimed at the confirmation of an alleged biological fact rather than at the establishment of legal relations. The Court finds, nonetheless, that the circumstances in the applicant's life in the spring of 1988, as described by the applicant himself, were such as to bring the facts of the instant case within the ambit of Article 8.'*

The fact that the biological link was contested was not fatal to the claim but caused the European Court to analyse the case as 'private life' rather than 'family life. For another reason discussed below in section 2.2.2.3 the European Court went on to hold the application inadmissible.

2.2.2.2. The Social Relationship Between the Mother and Father or Between the Father and the Child

The first step which the European Court takes when examining a complaint under Article 8 ECHR is to examine whether there is a relationship which can be qualified

219 Application nr. 27110/95, 29th June 1999.
220 *Rasmussen v Denmark*, ECtHR, 28th November 1984.

as 'private or family life' between the man alleging to be the father of the child and the mother. Family life can be established in one of two ways: if the relationship between the mother and the man alleging to be the father is of sufficient quality to qualify as 'family life', then the child who is born out of that relationship will be taken to have a relationship of 'family life' with the man concerned. Thus if the mother and father are married or have been, even though they have divorced by the time the child is born, there will be family life within the meaning of Article 8 ECHR.[221] If the mother and father have lived together in a stable relationship for a long time (in the case in question nineteen years) there will be family life, even if the mother was throughout married to someone else.[222] However even quite a short period of cohabitation, eleven months for example, may be enough to establish family life, if, for instance, the couple furthermore has marriage plans and the pregnancy was planned.[223] If the mother and father do not live together, but have a relationship of 'sufficient constancy' (in the case in question, they had four children together), there will also be family life.[224] In all these cases the European Court focuses upon the quality of the relationship between the parents and if on that basis 'family life' within the meaning of Article 8 ECHR is found to be present, the child is held to be included within that family life. Thus the European Court said in *Keegan v Ireland*:

> *'A child born out of such a relationship is ipso iure part of the "family" unit from the moment of his birth and by the very fact of it.'*[225]

If the man is not able to show sufficient quality in the relationship between himself and the mother he may nevertheless demonstrate that there is a relationship of 'family life' between himself and the child. In these cases the European Court focuses upon the quality of the actual contacts between the child and the man. However the European Court recognises that the mother has great power in this situation to thwart the development of social contacts between the child and the father. Thus the European Court has qualified even rather limited contacts between the child and the father, provided the father has shown consistent 'commitment' to the development of a relationship between himself and the child. Thus in *Lebbink v The Netherlands* the mother and father had lived together for about three years, but ceased cohabiting when the child was born. Perhaps this period of three years' cohabitation was already enough to qualify the relationship between the mother and father as family life, on the same basis as in *Keegan*. However the European Court went on to note that the father, although he had never lived with the child, was present at the birth, and had

---

221 *Berrehab v the Netherlands*, ECtHR 21st June 1988, Series A No. 138, § 21.

222 *Johnston v Ireland*, ECtHR 18th December 1986, Series A No. 112.

223 *Keegan v Ireland*, ECtHR 26th May 1994, Series A No. 291, §§ 44–45.

224 *Kroon v the Netherlands*, ECtHR 27 October 1994, Series A No. 297-C § 30.

225 *Keegan v Ireland*, ECtHR 26th May 1994, Series A No. 291, § 44.

visited her on several occasions and shown interest in the child's problems with her hearing. The totality of these factors supported a conclusion that there was family life between him and his daughter.[226] In conclusion: when the establishment of parenthood between the father and child is at issue, social factors are an important element in the European Court's case law. As suggested above, the situation when establishment of the father-child relationship is at issue probably contrasts with the situation when the mother-child relationship is at issue.

2.2.2.3. Presence or Absence of a Conflict of Interest Regarding the Establishment of Parenthood

Where there is no collision in the interests of the mother, father or child regarding the establishment of the father-child relationship, the European Court takes the view that national law should make provision for such legal establishment. Thus the European Court stated in *Kroon v The Netherlands*:

> *'According to the principles set out by the Court in its case-law, where the existence of a family tie with a child has been established, the State must act in a manner calculated to enable that tie to be developed and legal safeguards must be established that render possible as from the moment of birth or as soon as practicable thereafter the child's integration in his family (see, mutatis mutandis, the above-mentioned Keegan judgment, p. 19, para. 50).'*[227]

This principle is close to the principle quoted in section 2.2.1 above in the *Marckx case* in relation to the establishment of the mother-child relationship. The European Court, when regaled by arguments brought by the Dutch government as to why the father-child relationship should not be allowed to be recognised, responded:

> *'In the Court's opinion, "respect" for "family life" requires that biological and social reality prevail over a legal presumption which, as in the present case, flies in the face of both established fact and the wishes of those concerned without actually benefiting anyone. Accordingly, the Court concludes that, even having regard to the margin of appreciation left to the State, the Netherlands has failed to secure to the applicants the "respect" for their family life to which they are entitled under the Convention.'*[228] *(emphasis added)*

This approach, we suggest, is a key feature in the European Court's case law regarding parenthood. In the italicised phrase – referred to below as the 'biological and social reality rule,' the European Court is remarking *inter alia* that there is no conflict of

---

[226] *Lebbink v the Netherlands*, ECtHR, 1st June 2004.

[227] *Kroon v the Netherlands*, ECtHR 27th October 1994, Series A No. 297-C § 32.

[228] *Kroon v the Netherlands*, ECtHR 27th October 1994, Series A No. 297-C § 40.

interest between the mother, father and child regarding the establishment of the relationship between the father and child.

This principle was applied in *Nylund v Denmark*[229], discussed in section 2.2.2.1 above. Declaring the applicant's claim inadmissible, the European Court noted that the reason that the Danish Court of Appeal had rejected the applicant's claim was because allowing the DNA-testing would not have been in the child's interests. It also referred to the disturbance such an examination would cause to the family relationships in the child's family.

The question whether the establishment of the father-child relationship presents a collision between the interests of the mother, father and child is of greater weight in the European Court's case law than the question whether there are biological ties (issue (1) above) or social ties between the father and child (issue (2) above). This principle is shown by the case of *Yousef v the Netherlands.*[230] In *Yousef* there was no doubt whatsoever that the father was the child's biological father and furthermore the Dutch courts had allowed him to enjoy a right of access to his daughter. However the mother had always been opposed to the father being allowed to recognise the child. Under Dutch law her consent to recognition by the father was required; however the father was entitled to apply to the court for substitution of this consent. The father had made such application but the court had refused to substitute the mother's consent. Even after the mother died (when the child was seven) and the father applied once again for permission to recognise the child and thus to establish a legal affiliation link to her, the courts at all instances refused the permission. The father applied to the European Court alleging violation of Article 8 ECHR. When one considers the strength of the principle originated by the European Court in *Marckx v Belgium* and then applied in the cases of *Johnston v Ireland*, *Keegan v Ireland* and *Kroon v the Netherlands* as explained above (and quoted in the first quotation (from the *Kroon* case) in this section, it is clear that the father's claim to recognise the child was covered by the general rule. The European Court nevertheless upheld the decision of the Dutch courts, who judged that the child's interests would not be served by allowing the father to recognise her.[231] This case provides a very clear indication of the decisive effect in the European Court's case law of the presence of a conflict of interest (in the case in hand, between the father and the child) – coupled with the primacy of the child's interests – regarding the establishing of the father-child relationship.

---

229 Application nr. 27110/95, 29th June 1999.

230 *Yousef v the Netherlands*, ECtHR 5th December 2002, RJD 2002-VIII, p. 245.

231 *Yousef v the Netherlands*, ECtHR 5th December 2002, RJD 2002-VIII, p. 245, § 51.

2.2.3. *Legal Recognition of Family Life: The Criteria*

From the study of the European Court's leading case law on the establishment of the father-child relationship we have derived in the previous section three elements which play a role in the decisions: (1) a biological link; (2) the social factors, whether derived from the relationship between the father and the mother or between the father and the child or possibly a combination of both; (3) the presence or absence of a conflict of interest. These features apply in a given case in combination. We will now examine with a brief overview what the combined effect is of these features. The examination of the elements in combination will indicate the relative weight accorded by the European Court to the three elements.

In *Marckx v Belgium*, there was an undisputed biological link, and furthermore social links, although, as signalled above in part 2.2.1, in the case of the mother-child relationship a social link is probably not required. Furthermore, there was no conflict of interest regarding the establishment of the mother-child relationship. The European Court held that Articles 8, 14 and First Protocol, Article 1 ECHR were violated, and Belgium was required to adjust its laws in order to make possible the establishment of the mother-child relationship.

In *Keegan v Ireland*, there was a biological link between the child and the father, moreover there were sufficient social factors, qualifying as 'family life', to attract the protection of Article 8 ECHR. In this case there was no conflict between the interests of the mother, father and child regarding the establishment of parenthood. In that case what was at issue was the father's right to be informed that the mother had placed the child for adoption so that he was in a position to take steps to establish a legal affiliation link or other steps in relation to her. In this case there was no conflict of interest in fact as the child had long since been placed for adoption so that the father had no hope of exercising his rights. But on the hypothesis that he had been on time with his claim, there still would not necessarily have been a conflict of interest. The mother, by placing the child for adoption, had no interest in stopping the father from establishing a link to the child, at least in the absence of an indication that the establishment of the child-father relationship was against the child's interests. In *Keegan's case* the European Court found a violation of Article 8 ECHR by the fact that Irish law gave the father no right to be informed of the adoption and therefore no right to protect any rights regarding the legal affiliation link between himself and the child. In *Kroon v the Netherlands* the analysis is similar: there was a biological link between the father and child, there were social links and there was no conflict of interest between the mother and the father or between one of the parents and the child regarding the establishment of a legal affiliation link. The European Court held that the Netherlands had to change its law to make it possible to establish the legal affiliation link.

The break in the line is *Yousef v the Netherlands*, in which case there was a biological and social link between the child and the father. But in this case there was a conflict of interest: the courts were convinced that the establishment of the legal affiliation link between the child and father was not in the child's interests. In *Yousef's case* the European Court found no violation of Article 8 ECHR and there was no responsibility on the state to allow the legal affiliation link between the child and father to be created. This case confirms the overall picture that the presence or absence of a conflict of interest between the mother, father and child regarding the establishment of the legal affiliation link between the child and father plays a decisive role in the European Court's decision to intervene regarding the national rules on the establishment of parenthood.

2.2.4. Private Life and Legal Parenthood

In a number of cases the European Court has examined issues relating to parenthood in relation to the duty of the state under Article 8 ECHR to respect the 'private life' of the applicants. It is necessary to examine these cases to obtain a more complete picture of the vision which the European Court has developed regarding the minimum standards with which the member states are required to comply regarding the laws of parenthood or laws closely related therewith. These 'private life' cases will be examined in the light of the three elements given above.

In *Odièvre v France*,[232] the European Court was confronted with the question whether the system of *accouchement sous X* allowed by the French Civil Code is compatible with the right, guaranteed by Article 8 ECHR, to private life of the person who is born as a result of anonymous birth. (This system is referred to in part. 1.3.1.2 above, by footnote 68). The European Court had to balance, on the one hand, the interests which the system of *accouchement sous X* aims to protect, namely, the rights to privacy of the mother who has become pregnant in unhappy circumstances and the interests of the state in preventing resort by such desperate women to illegal abortion or child abandonment, and, on the other hand, the right or interest of the person thus born to know the identity of the mother and preferably also the father. The European Court held that France was entitled to preserve the secrecy of the mother's identity. The European Court contrasted the issue in *Odièvre* with the situation in *Mikulić v Croatia*,[233] where the issue raised was the slowness and ineffectiveness of the procedures to establish whether a certain man was the child's biological father. Regarding the conflict of interest the European Court in *Odièvre* said:

[232] *Odièvre v France*, ECtHR 13th February 2003.
[233] *Mikulić v Croatia*, ECtHR, 7th February 2002, RJD 2002-I.

'On the one hand, people have a right to know their origins, that right being derived from a wide interpretation of the scope of the notion of private life. .... On the other hand, a woman's interest in remaining anonymous in order to protect her health by giving birth in appropriate medical conditions cannot be denied. In the present case, the applicant's mother never went to see the baby at the clinic and appears to have greeted their separation with total indifference (see paragraph 12 above). Nor is it alleged that she subsequently expressed the least desire to meet her daughter. The Court's task is not to judge that conduct, but merely to take note of it. The two private interests with which the Court is confronted in the present case are not easily reconciled; moreover, they do not concern an adult and a child, but two adults, each endowed with her own free will.'[234] *(emphasis added)*

Applying the analysis as developed above, in *Odièvre's case* there was a biological link, but no social links between the child and the mother. For that reason the case was classified as 'private life' rather than 'family life'. There was a conflict of interest between the right to privacy of the mother and the child's right to know the identity of the person from whom she was biologically descended. That conflict of interest played a central role in the European Court's conclusion that Article 8 ECHR had not been violated by the rule protecting anonymous birth.

In *Znamenskaya v Russia* the European Court considered an application by Natalya Vasilyevna who had given birth to a stillborn child on 1st August 1997 after a pregnancy of thirty-five weeks. Her complaint concerned the refusal of the Russian authorities to allow her to record her deceased partner as the child's biological father, including the consequential change of the stillborn child's name to include the patronymic name. The partner had been put in a detention facility on 20th June 1997, some six weeks before the child was stillborn, when the pregnancy was about twenty-nine weeks advanced. The partner died in custody on 12th October 1997. Because of this detention, said the applicant, the partner had not been able to file a joint application with her to officially record the partner as the child's father. In her application based on Article 8 ECHR the applicant relied specifically[235] upon the 'biological and social reality principle' established in *Kroon v the Netherlands*, (and identified in part 2.2.2.3 above (second quotation in that part)) as establishing the relevance of an absence of conflict of interest when furthering a claim based on Article 8 ECHR. In *Znamenskaya* there was no dispute regarding the biological link, but the paternity established by law was alleged to conflict with the social facts.[236] In such case the role of social factors is considerable.

---

234 *Odièvre v France*, ECtHR 13th February 2003, §44.

235 *Znamenskaya v Russia*, ECtHR 12th October 2005, § 21.

236 In the absence of DNA-testing the assumption that there was a biological link between the father and child is risky as the father was dead and therefore not able to defend his interests.

The analysis of the social links in this case is rather strange. The European Court did not find sufficient social links to justify a finding of family life, but on the basis of the link between the mother and the unborn child found private life to be established. The European Court ignored the relationship between the mother and alleged father of the unborn child.[237] As shown in the quotation from *Kroon v the Netherlands* cited in part 2.2.2.3 above, the European Court's previous case law establishes that the relationship between the mother and father, if qualifying as 'family life', can be sufficient to establish 'family life' between the father and child. This would apply even though the father died before the birth, and thus, just like the father in *Keegan*, was unable to establish any social links to the child. The European Court seems to have overlooked this possibility, and in particular the mother's assertion – and its implications for the establishment of family life – that she had lived with the alleged father since 1994, meaning a cohabitation of between two and three years.[238] The fact that the mother was throughout the relevant period married to another man does not affect the relevance of facts tending to establish family life; in *Kroon v the Netherlands* Mrs Kroon was also married to one M'Hallem Driss throughout the period of her relationship with Zerrouk, the father of her four children. The lack of attention of the European Court in *Znamenskaya* for any social factors regarding the link between the father and the child is unsatisfactory, as it ignores the quality of the relationship between the mother and alleged social father. This point is recognised by the three judges who dissented; in fact this is the very reason for their dissent.[239] So, returning to our three-pronged analysis (part 2.2.3 above), we suggest that there were some social factors in *Znamenskaya*, namely the cohabitation between the mother and alleged father, which were relevant to the claim. Finally, was there a conflict of interest? We suggest that on the facts it was actually rather risky to conclude that the mother and alleged father wanted the same thing, since the latter was dead and had at no stage indicated whether he considered himself linked to the child. However, the European Court considered this a case in which the interests of all three parties (two of whom were dead) pointed in the same direction, as it said:

> 'According to the Court's case-law, the situation where a legal presumption is allowed to prevail over biological and social reality, without regard to both established facts and the wishes of those concerned and without actually benefitting anyone, is not compatible, even having regard to the margin of appreciation left to the State, with the obligation to secure effective "respect" for private and family life (*Kroon*, cited above, §40).There has been therefore a violation of Article 8 of the Convention.'[240]

---

237 *Znamenskaya v Russia*, ECtHR 12th October 2005, § 27.

238 *Znamenskaya v Russia*, ECtHR 12th October 2005, § 12.

239 Judges Rozakis, Botoucharova and Hajiyev.

240 *Znamenskaya v Russia*, ECtHR 12th October 2005, § 31–32.

The European Court invoked the 'biological and social reality' rule derived from the *Kroon* case again in the case of *Shofman v Russia*. Shofman was, by dint of the legal presumption of paternity, legal father of the child who had been born to his wife on 12th May 1995. In September 1997 he learned that he was not the biological father of the child. Due to the inflexible time-limits applied in Russian law, the applicant was time-barred from challenging the presumption of paternity. The applicant complained that Article 8 ECHR had been violated. Applying the scheme used above in part. 2.2.3 to examine the European Court cases, there is in this case no biological link. There were social factors, namely the marriage between the applicant and his wife, and between September 1995 and March 1996 the applicant lived with his wife and son and, in the belief that he was his biological son, treated him as his child. The European Court, holding that Russian law violated Article 8 ECHR by time-barring the applicant's challenge to the presumption of paternity in such circumstances, invoked the 'biological and social reality' rule, arguing that the time-bar was 'without regard to established facts and the wishes of those concerned'.[241] One might question whether this was a good example of a case to apply that rule, as the interests of the applicant in challenging the presumption of paternity was not self-evidently compatible with the interests of the boy, who was still very young and definitely in need of financial support, in having a legal father. Nevertheless one can see that the European Court finds the 'biological and social reality' rule a magic formula which readily provides the Court with the space it needs to find that the national rule has transgressed the ECHR.

In *Paulík v Slovakia*, the facts of which were closely similar to those in *Shofman v Russia*, concerning the applicant's inability to challenge the presumption of paternity due to time bars on the action, the European Court explored the nature of the conflict of interest between the applicant (man wishing to challenge the presumption) and his daughter. Again the European Court invoked the magic formula and said:

> 'As to the general interest, it is to be noted that the applicant's putative daughter is currently almost 40 years old, has her own family and is not dependent on the applicant for maintenance (contrast with *Yildirim*[242]). The general interest in protecting her rights at this stage has lost much of its importance compared to when she was a child. Furthermore, [the mother] initiated the DNA test and said that she had no objection to the applicant's disclaiming paternity. It therefore appears that the lack of a procedure for bringing the legal position into line with the biological reality flies in the face of the wishes of those concerned and does not in fact benefit anyone (see *Kroon and Others v. the Netherlands*, judgment of 27 October 1994, Series A No. 297 C, p. 58, §40).'[243]

241 *Shofman v Russia*, ECtHR, 24th February 2006, § 44.

242 *Yildirim v. Austria*, ECtHR 19th October 1999.

243 *Paulík v. Slovakia*, ECtHR 10th October 2006.

2.2.5. *The Significance of the European Court's Attention for the Presence or Absence of a Conflict of Interest*

What does all this have to do with harmonisation? We have shown in the foregoing, beginning at part. 2.2.2, that three elements feature in the judgments by the European Court in questions regarding the establishment of a legal affiliation link between the father and child in cases of natural parenthood: biological link; social links and the presence or absence of a conflict of interest. We have furthermore shown that the last element often plays a decisive role in the European Court's decision. In other words, the absence of a conflict of interest between the mother, father and the child provides a significant reason for the European Court to lay down a limit to the law of parenthood which the national rule has transgressed. But when we reflect on the overview of the national rules governing the law of parenthood (in part I above and most particularly part. 1.3) we see that the situations in which there is no conflict of interest between the parties are not the difficult questions. Whereas in part 1.3 we have identified a considerable number of rules in which there is marked discrepancy between the rules of the legal systems studied, these rules govern situations which will frequently be marked by a conflict of interest. It thus seems that the European Court, which in its decisions regarding natural parenthood seems to be increasingly addicted to the 'social and biological reality' rule, is not busy with formulating new rules which might resolve new types of conflicts in the law of parenthood. Were the European Court to undertake such activity, this would put the member states under increasing pressure to bring their laws concerning parenthood closer together. In the light of the foregoing (part 2 of this article), the task of the European Court seems to be rather more confined to identifying outdated, discriminatory rules which are of no benefit to anyone. In really ground-breaking conflicts of interest in cases such as *Odièvre v France*, discussed above or *Evans v the United Kingdom*[244] the European Court can be criticised for backing off from determining the real conflict of interest which is at the heart of the issue.

2.3. ASSISTED REPRODUCTION

It has been noted earlier that there is a recognised distinction between determination of parenthood in cases of natural reproduction and in cases of assisted reproduction. We have noted in part. 2.1 that when one considers the rule-making activities of the Council of Europe this distinction is not watertight. However, the European Court does make a sharp distinction. In *X, Y and Z v United Kingdom* the European Court was called upon to decide whether Article 8 ECHR was violated by the lack of a

244 *Evans v United Kingdom*, ECtHR 7th March 2006.

possibility for X to be registered as the father of the four children who were born to his partner, Y. X was a female-to-male transsexual, who had made his transformation with the full blessing and support of the British National Health Service. Furthermore, the children had also been conceived using sperm donation provided by the very same National Health Service. It is therefore not surprising that when the children were born the applicant was expecting to be able to establish in a formality that he was the children's legal father. Due to the law of the United Kingdom at that time, there was no possibility for X and Y to get married. Had X and Y been married, X would have experienced no difficulty establishing himself as the children's legal father, as he would have been presumed to be so by the presumption of legitimacy. Furthermore, had X not been a transsexual, he would have had the possibility, granted by the Human Fertilisation and Embryology Act, Section 27, to register himself, following conception by sperm donation with the full consent of both partners, as the children's legal father. None of this was possible for X, who therefore brought his case to the European Court, relying on Article 8 ECHR and the rule in *Johnston v Ireland*, *Keegan v Ireland* and *Kroon v the Netherlands*, cited in part 2.2.2.3 above, according to which the legal system should make it possible at the date of birth or as soon as possible thereafter, to establish the legal affiliation link between the father and child. Holding that Article 8 ECHR did not protect the applicant's claim to be registered as the legal father of his children, the Court said:

> 'It is true that the Court has held in the past that where the existence of a family tie with a child has been established, the State must act in a manner calculated to enable that tie to be developed and legal safeguards must be established that render possible, from the moment of birth or as soon as practicable thereafter, the child's integration in his family (see for example the above-mentioned *Marckx* judgment, p. 15, para. 31; the *Johnston and Others v. Ireland* judgment of 18 December 1986, Series A No. 112, p. 29, para. 72; the above-mentioned *Keegan* judgment, p. 19, para. 50; and the above-mentioned *Kroon and Others* judgment, p. 56, para. 32). However, hitherto in this context it has been called upon to consider only family ties existing between biological parents and their offspring. The present case raises different issues, since Z was conceived by AID and is not related, in the biological sense, to X, who is a transsexual.'[245]

As there was no common ground between the member states regarding the law applicable to the parenthood of transsexuals, the European Court saw no reason to find that Article 8 ECHR had been violated.[246] It is to be hoped that the law in this regard has been changed by the creative decisions in *Goodwin and I. v United Kingdom*,[247] on the question of civil status and the right to marry of transsexuals.

245 *X, Y and Z v United Kingdom*, 22nd April 1997, § 43.
246 *X, Y and Z v United Kingdom*, 22nd April 1997, § 44–45.
247 *Goodwin v United Kingdom, I. v United Kingdom*, 11th July 2002.

However an examination of that question would go outside the scope of this essay, which is to examine the role of the European Court in bringing about harmonisation in the law of parenthood.

2.4. ASSISTED REPRODUCTION: THE CRITERIA

It remains to apply our analytical scheme (the three-pronged criteria explained in part. 2.2.3) to the *X,Y and Z case.* In that case there was no biological link between the applicant and his children, however the European Court acknowledged there were sufficient social factors to enable the relationship between him, his partner and their four children to qualify for protection as 'family life'.[248] There was also no conflict of interest; all the parties wanted the same thing. However, the European Court introduced a new factor which seems inextricably linked to the newness of the claim and its character as concerning assisted reproduction; namely, there was no common ground.

3. CONVERGENCE OR DIVERGENCE?

We started with the assumption that in order to determine the harmonising effect of the case law of the European Court, one first has to determine how legal systems differ. After that, one has to analyse to what extent the case law of the European Court allows for the differences between the legal systems. So far, we have analysed these two aspects separately.

In the first part we have presented a model which systematically shows the differences between the laws on affiliation.[249] The model allows us to differentiate the grounds for legal affiliation and the 'secondary principles' on the basis of which a deviation from the basic principle is allowed. So for example, we have seen that genetic affiliation is the ground for legal paternity in case of natural reproduction in all the legal systems under consideration. However, some legal systems like the Dutch, the French and the German legal system allow for exceptions to this basic principle on the basis of secondary principles such as legal certainty and the protection of the private life of the members of the legal family.

The first conclusion which follows from the analysis of the national legal systems in the first part is that legal systems differ most profoundly from one another at the most elementary level of the model: the grounds for legal affiliation. It has been shown that legal maternity can be based either on apparent status or on the fact of giving

[248] *X,Y and Z v United Kingdom*, 22nd April 1997, § 36–37.

[249] Par. 1.1 A model for the comparison of national laws on legal affiliation.

birth. In case of legal paternity, the basis is either genetic paternity, apparent status or intention. It has been shown that legal systems do not only differ as to which grounds they use, but also as to the demarcation of the grounds: intention as a ground for legal parenthood under French law works differently compared to intention as a ground for legal paternity under English or Swedish law.[250]

The second conclusion is that, although legal systems share the same secondary principles, these principles have been worked out differently. This is evidenced by the different rules on periods of limitation, *locus standi* and the function of apparent status. The most important interests which are put forward to allow a deviation from the ground for legal affiliation are legal certainty and the stability of the child's legal affiliation status and the protection of the private life of the members of the legal family.[251]

In the second part we analysed the case law of the European Court in matters of legal parenthood. This analysis allows for two conclusions. In the first place, it has been shown by the Court's decision in *X, Y and Z v. United Kingdom* that its approach towards family life and legal parenthood depends on whether the case is about natural reproduction or artificial insemination. From a national perspective, such a differentiation gives no reason for surprise, because national legal systems do the same.

The second conclusion is however more revealing. It appeared that unlike in the case of national legal systems, it is hard to derive a basis for legal affiliation from the Court's case law. We have observed that when one considers the three criteria used by the European Court to determine whether a man has family life with a child which should be respected by the State, *i.e.* biological link, social relationship or the presence of a conflict of interest between the parties, that the last feature often plays a decisive role in the European Court's decision.[252]

A conflict of interest between the mother, father and child (in any combination of conflict of interest) forms a reason for the European Court not to intervene and to allow the State concerned a wide margin of appreciation to resolve the conflict of interest. This means that national systems are not, in the cases where there is a really difficult conflict to resolve, being pinned down by the European Court to comply with a minimum norm under Article 8 ECHR. We suggest that the European Court is rather more confining its task to smoothing things over in cases where the rules have already been established. A classical example is the case of *Marckx v Belgium*, in fact, where the judgment was founded upon an existing treaty obligation (with which, it must be agreed, not all states were in compliance). The fact that the European Court sometimes gets in a muddle with its ideas about a conflict of interest, as happened in *Znamenskaya v Russia*, does not, in our view, change the basic picture. In fact, in

250 Par. 1.2. Grounds for legal affiliation.
251 Par. 1.3. Establishment and annulment of legal parenthood.
252 Par. 2.2. Natural reproduction and legal parenthood.

the overall picture, we suggest that the role of the European Court is much less adventurous in relation to natural parenthood than, at first blush, might be expected, on the basis of the volume of case law, for example.

The absence of a basis for legal parenthood is even more apparent in the case of artificial reproduction.[253] Very explicitly, the European Court has made it clear in *X, Y and Z v United Kingdom* that it does not consider that it has a harmonising role to play.

If we combine the conclusions of the first and the second part, it follows that it is hard to apply the model we used to analyse the national legal systems to the case law of the European Court in matters concerning legal parenthood. Although, one could argue that in case of natural reproduction the basis for legal paternity is biological affiliation in combination with social factors (first layer of the model), it is not clear at all what the exceptions to this basis are (second layer of the model). It only follows from our analysis in the second part that in case of a conflict of interest the State has a wide margin of appreciation to solve that conflict of interest, but the Court gives no guidance as to how that conflict of interest should be solved. Moreover, in case of legal maternity and in case of legal parenthood following artificial reproduction the ground for legal affiliation is lacking completely.

What does this tell us about the harmonising effect of the Court's case law? Our analysis shows that the harmonising effect should not be overestimated. Apparently, the Court does not perceive its function as being the setting of Europe-wide standards for legal parenthood. The Court and its case law function as a complementary system next to national legal systems, to correct certain results following from the rigid application of national law on legal affiliation. In performing its corrective role in the field of legal parenthood the European Court, apparently, is lead by principles which are determined by the Member States and not vice versa.

---

253 Par. 2.4. Assisted reproduction: the criteria.

MATRIMONIAL PROPERTY LAW: DIVERSITY OF FORMS, EQUIVALENCE IN SUBSTANCE?[1]

BENTE BRAAT

1. INTRODUCTION

Are we moving towards harmonisation of matrimonial property law in Europe? Is there, well hidden behind the diversity of forms, an equivalence of substance?

Looking for an answer is like being a gold digger or a treasure hunter. This does not only mean that there may be a surprise at the end but also that there will be some traps to overcome and clues to solve. First of all, what are we exactly talking about? What is matrimonial property law? Answering this question in the light of one specific legislation may already not be an easy task but it gets even more complicated when trying to find a definition that would work in a European perspective, that is to say making it possible to determine whether we, in Europe, are moving towards harmonisation or not.[2]

Matrimonial property law is difficult to define, because, first of all, the notion as such has not always traditionally been used in all European countries.[3] It is also difficult

---

1 This title is directly inspired by the chapter on matrimonial property law of the book by ANTOKOLSKAIA, M., *Harmonisation of Family Law in Europe: A Historical perspective, A Tale of two Millennia*, Intersentia, Antwerp-Oxford, 2006, where she explains that researchers are looking at matrimonial property law on two different level: the functional level of functional solutions on the one hand and the formal level of legal techniques, concepts and rules on the other.

2 In international instruments the following terms are used: The Brussels II and IIbis Regulations (EC No. 1347/2000 and EC No. 2201/2003) both avoid the use of the concept matrimonial property law by using the term 'property consequences of the marriage'. The Green paper on conflict of laws in matters concerning matrimonial property regimes, including the question of jurisdiction and mutual recognition, (SEC(2006) 952) doesn't use the concept matrimonial property law but give a definition of matrimonial property regimes. They are 'the sets of legal rules relating to the spouses' financial relationships resulting from their marriage, both with each other and with third parties, in particular their creditors'.

3 ANTOKOLSKAIA, M., *Harmonisation of Family Law in Europe: A Historical perspective, A Tale of two Millennia* (2006), p. 481.

to define because it is situated at a crossroads: a crossroads of family law and property law but also of several parts of family law, as for example marriage law, succession law or maintenance law. The third difficulty of finding a well working and accurate definition ensues from the fact that the term matrimonial property law often encompasses two different things. It includes, on the one hand, some imperative rules influencing the spouses' financial relationship,[4] sometimes called the primary regime,[5] and on the other hand, rules focussing on the matrimonial property regimes itself, which may formulate a default regime[6] and in some legislations several other regimes spouses can choose to apply by way of a marital contract. One should therefore be careful when using the concept of matrimonial property law. Perhaps we do not really need to use it. In fact what we will try to find out here is whether the property situation of two married persons is, in Europe, ruled by look-alike principles. To answer this question we will look at several sub-questions: first how is the property of the spouses arranged during marriage (is there a community of assets, or do spouses hold their property separately?), secondly how is that property managed and by whom, thirdly what are the creditor's rights on that property and finally how is the property distributed upon dissolution.

The question of the definition is not the only difficulty we have to cope with. There is a second trap on our road to the treasure. It is a geographical one. To give a well justified answer to the question whether or not matrimonial property law is, in Europe, moving towards harmonisation, all European jurisdictions would have to

4 VERBEKE, A., *et al*, 'European marital property law. Survey 1988–1994', *ERPL* (1995), p. 445–482.

5 For example, in opposition to France or Belgium where the concept of primary regime is commonly used, this is not the case in German law, even if the part of the German civil code entitled 'Wirkung der Ehe in allgemeinen' (§§ 1353–1362 German Civil Code) fulfils the same function. See: MARTINY, D., 'Ein zusätzlicher Güterstand für Europa?', in: HOFER, S., KLIPPEL, D., WALTER, U., (eds.), *Perspektiven des Familienrechts, Festschrift für Dieter Schwab*, Gieseking Verlag, Bielefeld, 2005, p. 1189–1207. The use of the term primary regime in the Questionnaire for the Study in comparative law on the rules governing conflicts of jurisdiction and laws on matrimonial property regimes and the implementations for property issues of the separation of unmarried couples in the Member States (2003) directed by the Consortium Asser-UCL, has led to some misunderstandings as the term was sometimes understood as a synonym of default regime. See for example the Danish Report, See under Justice and Home Affaires: Studies in judicial cooperation in civil and commercial matters: http://europa.eu.int/comm/justice_home/doc_centre/civil/studies/doc_civil_studies_en.htm.

6 I.e. the legal non contractual marital property regime entering into force at the time of conclusion of the marriage in case the spouses did not draft a marital contract. See: VERBEKE, A., *et al*, 'European marital property law. Survey 1988–1994' (1995), p. 445–482.

be overviewed. This is beyond the scope of this paper.[7] The answer presented here, will therefore only be a partial one, including only some European countries.

Now that some of the traps have been revealed, the search can begin. Is there in Europe as far as the property situation of spouses is concerned a diversity of form (2) but an equivalence in substance (3)? This question will bring us some steps closer to an optional matrimonial property regime for Europe (4).

2. DIVERSITY OF FORMS REGULATING THE PROPERTY OF SPOUSES

European legislators certainly have a lot of imagination and a wide range of ways to regulate the effect of marriage on the property of spouses have been invented. Some prefer to reject the idea that marriage should have any influence (2.1) whereas others still think that marriage should influence the financial situation of spouses. But then they do not all have the same idea about what shape the influence should take (2.2).

2.1. MATRIMONIAL PROPERTY OR NO MATRIMONIAL PROPERTY REGIME? THAT IS THE QUESTION.

The main difference regarding matrimonial property law in Europe is the one of the existence or not of the institution of matrimonial property regime as such.[8] It is far from a secret: as far as English law is concerned marriage has no effect on the status of property of the spouses: each spouse holds his or her property separately, as if they were not married at all. There is no explicit legal regime, since there is no specific set of rules regulating the patrimonial consequences.[9] However, this does not mean that marriage has no effect at all. Indeed, as clearly stated in the interim report of the study

---

7 Several comparative law studies have been made encompassing several European legislations. See for example: VERBEKE, A., *et al*, 'European marital property law. Survey 1988–1994', *ERPL* 1995, p. 445–482; VERBEKE, A., *Goederenverdeling bij echtscheiding*, MAKLU, Antwerpen, 1991; HENRICH, D., SCHWAB, D., (eds.), *Eheliche Gemeinschaft, Partnerschaft und Vermögen im europäischen Vergleich*, Verlag Gieseking, Bielefeld, 1999; BOELE-WOELKI, K., *et al*, *Huwelijksvermogensrecht in rechtsvergelijkend perpectief*, Ars Notariatus CIII, Kluwer, Deventer, 2000; Study in comparative law on the rules governing conflicts of jurisdiction and laws on matrimonial property regimes and the implementations for property issues of the separation of unmarried couples in the Member States (2003). See under Justice and Home Affaires: Studies in judicial cooperation in civil and commercial matters: http://europa.eu.int/comm/justice_home/doc_centre/civil/studies/doc_civil_studies_en.htm.

8 CRETNEY, S., *et al*, *Principles of Family Law*, Sweet & Maxwell, London, 2002, para. 4–002, p. 102.

9 VERBEKE, A., *et al*, 'European marital property law. Survey 1988–1994' (1995), p. 445–482.

'Community of property. A regime for England and Wales': 'marriage affects property rights by subjecting them potentially to the court's discretionary jurisdiction on divorce'.[10]

2.2. MATRIMONIAL PROPERTY LAW IN EUROPE: A COLOURFUL PATCHWORK?

If we leave the situation of English law aside for a minute, what does the matrimonial property law in some of the other European countries look like?

2.2.1. Community or no Community During the Marriage

How is the property of the spouses arranged during marriage? Do they hold everything in common? Or is, on the contrary, everything separate? Or is it a combination of both situations? In a continental terminology, this is the question of the existence or not of a community during marriage and will influence the next three topics. Among the 25 member states of the EU a majority of legislations know a community of property as a legal regime. Since we wonder about the situation during marriage, the systems of deferred community or with another kind of participation taking place after dissolution belong to the category separation. In the category community property one can distinguish between the limited community of property (Art. 1398 ff Belgian Civil Code, Art. 1401 French Civil Code and Art. 1401 ff Luxemburger Civil Code, for example) and the total community of property (Art. 93 Book 1 Dutch Civil Code)).[11]

2.2.2. Management of Property

The second question regards management of property. Again a distinction must be made between systems of community and systems of separation. For community systems a distinction must be made between management of the community and management of the separate property.[12] In principle, in most of the legislations surveyed the management of the separate property is sole and exclusive and this is also sometimes the case of the community of property (at least in the Netherlands,

10 COOKE, E., AKOTO, T., BALOW, A., CALLUS, T., 'Community of Property – A Regime for England and Wales: Interim Report', *IFL* (2005), p. 133–137.

11 For some time now, the Dutch legislator is thinking about modifying some rules of matrimonial property law, and among other things to cut down the community up to a limited one excluding property acquired by inheritance or gift. See: Bill 'Aanpassing wettelijke gemeenschap van goederen', Dutch Second Chamber, File 28867, 2005–2006, n°9 and 10.

12 VERBEKE, A., *et al*, 'European marital property law. Survey 1988–1994' (1995), p. 445–482.

where every spouse manages the community property he/she acquires, see Art. 90 and 97 Book 1 Dutch Civil Code)[13], but most of the time the management of the community is concurrent (see for example Art. 1421 French Civil Code and Art. 1416 Belgian Civil Code). In regimes based on separation, each spouse manages its property, at least in principle, alone (see for example Sec. 16(1) Danish Act on the Legal Effects of Marriage).

In the systems with a community of property during the marriage but also to some extent in systems without community during the marriage and especially in those which guarantee a right of sharing at the end of the marriage, the principle of autonomy of management is mitigated by several imperative rules requiring consent of the other spouse for certain important acts.[14] In some legislations this set of rules obligatory to all the spouses regardless of their matrimonial property regime is called the primary regime. They are the consequence of the impact of, on the one hand, the need of protection of the living environment of the spouses[15] and, on the other hand, of patrimonial solidarity.[16] But here I am in fact already looking at the common core of European legislations. As you see when you do not go too much into detail, the common principles come to light and you can not help noticing them.

2.2.3. *Creditor's Rights*

The topic of the creditor's rights is certainly the one where the most diversity remains. This is, however, rather a consequence of the way the assets of the spouses are arranged during marriage than a proof of a diversity in Europe. As creditors may recover from the entire patrimony of their debtor, they can always seize all the debtor's income, regardless whether it is qualified as private or as community property. This principle has of course different meanings according to the way the property is arranged: in systems of separation of property, the creditor can in principle only seize the separate property of his debtor whereas in systems of community he may also have the possibility to seize a part of the community[17] or the whole community.[18]

---

13 The Dutch Bill also foresee to modify the management rules. Bill 'Aanpassing wettelijke gemeenschap van goederen', Dutch Second Chamber, File 28867, 2005–2006, n°9 and 10.

14 VERBEKE, A., *et al*, 'European marital property law. Survey 1988–1994' (1995), p. 445–482.

15 A spouse may often not dispose of the family home (and sometimes also not of the furniture) without the consent of the other spouse. See i.e., Art. 215 French Civil Code and Art. 88 Book 1 Dutch Civil Code.

16 See i.e., § 1365 German Civil Code and Art. 180 Italian Civil Code.

17 See i.e. Art. 1410–1413 French Civil Code.

18 See i.e. Art. 95 Book 1 Dutch Civil Code.

2.2.4. *Distribution of Property upon Dissolution*

Two questions must be distinguished. The first one concerns the mass which is the object of distribution and the second one concerns the method of distribution.

In the systems with a community during the marriage, the divisible mass consists of the community, which can be total or limited. In systems based on separation, the divisible mass may also be total (Sec. 15 Danish Act on the Legal Effects of Marriage) or limited (§1363 al. 2, 2nd sentence German Civil Code or §81 Austrian Marriage Act), but the divisible mass itself only arises after dissolution.

The existence or not of a community during the marriage has a strong impact on the question of distribution of property upon dissolution. In the community of property systems the main technique consists of dividing the community of property in to equal shares. But also in the legislations where the matrimonial property regime is based on separation, the need for a patrimonial correction at the end of the marriage has been recognised. But then the concrete way to realise this participation varies quite a lot. Three different techniques will be set out but in fact there are some more variations, which are however all on the same theme.

The first possibility is the one of a community arising after dissolution, the so-called deferred community. Community which will then be divided into two equal parts. It is for example, in principle, the system of Denmark (Sec. 15 and 16 Danish Act on the Legal Effects of Marriage). The second solution, consists of comparing the matrimonial gains of both spouses and to attribute to the spouse with less matrimonial gains a share in the gains of his former spouse. This is the German system (§1363 al. 2, 2nd sentence German Civil Code).[19] The third system is the one of equitable distribution and consists in giving all the power to the judge who will then decide on a reallocation of property. This is the English solution. Of course, as already said, other possibilities exist in Europe (see i.e. the Austrian system), and for example, a combination between, let's say, solution 1 and 3 can be found.

More than once in this part of this paper focusing on the diversity of forms or solution in Europe the resemblance of the principles behind the solution had to be mentioned. The next part will precisely address this issue.

---

19 In this system the initial assets are compared to the final assets. The difference between the two then constitute the matrimonial gains. STEENHOFF, G.J.W., 'A Matrimonial Property System for the European Union?', *IFL* (2005), p. 74–77.

3. EQUIVALENCE IN SUBSTANCE

Are there common principles to overcome the breach between common law and civil law in this area of matrimonial property law? And what about the diversity of forms in the other European systems, is this perhaps also only a façade?

3.1. THE GAP BETWEEN ENGLAND AND THE REST OF THE EU ISN'T THAT BIG AFTER ALL

First of all and this is perhaps one of the most important points, the gap between England and the rest of the EU isn't that big after all. One would not be too far from the truth when qualifying the English system as a legal regime of separation of property. So one can say in a way that some kind of matrimonial regime exists even if you have to read between the lines to find it.[20]

And that is not all, the House of Lords decision in *White v White*[21] already gave rise to claims that England and Wales have in practice adopted a system of deferred community of property. Indeed there is a separate property of spouses during marriage, followed by a requirement to measure the division of the parties' assets on divorce against a yardstick of equality. More recently the *Miller v Miller* and *McFarlane v McFarlane*[22] cases show the attempt to define and distinguish 'matrimonial assets' (which will include the matrimonial home irrespective of ownership, it seems, from other property owned by parties to a marriage), which again is another step towards a 'real' matrimonial property regime in England and Wales.[23]

---

20 PINTENS, W., 'Europeanisation of Family Law', in: BOELE-WOELKI, K., (ed.), *Perspectives for the Unification and Harmonisation of Family Law in Europe*, Intersentia, Antwerp-Oxford, 2003, p. 3–35 and COOKE, E., AKOTO, T., BALOW, A., CALLUS, T., 'Community of Property – A Regime for England and Wales: Interim Report' (2005), p. 133–137.

21 *White v White* [2000] 2 FLR 981.

22 *Miller v Miller* and *McFarlane v McFarlane* [2006] UKHL 24.

23 This paper was handed in at the end of January 2007. Therefore the latest 'Big money case' *Charman v Charman* [2007] EWCA Civ 503 [see http://www.bailii.org/ew/cases/EWCA/Civ/2007/503.html] examined by the England and Wales Court of Appeal at the 24th of May 2007 could not be taken into consideration. However, it seems that the Court of Appeal judges sent out a message to the civil law lawyers saying that: 'Almost uniquely our jurisdiction does not have a marital property regime and it is scarcely appropriate to classify our jurisdiction as having a marital regime of separation of property. More correctly we have no regime, simply accepting that each spouse owns his or her own separate property during the marriage but subject to the court's wide distributive powers in prospect upon a decree of judicial separation, nullity or divorce'. SCHERPE, J.M., 'Englisches Familienrecht: Miller und McFarlane – Das House of Lords entscheidet erneut über Güteraufteilung nach Ehescheidung', *FamRZ* 2006, p. 1314–1315. FROHN, E.N., 'Engels huwelijksvermogensrecht: White v White en verdere ontwikkelingen', *FJR* 2006, p. 304–308.

Not only the gap between England and the rest of the EU isn't that big after all but also the legal regimes of separation and community are getting closer, showing behind the scene the common principles of European matrimonial property law.

3.2. THE COLOURS OF THE PATCHWORK AREN'T THAT DIFFERENT AFTER ALL

3.2.1. Community or no Community During Marriage

In the systems of community of assets a difference is made between the community assets and the private assets, so to say a horizontal division. In the system without community, the distinction is vertical, between the assets of one spouse and the assets of his or her wife or husband. But then as it seems this distinction between the horizontal and the vertical division is less sharp than we might think at first sight. For example the absence of community during the marriage does not imply that there is no idea of sharing in these systems or that the solidarity inherent to the marriage has no actual influence on the situation on the assets during the marriage.

3.2.2. Management of Property

Also the question of management shows some common roots. In case of separation of property, one is in the habit of saying that spouses can act as if they were not married, i.e. independently from each other. Whereas in case of a system of community, the presence of a community is supposed to have an important influence on the freedom of management of each spouse. Here also in reality the breach between two systems is less important. On the one hand because even in systems of separation of property the independence of the spouse is somehow limited[24] and, on the other hand, because even in community systems the rules of management of the community are often based on the idea of independence of both spouses.[25]

As a conclusion of this question of management one may say that common roots are formulated in the sense of an independence for daily matters, usual acts and acts related to the profession of a spouse but solidarity and thus existence of an obligation to obtain the consent of both spouse for important/dangerous acts.

[24] I.e. § 1365 German Civil Code.
[25] I.e. Art. 180 Italian Civil Code.

3.2.3. Creditor's Rights

Regarding the question of the creditor's rights a large difference remains as a result of the presence or not of a community during the marriage. But here again the gap between the two types of matrimonial property regimes is a bit smaller than it might seem. For example in most of the systems both spouses are engaged and jointly liable for usual household debts[26] and symmetrically in some jurisdictions as for example France and Belgium the creditor of one of the spouse may not seize the entire community but only part of it (in France the income of his debtor).[27]

3.2.4. Distribution of Property upon Dissolution

The last topic, the distribution of property upon dissolution also enjoys some equivalence in substance. First this equivalence concerns the property that is subject of the division. It indeed most of the time consists at least of the gains acquired during marriage. And the second equivalence lies in the right to distribution; the rule is being of the time that of equal sharing.

In the end: matrimonial property law in Europe isn't perhaps that colourful. A lot of differences remain but the main principles behind the practical differences often show a lot of similarities. This is a starting point that justifies that we look at the feasibility of an European optional property regime.

4. AN OPTIONAL MATRIMONIAL PROPERTY REGIME FOR EUROPE

There are different roads which lead to the harmonisation of European family law.[28] One of them is to elaborate an additional family law people could choose to apply.

In his article entitled Towards a European family law, René de Groot, points out the main advantages of this solution:

- First, one can hope for the political willingness to collaborate to the elaboration of such an optional family law (which will be bigger in comparison with the willingness to think about a unified family law applicable all over Europe);

---

26 I.e. Sec 11 Danish Act regarding the legal effects of marriage; Art. 223 Belgian Civil Code; Art. 85 Dutch Civil Code.

27 I.e. Art. 1411 French Civil Code and Art. 1409 Belgian Civil Code.

28 GROOT, G.-R., DE, 'Op weg naar een Europees personen- en familierecht?', *1 Ars Aequi* (1995), p. 29–32.

- secondly, by choosing the applicability of such an optional family law, one can avoid the uncertainty of the private international law solution;
- thirdly, this optional law could be realised bit by bit;
- this optional law could also serve as an inspiration for national legislators who are willing to reform their national law;
- and finally it could be declared applicable to situations where somebody or a situation is linked with more than one European jurisdiction (unless this has expressly been rejected).

There are some strong arguments for starting drawing up additional family law with the topic of matrimonial property law.[29] Anders Agell was in 1995 one of the first to come up with the idea of an additional matrimonial property law. Since then the idea of such a regime has come back now and then. Couples with an international element (different nationalities, plans to move a lot around Europe) could choose for application of it.

However not everybody will agree with that point of view. First of all, problems could arise from the fact that this regime would have to be chosen in the form of a marital contract and thus must be considered binding,[30] which may cause some concern in some jurisdictions as for example in England and Wales.[31] And then of course, some scholars do not believe in matrimonial property anymore. In her Model Family Code, Ingeborg SCHWENZER leaves aside the idea of a matrimonial property regime but

29 AGELL, A., 'Towards uniforming spouses' property rights especially in international marriages?', in: Council of Europe, CONF/FA (95) 1, Proceedings of the 3rd European Conference on Family Law 1995, p. 63 ff.; AGELL, A., 'The division of property upon divorce from a European perspective', in: POUSSON-PETIT, (ed.), *Liber Amicorum Marie-Thérèse Meulders-Klein, Droit comparé des personnes et de la famille*, Bruxelles: Bruyant 1998, p. 1–20; MARTINY, D., 'Is Unification of Family Law Feasible or Even Desirable?', in: HARTKAMP, A., *et al* (eds.), *Towards a European Civil Code*, Nijmegen: Ars Aequi 1998; HENRICH, D., 'Die Zukunft des Güterrechts in Europa', *FamRZ 2002*, p. 1521–1526; HENRICH, D., SCHWAB, D., (eds.), *Eheliche Gemeinschaft, Partnerschaft und Vermögen im europäischen Vergleich*, Bielefeld: Verlag Gieseking 1999 ; VERBEKE, A., 'Perspectives for an international marital contract', *Maastricht Journal of European and Comparative Law* 2001, p. 189–200; STEENHOFF, G.J.W., 'Harmonisatie van huwelijksvermogensrecht binnen de EU: wat is voorlopig haalbaar?', in: BOELE-WOELKI, K., BRANTS, C., STEENHOFF, G.J.W., (eds.), *Het plezier van de rechtsvergelijking. Opstellen over unificatie en harmonisatie van het recht in Europa aangeboden aan prof. mr. E.H. Hondius*, Nederlandse Vereniging voor Rechtsvergelijking, n°63, Deventer, Kluwer, 2003, p. 87–101; STEENHOFF, G.J.W., 'A Matrimonial Property System for the European Union?', UK-German Judicial Family Law Conference, Cardiff 8–11 September 2004. MARTINY, D., 'Ein zusätzlicher Güterstand für Europa', UK-German Judicial Family Law Conference, Cardiff 8–11 September 2004; ANTOKOLSKAIA, M., *Harmonisation of Family Law in Europe: A Historical perspective, A Tale of two Millennia*, Antwerp, Intersentia 2006, p. 483.

30 This is the important question of the autonomy of the spouses with regard to their matrimonial property regime.

31 Indeed pre-nuptial agreements may have no effect at all. COOKE, E., AKOTO, T., BALOW, A., CALLUS, T., 'Community of Property – A Regime for England and Wales: Interim Report, *IFL* 2005, p. 133–137.

provides for financial consequences after dissolution of the partnership (marital or non marital relationship).[32] The idea does certainly look attractive but will for the moment be very difficult to implement. This is not the case of an optional matrimonial property regime.

4.1. THE BASIS: COMMON CORE AND BETTER LAW REGARDING MATRIMONIAL PROPERTY LAW

Now that the advantages and perhaps also the need for such an optional European matrimonial regime has been established, the next big question is: what should such a regime look like? Two things should be kept in mind in our search for it. First, one should look at the common core of the European legislation and secondly it is of utmost importance that the regime comply with needs and views of the European couples of today (or of the future). Here we have the eternal question of common core and better law.[33]

4.1.1. *First Step: Looking for the Common Core of European Matrimonial Property Law*

As far as common core is concerned, as presented in part 3 on the equivalence in substance, the following common principles can be mentioned as being of common influence in Europe. The first common principle concerns the impact of solidarity of spouses during the marriage. The second one is the principle of balance between independence and solidarity as far as management is concerned. Thirdly, an attempt to protect a part of the accrued gains from the other spouse's creditors can be discovered and finally, after dissolution, a principle of participation in the accrued gains.

4.1.2. *Second Step: Common Core is Not Enough, European Couples Need a Better Law*

4.1.2.1. Use of the Dutch Guidelines for a Default Regime

Which are the requirements a European additional regime has to meet? The report about matrimonial property law of the Dutch Ministry of Justice which was written during the preparatory stage of the bill aiming to modify the Dutch default regime

---

32 SCHWENZER, I., DIMSEY, M., *Model Family Code from a global perspective*, Antwerp, Intersentia/Stämpfli 2006.

33 ANTOKOLSKAIA, M., "'The Better Law' approach and the Harmonisation of Family Law", in BOELE-WOELKI, K., (ed.), *Perspectives for the Unification and Harmonisation of Family Law in Europe*, Antwerp, Intersentia 2003, p. 159–183.

of total community mentions the following guidelines for the most suitable regime of matrimonial property:[34]

1. First, the regime must be unambiguous and simple, the rule must be clear and understandable for every body;
2. Secondly, the regime must be broadly applicable and easy to handle;
3. The third point concerns the divisible mass: The property earned by one or both spouses during the marriage should be divided equally between the spouses in case of divorce;
4. And then, the regime must express the equality of the spouses;
5. In the end, the regime must not differ too much from the matrimonial property regime of foreign modern legislations.

Do these guidelines also hold for a European additional regime? Or are they specific to a default regime or even to the Netherlands? These Guidelines are certainly not only of importance for the Dutch bill but it is true that they are not all of the same importance as far as the European situation is concerned. The two first points are of less importance for the European situation because we are looking for a regime that the spouses will have to choose for expressly. Of course, theoretically one should always aim at simplicity. But can matrimonial property law really be simple and at the same time meet other requirements like equality of spouses and a good balance between independence and solidarity?[35] If simplicity is impossible to reach, we certainly should try to look for a regime that is easy to handle on a day to day basis. Indeed most people are not born accountants and do not want to be bothered about money in every moment of their life. The regime may become a bit more complicated after dissolution, but then most of the time there will be some specialist involved. Of course, the final result should still be foreseeable (legal certainty is essential). The three others points of the list above are applicable to the European situation. But here another question arises. We are looking for a regime applicable to a certain category of couples. Do these couples have some specific expectations? Do we have to broaden the Dutch list with some guidelines specific to the European situation?

4.1.2.2. Europeanisation of the Dutch Guidelines

Yes, some points have to be added. First of all, it is of course important that the regime be attractive to international couples. Secondly, it must be compatible with as many

---

[34] Ministerie van Justitie, 'Notitie huwelijksvermogensrecht', BOELE-WOELKI, K., *Algehele gemeenschap van goederen: afschaffen!?*, Ars Notariatus CVII, Deventer, Kluwer 2001, p. 11. Other guidlines have been exposed. See i.e. BOELE-WOELKI, K., *et al*, *Huwelijksvermogensrecht in rechtsvergelijkend perpectief*, Ars Notariatus CIII, Deventer, Kluwer 2000, p. 253 and HENRICH, D., 'Zur Zukunft des güterrechts in Europa, *FamRZ* 2002, p. 1521–1526.

[35] BRAAT, B., *Indépendance et interdépendance patrimoniales des époux dans le régime matrimonial légal des droits français, néerlandais et suisse*, Stämpfli, Bern, 2004.

European legislations as possible and especially with their imperative rules (sometimes called primary regime). Not all the European legislations have the same imperative rules even if they have a lot of those rules in common. Three types of rules influencing the property situation of spouses regardless of their matrimonial property regime can be distinguished. The joint liability for some debts, the protection of the living environment of the spouses and the protection of the property of one of the spouses against some actions from the other. They are all based on the idea that marriage goes hand in hand with solidarity but nevertheless the impact of that idea does not have the same weight everywhere. Let's take an example. Art. 88 book 1 of the Dutch Civil Code specifies a list of actions which need the consent of the other spouse. Among them, and beside the usual protection of the family home, there are other rules limiting the autonomy of spouses to act alone. For example one spouse can not contract security in favour of a third person without the consent of his/her spouse and this applies regardless of the matrimonial property regime.[36] Such a far-reaching limitation certainly does not exist in all European countries. This will then mean that even among couples having chosen the same matrimonial property regimes there might be some differences depending on the imperatives rules that may apply to their situation.

4.2. STARTING POINT FOR A EUROPEAN OPTIONAL MATRIMONIAL PROPERTY REGIME

Now that we have some ideas about the common core and some guidelines to establish the better law: what should such an additional regime look like? Anders Agell was the first one to raise the idea of an international regime of matrimonial property law. He mentioned the following guideline:

> 'an equal division at the dissolution of the marriage of property or gains acquired by spouses during the marriage (with the exception of property received through inheritance, a will or a gift by a third party)'.

He doesn't however give a clear answer to the question of the exact form of the regime, but shows a preference for a system with no community during the marriage.[37]

---

36 Art. 88 al 1 sub c book I Dutch Civil Code.

37 AGELL, A., 'Towards uniforming spouses' property rights especially in international marriages?', in: Council of Europe, CONF/FA (95) 1, Proceedings of the 3rd European Conference on Family Law 1995, p. 63 ff. AGELL, A., 'The division of property upon divorce from a European perspective', in: POUSSON-PETIT, J., (ed.), *Liber Amicorum Marie-Thérèse Meulders-Klein, Droit comparé des personnes et de la famille*, Bruxelles: Bruyant 1998, p. 1–20.

Other well known family law specialists as VERBEKE,[38] STEENHOFF[39] and MARTINY,[40] share his opinion about what an optional or additional matrimonial property regime should look like. The balance between independence and solidarity of spouses come better to existence in a system where there is a division of property (in nature or in value) that takes place after dissolution but where there is no community during the marriage.

Of course, we can only agree with their point of views. But is Europe really ready for a system based on a separation? Once a Swiss lawyer wrote the following about the Swiss legal regime which is based on separation during the marriage 'Le nouveau droit se justifierait donc plutôt comme un pari sur l'égalisation matérielle des conditions (au moyen de la disparition ou de la compensation adéquate des disparités et inégalités entre homme et femme), à très long terme.'[41] In other words, a system based on separation is a gamble on the financial equality of spouses. Because even if a division takes place in case of dissolution, independence during marriage can have some unpleasant consequences on the spouse staying at home.

Are spouses really equal today, at least economically? Are couples willing to choose for this additional regime likely to be so? Anyway, part of the answer is provided all by itself, as immediate community of property is, as far as England is concerned, a truly foreign form of ownership. It is literally unavailable there.[42]

So let's keep the idea of a deferred community (in nature or in value). But we should not forget to introduce a rule that gives, also during the marriage, a real autonomy to the spouse not earning any money.[43]

---

38 VERBEKE, A., 'Perspectives for an international marital contract', *Maastricht Journal of European and Comparative Law* 2001, p. 189–200.

39 STEENHOFF, G.J.W. 'A Matrimonial Property System for the European Union?', *IFL* (2005), p. 74–77.

40 MARTINY, D., 'Ein zusätzlicher Güterstand für Europa?', in: HOFER, S., KLIPPEL, D., WALTER, U., (eds.), *Perspektiven des Familienrechts, Festschrift für Dieter Schwab*, Gieseking Verlag, 2005, p. 1189–1207

41 PERRIN, J.-F., *Comparaisons pour la réforme du droit matrimonial*, CJR, Études et Pratiques, Lausanne: Payot 1985, p. 143.

42 COOKE, E., BARLOW, A., CALLUS, T., *Community of property. A regime for England and Wales*, The Policy Press, Bristol, 2006, p. 25–26

43 And there remains always the solution of proposing two different additional matrimonial property regimes. See: MARTINY, D., 'Is Unification of Family Law Feasible or Even Desirable?'; in: HARTKAMP, A., *et al* (eds.), *Towards a European Civil Code*, Ars Aequi, Nijmegen, 1998; PINTENS, W., 'Europeanisation of Family Law' (2003), p. 3–35; BRAAT, B., *Indépendance et interdépendance patrimoniales des époux dans le régime matrimonial légal des droits français, néerlandais et suisse*, Stämpfli Bern, 2004, p. 417; ANTOKOLSKAIA, M., *Harmonisation of Family Law in Europe: A Historical perspective, A Tale of two Millennia* (2006), p. 484.

PART IV
CONVERGENCE AND DIVERGENCE: PRACTICAL AND POLITICAL ASPECTS

BUILDING ON CONVERGENCE AND COPING WITH DIVERGENCE IN THE CEFL PRINCIPLES OF EUROPEAN FAMILY LAW

KATHARINA BOELE-WOELKI

Scholarly activities do not need 'legitimation' beyond scientific accuracy[1]

1. INTRODUCTION

Comparative law is an instrument to realise certain aims. Also in the case of the Commission of European Family Law (CEFL), the comparative research that has been undertaken since 2001, serves a specific purpose. The main objective of the CEFL, which represents 22 European jurisdictions, is the creation of a set of Principles[2] of European Family Law that are thought to be the most suitable for the harmonisation of family law in Europe.[3] CEFL's work is purely academic and involves finding, analysing and comparing rules and then formulating and presenting non-binding Principles. In doing so, the CEFL assists legislatures in their efforts to modernise family law legislation.

Before describing the route embarked upon by the CEFL when sailing so far between Scylla and Charybdis,[4] some preliminary remarks are made regarding the terminology which is used. Having already described and analysed CEFL's working method in an

1 ÖRÜCÜ, E., 'Viewing the Work in Progress of the Commission on European Family Law', *International Law FORUM du droit international* (2005), p. 219–227 (221).

2 See: ZIMMERMANN, R., *Die Europäisierung des Privatrechts und die Rechtsvergleichung*, Schriftenreihe der Juristischen Gesellschaft zu Berlin, Heft 179, 2006, p. 35: 'Die Erabeitung solcher Grundregeln ist in den letzten Jahren stark in Mode gekommen. ... Am Anfang dieser Entwicklung standen die Grundregeln des Europäischen Vertragsrechts, ... Sie sind heute das am gründlichsten vorbereitete, am weitesten fortgeschrittene und international am stärksten beachtete Projekt europäischer Rechtsvereinheitlichung in einem zentralen Bereich des Privatrechts.'

3 See: on the harmonising potential of the CEFL Principles on divorce: ANTOKOLSKAIA, M., *Harmonisation of Family Law in Europe: A Historical Perspective*, European Family Law Series No. 13, Intersentia, Antwerp-Oxford, 2006, p. 361–365.

4 Scylla and Charybdis became metaphors for a choice between equally dreadful alternatives.

earlier publication,[5] this fundamental issue will not be extensively addressed here. However, for those who are not yet familiar with the activities of the CEFL, I will briefly recall CEFL's "six-steps method" and the "five approaches". In that connection, I will take the opportunity to air some thoughts about the working method of international and regional organisations – more specifically the European Commission – that adopt international or regional instruments which are aimed at unifying or harmonising the law. These organisations are also faced with the same problems which the CEFL has to solve when drafting its Principles. In that sense the work of organisations that have legislative competence or, to put it differently, that are acting as "international legislatures", and, the CEFL project, are comparable. Finally, I will only focus on the content of the Principles of European Family Law in the field of Divorce and Maintenance between Former Spouses which were published in 2004.[6] Some examples will be provided as to how the CEFL is building on convergence and how it is coping with divergence. These examples will not include the Principles regarding Parental Responsibilities, which currently are being prepared. Already in 2004, however, in a work-in-progress report, reference was made to the generally accepted rule that common solutions will be applied (the presumption of similarity) with regard to many aspects in the Principles of Parental Responsibilities.[7] At this stage it can be noted that the final version of the Principles in this field will confirm this preliminary conclusion.

2. REMARKS ON THE TERMINOLOGY USED

2.1. CONVERGENCE AND DIVERGENCE AND SIMILARITIES AND DIFFERENCES

Apparently, a distinction is to be made between the antonyms of "similarities and differences" and "convergence and divergence".[8] Neither similarities and convergence,

---

5 BOELE-WOELKI, K., 'The Working Method of the Commission on European Family Law', in: BOELE-WOELKI, K., (ed.), *Common Core and Better Law in European Family Law*, European Family Law Series No. 10, Intersentia, Antwerp-Oxford, 2005, p. 15–38.

6 BOELE-WOELKI, K., FERRAND, F., GONZÁLEZ BEILFUSS, C., JÄNTERÄ-JAREBORG, M., LOWE, N., MARTINY, D., PINTENS, W. (eds), *Principles of European Family Law Regarding Divorce and Maintenance Between Former Spouses*, European Family Law Series, No. 7, Intersentia, Antwerp-Oxford, 2004.

7 BOELE-WOELKI, K., 'Parental Responsibilities – CEFL's Initial Results' in: BOELE-WOELKI, K., (ed.), *Common Core and Better Law in European Family Law*, European Family Law Series No. 10, Intersentia, Antwerp-Oxford, 2005, p. 141–168 (167–168).

8 According to ÖRÜCÜ, E., *The Enigma of Comparative Law*, Martinus Nijhoff, Leiden, 2004, p. 34, the cognition of the legal, social and cultural environments in which we live can best be done not just by discovering resemblances between similars or even similarities between differents, but more fundamentally by finding and explaining similarities among differents, and differences and divergences among similars.

on the one hand, nor differences and divergence, on the other, should be used as synonyms. They have different meanings. According to my understanding, convergence and divergence indicate a certain development of the law. Speaking of convergence means that certain developments are coming together – they are progressing towards a common goal or developing towards a common result – whereas in the case of divergence the developments are moving away from each other – in other words they are becoming more dissimilar. In addition, convergence and divergence are signalling developments in either this or that direction, whereas similarities and differences merely indicate a factual situation. Generally speaking, the term development is neutral; it can have positive or negative effects, although these connotations allegedly contain a value judgement. As a result, developments can, for instance, either be characterised as leading to expansion, improvement and progress or to restriction, control and constraints. Additionally, it should be stressed that even if national solutions differ, which by the way is always the case, convergence may be attained if the different solutions are pointing in the same direction. For instance, the national legislature allows, to a greater or lesser extent, party autonomy in the field of divorce. The spouses may not only agree that their marriage should be dissolved, but they may also agree on the consequences of the divorce. In that connection the national law may – to provide another example – require more or less public intervention by the competent authority regarding the consequences of the divorce as far as, in particular, children are concerned. Another example – which so far remains outside CEFL's ambit – is the increasing number of jurisdictions which have recently introduced new institutions for same-sex relationships which, despite their differences (there are no two identical schemes),[9] evidently confirm the modern trend, that in addition to the traditional concept of marriage, other relationships between two persons should be recognised by the law regardless of their gender.[10]

Considerable dissimilarities exist, for instance, with regard to the requirement of a minimum duration of the marriage before a divorce can be obtained. National systems may have an independent requirement, or a further condition may have the consequential effect of requiring a minimum duration of the marriage. This is the case in those systems where a divorce, based upon consent, requires a minimum period of separation. It is striking to note that especially separation time period tends to vary – at least if we take into account the 22 European jurisdictions that are represented in the CEFL. There are generally five different periods, namely six months, one year,

9 See: Boele-Woelki, K., Curry-Sumner I., Jansen, M., Schrama, W., *Huwelijk of Geregistreerd Partnerschap? Een evaluatie van de Wet openstelling huwelijk en de Wet geregistreerd partnerschap*, Ars Notariatus No. 134, Kluwer, Deventer, 2007.

10 See: Curry-Sumner, I., 'It's marriage Jim but not as we know it. Is the ban on same-sex marriage in the United Kingdom justified?', *I.J.F.L.*(2006), p. 2–10.

two years, three years and five years.[11] Despite the significance of the national solutions one should keep in mind that the different lengths of the separation time periods, as arbitrary as they might be, have been gradually reduced in the last 10–20 years and it is likely that more jurisdictions will follow this trend. Hence, taking all circumstances into account leads inevitably to the conclusion that, despite the great differences regarding the minimum duration of the marriage and the minimum duration of the separation, respectively, the systems are gradually converging. The lengths of all periods are being reduced and not extended.

Throughout the last fifty years considerable changes have taken place in family law.[12] In many countries family law often has become more permissive and, in this context, it goes without saying that the changes to the law largely depend on different factors, such as social, economic and political circumstances,[13] whereas cultural constraints, to my mind, no longer play such a dominant role in family law compared to some fifty years ago.[14] Understandably, convergence does not require total similarity between the solutions which are applied in the national systems and it already has been stressed that differences between the national systems always can be detected. Comparative law thrives on these differences,[15] whereas all those who are involved in the unification or harmonisation process concerning the law are challenged to categorise the differences in terms of almost being alike, bridgeable, conflicting, incompatible or irreconcilable.

2.2. COMMON CORE AND BETTER LAW

An additional remark should be made regarding the above-mentioned terms "common core" and "better law". One is not the opposite of the other. If a specific solution is applied in all legal systems, or at least in a significant majority of the jurisdictions surveyed, a common core can be easily identified. Logically, similarities are the fundamental components when identifying a solution as representing the

---

11 See: BOELE-WOELKI, K., et al, (eds.), *Principles of European Family Law Regarding Divorce and Maintenance Between Former Spouses*, (2004.), p. 17–19.

12 See: FRANK, R., 'Rechtsvergleichende Betrachtungen zur Entwicklung des Familienrechts', *FamRZ* (2004), p. 841–847.

13 See: BRADLEY, D., 'A Note on Comparative Family Law: Problems, Perspectives, Issues and Politics', *4 Oxford University Comparative Law Forum* (2005) at ouclf.iuscomp.org who distinghuishes between political ideology, political interests, political culture and political discourse. Also published in SMITS, J., (ed.), *Elgar Encyclopedia of Comparative Law*, Elgar, Cheltenham, 2006, p. 259–272.

14 See: CRETNEY, S., 'Breaking the Shackles of Culture and Religion in the Field of Divorce?', in: BOELE-WOELKI, K., (ed.), *Common Core and Better Law in European Family Law*, European Family Law Series No. 10, Intersentia, Antwerp-Oxford, 2005, p. 3–14 (14).

15 See: ÖRÜCÜ, E., *The Enigma of Comparative Law* (2004), p. 34.

common core. Additionally, the most likely conclusion is that the solutions, which are similar, have converged or are converging. Building solely on the "common core" could be a possible way to proceed. However, as already pointed out, the CEFL also has opted for the additional application of the "better law" approach.[16] This latter method operates on the assumption that it is not always the established common denominator that contains the best solution. In view of this, a better solution is chosen instead. It should be briefly added, however, that the use of the "common core" or the "better law" always requires that choices be made and the grounds for these choices also must be explicit. Thus, in the comparative research process, we have entered the stage where the analysis of the solutions is to be evaluated. In that process, both the convergence and the divergence of the solutions are to be taken into account.

In this context it should be stressed that the motto "building on convergence and coping with divergence" only partly characterises the way in which the CEFL operated in achieving its final results. In addition to either the choice for the common core solution, which almost immediately reflects convergence, or the choice for a better solution in the case of differences, which may be a sign of divergence, the CEFL also used its academic freedom to propose, where necessary, more modern, convincing and permissive rules than are commonly applied in the national systems. For instance, the abandoning of the irretrievable breakdown of the marriage as a ground for divorce, which clearly constitutes the common core of the European systems is the most illustrative example. This approach deviates from the common core because its solution was not considered as the best solution in view of the objective pursued by

---

16 It is to be regretted that in this respect CEFL's working method and results have been entirely misunderstood by VERSCHRAEGEN, B., 'Comments on the Principles of European Family Law: Divorce and Maintenance Between Former Spouses', in: BOELE-WOELKI, K., (ed.), *Common Core and Better Law in European Family Law*, European Family Law Series No. 10, Intersentia, Antwerp-Oxford, 2005, p. 135–138 (136): 'Some principles refer to the so-called 'common core', others focus on a 'better law', obviously in areas where a common core cannot be established. Upon analysis, therefore, the 'common core' remains extremely limited. This is not at all surprising. It may then be a wise decision of the Commission on European Family Law to suggest alternatives and/or, as the case may be, to refer to national law. By and large, the choice for a 'better law' and the reference made to national law demonstrate the limits of the harmonisation of family law.' Firstly, the 'better law' approach is not only applied if no 'common core' can be found. Secondly, not only in the field of divorce but in particular regarding maintenance between former spouses, a considerable amount of 'common core' for substantial aspects was detected. Thirdly, the CEFL has deliberately chosen not to propose alternative rules in order to provide a consistent model. Fourthly, reference to national law has been made with regard to those questions which should not be dealt with in the Principles on Divorce and Spousal Maintenance (e.g. the notion of children or long-term relationships). Fifthly, VERSCHRAEGEN'S overall conclusion that for all the reasons which she has provided, the limits of the harmonisation of family law are demonstrated, is not logical and therefore unconvincing. See for a detailed explanation and comparative tables which make a distinction between five different approaches that have been applied by the CEFL, BOELE-WOELKI, K., 'The Working Method of the Commission on European Family Law' (2005)), p. 31–37.

the CEFL. The drafting of a new rule also can be subsumed under the so-called better law approach. Consequently, the CEFL principles may – similar to the UNIDROIT Principles for International Commercial Contracts – be considered as "both restatement and prestatement reflecting the fact that they encapsulate the average of both existing and desirable modern and functional solutions."[17]

Generally speaking, the harmonisation of the law should not be only common core-based. This also applies in the field of family law, in particular to the model-providing project of the CEFL. Masha Antokolskaia convincingly stated that the use of the better law method is indispensable in order to achieve positive results that represent a high standard of modernity.[18]

2.3. UNIFICATION AND HARMONISATION

Finally, it is regrettable that not only in the field of (international) family law, the terms "unification" and "harmonisation" of the law are often used incorrectly.[19] The "unification" of the law leads to the application of identical rules. These uniform rules are to be applied, for instance, in all national systems which are bound by either the international or the regional instrument which contains these rules. Admittedly, differences can arise even in the case of uniform rules. In particular, if a supranational court has not been granted competence to determine the interpretation of uniform rules, national courts should only consider their international character and to the desirability of achieving uniformity in their interpretation and application. This is, for instance, the case in respect of all Hague Conventions of Private International Law.

17 See for this characterisation: KRONKE, H., 'Introduction' in: 'UNIDROIT Principles: New Developments and Applications', ICC *International Court of Arbitration Bulletin*, Special Supplement 1,7 (2005). See also: EUROPEAN GROUP ON TORT LAW, 'General Introduction', in: *Principles of European Tort Law: text and commentary*, Springer, Vienna, 2005, No. 31: 'The Principles are not a restatement of the law of torts in Europe. After all and despite the many similarities, there are too many differences among the respective national systems. So there is not yet a solid basis for 'restatement'.'

18 See: ANTOKOLSKAIA, M., 'The "Better Law Approach" and the Harmonisation of Family Law', in: BOELE-WOELKI, K., (ed.), *Perspectives for the Unification and Harmonisation of Family Law in Europe*, European Family Law Series No. 4, Intersentia, Antwerp-Oxford, 2003, p. 159–182 (180–182).

19 The most recent example can be derived from the Proposal for a Council Regulation amending Regulation (EC) No. 2201/2003 as regards jurisdiction and introducing rules concerning applicable law in matrimonial matters (17.7.2006), COM (2006) 399 final, in which the drafters of the explanatory memorandum constantly refer to 'harmonised conflict-of-law rules in matters of divorce' whereas undoubtedly the unification of these rules is what is meant.

In contrast, the "harmonisation" of the law is less far-reaching.[20] Similar rules indicate that the laws of the legal systems in a specific area are in harmony with each other. The differences are reduced to a minimum. The process of the harmonisation of the law is stimulated by either EU directives, binding decisions of supranational courts or model laws.

3. INTERNATIONAL AND REGIONAL ORGANISATIONS AND THE CEFL: A BRIEF COMPARISON OF THEIR WORKING METHODS

It already has been mentioned that the activities of international and regional organisations are actually comparable with those of the CEFL. A comparison also reveals significant differences. The CEFL has no legislative competence, it lacks democratic legitimation, its models may be considered as nothing more than a contribution to the scholarly debate on the harmonisation of family law in Europe and the drafters are not bound by political orders from national ministries, to name but a few differences. Nevertheless, the preparatory activities, undertaken before the adoption of an international or regional instrument, are very similar to those of the CEFL. Actually, almost the same process is applied. This does not only hold true for the drafting of questionnaires and national reports, the description and analysis of differences and similarities, but more importantly, for the choices regarding the rules to be adopted. These choices are also either common-core-based or inspired by a solution which is considered by the drafters to be the best in view of the objectives of the instrument to be adopted.

It is striking to note that there is a wide range of publications about the working methods of the many academic projects concerning the harmonisation of private law in Europe, whereas, in contrast, relatively little attention is paid to the explanation and justification of the working methods of those international and regional organisations which are predominantly working in the field of the unification and harmonisation of the law. There are several explanations for this observation. International organisations, for instance, have a long-standing tradition and working experience. This applies, for example, to the Hague Conference on Private Interna-

---

20 According to MEULDERS-KLEIN, M.-T., 'Towards a European Civil Code on Family Laws? Ends and Means', in: BOELE-WOELKI, K., (ed.), *Perspectives for the Unification and Harmonisation of Family Law in Europe*, European Family Law Series No. 4, Intersentia, Antwerp-Oxford, 2003, p. 105–117 (106) 'harmonisation' implies a concern to reconcile the preoccupations and the interests of the various systems so as to avoid conflicts and clashes whereas 'unification', on the contrary, means the voluntary or imposed uniformisation of different systems.

tional Law, which is frequently praised for its in-depth preparatory work and its openness regarding the coming into existence of its conventions. A regional organisation such as the European Commission, has a different working method, which includes consultations with advisory committees, tenders regarding the comparative research to be carried out, green papers, public hearings, proposals and revised proposals before the final instrument is approved. In the field of cross-border family relationships, this already has resulted in binding instruments for 24 European Member States.[21] In international and regional organisations, national delegates represent their countries, more specifically their jurisdictions. The instruments to be adopted are subject to negotiations in which political interests play an important role. In the case of different positions frequently compromises are reached, which make the rules often complicated and consequently difficult to apply. Even if compromises cannot be reached, certain issues are excluded from the scope of the instrument, or are not dealt with at all.

In contrast, the drafting of Principles of European Family Law differs significantly. Most decisively, the drafters lack a political mandate. They do not represent their national system. Instead they distance themselves from their own legal background because the European perspective ultimately should prevail. In any case, the adopted results require justification of the choices that were made. It is absolutely vital to reveal the criteria which were considered to be decisive. This aspect is one of the major objectives and, as a result, the concerns of the CEFL, because its Principles may only aspire to be used not *ratione imperii*, but *imperio rationis.*[22] Therefore, the utmost care has been devoted to the explanation of both the commonly shared desires and the underlying considerations, which are either of a general or specific nature. The comments associated with each Principle contain this fundamental information.

Similarly, the explanatory reports, written by one of the experts who has taken part in the negotiations on a Hague Convention, contain extensive information about the provisions and their backgrounds. In contrast, the European Commission, in its recent preliminary documents on EC regulations in the field of cross-border relationships, only drafts an Explanatory Memorandum, which explains the grounds for, and the

---

21 Brussels IIbis (divorce and parental responsibilities) replaced Brussels II from 1st March 2005 onwards and Brussels I (maintenance) became effective on 1st March 2002. See also: BOELE-WOELKI, K., GONZÁLEZ BEILFUSS, C., (eds), *Brussels IIbis: Its Impact and Application in the Member States*, European Family Law Series No. 14, Intersentia, Antwerp-Oxford, 2007.

22 See: HARTKAMP, A., 'Principles of Contract Law', in: HARTKAMP, A., et al, (eds.), *Towards a European Civil Code*, Ars Aequi Libri, Nijmegen, 2004, p. 125–143 (131) who expresses this hope for both the UNIDROIT Principles of International Commercial Contracts and the Principles of European Contract Law.

objectives of, a proposal for a regulation.[23] Only parts of this explanation are transformed into the considerations, which precede the text of the regulation. These considerations do not replace an explanatory report.[24] It is, therefore, difficult to discover why certain rules have been adopted in the recent EU regulations regarding cross-border relationships.[25] Without doubt, it would be preferable to have more openness in terms of justification, the grounds for, and the explanation of, the rules. Regrettably, this is not common practice in European lawmaking and this will almost certainly not change in the future. In that respect, the European legislature certainly does not win the beauty contest!

After these long preliminary remarks, concrete examples should be provided which exemplify the motto of this contribution. I start with examples which indicate differences between the national systems. Obviously those differences, which in some cases were also a sign of diverging tendencies, required more consideration than similarities.[26]

4. CEFL'S SIX STEPS AND FIVE APPROACHES

First of all, I will provide a brief overview of CEFL's working method, where six steps are to be distinguished. The *first step* is to select the fields of family law most suitable for harmonisation. The *second step* is to draft a questionnaire that embodies the functional approach. According to this problem-oriented approach, questions are posed in purely functional terms, without any reference to the concepts of a specific legal system, thus asking what is the underlying problem that a certain legal provision intends to redress. The *third step* is to draw up national reports which not only take the law in the books into account, but also the law in practice. Each legal system may prescribe its list of official sources, but this list, which is only designed to bind judges and courts internally, does not necessarily bind a comparatist. The practical

---

23 See: the Proposal amending Brussels IIbis, note 19.

24 Critically LINKE, H., 'Die Europäisierung des Unterhaltsverfahrensrechts', *Familie, Partnerschaft, Recht* (2006), p. 237–240 (240): 'Bei derart umfassenden Regelwerken (The author discusses the Proposal for a Council Regulation on jurisdiction, applicable law, recognition and the enforcement of decisions and cooperation in matters relating to maintenance obligations, COM (2005) 649) ist eine Entwurfsbegründung unverzichtbar, damit der Rechtsanwender überhaupt Sinn und Zielsetzung mancher Vorschriften nachvollziehen kann. Anderfalls wird es eine auseinanderdriftende Interpretation durch die Instanzgerichte geben, die die allein vorlageberechtigten höchsten Gerichte nicht auffangen können.'

25 See: BOER, TH. M., DE, 'Jurisdiction and Enforcement in International Family Law: A Labyrinth of European and International Legislation', *NILR* (2002), p. 307–351.

26 The decision to deviate from the common core regarding the generally applied divorce ground, namely the irretrievable breakdown of the marriage, does, however, exemplify the exception to this rule. See: Comment 3 under Principle 1:8.

importance of the law, as it appears in action, also holds true in the field of family law. The national reports are aimed at discovering what practitioners are actually doing with the legal rules. The *fourth step* is to collect and to disseminate the comparative material. In addition to publishing the country-by-country reports, which are accessible on CEFL's website, there is an integrated and printed version laid out according to the question numbers. This integrated version provides a rapid overview and a straightforward simultaneous comparison of the different solutions within the national systems. The *fifth step* is to draft the Principles of European Family Law. Proposals are made by the members of the Organising Committee, which are discussed with the authors of the national reports (the Expert Group). It is at this stage where a decision must be made whether to adopt the "common core" and/or the "better law" approach. The *sixth* and *final step* is to publish the Principles which consist in the case of divorce and maintenance between former spouses, of three parts: firstly, the provisions, secondly, the comparative overviews which refer to the national reports and, thirdly, the comments, which elucidate the provisions. Due to the importance of international instruments in the field of parental responsibilities, the respective Principles will, in addition, specifically refer to them before providing the comparative overviews and the comments.

The process of evaluation frequently has been considered to be the best step in the entire comparative research process.[27] In the case of the CEFL project this is the fifth step, where choices are made between the solutions offered in the national systems. It is the stage where one expresses one's true colours. This also applies to the common solutions. In view of the goal and perspective of the project, do they really represent the best solution? This had to be kept in mind throughout the whole drafting process. The first set of CEFL's Principles disclose the following five different approaches:[28]

The common core was found and selected as the best solution.[29]
The common core was found, but a better solution was selected.[30]
The common core was found, but the solution was left to national law.
No common core was found and the best solution was selected.
No common core was found and the solution was left to national law.

Keeping in mind the motto of this contribution, I mainly will focus on examples which illustrate the first approach (the common core was found and selected as the

27 See: KOKKINI-IATRIDOU, D., 'Some Methodological Aspects of Comparative Law', *NILR* (1986), p. 143–194 (191).

28 See: BOELE-WOELKI, K., 'The Working Method of the Commission on European Family Law', (2005), p. 32–35.

29 The common core and the selected solution are thus identical.

30 The common core and the selected (better) solution can be compared.

best solution) and the fourth approach (no common core was found and the best solution was selected), although the other three approaches also show how the CEFL has built on convergence and coped with divergence.[31]

4.1. COPING WITH DIVERGENCE

With regard to some aspects of divorce law, CEFL's comparative research confirms that it was not possible to derive generally applied solutions in the national systems surveyed. Consequently, the drafters were prompted to decide which of the offered solutions should be selected. Another option was the drafting of a new rule. Both methods belong to the better law approach.[32] This paragraph mainly focuses on differences which exist regarding the following questions:

- Should only one or multiple grounds for divorce exist?[33]
- Does the mutual consent of spouses also require a factual separation?[34]
- Does the mutual consent of spouses to dissolve their marriage require that they have reached an agreement regarding the consequences thereof?[35]
- Should the agreement on the consequences of the divorce cover all aspects?[36]
- Should this agreement be in a written form?[37]

Also, with respect to spousal maintenance, no common core could be detected regarding the following questions:

- Should the income and the assets of the spouses be taken into account when assessing the conditions for maintenance?[38]

---

31 See in particular: ROTH, M., 'Future Divorce Law – Two Types of Divorce', p. 41–57; FERRAND, F., 'Divorce and Spousal Agreements'; GONZÁLEZ BEILFUSS, C., 'CEFL's Maintenance Principles: The Conditions for Maintenance', p. 83–10, all in: BOELE-WOELKI, K., (ed.), *Common Core and Better Law in European Family Law*, European Family Law Series No. 10, Intersentia, Antwerp-Oxford, 2005.

32 See the explanation given under para. 4 regarding the five approaches that the CEFL has applied.

33 Principle 1:3 opts only for two types of divorce.

34 Principles 1:4 para. 1 sentence 2 states that no period of factual separation should be required.

35 Principle 1:4 states that the mutual consent of the spouses refers to the dissolution of their marriage. No agreement on the consequences is required.

36 Principle 1:6(1) enumerates the following aspects: (a) parental responsibility, where necessary, including the residence of and the contact arrangements for the children, (b) child maintenance, where necessary, (c) the division or reallocation of property, and (d) spousal maintenance.

37 Principle 1:6(2) requires a written form.

38 CEFL's answer is positive. Comment 2 under Principle 2:3 states that in determining the creditor spouse's needs and the debtor spouse's ability to satisfy those needs, account should particularly be taken of each spouse's income and assets.

- Should the standard of living during the marriage, as well as a new long-term relationship of the debtor spouse, be taken into account when determining claims for maintenance?[39]

This overview demonstrates that, only in relation to a few aspects, no common core actually exists. The maintenance aspects are of minor importance. This also applies to the first and last question under the divorce part. However, the questions about the requirements of a consensual divorce divides the jurisdictions surveyed into two blocks and, in relation to these aspects, diverging tendencies can be noticed. The first issue, which has been solved differently, concerns the separation of the spouses who both want a divorce. In twelve of the twenty-two jurisdictions surveyed, mutual consent of the spouses does not require that the spouses have lived apart for a certain period of time before they are allowed to file for a divorce. In contrast, the other jurisdictions require a separation period to prevent hasty decisions and to facilitate attempts at reconciliation. Within these jurisdictions, the length of the separation period differs considerably, from six month to even four years.[40] Consequently, with regard to the separation periods, no significant common factor could be found among the twenty-two systems. The CEFL had to make a choice between two different solutions. Should a period of separation be required if the spouses agree that their marriage should be dissolved? Is there any justification to bind spouses against their corresponding clear and free will? According to the opinion of the CEFL, the answer to both questions is negative. In view of the general objective of the drafters that consensual divorce should be favoured, the separation period was abandoned. The mutual consent of the spouses should be considered to be of overriding importance and it should prevail under all circumstances. However, the argument that hasty decisions should be prevented has also to be taken into account. Regarding this important aspect the CEFL decided that under specific circumstances, for instance, the spouses have children or they have not agreed upon the consequences of their divorce, a certain period of reflection should be required. During that reflection period, which is regulated in Principle 1:5, the spouses do not need to live separately.

The second issue relates to the so-called package deal. The more stringent view, represented by half of all jurisdictions surveyed, requires that mutual consent should include all consequences, whereas, according to the more practical solution, which is applied by the other half of the jurisdictions, all that is required is an agreement on the dissolution of the marriage.[41] It has been extensively discussed whether the CEFL should discard the package deal or opt instead for a Principle which favours

[39] According to Principle 2:4 both aspects should be taken into account.

[40] See: Principle 1:4: Comparative overview and Comment.

[41] See the comparative overview under Principle 1:6.

consensual divorce. In the end, the latter alternative was chosen as the better law rule. Hence, Principle 1:4(2) considers consent with respect to the divorce itself, and consent with respect to the consequences thereof, as two separate issues. For the same reasons that justify the lack of any impediment regarding the separation period, a divorce by mutual consent should be possible, even if the spouses do not agree on the consequences. In such a case, the competent authority determines the consequences of the divorce according to Principle 1:7.[42] Also Principle 1:4(2) should be read not only in conjunction with Principle 1:5, which proposes a reflection period in order to give the spouses the opportunity to come to an agreement on the consequences of their divorce, but also with Principle 1:6, which favours the spouses' consent and agreement concerning the main consequences of the divorce.

4.2. BUILDING ON CONVERGENCE

The comparison between CEFL's five approaches in drafting its Principles reveals that, with regard to the following aspects of divorce law, a common core was found:

- The law permits divorce;[43]
- The divorce procedure is determined by law;[44]
- Divorce is permitted upon the basis of the spouses' mutual consent;[45]
- The agreement containing the mutual consent regarding the dissolution of the marriage is expressed either by a joint application of the spouses or by an application by one spouse with the acceptance of the other spouse;[46]
- The competent authority determines the consequences for the children (parental responsibility, including the residence of, and the contact arrangements for, the children and child maintenance). An agreement between the spouses is taken into account insofar as it is consistent with the best interests of the child;[47]
- The competent authority scrutinises the validity of the agreement on the division or reallocation of property and spousal maintenance;[48]
- The divorce is permitted without the consent of one of the spouses if they have been factually separated for a certain period of time;[49]

[42] See: ROTH, M., *ibid.*, note 5, p. 45–46.
[43] See: Principle 1:1(1).
[44] See: Principle 1:2(1).
[45] See: Principle 1:4(1).
[46] See: Principle 1:4(3).
[47] See: Principle 1:7(1).
[48] See: Principle 1:7(2).
[49] See: Principle 1:8 (the period of separation and the meaning of separation).

- In cases of exceptional hardship to the petitioner, the competent authority grants a divorce where the spouses have not been factually separated for a certain period;[50]
- In the case of a divorce without the consent of the other spouse, the competent authority determines, where necessary, parental responsibility, including the residence of and contact arrangements for the children and child maintenance.[51]

The Principles in the field of maintenance between former spouses contain even more issues that represent the common core:

- Maintenance between former spouses is subject to the same rules regardless of the type of divorce;[52]
- Each spouse is obliged to provide for his or her own support after divorce;[53]
- Maintenance after divorce is dependent upon the creditor spouse having insufficient resources to meet his or her needs and the debtor spouse's ability to satisfy those needs;[54]
- In determining a claim for maintenance, certain factors should be taken into account, such as: the spouses' employment ability, age and health; the care of children; the division of duties during the marriage; the duration of the marriage; and any new marriage;[55]
- Maintenance is provided at regular intervals and in advance;[56]
- In cases of exceptional hardship to the debtor spouse, the competent authority denies, limits or terminates maintenance because of the creditor spouse's conduct;[57]
- In determining the debtor spouse's ability to satisfy the needs of the creditor spouse, the competent authority gives (a) priority to any maintenance claim of a minor child of the debtor spouse; (b) takes into account any obligation of the debtor spouse to maintain a new spouse;[58]
- The competent authority grants maintenance for a limited period, but in exceptional cases, does so without any time limit;[59]

50 See: Principle 1:9.
51 See: Principle 1:10(1).
52 See: Principle 2:1.
53 See: Principle 2:2.
54 See: Principle 2:3.
55 See: Principle 2:4. The standard of living during the marriage and a new long-term relationship of the debtor spouse fall under the better law approach. Regarding these circumstances no common core was found.
56 See: Principle 2:5(1).
57 See: Principle 2:6.
58 See: Principle 2:7.
59 See: Principle 2:8.

- The maintenance obligation ceases if the creditor spouse remarries or establishes a long-term relationship;[60]
- After its cessation, the maintenance obligation does not revive if the new marriage or long-term relationship comes to an end;[61]
- The maintenance obligation ceases upon the death of either the creditor or the debtor spouse;[62]
- Spouses are permitted to make an agreement as to maintenance after divorce. The agreement concerns the extent, performance, duration and termination of the maintenance obligation and the possible renouncement of the claim to maintenance;[63]
- This agreement must be in writing;[64]
- The competent authority scrutinises at least the validity of the maintenance agreement.[65]

This long list of aspects, in respect to which the CEFL was able to detect a common core as well as converging tendencies, forms the constituent part of the CEFL Principles. It was discovered that more countries now take the same approach and, within a certain approach, the differences are becoming less pronounced. After evaluating their effectiveness and suitability, the common solutions[66] were considered to be the best solutions. In providing explanations, using the common core approach undeniably is the easier method to use, because it makes justification simpler by restating what represents the majority.[67]

5. FINAL REMARKS

(1) The comparison of the present situation with the situation some 20–25 years ago[68] demonstrates that the European family law systems follow common solutions to a

---

60 See: Principle 2:9(1).
61 See: Principle 2:9(2).
62 See: Principle 2:9(3).
63 See: Principle 2:10(1).
64 See: Principle 2:10(2).
65 See: Principle 2:10(3).
66 According to ANTOKOLSKAIA, M., *Nederlands echtscheidingsrecht and the CEFL Principles on Divorce*, Inaugural lecture, VU, Amsterdam, 13th September 2006, p. 4, however, the possibilities of the common core approach are limited in the field of divorce. In her view only half of the CEFL Principles were based on the common core of the national systems surveyed.
67 See: ÖRÜCÜ, E., 'Viewing the Work in Progress of the Commission on European Family Law' (2005), p. 224–225.
68 See: SCHWENZER, I., *Model Family Code: From a Global Perspective*, European Family Law Series No. 12, Intersentia, Antwerp-Oxford, 2006, p. 22–32 and ANTOKOLSKAIA, M., *Harmonisation of Family Law in Europe: A Historical Perspective* (2006), p. 359–361.

very large extent in those fields that are covered by CEFL's first Principles. The European family law systems in the area of divorce, maintenance between former spouses, came, and are still coming, together and the challenges for more harmonisation are already imminent.[69] CEFL's next set of Principles will demonstrate that this also applies in the field of parental responsibilities. My prediction for the future is that this convergence, which has been demonstrated by the twenty-two national reports which were drafted under the auspices of the CEFL, will even increase in the coming years due to, among others, the EU freedoms, the rapid changes of family law based on political and economic circumstances, the progressing unification of the rules regarding cross-border family relationships[70] and the decisions of the European Court of Human Rights.[71]

(2) In this contribution an attempt also is made to clarify some terminological aspects that are intrinsic to the harmonisation process of family law in Europe. The role which the CEFL's Principles may play in this process has been emphasised. Building on convergence, and coping with divergence, relates to all kinds of projects in the field of the harmonisation and unification of legal systems. The applied working method should always be explained and exemplified. Moreover, comparative research requires scientific precision. In this respect the CEFL has tried to meet the necessary standards. In particular, a great deal of consideration has been given to the explanation as to why a certain Principle has been adopted. In this process, differences have been faced and definitely not denied. From a purely scholarly point of view it is a challenge not only to build on convergence, but more importantly, to cope with divergence. It is for outside observers to determine whether the CEFL has succeeded in this endeavour.[72]

---

69 BRADLEY, D., *ibid.*, note 13, holds a different view. He provides examples which do not only refer to Europe and which cover different aspects of family law: marriage, pension rights and child law in general.

70 See: BOELE-WOELKI, K., 'The European agenda: an overview of the current situation in the field of private international law and substantive law', *IFL* 2006, p. 149–154.

71 See, for instance: ECHR 13 September 2005, Case of B. and L. v. the United Kingdom (Appl. No. 36536/02) where the Court decided that the prohibition on parents-in-law marrying children-in-law under United Kingdom law constitutes a violation of Art. 12 ECHR. In many other European countries these bars on marriage were lifted some years ago as serving no purpose. See in general on the influence of the decisions of the ECHR on national family law: GRUNDERBEECK, D., VAN, *Beginselen van personen- en familierecht. Een mensenrechtelijke benadering*, Intersentia, Antwerpen, 2003.

72 See: LANDO, O., 'Can Europe Build Unity of Civil Law Whilst Respecting Diversity?', *Europa e diritto privato* 2006, p. 1–18 (13): 'The members of the Commission on European Family Law know the problems and the laws. They can tell Europe which rules are useful and reasonable for the countries of a Union that by and large have come to share the same legal values. As far as is known the European Commission has not yet taken any steps to harmonize the substantive rules of family law. But that may come.' See for a different view: BRADELY, D., 'A Note on Comparative Family Law: Problems, Perspectives, Issues and Politics', *4 Oxford University Comparative Law Forum* (2005), p. 263: 'The Commission's method, which has involved dissecting and isolating aspects of legal policy prior to constructing model laws, indicates its lack of concern with factors

In doing so, it should be kept in mind that its Principles are neither part of an institutional design, nor do they claim to produce anything beyond a frame of reference.[73] There is every reason that they once will contribute to something similar to the Common Frame of Reference which is currently being prepared in the field of European contract law.[74]

determining divorce and support legislation in different jurisdictions and, in particular, with integration of legal policy in particular political programs.'

73 Örücü, E., 'Viewing the Work in Progress of the Commission on European Family Law' (2005), p. 221.

74 See: COM (2003), 68 final, OJ C 63/1 (15/3/2003).

TOWARDS A UNIFORM EUROPEAN FAMILY LAW? A POLITICAL APPROACH

General Conclusions

MARIE-THÉRÈSE MEULDERS-KLEIN

1. INTRODUCTION

Undoubtedly, the theme of a Uniformisation or a Unification of national substantive Family laws among European countries has recently become more and more prominent due to the activities of the *Commission on European Family Law* (CEFL).[1] Self appointed and founded in 2001 at the University of Utrecht with the support of the European Commission,[2] three years ago the CEFL organized an international Conference "to study the feasibility of the harmonization of family law in Europe and to initiate practical steps to that end under the title: '*Perspectives for the Unification and Harmonization of Family Law in Europe*'.[3] At this time the CEFL's main objectives were defined as being 'to study the feasibility of the harmonization of family law in Europe, to initiate practical steps to that end, to provide a strong and very necessary impetus in European countries, to seriously consider the problems and possible solutions for reshaping national family laws in accordance with the needs and purposes of the emerging "European Citizenship".[4] At the same conference even the

---

1 Unfortunately a misleading name.
On the origin of the CEFL, its organisation and functioning see PINTENS, W., 'Europeanisation of Family Law' in: BOELE-WOELKI, K., (ed.), *Perspectives for the Unification and Harmonisation of Family Law in Europe*, Intersentia, Antwerp, 2003, p. 3–35.

2 Financed under the programme *Judicial Cooperation Civil Matters.*

3 See the conference book: *Perspectives for the Unification and Harmonisation of Family Law in Europe*, Intersentia, Antwerp, 2003, op. cit. note 1.

4 Preface to BOELE-WOELKI, K., (ed.), *Perspectives for the Unification and Harmonisation of Family Law in Europe*, Intersentia, Antwerp, 2003.

drafting of a European Civil Code of Family Law was on the agenda.[5] Thus the aim was not only a scientific comparative stock-taking of the current state of family law in the European Nation States, but also the political drafting of a Uniform European Family Law.[6]

Three years later and after intensive comparative research by the experts of CEFL[7] in a number of different European countries,[8] the present international conference on "*Convergence and Divergence of Family Law in Europe*" is directed to the same goals and – thanks to its convener, Professor Masha Antokolskaia, and to all its distinguished speakers – it has been a most illuminating experience.

It appears indeed that the topic chosen is not only intended to serve as the basis for a high-level scientific discussion on European comparative law, but primarily as a means of achieving a political objective raising a question of vital importance for all European States at the crossroads where they stand today i.e. whether, especially within the European countries, a spontaneous or forced *movement* exists towards a uniformisation of family laws, with the attendant risk for their democratic freedom to choose their own laws in this fundamental and specific area.

2. SPECIFICITY OF FAMILY LAW

What lends the topic chosen its unusual flavour is the fact that in every nation, of all branches of law, family law is as a rule the most autonomous and the most specific, being as it is so deeply "embedded" in history and a cornerstone of their future development,[9] but also linked with the development of each individual. The values with which it is charged, its role in the attribution of legal personality, bonds of kinship, the identity and the personal status of the individual and the way families

---

5 Meulders-Klein, M.-T., 'Towards a European Civil Code of Family Law? Ends and Means', in: Boele-Woelki, K., (ed.), *Perspectives for the Unification and Harmonisation of Family Law in Europe*, European Family Law Series No. 4, Intersentia, Antwerp, 2003, p.105–116.

6 Pintens, W., 'Europeanisation of Family Law' (2003), op. cit. note 1, p. 4–33.

7 On the working method of the CEFL, see: Pintens, W., ibid, and Boele-Woelki, K., 'The Working Method of the Commission on European Family Law', in: Boele-Woelki, K., (ed.), *Common Core and Better Law in European Family Law*, European Family Law Series No. 10, Intersentia, Antwerp, 2005, p. 15–41. See also M. Antokolskaia, note 35 hereafter.

8 See the national reports in: Boele-Woelki, K., Braat, B., Sumner I., (eds.), *European Family Law in Action*, Vol. I: Grounds for Divorce, European Family Law Series No. 2, Intersentia, Antwerp, 2003 and Boele-Woelki, K., Braat, B., Sumner I., (eds.), *European Family Law in Action*, Vol. III, Family Law Series No. 9: Parental Responsibilities, Intersentia, Antwerp, 2005.

9 Comp. further the so-called "*Cultural Constraint argument*" bitterly criticised by the CEFL, and especially by Antokolskaia, M., in: *Harmonisation of Family Law in Europe: A Historical Perspective. A Tale of Two Millennia*, Intersentia, Antwerp, 2006, Part I, Chap. 2, Part I and II.

are structured, all these place family law at the very crux of society in every country. This being so, it should come as no surprise that every nation has an interest in keeping a close eye on its law regarding the status of the individual and the family which, being a *matter of public policy*, is off-limits, – *d'ordre public et indisponible* –, and mostly placed under the protection of the national Constitutions.[10] Since the duty falls upon the law to instil order into the natural disorder of things, family law especially has to secure the coexistence and the survival of the groups and their members on the basis of two overlapping, albeit formally different norms, namely Marriage and Filiation that are present in all societies as it has been described by the most famous anthropologists and sociologists.[11]

Comparative law in this field brings out the diversity of substantive law from one society to another in the light of their values and beliefs – what David Bradley terms 'the Intimacies of Nations'[12] – even if some more or less converging trends have gradually emerged in the closing decades of the 20th century as a result of the combined impact of unprecedented sociological, ideological, political, economic and scientific changes whose rhythm and intensity vary from one State to another. Hence the various divergences and convergences from one country to another.[13]

The present question of a voluntary *harmonization* or even more of a directly or indirectly forced *unification* of European substantive Family laws thus has nothing to do with a spontaneous return to the medieval *Ius commune* of the Pandectists that is so often evoked as a model[14] nor with the Church Canon Law,[15] but is an idea that has arisen only recently, more specifically in the aftermath of the *Maastricht Treaty* and the creation of the *European Union* (1992). True, the *Council of Europe* had already prompted its 47 Member States towards diplomatic co-operation by means

---

10 See: MEULDERS-KLEIN, M.-T., 'Family Law, Human Rights and Judicial Review in Europe – Heterogeneity and Complexity, in: LØDRUP, P., MODVAR, E., (ed.), *Family life and Human Rights*, Gyldendal, Oslo, 2004, p. 477–495.

11 cf. MAINE, LEWIS MORGAN, MALINOWSKI, CL. LEVI-STRAUSS, DURKHEIM, W.J. GOODE, etc.

12 BRADLEY, D., 'A Family Law For Europe? Sovereignty, Political Economy and Legitimation', in: BOELE-WOELKI, K., (ed.), *Perspectives for the Unification and Harmonisation of Family Law in Europe*, Intersentia, Antwerp, 2003, p. 65 ff. See also below: D. BRADLEY, note 31.

13 GLENDON, M.-A., *The Transformation of Family Law – State, Law and Family in the United States and Western Europe*, The University of Chicago Press, Chicago, 1984; MEULDERS-KLEIN, M.-T., *La personne, la Famille et le Droit – Trois décennies de mutations en Occident*, Bruylant, Bruxelles and LGDJ, Paris, 1999.

14 Remind KAHN-FREUND, O., 'On uses and misuses of Comparative Law in the process of Law-Making', *1 Modern Law Review 37* (1974), p. 1–27.

15 ANTOKOLSKAIA, M., *Harmonisation of Family Law in Europe: A Historical Perspective*, Intersentia, vol. 13, 2006, Part I and II.

of *conventions*[16] in order voluntarily to harmonize certain matters pertaining to persons' status, and the *European Court of Human Rights*, as we know, has already made irreversible inroads into the States' legislative autonomy with its judgment in the *Marckx v/ Belgium* case (1979).[17] However, a progressive approach to a true harmonization or even deliberate uniformization of European substantive family laws was not set in train until after Maastricht (1992) and the creation of the European Union. On the contrary, the European Commission itself had previously enjoined the *Observatory of Family Policies* that it created in 1988 further to the Single Act – and in which I participated for several years under the presidency of Jacques Delors to deal with family matters "only from the outside" by means of appropriate social policies and "without trespassing on the autonomy of Member States in the field of substantive law".[18] We realize today, however, that in the meantime there has been a *volte-face* and that the European institutions – be it in the case law of the European Court of Human Rights since the landmark judgment in the case of *Marckx v. Belgium* (1979) to which I shall revert later, or in the Community legislation and the case-law of the Court of Justice in Luxembourg which applies the European Convention of Human Rights by way of "general principles" – are increasingly moving into the civil field of family law by unforeseeable and imperceptible sideways approaches that take them also into the realm of substantive law. Further, the fact that the European Commission itself sponsors this movement in various European universities is evidenced in particular by the continuing work of the CEFL. However, to what purpose does this process serve? By what means should it be carried through? How far should it go? Is it then to be an evolution through an obscure sideways approach?[19] If so, then on what basis?

---

16 KILLERBY, M., 'Family Law in Europe- Standards set by the Member States of the Council of Europe', in: POUSSON-PETIT, J., (ed.), *Droit Comparé des personnes et de la Famille. Liber Amicorum Marie-Thérèse Meulders-Klein*, Bruylant, Brussels, 1998, p. 351 ff.

17 See MEULDERS-KLEIN, M.-T., 'Internationalisation des droits de l'homme et évolution du droit de la famille: Un voyage sans destination' in *La Personne, la Famille et le Droit* (op. cit. note 13, p. 495–525) and 'Family Law, Human Rights and Judicial Review in Europe – Heterogeneity and Complexity' in LODRUP, P. and MODVAR, E. (eds.) (op. cit. note 10). Comp. AGELL, A., 'The Swedish Legislation on Marriage and Cohabitation. A Journey Without a Destination', *Am Journal of Comp. Law*, 1981, vol. 29, p. 285 and following – See also M. ANTOKOLSKAIA 'Human Rights as a basis for the Harmonisation of Family Law?' in LODRUP and MODVAR, p. 29–47. Comp. the critics of GLENDON, M.-A., *Rights Talk: The Impoverishment of Political Discourse* – Free Press, New York, 1991.

18 *Journal Officiel des Communautés européennes*, 31 octobre 1989, n°C 277/2.

19 See namely: MCELEAVY, P., 'First steps in the Communitarisation of Family Law: Too Much Haste, Too little Reflection?', in: BOELE-WOELKI, K., (ed.), *Perspectives for the Unification and Harmonisation of Family Law in Europe*, Intersentia, Antwerp, 2003, p. 509–526.

3. EUROPEANISATION OF FAMILY LAWS

Around 1965, Europe witnessed the emergence of changing but converging patterns in people's perceptions and outlook in matters pertaining to the family. Even today sociologists are still unable to explain this sudden phenomenon save to indicate perhaps an unprecedented ideological, sociological, political and economic climate together with the impact of unparalleled progress in media, sciences, biology and technologies. From then on many European States spontaneously set about reforming their legislation relating to marriage, divorce, filiation, etc., but at varying speeds and with differing content as we have seen throughout the present Conference. Hence their diversity and the question marks: "Convergence or divergence?" "Harmonization or unification?" "For what purpose? Economic? Ideological? Political? By what means?" – not to overlook the fact that there are "two Europes" endowed with different institutions and powers: that of the *Council of Europe* and that of the *European Union*, respectively comprising at present 47 and 27 nations.

4. THE COUNCIL OF EUROPE

In the case of the Council of Europe, what turned out to be the real earthquake made its irreversible entry on to the European stage in the shape of the judgment in *MARCKX v. Belgium* (1979), handed down by the European Court of Human Rights in Strasbourg which took upon itself the power to condemn not only *acts by governments* held to be in breach of the fundamental rights of which it is the custodian, but for the first time a democratic *Act of Parliament* itself and hence the whole body of family law through judicial interpretation of the vague notions of "Private life" and "Family life" (Art. 8 ECHR) as well as of the all-embracing right to "non-discrimination" – even between non comparable situations – enshrined in the henceforth autonomous Article 14 ECHR. Combined with the immediate and self-executing nature of the Court's interpretative judgments in all Member States, these two Articles on their own are sufficient to undermine "a whole code of family law"[20] and to substitute the unpredictable rule of case-law and the government of judges for the sovereignty of the States.[21]

---

20 See dissenting opinion of the Judge Sir Gerald Fitzmaurice in *Marckx v. Belgium*. ECHR (1979).

21 MAHONEY, P., 'Judicial activism and Judicial self-restraint in the European Court of Human Rights: Two sides of the same coin', *1–2 Human Rights Law Journal 11* (1990). See also M.-T. MEULDERS-KLEIN, 'Internationalisation des droits de l'homme et évolution du droit de la famille: un voyage sans destination' in *La personne, la Famille et le Droit* (op. cit. note 17, p. 495-525).

This is a basis for saying ironically that, in a way, the binding case-law of the Strasbourg Court and its direct application to all Member States of the Council of Europe is likely to make paradoxically a significant contribution to an "approximation" of European family laws by "deconstructing" national family rules piece by piece on an unforeseeable basis. This in particular is the path that led to the splitting of the link between marriage and filiation and to the belief that marriage has outlived its usefulness. Consequently, the emergence of the phenomenon of "unmarriage" – the so-called "démariage" in French – although the "right to marry" is at the same time heralded as a conquest in other unprecedented circumstances such as same-sex or transsexual marriages. This statement notwithstanding, there can be absolutely no question of criticizing the principle of the equal right of the child born out of wedlock to have a "*normal family life*", that is to have a *mother* (judgment in *Marckx v. Belgium*, 1979) and a *father* (judgment in *Johnston v. Ireland*, 1986) and the same rights as a legitimate child. Far from it indeed... Long before I myself pleaded for the equality of children whether born in wedlock or not. However the over-ideologisation of Human rights and their constantly changing and unpredictable interpretation by the European judges are obviously a roadmap for a "Journey without a destination"[22] and may still hold many a surprise in store. Indeed, Article 8 ECHR itself, combined with Article 14 on non-discrimination contains a clear potential antagonism between "private life", interpreted as an increasingly unfettered individual liberty of the ones versus the equal right to a "normal family life" of the other family members who deserve the same protection: this is especially the case of the child for instance, born by whatever stratagem and in whatever circumstances – contrary to the ONU Children's Rights Convention 1989.[23] Nor does the Strasburg Court of Human Rights case-law unify the national rules of paternity or maternity establishment.[24] The same is true for divorce legislation.[25] So far, there is no real convergence among European family legislations, but to that extent, the new European legal notion of family is clearly becoming something of a "will-o'-the-wisp" according to the unforeseeable interpretation by a majority of judges case by case and to the random composition of the judiciary. Moreover, in this context, sex, procreation and parentage are increasingly in the eye of the ideological storm described by Professor

---

22 See the excellent report of: FORDER, C. and SAARLOOS, K., 'The establishment of Parenthood: A Story of a successful convergence?' in this book.

23 See for instance the child's discrimination bound to the legal anonymity of the birth mother, or of the child of same-sex parents (cf. Marckx and Johnston cases, supra).

24 See: FORDER, C. and SAARLOOS, K., 'The establishment of Parenthood: A Story of a successful convergence?' in this book.

25 See: contribution of Bea VERSCHRAEGEN in this book, and comp. ANTOKOLSKAIA, M., 'Convergence and Divergence of Divorce laws in Europe', in: *3 Child and Family Law Quarterly 18*, (2006), p. 307–330.

Swennen:[26] namely sex and procreation would also include at will the right to incest, polygamy, same-sex marriage and parentage,[27] procreation and parentage by any ways including Internet bargaining, as in Belgium, and even sadomasochist practices as compatible with Human Rights provided they are consented to by the victim.[28] All this in the name of Human Rights. "A world without limits" although some lawyers claim that it is still too narrow.[29]

In this context not only is the concept Family becoming a mess but Family Law becomes a powerful tool to change society, as has been the case with the three major historical Revolutions – French, Soviet and Chinese – as was once rightly pointed by Professor Müller-Freienfels.[30]

By the same token David Bradley clearly asserts that political considerations and politicians influence voluntarily the evolution of family laws, and that divergences or convergences reflect not only culture or heritage. They assume an active role in promoting political and economic goals. Economic factors become prominent at the same time as new ideologies.[31] And new ideologies and ideologists work very hard to change peoples opinions *bottom down*.

Hence the quest for a new Uniform European Family Law as a political tool.[32]

Paradoxically, on what then, might we ask, could this constantly evolving "common" European family law be based if the European Courts, as supreme oracles, claim that they follow the evolution of peoples' ideas, mores and morals, and the latter follow the increasingly exponential and irreversible extrapolations of the supranational courts in a perfect vicious circle?

It is therefore necessary to clarify what is involved in the attempt to construct an all-embracing Pan-European Family Law.

---

26 See: SWENNEN, F., 'The Evolving Marriage Concept and the Impediments to Marriage', as symbol of 'a cultural sexual revolution', in this book.

27 See: SCHWENZER, I., 'Convergence and Divergence in the Law on Same-Sex Partnerships' in this book.

28 CEDH, 1 Sect.17.2.2005, *K.A. & D.A. v / Belgium*. In that case the wife was the "consenting" victim.

29 MCGLYNN, C., 'Families and the European Union Charter of Fundamental Rights: progressive change or entrenching the status quo?' (2001), 26 *European Law Review*, p. 582–596.

30 See MÜLLER-FREIENFELS, W., 'Zur revolutionären Familien Gesetzgebung insbesondere zum Ehegesetz des Volksrepublik China vom 1 Mai 1950', in: CAEMMERER, E., VON MENTSCHIKOFF, S., ZWEIGERT, K., (eds.), *Ius privatum gentium: Festschrift für Max Rheinstein*, Mohr Tübingen, 1969.

31 BRADLEY, D., 'A political and institutional perspectives on Convergence in Family Laws'. Note on Comparative Family Law: Problems, Issues and Politics – Oxford University Comparative Law Forum, 4, 2005.

32 My opinion.

5. THE EUROPEAN UNION

Turning now to the European Union, the most peculiar feature of all this is that the EU itself has charged in a roundabout manner into a field in which it has basically no competence – that of substantive Family law – supposedly under the banner of the "free movement of persons, goods and services in the European Space" supported by means of judiciary Regulations which are theoretically in accordance with the economic logics of the free market and globalization beyond Brussels II and Brussels IIbis. This all together with the declarations of the Laeken Summit of 2001.[33]

More surprising still is the new *European Charter of Fundamental Rights* (2000) which copies the ECHR, even to the extent of straying into the field of the basic conditions governing marriage (Art. 9) and more generally with Article 52 as if in an attempt to make the EU with its constraints more attractive in the matter of Fundamental Rights within the so-called new "*Space of Justice, Security and Liberty*" including even the domain of substantive family law. However, still not enough. Thus, for economic, political and ideological reasons, the ambition of the EU to become a player directly or indirectly in the family branch of civil law is only one step further away, as indeed is the scrutiny by the Court of Luxembourg basing itself on "general principles" pending the entry into force of the European Charter which is stronger than the CEDH, and with the inherent risk of conflicts of jurisdiction and interpretation between the two European Courts. This all under the veil of the Economy combined with a Pan–European vista and even *under pressure*, as was recently the case for Bulgaria whose entry into the EU was made conditional on its prior acceptance of following the "principles of family law" of the CEFL.[34]

Hence the central question: namely, whether the Member States are still free to decide on their own substantive family rules, or only under the governance of a benevolent *Big Brother*. Moreover, how much further might this new imperialism grow by unpredictable side roads approaches? It is at this point that we discover that the standing claim of the CEFL against the "embedded cultural constraint argument" becomes outdated and irrelevant. Paradoxically, indeed another kind of constraint seems to be born. And this despite the obvious fact that all the peoples of all democratic nations deserve respect for their opinions, values, cultures and beliefs, lest they fall themselves prey to tyranny.

---

[33] European Council of Laeken, 14–15 December 2001. See: PINTENS, W., 'Europeanisation of Family Law', op. cit. (note 1) *supra*, p. 20–27.

[34] On the pressure exerted on Bulgaria see: TODOROVA, V., 'The Accession of Bulgaria to the European Union: A Path to the Harmonisation of Family Law' in this book.

6. THE COMMON CORE OR THE BETTER LAW?

By way of conclusion, it should be said that the Comparative Law survey carried out here has been methodological – *de lege lata* and *de lege ferenda* – in an attempt to determine whether the family laws of European countries are spontaneously converging – about which there is still room for doubt or – failing that, how to seek theoretical and technical legal ways and means of harmonizing or even unifying legal systems and domestic legislation among EU member States. For this purpose CEFL has resorted to two methods: to identify a "Common Core" that may already exist among a majority of EU members, or to define a "Better Law" on the basis of the majority views of its individual members.[35]

According to Professor Masha Antokolskaia the difference between the two lies in the fact that the search for a "Common Core" must be based on *objective cogent findings* showing the spontaneous emergence of common trends in the majority of European countries, ...whereas the alternative approach is based on *subjective personal preferences* of the members of the CEFL Organizing Committee and eventually on the outcome of votes on what should be held to be the "Better law" even in the details.[36]

Moreover the author adds: " *A Common core is defined as a solution shared by a significant majority of legal systems. Nevertheless, if this common denominator lies below the drafters of the Organizing Committee requirements as to the quality and the modernity of the rules they wish to make, or if there is no Common Core to find, the drafters are allowed to move towards the Better Law method, or either to formulate a new rule themselves...*" And further: "*By the same way in choosing one of those solutions above the others, the drafters of the Organizing Committee of the CEFL unavoidably take sides in this political debate and implicitly express their own value judgements within the conservative-progressive divide in Europe...*" Whereas this task belongs clearly to national Parliaments.

This is why honestly, and with all respect for my excellent colleagues, I must express my own concern about the political work of the self appointed Organizing Committee of the CEFL with the support of such a powerful institution as the European

---

35 See ANTOKOLSKAIA, M., in *Perspectives for the Unification of Family Law in Europe*, 2003, p. 159–181, Chap. 14 – On Divorce.

36 See on that important point: ANTOKOLSKAIA, M., *Harmonisation of Family Law in Europe: A Historical Perspective* (2006), p. 361–365: The Harmonizing Potential of the CEFL Principles of Divorce.

Commission itself and out of knowledge of most of the European peoples or even authorities.

7. CONCLUSION

"Better Law"? The concept is difficult to grasp. Does it mean the "Best Law" or the "Preferable one"? And if so, on the basis of what criteria? The personal opinions of those who know best? Politicians? Academics? Judges? Or general common sense in a democratic political system?

Setting aside any preconceived ideas, religious and doctrinal prejudices or ideological bias, we may find the answer to the question in the "Pragmatism" of the late 19th century American philosophers William JAMES[37] and John DEWEY according to whom the "preferable law" is that which, albeit not infallible, is *the least dogmatic and intransigent,* and that which engenders the fewest evils and the greatest harmony between human beings. In this sense any kind of dogmatism, be it religious, ideological, economic, missionary or intolerant, becomes hateful as a basis for the production of laws or arbitrary judgments. This is precisely the danger that looms over the European institutions: that of succumbing to a new libertarian dogmatic or utilitarian imperialism, not only under the guise of economy and profit, but of a kind of new illiberal morality and the myth of globalisation.

It is also on that ground that, according to reason and the wisdom of nations, the tree should be judged by its fruits. If the fruits that fall are bad, so is the tree itself. Elevated to a dogma, individual freedom may also produce bitter fruits in the lives of families, new inequalities for the weakest and too great misfortunes for those left by the wayside. A look at the present statistics and individual trajectories through life is enough to enable us to see this and shows clearly that the most permissive law, also called "Progressive Law", is not always the "Better Law" – far from it. Nor is "Modernity" an infallible "Progress".

Finally, if the upheaval we are now experiencing in what is dearest to us and constitutes the foundation of any society is to be ascribed to the Age of Enlightenment and to Modernity, or even Post-Modernity, I would like to conclude by offering here a quotation from a French sociologist who writes:

---

37 JAMES, W., *Pragmatism. A New Name for some Old Ways of Thinking*, 1907, reprinted by Harvard University Press, 1975.

"Modernity is that moment when man reappropriates the world and styles himself as the sole source of meaning and as the foundation of the powers to which he submits himself... But it is also that moment when, the Promethean vapours having dissolved, man discovers the disenchantment of a finitude from which no infinite can delude him." (André Arkoun)

1. *Legal Recognition of Same-Sex Couples in Europe*, K. Boele-Woelki and A. Fuchs (eds.)
2. *European Family Law in Action Volume I: Grounds for divorce*, K. Boele-Woelki, B. Braat and I. Sumner (eds.)
3. *European Family Law in Action Volume II: Maintenance Between Former Spouses*, K. Boele-Woelki, B. Braat and I. Sumner (eds.)
4. *Perspectives for the Unification and Harmonisation of Family Law in Europe*, K. Boele-Woelki (ed.)
5. *Family Law Legislation of the Netherlands*, I. Sumner and H. Warendorf
6. *Indépendance et interdépendance patrimoniales des époux dans le régime matrimonial légal des droits néerlandais, français et suisse*, B. Braat
7. *Principles of European Family Law Regarding Divorce and Maintenance Between Former Spouses*, K. Boele-Woelki, F. Ferrand, C. González Beilfuss, M. Jänterä-Jareborg, N. Lowe, D. Martiny and W. Pintens
8. *Inheritance Law Legislation of the Netherlands*, I. Sumner and H. Warendorf
9. *European Family Law in Action Volume III: Parental Responsibilities*, K. Boele-Woelki, B. Braat and I. Curry Sumner (eds.)
10. *Common Core and Better Law in European Family Law*, K. Boele-Woelki (ed.)
11. *All's well that ends registered?*, I. Curry-Sumner (ed.)
12. *Model Family Code – From a global perspective*, I. Schwenzer and M. Dimsey
13. *Harmonisation of Family Law in Europe. A Historical Perspective*, M. Antokolskaia
14. *Brussels II bis: Its Impact and Application in the Member States*, Katharina Boele-Woelki and Cristina González Beilfuss (eds.)
15. *Tensions between Legal, Biological and Social Conceptions of Parentage*, I. Schwenzer (ed.)
16. *Principles of European Family Law Regarding Parental Responsibilities*, K. Boele-Woelki, F. Ferrand, C. González Beilfuss, M. Jänterä-Jareborg, N. Lowe, D. Martiny and W. Pintens (eds.)
17. *Juxtaposing Legal Systems and the Principles of European Family Law on Divorce and Maintenance*, E. Örücü and J. Mair (eds.)
18. *Convergence and Divergence of Family Law in Europe*, M. Antokolskaia (ed.)

www.ingramcontent.com/pod-product-compliance
Ingram Content Group UK Ltd.
Pitfield, Milton Keynes, MK11 3LW, UK
UKHW051926100926
8556IPUK00022B/1399